1⁰⁰

PAGEMAKER 4
BY EXAMPLE

PC EDITION

PageMaker 4
by Example

PC Edition

TONY WEBSTER AND PAUL WEBSTER

M&T Books
A Division of M&T Publishing, Inc.
411 Borel Avenue
Santa Clara, CA 94402-3522

Library of Congress Cataloging in Publication Data

Webster, tony, 1940-
    PageMaker 4 By Example: PC Edition / Tony Webster and Paul Webster. — 1st ed.
       p.   cm.
    Includes index.
    ISBN 1-55851-149-0 (book) —ISBN 1-55851-151-2 (book / disk)
    1. Desktop publishing — Computer programs. 2. PageMaker (Computer program) 3. Micro-computers — Programming. I. Webster, Tony, 1940-. II. Title.
Z286.D47W44s 1991   91-19275
686.2'2544536 — dc20   CIP

Trademarks:
PANTONE® is a registered trademark of Pantone, Inc. All products, names, and services are trade-marks or registered trademarks of their respective companies.

Cover Design: Lauren Smith Design

Project Editor: Sarah Wadsworth

---

94 93 92   4 3 2

Preface

This book has been written to make PageMaker 4 as easy to understand and use as possible.

Its contents and approach are based on over 1000 hours of classroom training with a variety of desktop publishing packages. It can be used as a self-paced training book for individual teaching, or it can be used as the workbook for classroom training.

The book is broken up into modules which cover progressively more detailed operation of PageMaker. Each module includes an information section as well as a detailed exercise (except for Module 1).

Self-Paced Operation

For those PageMaker users who purchase this book to help them learn the many new concepts of version 4, the approach outlined in the following paragraphs is suggested.

As indicated above, each module contains an information section which is designed to introduce and outline the associated concepts. This part of each module should be read first. This information section complements the PageMaker manuals by providing many examples of how different concepts are utilized. Extensive use of screen illustrations helps to reinforce the learning process.

Following each information section is an exercise for each module (except the first). These exercises are summarized on one page at the front, so that people of all levels of experience with PageMaker can use them to gain maximum benefit. Those people, for example, who are feeling confident can attempt the exercises without further assistance. For those who need additional prompting, the detailed steps for each exercise are also included. Again, extensive screen illustrations are provided with each exercise solution, making them as simple as possible to understand.

These exercises use sample files that are included with the PageMaker system. Depending upon your geographical location, publications or templates that you open with PageMaker may be designed for A4 or Letter pages. In some cases, your sample files may differ slightly from those contained in our exercises. This should not make any difference to the performance of these exercises, however.

Classroom Operation

In classroom use, the attendees work through each module together with the course instructor. Instead of the user reading the information section of each module, the instructor should explain the concepts in front of the class. Attendees are strongly recommended to keep this information on hand for future reference.

The exercise sections are then attempted by the attendees on their own as part of the classroom tutorial. As for the self-paced approach, these exercises may be attempted without assistance, or worked through by following the detailed steps that are included.

There are nineteen modules contained within this book. Each one covers a separate facet of PageMaker and can be considered individually. Later modules, however, require knowledge which is explained in earlier sections.

Good luck in learning PageMaker. We hope this book contributes to your success with this package.

Acknowledgments

We would like to acknowledge the assistance of the following organizations and people who helped in the production of this book:

- Aldus Corporation, including Freda Stephen and Craig Danuloff
- Brenda McLaughlin of M&T Publishing
- David Webster and Caroline Webster who adapted this book to PageMaker 4

Contents

LEARNING THE BASICS

Module 1

Learning the Basics

In this first module we are going to look at PageMaker basics, including the screen, menus, palettes, and other tools, and see how these are used together to create, modify, close, and open your publications.

This training material is not designed to teach you how to use a PC. It is assumed throughout that you know how to work with the system and how to do all the necessary things such as operating the mouse, opening and closing documents, and working with drop-down menus.

We will be starting from the position as shown in Figure 1 — a view of the Windows desktop with PageMaker 4 installed.

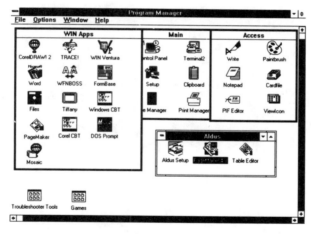

Figure 1. Here, PageMaker 4 is installed in the Aldus Group window within the Program Manager.

To start PageMaker, all you need to do is click on the PageMaker icon to highlight it and choose *Open* from the **File** menu. Alternatively, quickly double-clicking on the PageMaker 4 icon will open the program.

After performing the operation as listed above, your screen will appear as shown in Figure 2. This is the PageMaker desktop — at this stage we have not yet created a new publication or opened a current one. This requires additional steps.

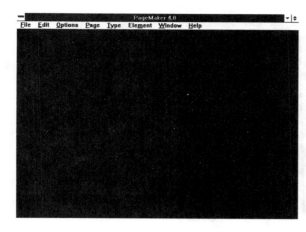

Figure 2. Upon opening PageMaker, after the Aldus PageMaker 4 screen has briefly come and gone, you will be greeted with a screen similar to this one.

Menus and commands

For the moment, let's look at PageMaker's menus (Figure 3).

These are the names at the top of the screen — names that include: **File, Edit, Options, Page, Type, Element, Window,** and **Help**. Each one of these menus contains several commands that are used to help put a publication together.

To see the contents of these drop-down menus, move the mouse over any of the menu names and click the mouse button. What will drop is the list of commands relevant to that menu (Figure 4). To get rid of the menu invoked, move the mouse away from that menu and click the mouse button. The menu will then disappear. Menus can either be selected by holding the mouse down on the menu or clicking on it once and taking your finger off the mouse.

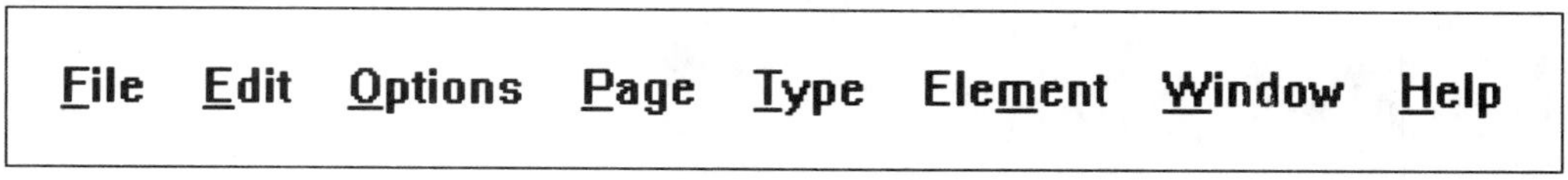

File   Edit   Options   Page   Type   Element   Window   Help

Figure 3. The PageMaker 4 menu bar.

In any particular menu, there are a varying number of commands listed. Some of these commands appear in black, while others are listed in gray. If a command is listed in gray, it cannot be selected at the current time. Some other function must be performed before the command can be selected.

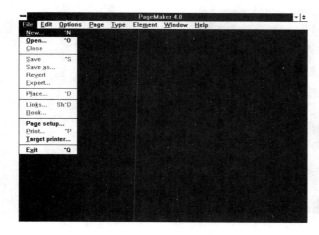

Figure 4. A menu is activated by moving the mouse so that the cursor is on top of one of the eight menu names, and then clicking the mouse button.

Commands listed in black are selected by running the mouse down the column after a menu has been invoked, until a command in the menu is highlighted in reverse video (Figure 5). Release the mouse button, if you still have your finger on it, and the highlighted command will be selected. If you activated the menu without holding the mouse button down (i.e., just clicking on it), a command is selected by clicking the mouse once over the required command.

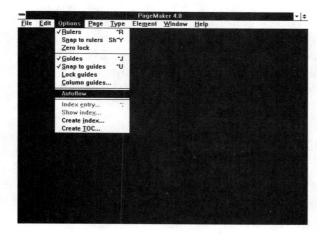

Figure 5. A command is activated by holding the mouse button down on the menu name and running it down the menu, highlighting commands as you go. Release the mouse button on the command you would like to use.

Alternatively, you can click on the menu once, and then once again on the desired command.

An alternative to selecting a command in this fashion is to select a command using the shortcut key method. Note that to the right of many menu commands there are several keys listed (Figure 6). These are the shortcut keys for invoking that special command.

For example, holding down the Control key while typing *R* will activate the rulers. There is no need to invoke the menu (in this case the **Options** menu) if you use the shortcut keys to select a command.

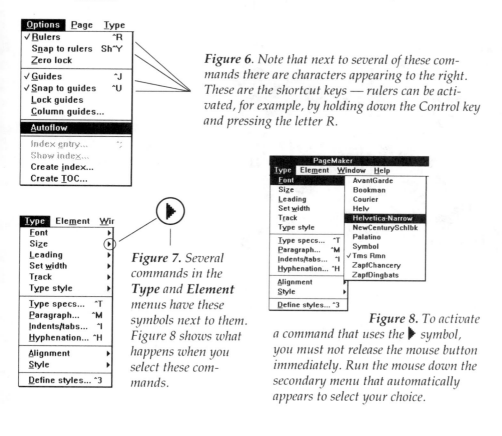

Figure 6. Note that next to several of these commands there are characters appearing to the right. These are the shortcut keys — rulers can be activated, for example, by holding down the Control key and pressing the letter R.

*Figure 7. Several commands in the **Type** and **Element** menus have these symbols next to them. Figure 8 shows what happens when you select these commands.*

Figure 8. To activate a command that uses the ▶ symbol, you must not release the mouse button immediately. Run the mouse down the secondary menu that automatically appears to select your choice.

If a menu command is followed by the ▶ symbol (see Figures 7 and 8), this means that that command must be selected in a slightly different way. You will find that when the mouse is held down on one of these commands, a secondary menu is immediately invoked to the right of that command. To select a choice from this menu, you must keep the mouse button held down and move it down the new list of choices. Release the mouse button on the choice you would like to select from those offered. These types of menu commands are found exclusively in the **Type** and **Element** menus.

Other commands within different menus have ellipsis marks following them: for example, the *New, Open, Save as, Export, Place, Links, Book, Page setup, Print,* and *Target printer* commands from the **File** menu (as shown in Figure 9). Each of these commands (and they occur in a number of different menus) opens a dialog box.

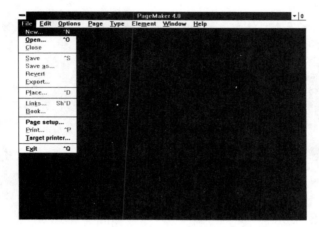

*Figure 9. Notice the different commands within the **File** menu that include the ellipsis.*

A dialog box (Figures 10 and 11) is basically a number of choices presented to invoke the selected command. A dialog box appears as a rectangular outlined window sitting within the page, containing several choices. Many commands use dialog boxes, and most dialog boxes, although different in content, offer similar operational functions.

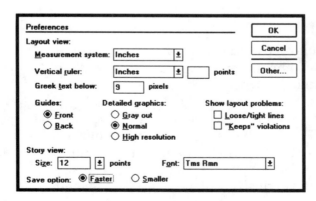

*Figure 10. Dialog boxes appear after invoking many of the commands in the PageMaker menus. A dialog box gives you additional choices over the execution of the command you have chosen. This dialog box represents the Preferences command from the **Edit** menu.*

20

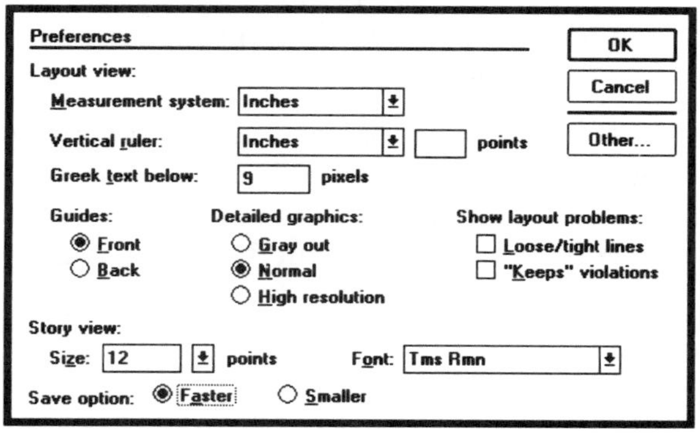

Figure 11. Choices can be made from the dialog box by clicking the mouse button in the circles, boxes, or text areas.

Although circles and boxes within a dialog box represent options to be selected, a group of circles usually means only one of this group can be selected at any given time. Small squares usually represent several options which can be invoked together. A filled circle or a checked box is a selected option.

With the larger rectangles in dialog boxes, you have several options. First, there are the rectangles with a downwards facing arrow at the right (such as *Vertical ruler* in Figure 11, above). By clicking on this arrow, a drop-down list of options occurs, allowing you to choose another option. Other boxes (such as *Greek text below* in Figure 11) allow you to click in the squares with the mouse and use the backspace or delete key to erase the current words or numbers (if there are any), then use the keyboard to insert the new values. Alternatively, if you double-click in such a rectangle, it then assumes a reverse video appearance allowing you to type in directly, deleting anything already in there.

For example, see Figure 13. Under *Page*, the *Letter* selection is showing. Figure 14 shows the drop-down list available with the *Page* options, which is achieved by clicking on the downwards arrow. A new option is selected by clicking on it with the mouse. To the right of *Options* are the small squares and in our case we have checked two of them. The *Orientation* may be *Tall* or *Wide*, but not both. The larger text squares include the different *Margin* dimensions. We have left the default values in these. After selecting all the choices you like within a dialog box, either select OK by clicking on it or press the Enter key.

If you invoke a dialog box by accident, or you select options within a dialog box you do not wish to use, click on the *Cancel* button.

Three things may happen after selecting a command in a menu. First, it may appear as though absolutely nothing has happened. In this case, you may simply have activated a command that does not become apparent until a certain task is performed. Second, you may be confronted with a dialog box. Third, a visible change may take place on the screen.

Starting a PageMaker document

A PageMaker document is referred to as a *publication*. We can create new publications or edit existing publications. By opening a publication we bring it into the computer's memory and onto the screen.

As you open PageMaker, you are not immediately thrust into a new publication as we indicated above. It is up to you to decide whether you want to open up a new or an existing publication.

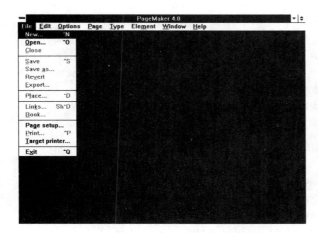

Figure 12. *A new Page-Maker publication is opened by selecting the* New *command from the* **File** *menu. Alternatively, you could have chosen an existing publication by selecting* Open.

To open up a new publication you must select the *New* command from the **File** menu (Figure 12). Upon doing so, you will be presented with the dialog box of Figure 13. This is the dialog box you will be confronted with every time you wish to create a new publication.

```
┌─────────────────────────────────────────────────┐
│ Page setup                          ┌──────────┐ │
│                                     │    OK    │ │
│ Page:  Letter      ±                └──────────┘ │
│                                     ┌──────────┐ │
│ Page dimensions:  8.5   x  11       │  Cancel  │ │
│                           inches    └──────────┘ │
│ Orientation: ◉ Tall  ○ Wide         ┌──────────┐ │
│                                     │ Numbers… │ │
│ Start page #: 1    Number of pages: 1└──────────┘│
│                                                  │
│ Options: ☒ Double-sided  ☒ Facing pages          │
│          ☐ Restart page numbering                │
│                                                  │
│ Margin in inches:                                │
│    Inside  1          Outside  0.75              │
│    Top     0.75       Bottom   0.75              │
│                                                  │
│ Target printer:   PostScript Printer on LPT1:    │
└─────────────────────────────────────────────────┘
```

Figure 13. Every time the New command is activated, this dialog box appears. Basically, it is asking what kind of page (and how many) you want to use for this new document.

Your first choice is what page size to use (Figure 14). All the traditional sizes are included, but if they are not appropriate you can create your own special page. Every time a page size is selected, its actual size is listed in the two boxes next to the words *Page dimensions*. If you want to create a special page, select *Custom* by highlighting it and insert whatever page size you like in the two boxes to the right. International versions of PageMaker also offer A3-A5 and B5 paper sizes.

```
Page:  ┌────────────┬───┐
       │ Custom     │ ± │
       ├────────────┴───┤
       │ Letter         │
       │ Legal          │
       │ Tabloid        │
       │ Custom         │
       └────────────────┘
```

Figure 14. The Page *size options for US versions.*

```
Page dimensions:  ┌───────┐   ┌───────┐
                  │ 8.5   │ x │ 11    │  inches
                  └───────┘   └───────┘
```

Your next choice is whether to use a *Tall* (vertical or portrait) or a *Wide* (horizontal or landscape) page (Figure 15). These two types of pages cannot be mixed in the same publication.

Orientation: ◉ Tall   ○ Wide

Figure 15. The Page Orientation *options.*

The next line asks you what page number you would like to start with and how many pages you would like to use in this publication (Figure 16). Keep in mind that any of the choices made in this dialog box can be altered after the publication has been opened, except for the number of pages. (This is changed differently as we will see later.)

Start page #: 1   Number of pages: 1

Figure 16. The Start page *and* Number of pages *options.*

Your further options are whether to use *Double-sided* pages, and whether or not to use *Facing pages* (Figure 17). You will find that it becomes much easier if both of these commands are selected (they are selected if a cross appears in the little box next to each command). When these two choices are selected, it is possible to view and work with two pages at one time.

Restart page numbering, when checked, ensures that page numbering always starts at the number specified in *Start page #* (see Figure 16).

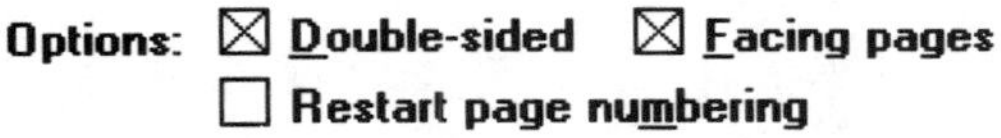

Options: ☒ Double-sided   ☒ Facing pages
☐ Restart page numbering

Figure 17. The Double-sided *and* Facing pages *options.*

Your final choices are the *Margins* for your particular page (Figure 18). These will cause guides to appear on the page — guides that will not print, but guides that will display to make sure text and graphics are contained in the right position on the page.

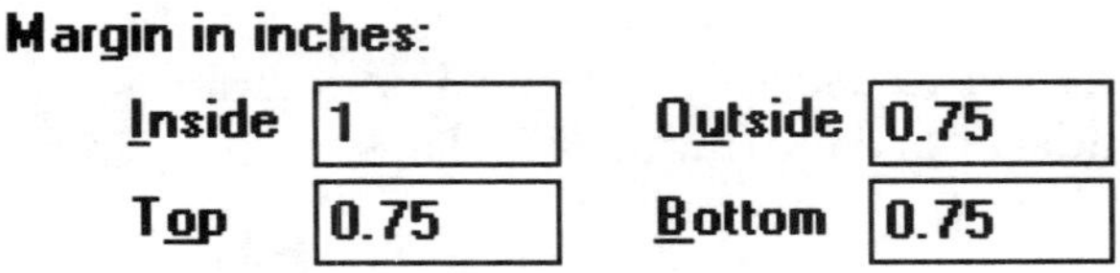

Margin in inches:
Inside 1   Outside 0.75
Top 0.75   Bottom 0.75

Figure 18. The page Margin *options.*

After choosing the correct page setup details as shown in Figures 13 through 18, you then click on OK (or press the Enter key) to get into the initial publication window. This is shown in Figure 19.

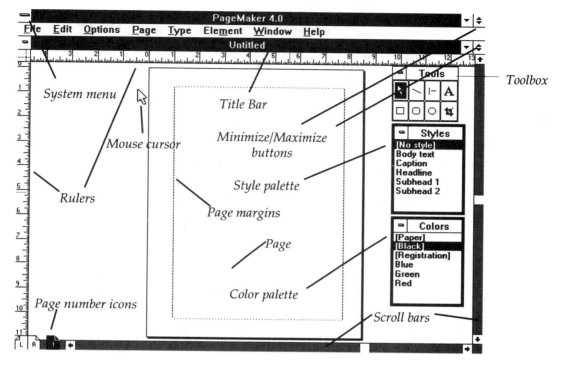

Figure 19. *The initial publication window. Not everything in this window may appear on your screen at first, so there is no need to panic.*

The menu box and menus have already been discussed. We will now look at the other major screen components in Figure 19 in more detail.

Before looking at the page itself, note that the *Page setup* command in the **File** menu, once invoked, uses a dialog box similar to that of *New* (Figure 13). The majority of the options selected when you choose *New* can be altered using this *Page setup* command, while inside your publication.

Title bar

The title bar is the shaded strip just below the menu names. At this stage, the name in the middle of this bar of Figure 19 reads "Untitled." This means that a new publication has just been opened and has not yet been saved. After a publication has been saved, its name replaces the word "Untitled."

The title bar also has three other properties. First, if the current window is not maximized (see description below) and the mouse button is held down anywhere in the title bar, moving the mouse will result in the entire PageMaker window also being moved. As the mouse button is released, the window will reformat in its new position (see Figure 20).

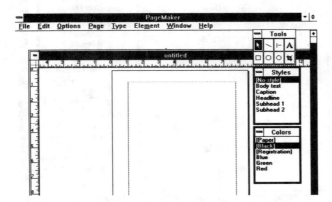

Figure 20. Holding the mouse button down on the title bar when the window is not maximized will result in the PageMaker window being dragged with the mouse.

Second are the minimize/maximize arrows in the top right-hand corner of the title bar. These arrows, when clicked, will cause the PageMaker publication to either expand or decrease in size on the screen. The current document can be either maximized to the whole screen by clicking on the up arrow, reduced slightly by clicking on the double-sided arrow button, or reduced to an icon by clicking on the down arrow. The same thing can also be done to the entire PageMaker program by clicking on the up/down arrows in the PageMaker 4 line at the top of the screen. These arrows are common to all Windows programs.

Third, the title bar contains the **System** menu, a small button in the top left-hand corner of the title bar. This button activates a menu that lets you minimize or maximize PageMaker on your screen or close the current PageMaker publication. This **System** menu is common to all Windows programs. There is also another **System** menu above this one, in the top line that reads PageMaker 4. This works in the same way, but will now affect all of Page-

Maker, not just the current publication. This combination of **System** menus and minimize/maximize buttons makes it possible to minimize/maximize or close the PageMaker document you are working on without affecting the whole program.

The Toolbox

The Toolbox (Figure 21) is a feature of PageMaker that is used very heavily. It is, literally, the box from which you select a tool to achieve a certain task. To select a tool, simply click the mouse on it.

Before looking at each of the available tools in more detail, note that the Toolbox has its own title bar and **System** menu, with similar properties to the publication title bar and **System** menu. The Toolbox can be closed or moved in the same way as described previously. If you accidentally remove the Toolbox from the screen, select the *Toolbox* command from the **Window** menu. The Toolbox will then re-appear on screen.

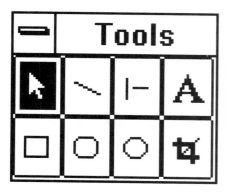

Figure 21. A blown-up picture of the Toolbox — usually situated near the top right-hand corner of the screen, although it can be moved around at will. Currently the pointer tool is selected.

The first tool in the Toolbox is the pointer tool. This tool is used most of the time, as it is the one that must be used to select most elements on the page. Its use will become more apparent as you use PageMaker more and more.

Figure 22. The pointer tool.

Figure 23. The diagonal-line drawing tool.

The second tool is the diagonal-line drawing tool, which allows straight lines in any direction to be created. Freehand drawings cannot be created within PageMaker. Holding down the shift key makes the tool identical to the perpendicular line drawing tool (below).

Figure 24. The perpendicular-line drawing tool.

The third tool is the perpendicular-line drawing tool. This tool allows only straight lines in 45 degree increments to be created. This is especially useful for creating forms, intercolumn rules, and for any lines that must be either horizontal or vertical.

Figure 25. The text tool.

Following the perpendicular-line drawing tool is the text tool. This tool is the one to select to edit text in PageMaker, to create text, or to change the properties of existing text.

Figure 26. The square-corner drawing tool.

Next we have the square-corner drawing tool, used for creating rectangles of any size. Holding down the Shift key when using this tool will create squares.

Figure 27. *The rounded-corner drawing tool.*

The rounded-corner drawing tool is used in much the same way as the previous tool, although the rectangles or squares can now be made with rounded corners.

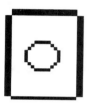

Figure 28. *The oval drawing tool.*

The oval drawing tool is simply used to create ellipses and circles of any shape or size on the page. Circles are created by using this tool in conjunction with the Shift key.

Figure 29. *The imported graphics cropping tool.*

Finally, the last tool in the Toolbox is the graphics cropping tool. This tool is used to remove portions of imported graphics — much like a knife.

Style and Color palettes

Figures 30 and 31 display the *Style* and *Color* palettes offered with PageMaker.

The *Style palette* allows you to select text and change its style according to a preset style type. For example, you may decide that your normal text within a publication is to be set at 10-point Palatino with 12-point leading, 2-point spacing after each paragraph, justified, a first line indent, and two tabs set at particular intervals. This can all be preset and named as a style type. Any text brought into the publication can be selected and applied this style type.

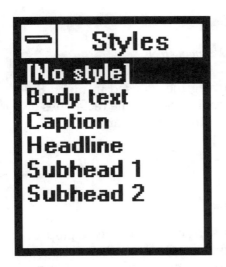

Figure 30. Style palette.

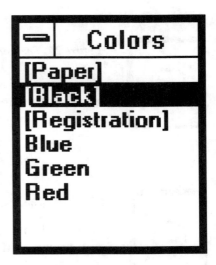

Figure 31. Color palette.

Similarly, subheadings can be, say, 12-point Bold Palatino with certain spacing above and below, with or without indenting. Again, this can be preset, given a name and applied to all relevant subheadings. This approach to document assembly leads to increased productivity and a more consistent publication layout. A style's specifications may be revised at any time. PageMaker will then apply those new specifications to any paragraphs that have been applied that style.

PageMaker comes initially with five default styles: Body text, Caption, Headline, Subhead 1, and Subhead 2.

The *Color palette* allows color to be added to selected text or graphics. Again, any number of color types can be named, specified, and added to the Figure 31 palette. If you have a color monitor, the results will be immediately apparent. The color approach still works with black and white monitors — the resulting printout on a color printer will then indicate the results.

Preset colors defined for PageMaker 4 include: Paper, Black, Registration, Blue, Green, and Red.

Don't try to use too many of these tools or palettes yet — all are covered in great detail in following modules. If you are still unsure as to the function of these tools, don't worry — you are not yet expected to understand them completely.

Page number icons

Down in the bottom left-hand corner of the page are the page number icons. Depending on how your document is set up, you may see many icons in this area or just a few. Quite probably, you will see an *L*, an *R*, and a *1*. The *1* tells you this is page 1 of the current document. As we start creating larger documents, the *1* icon will be accompanied by a *2*, a *3*, a *4*, and any number of icons up to 999. The icon currently highlighted in reverse video is the page currently being viewed on the screen. In this way, you can move to a specific page in your document simply by clicking on its page number icon.

The *L* and the *R* represent the master pages. The use of these master pages is covered in detail in later modules.

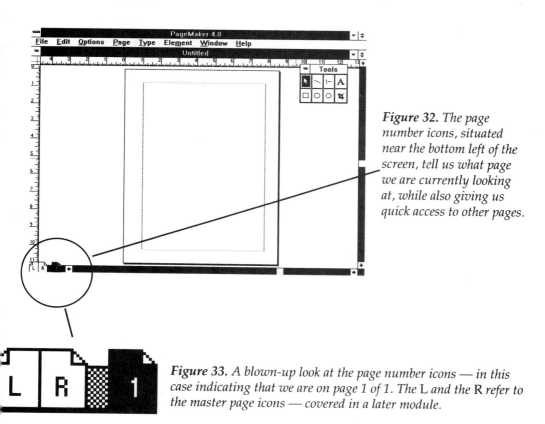

Figure 32. The page number icons, situated near the bottom left of the screen, tell us what page we are currently looking at, while also giving us quick access to other pages.

Figure 33. A blown-up look at the page number icons — in this case indicating that we are on page 1 of 1. The L *and the* R *refer to the master page icons — covered in a later module.*

Any single PageMaker document can hold up 999 pages. It is not possible to show this many page icons at the bottom of the screen. Depending on your screen size, no more than about thirty will be present. To accommodate the extra pages, left and right facing arrows at the beginning and end of the page icons will appear (Figure 34). The right facing arrow lets you scroll through the page numbers in ascending order. The left facing arrow is for scrolling back to find previous pages.

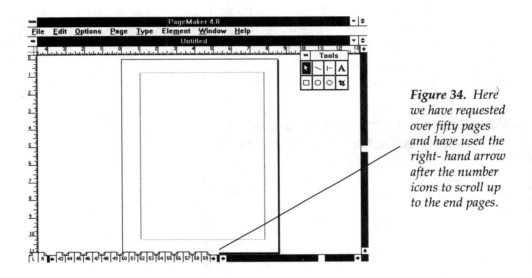

Figure 34. Here we have requested over fifty pages and have used the right- hand arrow after the number icons to scroll up to the end pages.

Although 999 pages is the maximum size of a publication, it is possible to number pages up to four digits in length. The maximum (automatic) page number allowed in PageMaker 4 is therefore 9999, subject to the overall publication being no larger than 999 pages.

The page

Probably, the first thing you will notice in opening a new publication is the representation of the page on the screen. This representation is based on the choices you selected upon opening up a new document. The outline of the page itself should be visible, as should the dotted margins defined for that page (Figure 35). If we had columns defined for this page, column guides would also be visible.

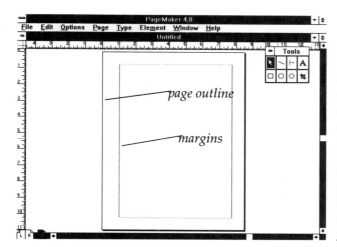

Figure 35. The outline of the page itself is very easy to spot. The dotted lines on the inside of the page indicate the page margins as described in the Page setup *dialog box of Figure 13 (the dialog box that appears after selecting* New *from the* **File** *menu).*

The pasteboard

The pasteboard is the area around the page that can be used to store any imported or created text or graphics. If we look at the page as an actual page, then the pasteboard should be viewed as the desk around the page. It can be used to great effect — it is a kind of visual computer memory. We can place all possible articles and pictures in this pasteboard area and choose visually between them. This pasteboard area remains constant no matter what page you are looking at in the publication. Nothing in the pasteboard area will print, and the pasteboard is always saved with the publication.

The rulers

Through the *Rulers* command in the **Options** menu, it is possible to choose to display, or not display, horizontal and vertical rulers on the screen. Figure 36 shows the rulers displaying. These rulers can be of considerable assistance in placing text and graphics on the page and can be used in conjunction with special horizontal and vertical ruler guides.

Figure 36 indicates the top left-hand corner of the page. Normally, for a single page viewed on screen, the ruler's zero position will begin at this point. For *Facing pages* view, this is not necessarily true. In either case, it is possible to change the zero position both horizontally and vertically.

The use and flexibility of rulers are explained in more detail in a later module.

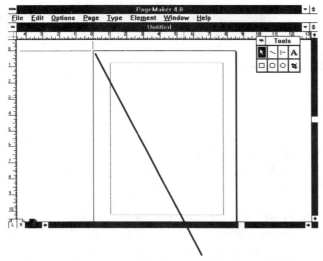

Figure 36. The ruler zero point can be seen at the top left-hand corner of the page.

Notice the 0,0 horizontal and vertical ruler positions are aligned with the top left-hand corner of the page.

The scroll bars

Along the bottom and right-hand side of the page are the scroll bars. These are the bars that allow you to move around the page to view different sections of the page in certain views.

On large high-resolution screens, scroll bars are used very little. When the whole page can be viewed and read at the same time, there is no real need to use the scroll bars. To read the text on a small screen, you will find that you will only be able to see about one third of the page at a time. Consequently, the scroll bars must be used to move yourself around the page. They can be manipulated in a variety of ways as described below.

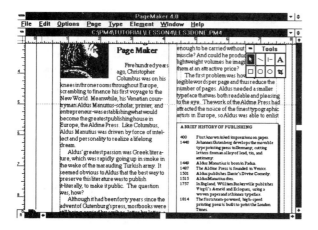

Figure 37. Scroll bars help to move the page around in order to edit different sections of that page. Compare this figure with the one below.

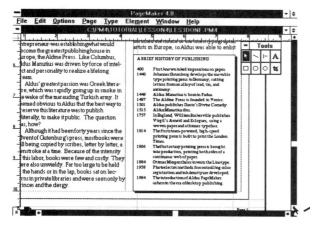

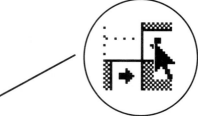

Figure 38. In this figure you will notice that a little more of the bottom and the right of the page is visible. Note also where the mouse cursor was clicked to achieve this page movement.

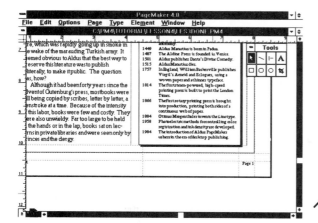

Figure 39. Here, even more of the bottom of the page can be seen after clicking on the down arrow again.

Both sets of scroll bars have an arrow in each corner (top, bottom, left, and right). Clicking on any arrow will move you in that direction in relation to the page. Many people get a little confused here — they tend to think that clicking on a certain arrow is going to take them in one direction, when in fact, it takes them in the other. Experiment to see which way clicking on a certain arrow is going to take you. Without having text on the screen, it can be a little tricky following exactly which way the scroll bars are moving.

Clicking on these arrows is the slow way to move around the page. If you click on the gray areas in the scroll bars you will move around much more quickly — on the smaller screens about a screen at a time. Before you try this, however, note one thing about the scroll bars; they both have a little white square in them. This white square represents what part of the page you are looking at in relation to the total screen area.

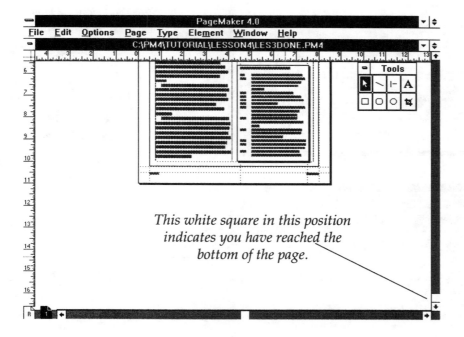

Figure 40. *Even in reduced (Fit in window) view (described in the next section), the screen can be scrolled. When we are looking at the bottom of the page, note where the white square is situated in the vertical scroll bar — also at the bottom.*

For example, if this white square is situated near the bottom of the right hand side scroll bar, this means that you are looking at or near the bottom of the page. If the square is near the top of the scroll bar, you are looking somewhere near the top of the page. When you click in the gray area of the scroll bar to move around, whatever side of the white square you click on is the direction you are going to move. As you scroll, watch the white squares change position in the scroll bars.

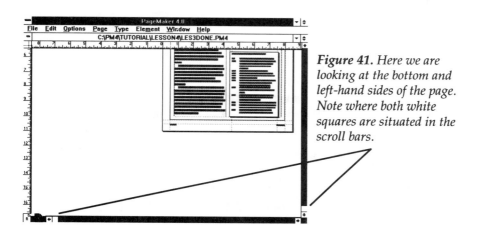

Figure 41. Here we are looking at the bottom and left-hand sides of the page. Note where both white squares are situated in the scroll bars.

Another way to scroll around the screen, and perhaps the easiest way, is to hold the mouse button down on one of the white squares, and move it up or down (or left or right). Release it when it appears that the white square is going to be situated where you want the page to be.

For example, if you are looking at the top of a page and would like to look at the bottom, hold the mouse button down on the right-hand white square, move the mouse down the page until the white square is situated near the bottom of the scroll bar, and release the mouse button. The whole PageMaker screen will reformat so that you are looking at the bottom of your page.

The final way to move around the PageMaker screen is to use the grabber hand. By holding down the Alt key and the mouse button, the pointer turns into a hand. The screen then moves in the direction that the mouse is moved. Holding down the Shift key restrains the movement, horizontally or vertically.

Resizing your window

The window that is holding the current PageMaker publication you are working on can be resized so that if you are working with two different applications at once, you can have them running side by side. The window can only be resized when it has not been maximized to its full size on screen. When the window is not maximized, move the mouse over either of the four edges of the window so that a double-headed arrow appears. By holding the mouse down and dragging it once you have a double-sided arrow, the window will change size.

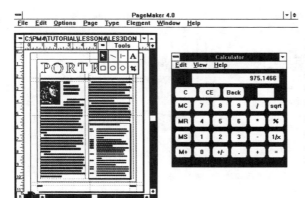

Figure 42. The current screen can be resized when it has not been maximized so that another application, such as the Windows calculator, *can also be viewed on screen.*

Page views

Before going any further, you should experiment with the different ways to view the PageMaker publication currently open. In Figure 43 you are viewing the full page of a document. This is generally the default way to view the page, and is called the *Fit in window* view.

To view the overall layout of your page, *Fit in window* is generally the best choice. When *Fit in window* is selected (**Page** menu), the page appears as big as possible given the current screen size. However, many screens are of a size that makes it impossible to do any editing when a page is at *Fit in window* size. There are other choices, however.

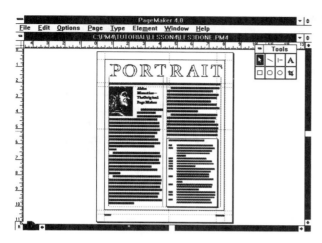

Figure 43. Here you see a publication opened in reduced, or Fit in window, view.

Listed in the **Page** menu are all the possible page sizes that can be selected to view the page. Experiment yourself by selecting different page views to see how a certain page size can be used for editing, another for viewing layout, another for precisely aligning graphics, and so on. PageMaker has a great variety of ways to view the currently open publication.

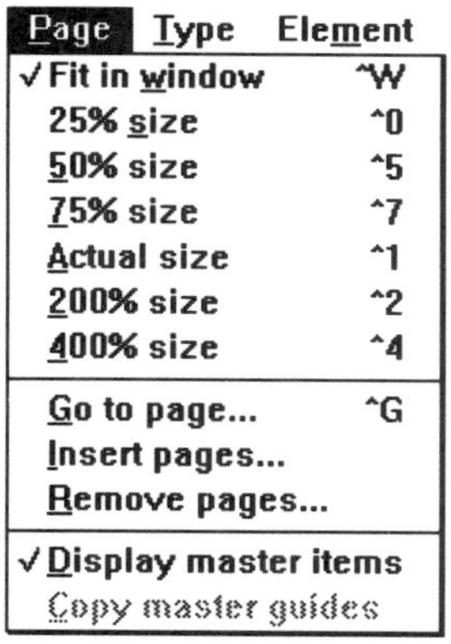

Figure 44. The Page menu gives you a wide range of ways to view your PageMaker publications.

One additional page view is achieved by holding down the Shift key while selecting *Fit in window* from the **Page** menu. What you get in this case is shown in Figure 45 — the whole pasteboard area as well as the page or pages. This is useful when you wish to view the whole pasteboard area. Figures 46 through 51 show six different views of the same publication.

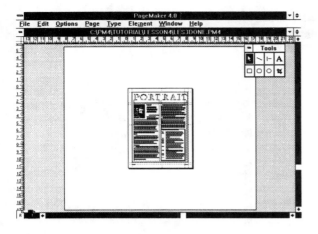

Figure 45. *This view, showing you the total pasteboard area around the page or pages, is achieved by using the Shift key while selecting* Fit in window *view.*

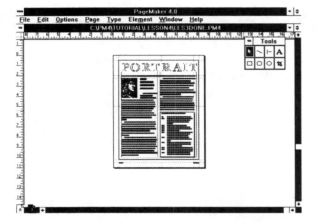

Figure 46. *Here we see the same page as Figure 43, at 25% size. . .*

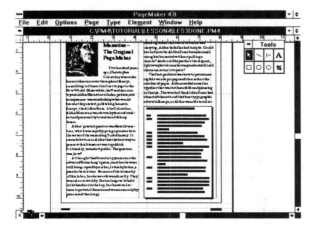

Figure 47. *. . . and again, at 50% size. . .*

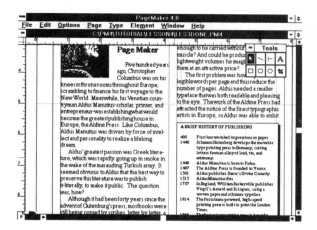

Figure 48. . . . at 75%. . .

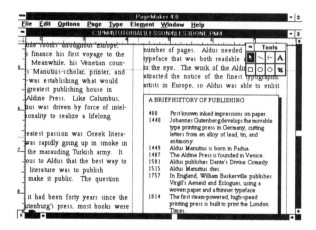

Figure 49. . . . at Actual size. . .

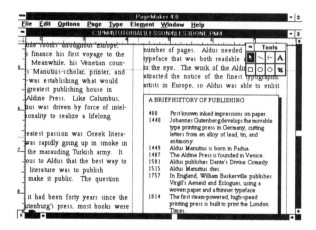

Figure 50. . . . now at 200% size. . .

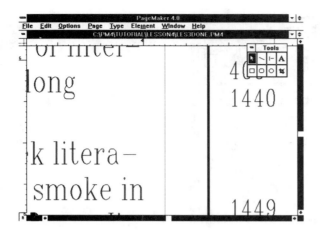

Figure 51. . . . *and finally, at* 400% size.

The Preferences command

It's a good idea to look at the *Preferences* command before you go any further, as it helps to customize PageMaker to your own liking. Invoke the *Preferences* command in the **Edit** menu now.

From this command there is a major choice to be made — which measurement units should be used. There are several units to choose from, so choose wisely — measurement units turn up everywhere in PageMaker. Whichever measurement unit is chosen is the one that appears in all future dialog boxes. This may be overridden at any time, as we will see later. It is also possible to set different measurements for the horizontal and vertical rulers in the dialog box of Figure 52. Again, this will be discussed in a future module. Other choices within the *Preferences* dialog box will be discussed in later modules.

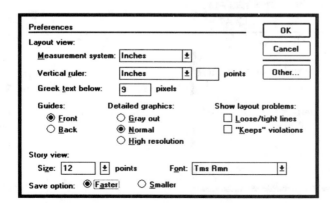

Figure 52. The choices in the Preferences *dialog box, accessed through the* Preferences *command in the* **Edit** *menu, help to customize PageMaker to your special preferences.*

Undo command

Located at the top of the **Edit** menu is the *Undo* command. This is a safety factor that allows you to undo virtually all PageMaker functions — including moves, deletes, copies, pastes, and so on. Always remember this command is here — however, remember it cannot undo everything, and it will only undo the very last step you have taken.

Close command

The *Close* command in the **File** menu (Figure 53) is used to close the currently open publication. As you choose *Close*, you will be prompted to save the changes you have made to this publication (unless you had just saved those changes). You can choose *Yes*, *No*, or *Cancel* (Figure 54). *No* closes the publication without saving changes — everything you changed since you last saved has been lost. *Cancel* takes you back to the PageMaker page. *Yes* will save all changes to the publication. The saving process is discussed in more detail later.

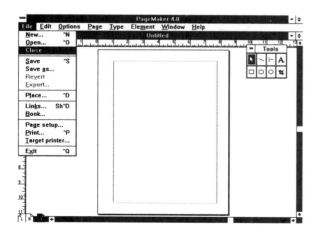

Figure 53. The Close *command will remove the currently open publication from the screen — regardless of whether it was a new publication or an existing one.*

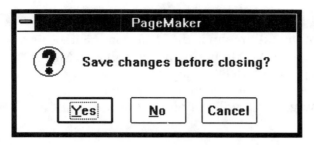

Figure 54. This warning will appear if you have not saved your work before quitting. As we will be discussing saving in a later module, if you are confronted with this warning now, click on Cancel.

The Exit command

The *Exit* command from the **File** menu (Figure 55) closes the entire PageMaker program and returns you to the Windows Program Manager.

At the conclusion of every information section and exercise you are working on in this book, you should close the current publication without saving the changes.

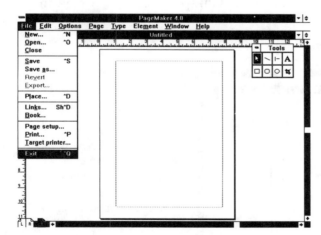

Figure 55. The Exit command, located at the bottom of the **File** menu, will return you to the Windows Program Manager.

Opening an existing publication

In this module, we have looked at ways to start up PageMaker as a new publication, including major options. For loading and opening previously saved publications, please refer to Module 2.

LOADING FILES

Module 2

Loading Files

PageMaker is a tool that allows you to manipulate and put together files that are generally, and most easily, created using other computer applications. Although we can create many publications using PageMaker alone, its real strength lies in the fact that it can accept formatted files from virtually all other major PC applications. Text files are best created in dedicated word processor packages, like Microsoft Word (Figure 1) or WordPerfect, while far more effective and professional graphics can be created in packages such as CorelDRAW! (Figure 2), Illustrator, and PC Paintbrush (Figure 3). Files created in these and other applications can be placed directly into PageMaker.

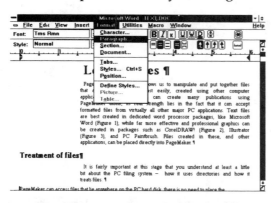

Figure 1. Word processor files can be imported directly into PageMaker.

Figure 2. CorelDRAW! files can be used in PageMaker.

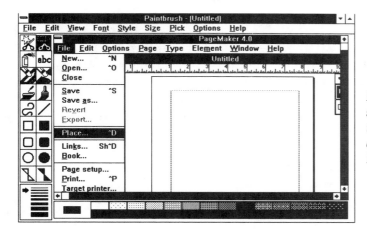

Figure 3. All the
screen shots for
this book can be
edited in PC
Paintbrush.

Treatment of files

It is fairly important at this stage that you understand at least a
little bit about the PC filing system — how it uses directories and
how it treats files.

PageMaker can access files that lie anywhere on the PC hard disk;
there is no need to place the files in the same directory as Page-
Maker before using them. Further, PageMaker takes a copy of
every file that's loaded into it — the original text or graphic file
remains untouched. This has several advantages — in that the
original file can now be used in other applications as well, and that
the PageMaker publication is treated as one file rather than a
mixture of several. Files imported to PageMaker from graphics or
word processing programs can now also be linked to your Page-
Maker file, so that any changes made in either PageMaker or the
outside program will be reflected in both files. (See Module 15, on
Linking Files.)

Outside files, most of the time, can be accessed in their original
form. Occasionally, you may have to do something a little different to a file to allow it to be used in PageMaker. For example,
PageMaker cannot accept CorelDRAW! files in the CorelDRAW!
format — the default format for such files. PageMaker can, however, accept CorelDRAW! files in their EPS format. Other packages have similar options for saving their graphics in a compatible
format.

Loading files

All types of files, whether they be text or graphics, are accessed through the *Place* command (Figure 4) in the **File** menu. After selecting this command, you will be presented with the dialog box of Figure 5. To help you understand the concepts of this module, you may find it useful to follow through our discussion by working with PageMaker as you read our comments.

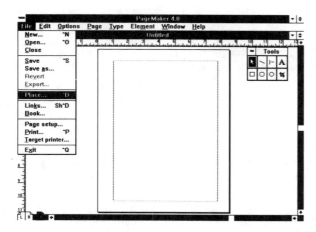

Figure 4. The Place *command is used to gain access to the files on the hard disk and/ or floppy disks.*

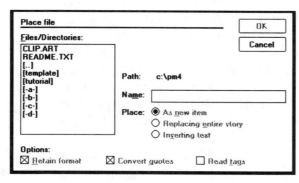

Figure 5. This is an example of the dialog box that appears on selecting the Place *command. Your* Files/Directories *list may look a little different.*

This is where the idea of directories becomes so important. In order for you to change directories to access different files, it is vital that you understand what you are doing.

In Figure 5, you are viewing files and sub-directories from the directory in which the PageMaker program is resident. This is named pm4, and this name is shown in the *Path* section of the dialog box.

Compatible files will be the only files that appear in this list. Incompatible files will not be listed at all. Other directories and/ or sub-directories that are included in the list are enclosed in brackets. See Figure 6 for a description of the *Place* command dialog box.

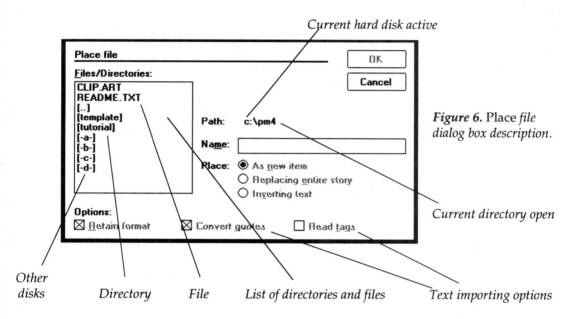

Figure 6. Place *file dialog box description.*

Most of the time you will find that the file you are after is not resident in this current directory at all, so you must change directories. There are two possibilities here, depending on whether the new directory is contained within or outside of the current directory.

To move to a sub-directory within the current directory, move the mouse over the name of that directory and click the mouse button quickly twice in succession . You will then be viewing the files and sub-directories from within the new directory (Figures 7 and 8). Alternatively, you can click on the new directory once to select it, and then click on the OK button.

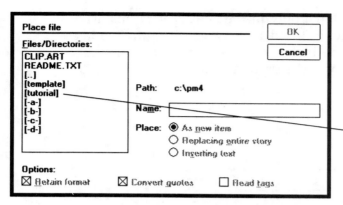

Figure 7. To gain access to the files and sub-directories in the tutorial directory, which is within the pm4 directory, you must double-click on that directory name. Alternatively, you may select that directory by clicking on it once, and then clicking on the OK button. Figure 8 now lists all files and sub-directories within the tutorial directory.

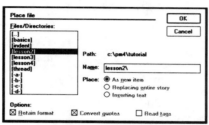

Figure 8. The file we want to place later in this module is called LEADSTRY.RTF, inside the directory lesson2, which is inside the tutorial directory. Once you have located the lesson2 directory as shown, you can select LEADSTRY.RTF using the methods described later in this module.

In Figures 7 and 8, we have moved to files and directories within the pm4 directory. Figures 9 and 10 show how to move to files and directories outside the pm4 directory.

To change to other directories outside the pm4 directory, which is often the most common first move, a different technique must be used. You must move the mouse over the two dots inside the brackets, which will be sitting below any compatible files but above any directories and disk drives.

Each time you locate and click on these two dots, it will take you one step closer to the main or root directory on the current drive. Depending on how far the pm4 directory was buried on your machine, the number of times you have to click on these two dots will be different. You also have the option to change the current drive by clicking on the letter representing the alternate hard drive, or you may select (a) or (b) if you wish to read from one of your floppy drives.

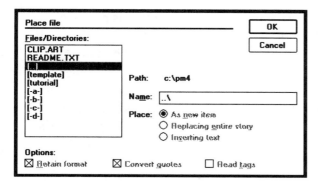

Figure 9. This is the same dialog box as Figure 7. Now, instead of moving to within the pm4 directory, you wish to move up towards the root directory. Double-click on the two dots in your list of files or directories as many times as it takes to get to the root directory. In our case one double-click will return us to the C drive root directory.

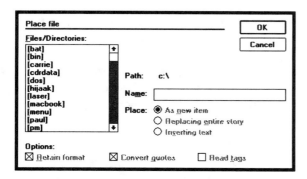

Figure 10. Double-clicking on the two dots inside the pm4 directory returns us to the root directory. Every name in the list is a directory.

Once you are looking at the root directory of Figure 10, you should see mainly a list of directories rather than files. From here, you can select the directory to move down to using the technique described below. You may need to scroll down this list of directories if it contains any more than ten or so names.

When you find the name of the directory you would like to move into, click on it twice. From within this directory, you may either select the file you are after, or move down another sub-directory level. Finding directories or files within different levels of directories is called "hierarchical filing." It is the standard method within the PC environment. If you are familiar with the PC, then you will be familiar with this filing structure. If you are not, however, do not worry if you find it confusing. Imagine it to be like a normal filing cabinet where you may place a number of files within one folder (directory). It is a very effective way to build up your library of information rather than having it all resident at the same level.

If you are sure the file exists in your directory but it is not listed in this window, it may well exist in a format incompatible with PageMaker. Return to the program in which it was created to change its format.

If you wish to follow through the next steps, locate the LEADSTRY.RTF file by following the steps outlined in Figures 7 and 8. To load this file, you can choose one of the two methods discussed above for moving into directories. Click on LEADSTRY.RTF and then click OK, or, alternatively, just double-click on the file. Additional options required in selecting your file are described at the end of this module.

After a few seconds (the length of time depends upon the format and the size of the file being loaded), you will be returned back to the PageMaker page with very little apparent difference. However, the mouse cursor will have changed its appearance once again depending on the type of file that is being loaded. If you have just loaded PageMaker and not changed any default settings, it will look like Figure 11.

Text files loaded in will cause the mouse cursor to change its appearance to any one of the three options shown in Figures 11, 12, and 13. Graphics files, however, will cause the mouse cursor to take on a variety of different forms, depending on their format. These are shown in Figures 14 through 17. The different text and graphics possibilities are briefly discussed below. The detailed operations of these different place methods are described in future modules.

Figure 11. When text has been selected to load into PageMaker using the Place *command, the mouse cursor may change appearance to look like this. This is called manual text flow and is the PageMaker default text input mode.*

Figure 12. This is the semi-automatic text flow cursor appearance.

Figure 13. This is the automatic text flow mode.

Figure 14. *This is the EPS or PostScript mouse cursor.*

EPS graphic files will cause the mouse cursor to look like Figure 14. Files from programs such as Adobe Illustrator and CorelDRAW! could be imported in this format.

Figure 15. *This is the draw-type cursor.*

Draw (or PICT) type files will cause the mouse cursor to take on this appearance. Files from CorelDRAW! can be imported in this format.

Figure 16. *This is the TIFF, or scanned image, cursor.*

TIFF files, which are usually scanned files, will cause the mouse cursor to take on the appearance shown in Figure 16.

Figure 17. *The paint-type mouse cursor.*

Paint files, such as those from PC Paintbrush, cause the mouse cursor to take on the appearance of a paintbrush.

Once you have changed the mouse cursor through the *Place* command to indicate a file has been loaded, you must get the file from memory to the page. In Figure 18, we are about to load the file LEADSTRY.RTF through the process described earlier in this module.

Before you click the mouse button, you must locate the mouse cursor where you would like the text or graphic to be placed. If it is a text file you are loading (as in our case), make sure that the mouse cursor is flush with the left margin of the page. It should snap to this margin (see Figure 18). If you click the mouse cursor now, the text will flow from where the mouse is located, across and down the page (Figure 19). This text file is now loaded. Such an operation may take a few seconds.

Before clicking the mouse, ensure that the mouse cursor looks the same as Figure 18 (which is the manual text flow mode as illustrated also in Figure 11). If it doesn't, go to the **Options** menu and choose the *Autoflow* command. (The reasons for doing this are explained in the next module.)

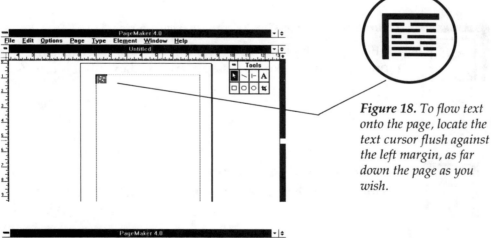

Figure 18. To flow text onto the page, locate the text cursor flush against the left margin, as far down the page as you wish.

Figure 19. Here we located the text cursor in the top left-hand corner of the margin before we clicked the mouse button.
The text flows within the bounds of the left, right, top, and bottom margins.

There is a second method that can be used to flow text and/or graphics onto the page (this is the method that should always be used with graphics). Position the mouse where you would like the top left-hand corner of the file to be and hold down the mouse button. Now move the mouse down and to the right of the page, keeping the mouse button held down. A box will be drawn indicating the area in which the text or graphics is going to flow. Once the mouse button is released, the text or graphics will flow into the area bounded by the box. See the example shown in Figures 20 and 21.

If you have already flowed your text, go back to earlier in this module and repeat the steps to load LEADSTRY.RTF. If the file you have just loaded fills the page, perform these steps in the pasteboard area at the side of the page.

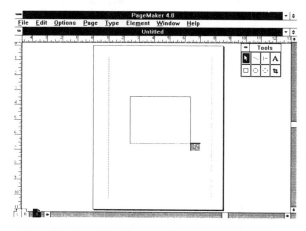

Figure 20. This method of loading the text onto the page is an alternative to Figures 18 and 19. After you have chosen LEADSTRY.RTF, through the Place *command and you are returned to your page with the text cursor of Figure 11, hold down the mouse button and drag the mouse diagonally to the right and down the page. Now see Figure 21.*

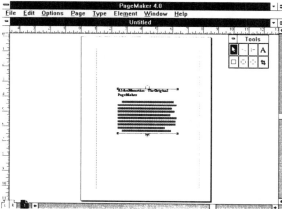

Figure 21. Release the mouse button when the box is the size you wish it to be. The text now flows to fill this box.

In Figures 22, 23, and 24, we are loading the ANCHOR.TIF file from within the lesson4 directory using the *Place* command. This is being loaded using the method described in Figures 20 and 21 — i.e., loading a file into a designated box area. You may note that it is possible, with this approach, to upset the correct proportions of a graphic. Don't worry; this is easily fixed and is explained in Module 7.

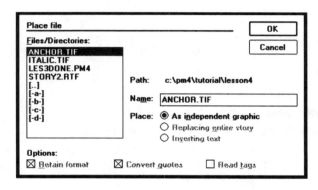

Figure 22. The file ANCHOR.TIF is selected — ready to load onto the PageMaker page. Now click on OK to get to Figure 23.

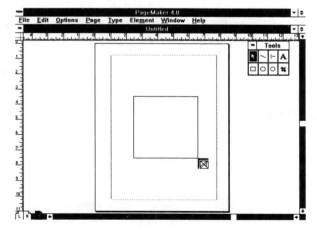

Figure 23. Hold the mouse button down and once again draw a box the size that you would like your picture to be. If the page is filled with text from the previous examples, use the area on either side of the page.

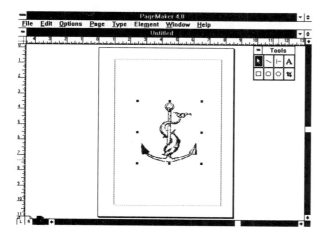

Figure 24. When you release the mouse button, the image fills the box you created for it.

If you need to clear your page at any time, select the text or graphic(s) with the pointer tool (the arrow in the Toolbox in the top right of the screen) and press the delete key.

In summary, to load files into PageMaker, choose the *Place* command, select your file, and flow it onto the page. The following modules will look at ways in which these files, including both text and graphics, can be manipulated once they have been imported.

Saving Files

The *Save* command in the **File** menu (Figure 25) will save all changes that you recently made to the publication you are currently working on. The *Save* command can be used at any time without your having to leave the work you are doing. The saving of both text and/or graphics forms a PageMaker publication. The first time you execute the *Save* command, the *Save publication as* dialog box (Figure 26) will appear. This lets you give your publication a name and lets you choose where you want to save this publication. The *Save as* command can also be used at any time during your work on a publication. If your publication has already been named, the *Save as* command lets you re-name it and/or change the disk or directory it is in. The *Save as* command will also reduce the size of your publication, after editing, which means less disk space is used. Other options within Figure 26 are discussed in later modules.

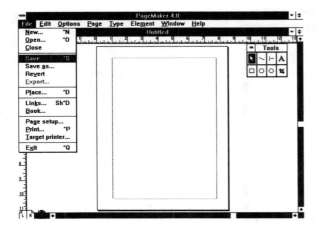

Figure 25. The Save *command in the* File *menu will save all changes you have made to the current publication. It is a good idea to use this command often to prevent the loss of valuable work you are doing in PageMaker.*

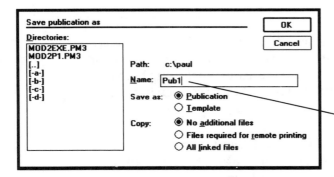

Figure 26. The Save publication as *dialog box appears either by selecting the* Save *command in a publication for the first time, or selecting the* Save as *command in the* File *menu. After moving around the directories and files on your machine to the place you would like your file to be saved, type in the name you would like to give the publication, as we have done here.*

Opening an existing publication

So far we have discussed opening PageMaker for a new publication. Opening previously saved publications can be done in one of two ways. The first way we will talk about is opening the saved publication from within PageMaker 4 using the *Open* command. Start up PageMaker as normal, and instead of choosing *New* from the **File** menu, choose *Open* (Figure 27). The *Open* publication dialog box will now appear (Figure 28). This gives you the opportunity to move around the files and directories on your PC to where you saved your PageMaker 4 publication. Once it is located, it's just a matter of double-clicking on the appropriate name or highlighting it with your mouse and clicking on OK. Figures 27 and 28 show how this is done.

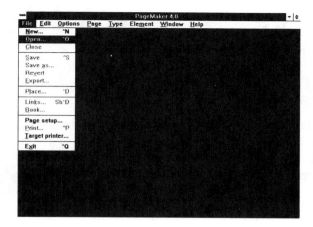

Figure 27. After starting up PageMaker from the desktop, the Open *command instead of the* New *command is selected in order to open a previously saved PageMaker publication.*

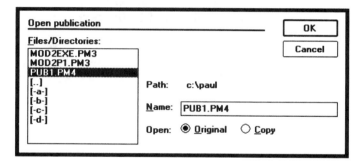

Figure 28. Once your PageMaker publication has been located, double-click on it, or select it and click on OK, to open the publication.

It is also possible to open an existing PageMaker 4 publication from the Windows MS-DOS Executive or File Manager programs. This is done by double-clicking on the file name once you have located it from the list of directories and files (Figure 29).

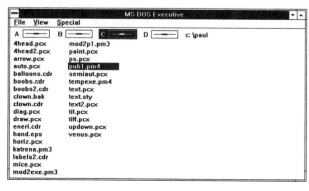

Figure 29. To open an existing PageMaker 4 file from the MS-DOS Executive, double-click on the file name once you have located it.

Options for importing text

You may have noticed several choices that can be made when importing text files — the choices that appear along the bottom of the *Place* dialog box. These include *Retain format, Convert quotes,* and *Read tags* (Figure 30).

Retain format will make sure that any formatting applied to text at the word processor level still applies in PageMaker. If it is not selected, the text will not come through with any of the formatting applied in the word processor.

Convert quotes will convert the " and ' quotes often used by word processors to the more professional ", ", ', and '.

Read tags (which is discussed in more detail in Module 11, **Style Sheets**), will read formatting codes imbedded in the text at the word processor level.

The other options, located to the right of the window include: *As new story, Replacing entire story,* and *Inserting text.* These are discussed in Module 10, **Templates.**

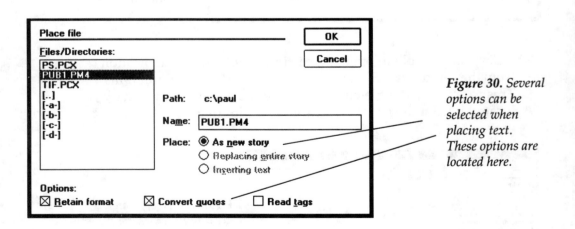

Figure 30. Several options can be selected when placing text. These options are located here.

EXERCISE: LOADING FILES

Loading Files

In this exercise you are going to load files into PageMaker, both graphics and text. You will also go through the process of locating these files on the hard disk using the PageMaker *Place* command dialog box.

This training material is structured so that people of all levels of expertise with Page-Maker can use it to gain maximum benefit. In order to do this, we have structured the material so that the bare exercise is listed below this paragraph on just one page, with no hints. The following pages contain the steps needed to complete this exercise for those who need additional prompting. The **Loading Files** module should be referenced if you need further help or explanations.

Module 2 exercise steps

1. *Start PageMaker.*

2. *Create a new PageMaker document, using these parameters:*

    > *Letter page*
    >
    > *0.75" margins all around the page*
    >
    > *Double-sided, Facing pages*
    >
    > *Four pages long*
    >
    > *Orientation tall (portrait)*

3. *Set the measurement preferences to inches.*

4. *Load in a text file called LEADSTRY.RTF from the lesson2 directory, which is located in the tutorial directory. Flow this text onto the first page using the manual flow method.*

5. *Load in the graphic LOGOTYPE.TIF from the lesson2 directory and place it at the bottom of the page.*

6. *Change the page view to* Actual size *and scroll to the top right-hand corner of the page.*

The detailed steps to complete this exercise are located on the following pages.

The steps in detail

1. Start PageMaker.

This first step is achieved by locating the PageMaker 4 icon in the Windows Program Manager. Double-click on this icon to load PageMaker (Figures 1 and 2).

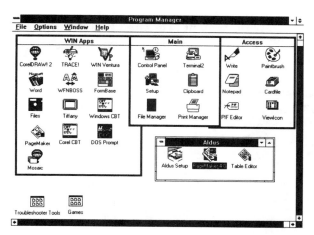

Figure 1. Although there is very little chance that your Program Manager will look anything like this one, there should be a window where PageMaker 4 is located.

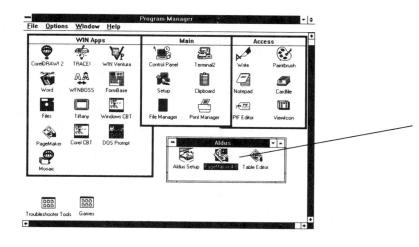

Figure 2. Double-click on the PageMaker 4 icon to start the program.

2. *Create a new PageMaker document using these parameters:*

    Letter page

    0.75" margins all around the page

    Double-sided, Facing pages

    Four pages long

    Orientation tall (portrait)

After starting PageMaker, a new document is created by selecting the *New* command (Figure 3) from the **File** menu. From this command comes the dialog box in Figure 4.

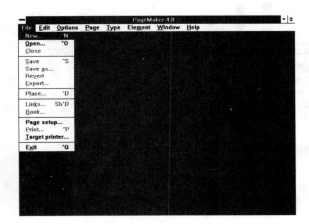

Figure 3. The New *command from the* **File** *menu must be used to create a new Page-Maker publication.*

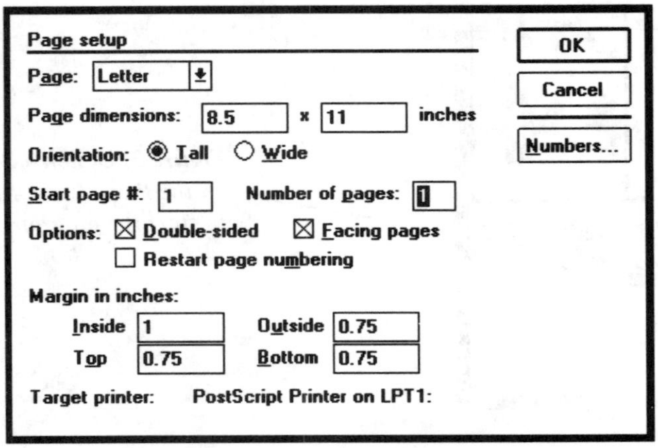

Figure 4. The New *dialog box contains all the options you need to create the page described in step 2 of this exercise. This figure shows current default values. Figure 5 shows the new values required for this exercise.*

In this dialog box, the default parameters of *Letter* size, *Double-sided*, *Facing-pages*, and *Orientation* (*Tall*) do not have to be changed. Just change the number of pages to 4 and the *Inside* margin to 0.75. Click on OK once this is done.

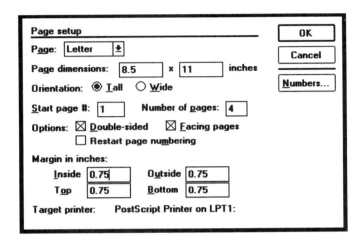

Figure 5. Your dialog box should be set up exactly like this one.

3. Set the measurement preferences to use inches.

These preferences are set using the *Preferences* command in the **Edit** menu. Invoke this command (see Figure 6) and set up the dialog box as shown in Figure 7.

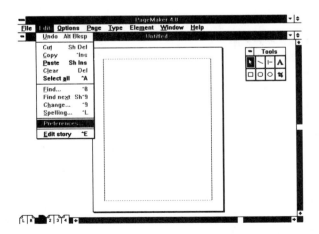

Figure 6. Use the Preferences *command to set measurement units.*

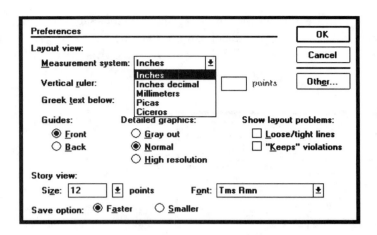

Figure 7. Select the correct measurement unit and click on OK.

As this is only an example of using the *Preferences* command, you may, in fact, prefer to set the measurement units to something else more suitable to you — perhaps millimeters. Remember, this unit of measure can always be overridden by inserting *m* for millimeters, *p* for picas, and *i* for inches in any dialog box after you insert the desired value.

4. *Load in a text file called LEADSTRY.RTF from the lesson2 directory, which is located in the tutorial directory. Flow this text onto the first page using the manual flow method.*

The first step here is to use the *Place* command from the **File** menu (Figure 8). From there you will be presented with the dialog box of Figure 9.

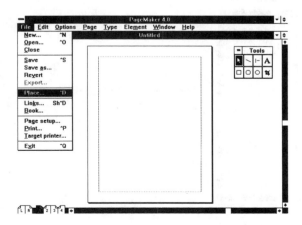

Figure 8. The Place *command is the one used to import all files into PageMaker.*

66

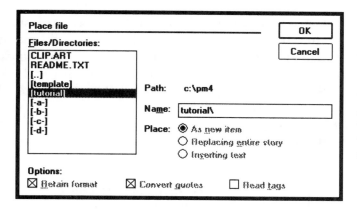

Figure 9. *If you opened PageMaker from the pm4 directory, you will be presented with a list containing the tutorial directory, which includes the lesson directories.*

If the PageMaker directory is the currently active directory, you will be looking at something similar to what is shown in Figure 9 — the tutorial directory should be listed. If it is, double-click on [tutorial]. If it's not, search through the computer's hard drive and directories for the pm4 directory (or something similar), and then for the tutorial directory within this.

Once you have entered the tutorial directory, you will have no trouble locating the lesson2 sub-directory (Figure 10(a)). Double-click on this, and then on LEADSTRY.RTF (Figure 10(b)) and wait a few seconds to be returned to the PageMaker page (Figure 11). Your tutorial or lesson2 directories may have slightly different files from ours. This doesn't matter — just find and select LEADSTRY.RTF (Figure 10(b)).

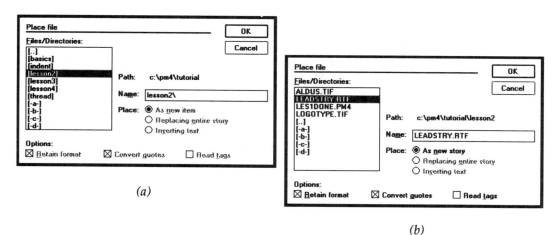

(a)

(b)

Figure 10. *Double-click on the tutorial directory in Figure 9, and on lesson2 (Figure 10(a)), and double-click again on the file LEADSTRY.RTF*

Your mouse cursor will, of course, change shape after the procedures shown in Figures 9 and 10. It should be the same as shown in Figure 11 — the manual flow mode. If it is not, go to the **Options** menu and choose the *Autoflow* command. To load this file onto the page, move the mouse cursor to the top left-hand corner of the page margins (Figure 11) and click the mouse once. The text will then flow onto the page (Figure 12).

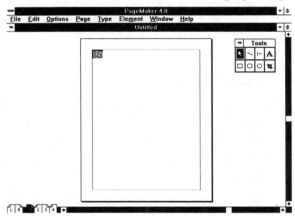

Figure 11. Note the shape of the mouse cursor, denoting a file is waiting to be loaded in manual mode. Position the mouse cursor where you want the text to flow from (normally the top of the page).

Figure 12. The text will flow across and down the page until it runs out.

5. *Load in the graphic LOGOTYPE.TIF from the lesson2 directory and place it at the bottom of your page.*

The *Place* command, once again, is used to load in a file, no matter what format it exists in. This time however, you will be immediately looking at the contents of the lesson 2 directory (Figure 13)— as this is where you retrieved your last file (LEADSTRY.RTF).

Locate the file LOGOTYPE.TIF and double-click on the filename (Figure 13). You will then be returned to the PageMaker page (Figure 14).

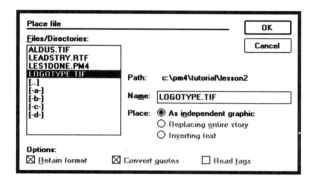

Figure 13. The Place *command will take you to the same directory as you retrieved the last file from — in our case the lesson2 directory. Select the file LOGOTYPE.TIF by double-clicking on it.*

To place this file at the bottom of your page, move the mouse down to this area (see Figure 14). You can deposit the graphic using one of two techniques — either the one click method you used above for the text flow or the box-draw method. To use the latter method, hold down the mouse button, move the mouse down and across to the right of the page, and release it when the box is the right size (Figures 14 and 15).

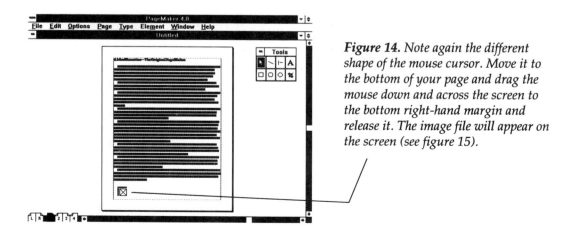

Figure 14. Note again the different shape of the mouse cursor. Move it to the bottom of your page and drag the mouse down and across the screen to the bottom right-hand margin and release it. The image file will appear on the screen (see figure 15).*

Figure 15. The graphic at the bottom of the page.

6. *Change the page view to* Actual size *and scroll to the top right-hand corner of the page.*

The page view is changed via the **Page** menu. Select the command *Actual size* from this menu (Figure 16).

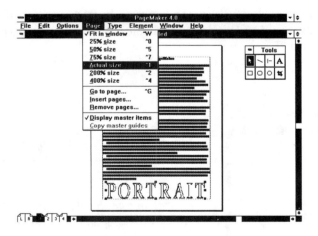

Figure 16. Changing to Actual size *view can be done in a variety of ways, but this way is the most straightforward.*

Initially, you may not be looking at the top right-hand corner of the page — in fact, it could be anywhere on the page. The scroll bars must be used to move the page around.

Figure 17. Initially, changing to Actual size *could put you anywhere on the page.*

These are the two areas that move you to the top right of the page. Two mouse clicks in each of these areas could be used to get you to the area you are after (depending, of course, on your screen size and type). You could also use the arrows circled in Figure 18, but this would be slower.

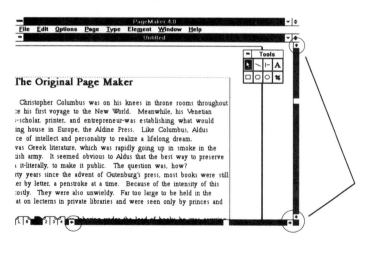

Figure 18. We clicked twice in the areas indicated in Figure 17 to get this result — a look at the top right-hand corner of the page. It is also possible to move around the page (more slowly) by clicking in the circled arrow areas.

After completing this exercise you will be familiar with the basic techniques involved in the use of PageMaker — how menus work, how dialog boxes work, how to load files, and how to move around the screen. This is a good start for moving to the next module.

WORKING WITH TEXT BLOCKS

Working with Text Blocks

As we have already seen, we can import text from other applications onto the PageMaker page. We need to have far more control, however, over the text than we did in the last module. We need to be able to manipulate a block of text in many different ways.

If you wish to follow through with us in this module, load any text onto the page. The LEADSTRY.RTF file as loaded in Module 2 would be suitable. Use the load method discussed in Figures 20 and 21 in Module 2 to get your text onto the page similar to the text shown in Figure 1.

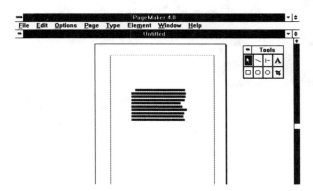

Figure 1. Make sure that you have a block of text on your page similar to this, if you wish to move through this module with us.

Before you start this module make sure that you have the selector (pointer) tool activated in the Toolbox. This will allow you to select and manipulate the text (Figure 1).

What you now have on the page in Figure 1 is referred to as a "text block." We are not going to be looking at sentences, letters, and words in this module, but rather the manipulation of the whole block of text as one unit.

If it is not selected, click on the block of text, anywhere, just once. Once selected, you should see several things appear around the edge of this text block (Figure 2). These include a line above and below the text, a "windowshade handle" above and below the text, and a dot (or small square) in each corner of the text block. These indicate that the text block is, in fact, selected, and each one of these selection indicators can be used in a different way to manipulate that text block.

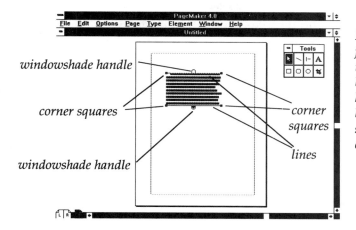

Figure 2. Note the features of the selected text. A line above and below, a windowshade handle above and below, and a dot or small square in every corner.

Moving text

Any text block can be easily moved to anywhere else on the page without changing its shape in any way. There are, in fact, two ways to do this. First, position the mouse on the block of text, somewhere near the middle of the block. Next, hold the mouse button down and don't move the mouse for a few seconds. The arrow cursor changes to a four-arrow type, the handles and corner squares disappear, and the text is bounded by dotted lines. Now move the mouse anywhere on the desk, with the mouse button still held down, and the text will move anywhere on the screen that you wish. This method is illustrated in Figure 3.

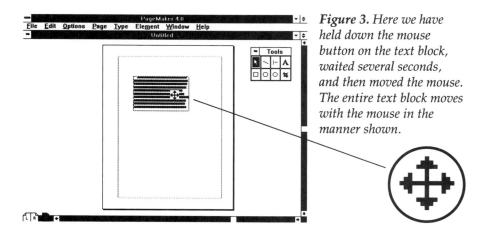

Figure 3. Here we have held down the mouse button on the text block, waited several seconds, and then moved the mouse. The entire text block moves with the mouse in the manner shown.

Alternatively, you can hold the mouse button down on the text and move the mouse immediately. What this will do is move the selected text block, but only in a boxed outline form. Once the mouse button is released, the text will reformat in its new position. This is illustrated in Figure 4.

Clicking anywhere outside the text block will deselect that block.

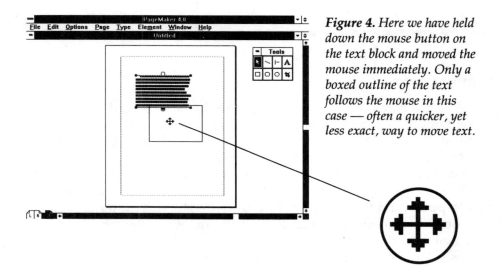

Figure 4. Here we have held down the mouse button on the text block and moved the mouse immediately. Only a boxed outline of the text follows the mouse in this case — often a quicker, yet less exact, way to move text.

Resizing text blocks

Text blocks can be resized as simply as they can be moved. Once again, there are several ways in which a text block can be resized. We will look at each one in turn.

People often think they must define their column width, number of columns, page breaks, and so on from the word processor they used to create the text. However, all this kind of work is done from within PageMaker and can be altered at will, regardless of how the text was created in the word processor. The word processor is used basically as a text input medium — very little formatting work need be done at this early stage.

Resizing vertically

The method we are about to describe is used to resize a text block vertically — the width of the text block is not altered at all. Before you do this, however, let's get one thing straight — there is no way, using these methods, that you will lose any text. It may look as though text has disappeared, but rest assured, it will come back.

With reference to Figure 5, note the handles above and below the selected block of text. The top handle should be empty, while the bottom handle has a small down arrow (▼) in it. This indicates that the text block contains more text than is currently visible. If the handle had no symbol, this would indicate the end of a particular text block.

Let's now say that you want to alter the length of this text block vertically. The way this is done is as follows. Hold the mouse button down on the bottom handle (with the down arrow sign). You must be fairly exact when doing this, and you must make sure that you do not simply click once — you must hold the mouse button down. Once you have done this, you can move the mouse up and down, keeping the button down, as much as you like. Where you release the mouse button is going to determine the new length of the text block (see Figures 5 and 6). If you moved the mouse up, text will have disappeared from the page. However, if you moved the mouse down, more text will have appeared on the page. (Unless, of course, the text file ran out of text; in which case the bottom handle will be empty.)

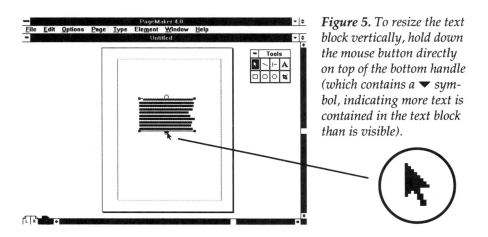

Figure 5. To resize the text block vertically, hold down the mouse button directly on top of the bottom handle (which contains a ▼ symbol, indicating more text is contained in the text block than is visible).

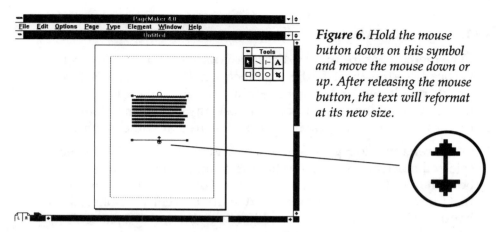

Figure 6. Hold the mouse button down on this symbol and move the mouse down or up. After releasing the mouse button, the text will reformat at its new size.

Alternatively, the text block could have been resized using the same method on the top handle. Holding the mouse button down on this handle will allow you to resize the text in the exact same way (Figure 7). However, if you shorten the text block from the top, the text will disappear from the bottom of the block. You cannot hide text from the top of a block using this method.

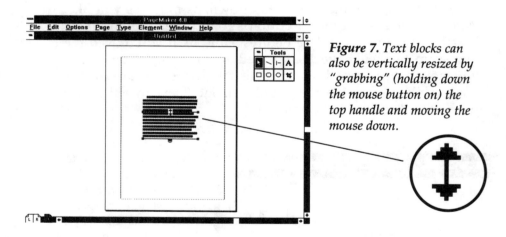

Figure 7. Text blocks can also be vertically resized by "grabbing" (holding down the mouse button on) the top handle and moving the mouse down.

Resizing horizontally

If you would like to increase or decrease the width of a text block horizontally, hold down the mouse button on any dot in any corner of the text block. You must be fairly exact when doing this, and you may at first miss the dot altogether. If you do, reselect the text block and try again till you get it. You will know when you have selected it correctly when moving the mouse button causes the effect shown in Figure 8 to appear.

This method of grabbing a corner dot with the mouse can, in effect, allow you to resize text both horizontally and vertically at the same time.

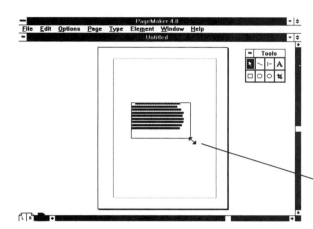

Figure 8. To resize text blocks horizontally, hold down the mouse button on any corner of a selected text block. In every corner of this block there should be a dot — this is what you grab. As you move the mouse, a rectangle is created on screen indicating the new size of the text block. Text blocks can also be resized vertically in this fashion.

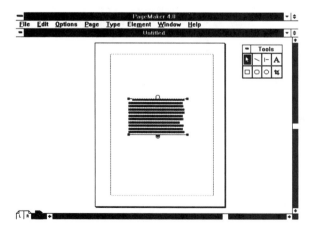

Figure 9. After you release the mouse button, the text block formats to the exact size of the rectangle of Figure 8.

The box which appears on screen is letting you know what the new dimensions of the text block will be when you release the mouse button. You will find that the text block can be adjusted both horizontally and vertically at the same time, and the text will reflow immediately.

Column guides

There are several guides that exist in PageMaker for exercising control over text blocks. Perhaps the most common guides that you will use are the column guides.

To adjust the number of columns on the page, select the *Column guides* command from the **Options** menu (Figure 10). You will be presented with the dialog box of Figure 11.

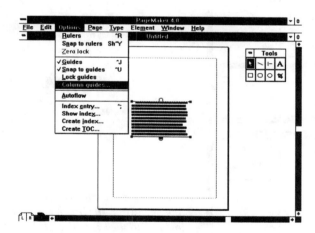

Figure 10. The Column guides *command in the* Options *menu is used to select the number of columns for the page.*

Within this dialog box, you first input the number of columns you want, and then the amount of space to be included between the columns. Upon clicking OK, you will notice column guides have been added to the page (Figure 12).

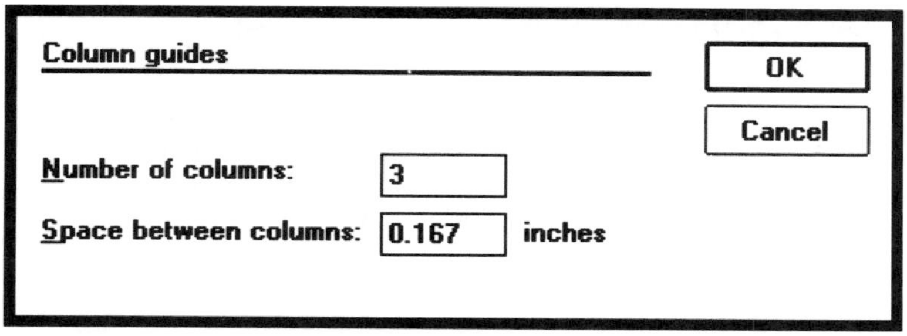

Column guides   [**OK**]

[**Cancel**]

Number of columns: [3]

Space between columns: [0.167]   inches

Figure 11. The
Column guides
command dialog
box. Here we
have defined
three columns
with .167"
between each
one.

Text already on the page will not immediately flow into these new columns — it is up to you to flow the text into these columns. The column guides initially appear in the background. Text currently on the page stays in its previously defined area.

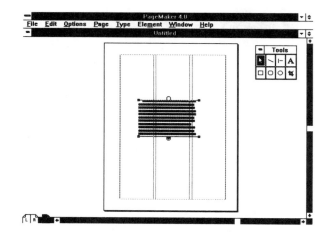

Figure 12. Although existing text on the page will not flow into the three columns automatically, the guides will appear on the page, and any text now added will flow into these new columns.

If you wish to continue following our operations, select your text as shown in Figure 12 and press the Delete (or Backspace) key. This text is then deleted. Choose the LEADSTRY.RTF example file with the *Place* command and flow it down column 1 of the page as shown in Figures 13 and 14. To find this file, double-click on tutorial in the pm4 file, and then again on lesson2.

Whenever a new text file is flowed, it will obey the bounds of a column guide. See Figures 13 and 14, which illustrate this point.

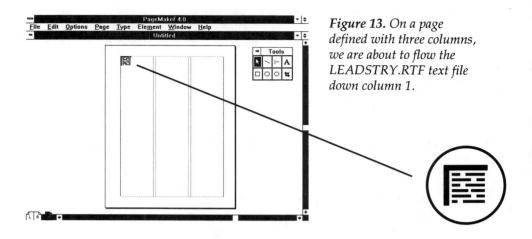

Figure 13. On a page defined with three columns, we are about to flow the LEADSTRY.RTF text file down column 1.

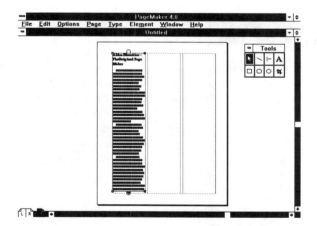

Figure 14. Note how the text flows down the first column, rather than across the whole page, as it would if no columns were defined.

The *Column guides* dialog box only selects equal size columns. Irregular columns may be achieved by manually moving the column guides. To do this, hold down the mouse button directly on a column guide, away from text if possible, and move the mouse button to the left or the right. The column guide will move with the mouse. You cannot pull just one column guide. The set of column guides moves together, as shown in Figure 15.

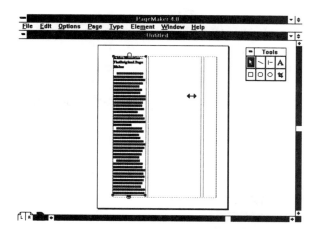

Figure 15. Irregular columns can be created by holding the mouse button down on a set of column guides and "dragging" it to the left or right.

Margin guides

Margin guides have already been discussed in Modules 1 and 2: these are the guides you can see around the inside edges of the page. They are defined when you open a particular publication; however, they can also be altered manually if you wish. To do this, hold down the mouse button on either the left or the right margin and move the mouse to the left or the right. A dotted margin guide will follow the mouse, and where it is released will be the new text margin (Figure 16). Any text now flowed onto this page will observe these new margins.

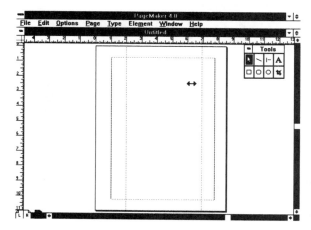

Figure 16. The left and/or right margin guides can be altered from within a publication by holding down the mouse button on the left or right margin, and dragging them where desired. To better illustrate this, we have temporarily changed from 3 columns to 1 column through the dialog box in Figure 11.

All guides on the page, whether they be margin, column, or even ruler (which we look at a little later on), are affected by several commands in the **Options** menu. Bear in mind these guides never appear on the printed output. They are simply there to help you control the layout of your document. The first command which modifies guides is the *Guides* command. This command hides or shows all guides (Figures 17 and 18).

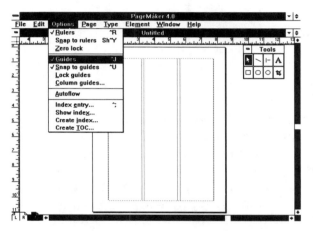

Figure 17. Selecting the Guides *command will alternately hide and show column guides on the screen. Note that with all such commands, a check to the left indicates that the option is turned on.*

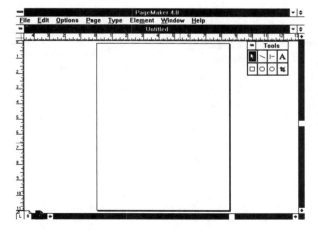

Figure 18. Here the guides are hidden from the page, giving a better indication of what the page will look like when printed.

Snap to guides is a command (Figure 19) that allows all text and graphics on the PageMaker page to "magnetically snap" to the various page guides whenever they are in close proximity. This feature is usually best left on since it makes sure that all text and graphics blocks are flush with margins, which is generally the requirement. It is often turned off when working close to a particular guide that you do not want to be flush with.

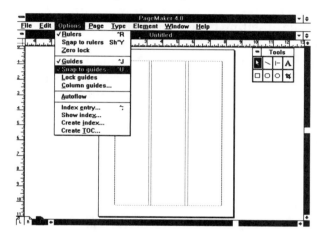

Figure 19. Selecting the Snap to guides *command, which will be on by default, allows text and graphics to snap flush to guides they are close to.*

Lock guides is, as the name suggests, a lock for all guides on the page (Figure 20). With this command activated, no guides can be moved at all until this command is reselected. It makes sure you don't accidentally move any guides that have been accurately positioned.

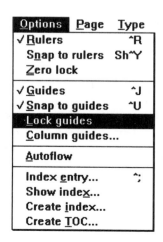

Figure 20. All guides can be locked into position using this command, to prevent accidental movement of correctly placed guides.

Warning about guides

All guides on the page can occupy a position above or below that of any text or graphic objects on the page. What this means is that if you try to select text or graphics exactly where a guide is, the guide or the object may be selected first.

This can be controlled through the *Preferences* command in the **Edit** menu (Figure 21). The associated dialog box (Figure 22) provides you with a choice of setting the guides at either the front or the back. Alternatively, even if the guides are set to the front, it is possible to choose the *Guides* command in the **Options** menu to hide the guides from the screen temporarily. The object can then be selected. Another way to select an object behind a guide is to hold down the Control key while selecting.

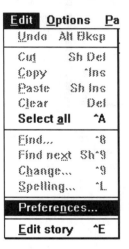

Figure 21. To control whether guides should be behind or in front of other objects on the screen, first choose the Preferences *command from the* **Edit** *menu . . .*

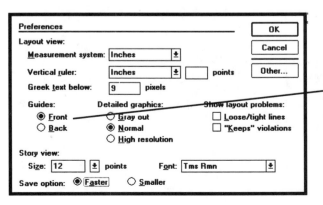

Figure 22. . . . then, from the dialog box that appears, make your choice. We have chosen to have the guides appear at the front.

Reflowing text

By now, several questions about the movement of text may have entered your mind. How do you get to see all of a text file? How do you flow the same file down several columns? How do you continue a text file from one page to the next? Right now we will look at exactly how to do these things.

The first thing we will look at is how to continue text from one text block to another. This will have to be done if you want to flow text down several columns on the same page, or even if you want to flow text from one page to another. As you might have guessed, there are several ways to do this.

Figures 23 through 31 on the following pages show how to flow text manually into three columns across the page. If you wish to follow this approach, define three columns and select the example file LEADSTRY.RTF through the *Place* command in the **File** menu. After a few seconds, your screen will look like Figure 23. Now, flow the text down one column as shown in Figure 24. Any text or graphics currently on the page can be erased by clicking on it to select it and pressing the Delete or Backspace key.

The first (and easiest) way to continue text from an existing block to a new one is as follows. Using the pointer tool, select the text block containing the currently hidden text (such as column 1 of Figure 24) that you would like to continue flowing onto the page. Click once on the bottom handle that contains a down arrow symbol (Figure 25). After doing this, you will have a new text paragraph mouse cursor — the same one that appears immediately upon loading a new file (Figure 26). You can now flow text anywhere or anyhow you like, with the knowledge that the text block you are about to create picks up exactly where the text block you just selected leaves off.

Follow Figures 27 through 31 to flow a full text file across multiple blocks. For a summary of this operation, study the captions of Figures 23 through 31 carefully.

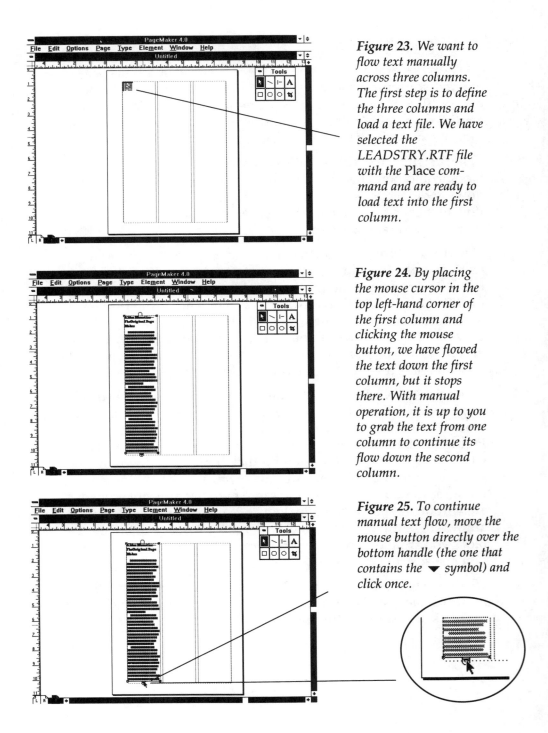

Figure 23. *We want to flow text manually across three columns. The first step is to define the three columns and load a text file. We have selected the LEADSTRY.RTF file with the Place command and are ready to load text into the first column.*

Figure 24. *By placing the mouse cursor in the top left-hand corner of the first column and clicking the mouse button, we have flowed the text down the first column, but it stops there. With manual operation, it is up to you to grab the text from one column to continue its flow down the second column.*

Figure 25. *To continue manual text flow, move the mouse button directly over the bottom handle (the one that contains the ▼ symbol) and click once.*

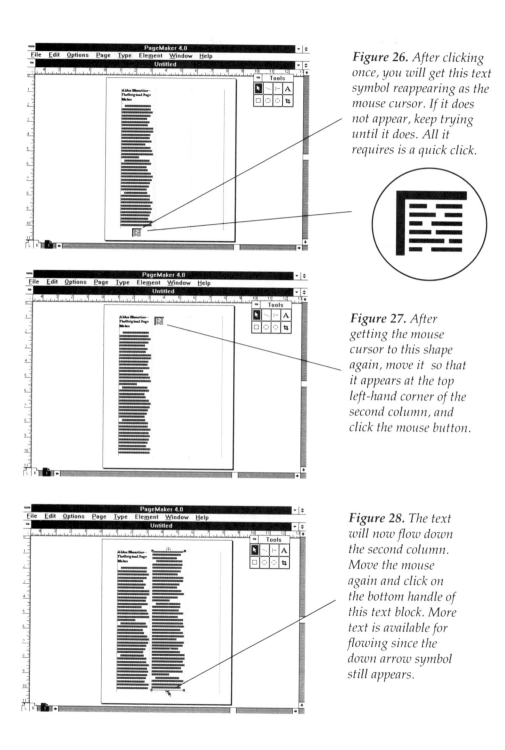

Figure 26. *After clicking once, you will get this text symbol reappearing as the mouse cursor. If it does not appear, keep trying until it does. All it requires is a quick click.*

Figure 27. *After getting the mouse cursor to this shape again, move it so that it appears at the top left-hand corner of the second column, and click the mouse button.*

Figure 28. *The text will now flow down the second column. Move the mouse again and click on the bottom handle of this text block. More text is available for flowing since the down arrow symbol still appears.*

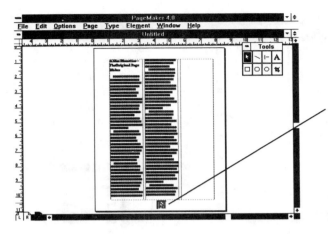

Figure 29. *Once again, the mouse cursor will change shape.*

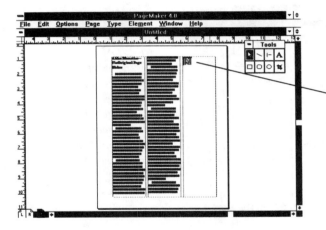

Figure 30. *Now move the mouse cursor so that it appears at the top left-hand corner of the third column and click the mouse button.*

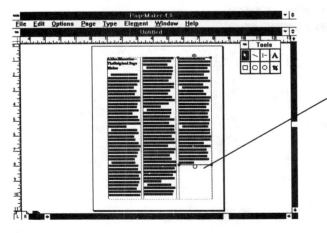

Figure 31. *In our case, the text in the file we were using ran out before it reached the end of the column. Apart from the fact that it does not fill the column, you are aware of this because the bottom handle of the third text block is empty.*

If a text block contains the ▼ symbol in its bottom handle, this means that it can be clicked on again and the text that follows can be flowed into a new text block. If you click on this handle by accident and get the paragraph mouse cursor when you don't want it, simply reselect the pointer tool and it will disappear.

In Figure 31, we know we have reached the end of the text file, since the bottom handle of the third column is empty and does not contain a ▼ symbol.

Automatic text flow

Text can be made to run across columns and pages automatically, without operator intervention. To do this, select the command *Autoflow* from the **Options** menu (Figure 32). When this command is selected, the mouse cursor will look like this ⎍ rather than like this ▤ (Figure 33). When you click the mouse to flow the text, it will flow across columns and pages fairly quickly, creating any pages it needs as it goes along (Figure 34). This process, which can take a bit of time with large text files, can be stopped by clicking the mouse button.

Options Page Type
√ **Rulers**   ^R
Snap to rulers Sh^Y
Zero lock
√ **Guides**   ^J
√ **Snap to guides** ^U
√ **Lock guides**
Column guides...
Autoflow
Index entry...   ^;
Show index...
Create index...
Create TOC...

Figure 32. Selecting the Autoflow *command in the* **Options** *menu, before text is flowed, allows text to run automatically across columns and pages.*

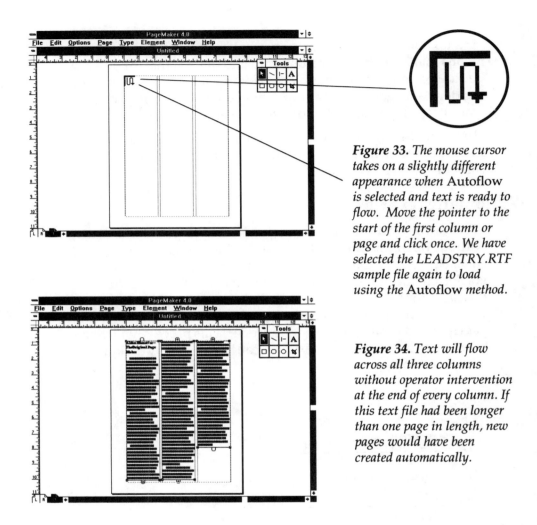

Figure 33. *The mouse cursor takes on a slightly different appearance when* Autoflow *is selected and text is ready to flow. Move the pointer to the start of the first column or page and click once. We have selected the LEADSTRY.RTF sample file again to load using the* Autoflow *method.*

Figure 34. *Text will flow across all three columns without operator intervention at the end of every column. If this text file had been longer than one page in length, new pages would have been created automatically.*

Semi-automatic text flow

Semi-automatic text flow is just as it sounds — a midway point between manual and automatic text flow. In manual flow, you must click the loaded mouse cursor at the top of every column or page, go to the bottom of that column or page, click on the bottom windowshade handle to reload the cursor, go to the top of the next column or page, and repeat the steps. With automatic text flow, you simply click the loaded mouse cursor on the first column or page, and the rest is done automatically.

If you hold down the Shift key when you are about to click the mouse cursor to flow the text for the first time (regardless of whether the *Autoflow* command has been selected or not), the mouse cursor will change appearance to look like this: |[⬇. When it does, the text will flow down the first column or page and stop, and the mouse cursor will be loaded automatically as the text finishes flowing down that column or page. You are then free to click at the top of the second column or page, without having to click first on the bottom windowshade handle of the first column.

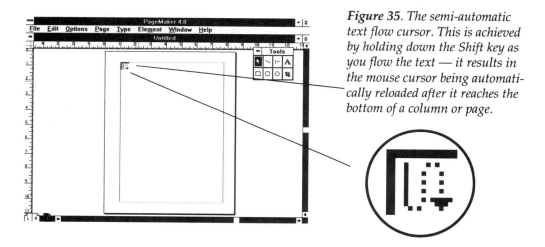

Figure 35. The semi-automatic text flow cursor. This is achieved by holding down the Shift key as you flow the text — it results in the mouse cursor being automatically reloaded after it reaches the bottom of a column or page.

Semi-automatic text flow is perhaps best used when you want to flow text more quickly than you can manually, but not regularly across the full length of all columns and pages, as automatic text flow does by default.

Temporarily changing text flow modes

Automatic to semi-automatic

1. Select *Autoflow* from the **Options** Menu.

2. Hold down the Shift key, position the mouse cursor where text is to reflow, and click on the mouse button.

The mouse icon changes to the semi-automatic icon and returns to automatic when the Shift key is released.

Automatic to manual follows similar steps except that the Control key is used instead of the Shift key.

Manual to semi-automatic

1. Select manual text flow mode (*Autoflow* off in the **Options** menu).

2. Press the Shift key and click the mouse button.

The mouse icon changes to the semi-automatic icon and returns to manual when the shift key is released.

Manual to automatic follows similar steps except that the Control key replaces the Shift key. Text will flow to the end of the file or until you click the mouse button again.

Resizing multiple text blocks

Whenever a text block is split up into several text blocks, any of the individual blocks can be resized and moved without losing any continuity of text between the blocks. When the first block in a series of blocks is resized, for example, by raising the bottom windowshade handle (Figure 36), text is forced back into the following text blocks. Note that the third text block in Figure 36 has increased in length, reflecting the extra text now available.

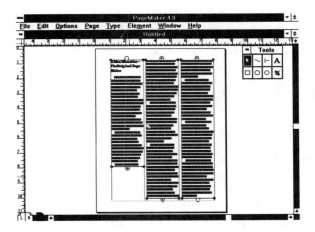

Figure 36. Any text block in the sequence can be resized without drastic consequences or loss of text. Here we have resized the first column of the page in Figure 34. Note the third column has now changed size to accommodate the extra text now available.

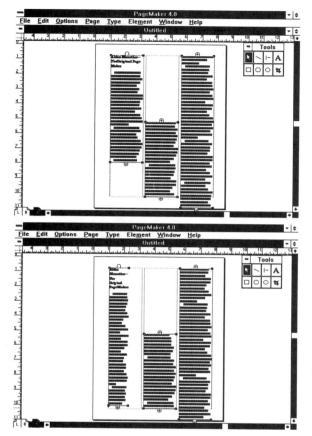

Figure 37. Even the middle block in a series of text blocks can be resized without losing text or continuity.

Figure 38. Here, the first column has been narrowed, still without any loss in the flow and readability of the text. Column 3, in both Figures 37 and 38, has changed in length to accommodate the extra text.

Removing text blocks

Text blocks can be selected with the pointer tool and then deleted using the *Cut* or *Clear* commands from the **Edit** menu. The Delete or Backspace keys also delete a text block, once selected. When this happens, that text block is removed from the "chain." In other words, the text loses its continuity. Because of this, never use these commands to remove a text block if you want to maintain text continuity.

The simplest way to remove a text block is similar to the way we resized text blocks earlier. However, instead of resizing the text block a little, hold down the mouse button on the bottom handle and pull the mouse cursor up to the start of the text block (Figures 39 through 42). The entire text block will disappear with only the two handles remaining, as shown in Figure 42.

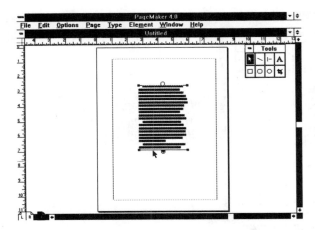

Figure 39. *Let's say that you want to get rid of this text block. You initially act as though you are going to resize it.*

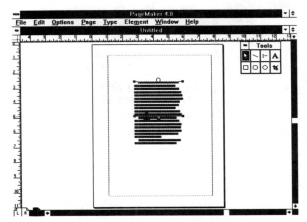

Figure 40. *Hold down the mouse button on the bottom handle, and pull the mouse cursor up the page. However, instead of releasing the mouse button half-way up the column. . .*

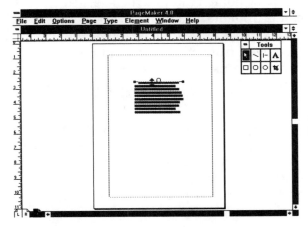

Figure 41. *. . . take it all the way to the top.*

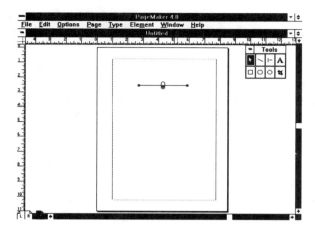

Figure 42. After releasing the mouse button above the text block, the two handles will appear together on the page.

When just these two handles remain, there are two things you can do. First, if you click anywhere else on the page, the handles will disappear. Second, if you click on the bottom handle once, they will both still disappear, but you now have a loaded mouse cursor with which you can reflow the text elsewhere (Figure 43).

This method could have been used to remove the middle column of text in, say, Figure 34. Text continuity is not lost: all the text in the middle block that is removed using the above method moves into the third column and is available for flowing into the rest of the column and onto another page, if necessary.

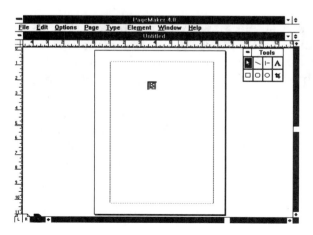

Figure 43. If the mouse button is clicked on the bottom handle of the text block in Figure 42, the text can be completely reflowed. Text will never be lost — nor will continuity — if this method is used.

Separating a text block

When a text block has flowed onto the page, it may not be in the desired layout or format. For example, the page may have three columns although your text occupies only the first column. Instead you would like it to be placed in the top half of the page, with sections of text in all three columns. This is achieved by breaking the text block in the first column into two more sections. These two sections can then be placed in the two additional columns. If you want to follow through with us in this section, make sure you have a page with three columns and enough text to fill the first column.

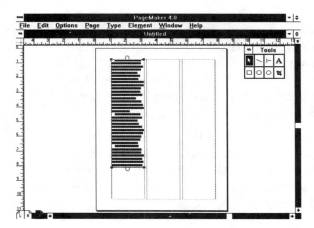

Figure 44. The text on this page occupies the first column only. If this is not how you want your layout to look, you can break a larger text block into smaller text blocks so they can be moved around individually. The first step in breaking apart a text block is to select it with the pointer tool and then place your mouse over the bottom window-shade handle.

To break the text block, first select it with the pointer tool (Figure 44). Then, with your finger on the mouse button, move the bottom windowshade handle up to where you would like the text in the first column to end. Upon stopping, you'll notice the bottom text handle now has the down arrow symbol inside it. By clicking once on the down arrow, you will get either the manual flow icon or the autoflow icon, depending on whether *Autoflow* from the **Options** menu has been selected or not. For this exercise, *Autoflow* should be switched off. Next, flow the text into the second column. Follow the same steps with the text block in column 2, to create a third text block. Figures 45 through 49 explain these steps in detail.

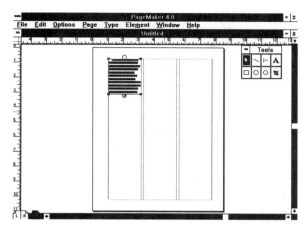

Figure 45. *Push the bottom middle handle up as though you were resizing the text block. Once you've released your finger from the mouse at the desired point, the bottom text handle will display the down arrow symbol.*

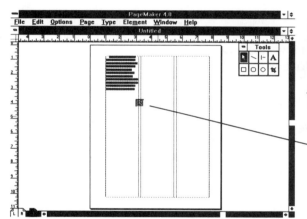

Figure 46. *Upon clicking on the down arrow symbol, the text flow icon will appear. If the Autoflow icon appears, go to the **Options** menu and deselect Autoflow.*

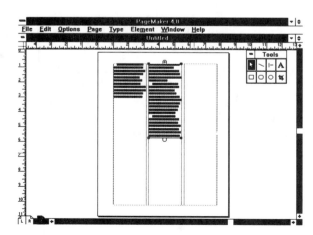

Figure 47. *Now, flow text into the second column.*

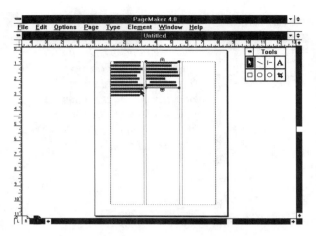

Figure 48. *Follow the same steps with this text block that you did with the first one. Push the bottom handle up to the place in the text where you wish to break the block. Click the mouse on the down arrow and you will get the manual text flow icon again.*

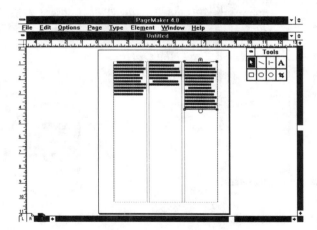

Figure 49. *Again, reflow the text, but this time flow it into the third column. Now you have three individual text blocks.*

These three text blocks can be moved anywhere around the page without affecting one another. Note that these three text blocks are still threaded together and form what PageMaker calls a "single story." Resizing any of these text blocks will not affect text continuity. The resizing features will be the same as those discussed earlier in Figures 36, 37, and 38.

Combining text blocks

If your current document is made up of numerous text blocks, you may wish to join some or all of them, making it easier to move text around. If there are two text blocks which are part of the same story, first select the second one with the pointer tool. Place the mouse over the bottom windowshade handle and pull it all the way up to the top, as you did in Figures 40 and 41 in this module. Figures 50 and 51 repeat this operation.

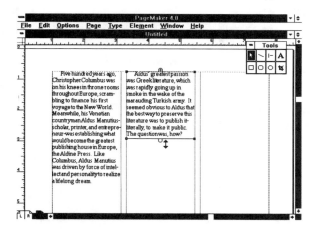

Figure 50. Hold the mouse down on the bottom handle and start pulling it all the way up to the top handle.

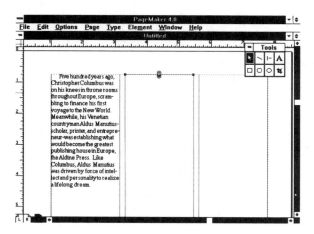

Figure 51. You should be left with no text from the second block and the two handles showing a plus in the top one and a down arrow symbol in the bottom one.

Now there should be a plus symbol and a down arrow symbol left in the handles of column 2 (Figure 51). Select the first text block. Once selected, the bottom window handle will show the down arrow symbol. Place your mouse over this handle, and pull it down to reveal the text you have recombined with the text of column 1.

Alternatively, you could have just selected the column 1 text and pulled down on the bottom windowshade handle. The text from column 2 would have flowed into column 1.

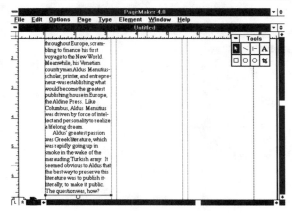

Figure 52. The mouse is held on the down arrow and pulled down to reveal the text we have just recombined from column 2 into column 1.

If you have more than two text blocks of the same threaded story to join, you could continue doing what we have just described for multiple blocks. Alternatively, use the text tool and place the flashing cursor at the end of the first text block.

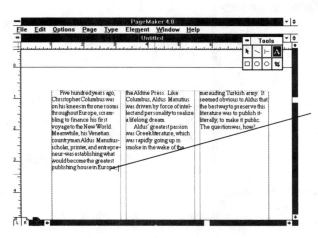

Figure 53. These three text blocks are to be joined. To do this, place the text cursor at the end of the first text block.

The next step is to choose the *Select all* command from the **Edit** menu. All your text should be selected and shown on the screen in reverse video (Figure 55). From the **Edit** menu, next choose *Cut*. All text on your screen will totally disappear — but don't worry. If you now select *Paste* from the **Edit** menu, all the text will flow back onto your screen as one block.

Figures 53 through 57 summarize this process.

Figure 54. *Following from Figure 53, you should next choose* Select all.

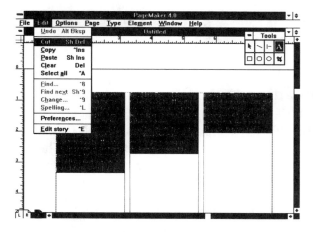

Figure 55. *After all the text is selected, you then execute the* Cut *command. All text on your screen will disappear.*

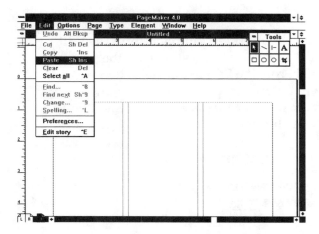

Figure 56. To finalize the joining of multiple text blocks, select the Paste command from the **Edit** menu. Note that all text has disappeared from the page prior to executing the Paste command.

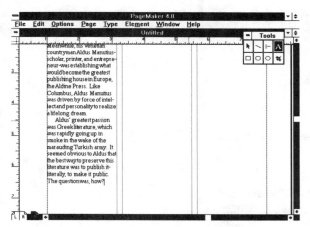

Figure 57. After the Paste command is used, the text reflows as one block. The finished result is obvious when you look at the page in reduced view. The three text blocks have become one larger text block. If your text is longer than one column, you will have to continue reflowing it until all text is placed.

Unthreading and threading text

Unthreading text occurs when text blocks that belong to the same story are separated so they become individual text blocks. The new text blocks will remain unaffected by changes made to text blocks that were once part of the same story. That is, if you have a text block which is part of a large story, and you would like to edit or change its layout without affecting the rest of the text, you can unthread the text block and make necessary changes. This un-threaded text block can always be rethreaded back into the origi-nal story. Figures 58 through 62 explain this process in detail.

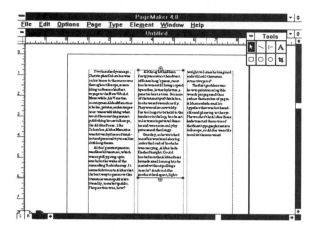

Figure 58. *When un-threading text blocks that belong to the same story, first select the text block you wish to separate with the pointer tool (in this example, the middle text block).*

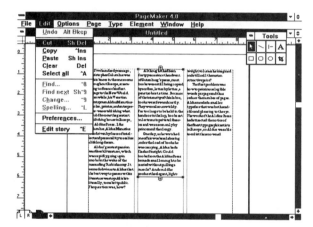

Figure 59. *After selecting the appropriate text block, you then move to the* Cut *command in the* **Edit** *menu.*

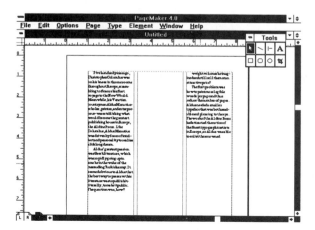

Figure 60. *The selected text block has been cut from the screen.*

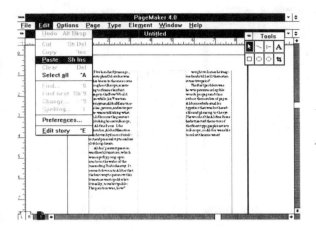

Figure 61. *The next step is to select the* Paste *command from the* **Edit** *menu.*

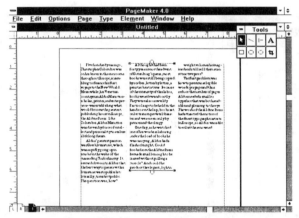

Figure 62. *The text block has been pasted back onto your page, but as a separate and individual text block. You can now edit, manipulate, and change the layout of this text block without affecting the other text blocks on the page.*

Because the text block you unthreaded is no longer part of the larger story, any changes you make to the whole story will not affect the unthreaded text. Therefore, once you have made changes to the unthreaded text, you may wish to rethread it back into the larger story.

To rethread the text block, first select it with the pointer tool. Then choose the *Cut* command, and the text block will disappear from the screen. Next, place the text cursor at the point at which you would like to rethread your text. The text block does not have to be rethreaded into the story at the place it was unthreaded. After you select the *Paste* command, the text will flow back onto the page as part of the larger story.

See Figures 63 through 68 for a detailed description.

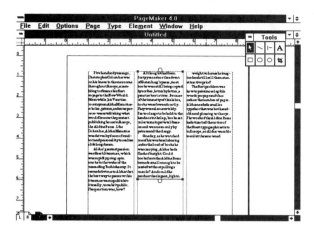

Figure 63. *To rethread the middle text block back into the larger story, you first select it with the pointer tool.*

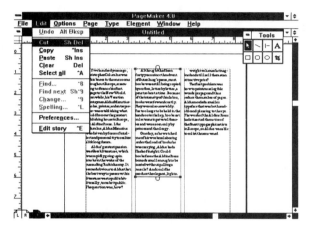

Figure 64. *The Cut command is then executed.*

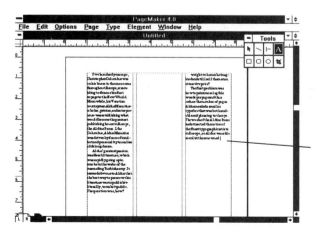

Figure 65. *After cutting the text block from the page, select the text tool and place the cursor in the story where you would like to rethread the text. In our case, we placed the flashing cursor at the end of the text block in the third column.*

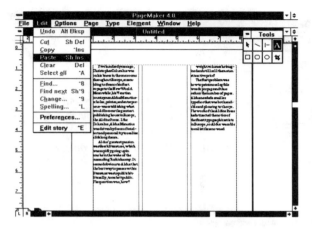

Figure 66. After placing the text cursor where you wish (in our case at the end of the text in the third column), you then select the Paste command.

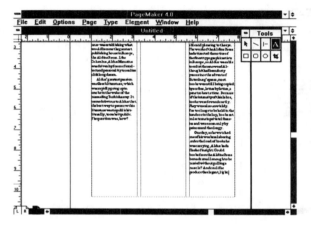

Figure 67. The text flows back onto the page and has been rethreaded into the original story.

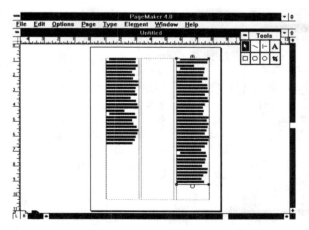

Figure 68. On selecting the longer text block with the pointer tool, you can see that there is no more text to flow. This larger text block can now be broken down into smaller text blocks or moved around the page. Now that the text blocks form one story again, any changes made to the story will affect the whole text.

Rotating text blocks

The *Text rotation* command is contained within the **Element** menu. With this command, you have the ability to rotate text blocks in 90 degree angles. Text that you want rotated must be selected by the pointer tool, and only one text block can be rotated at a time. If you wish to work with us, type your name anywhere onto an empty PageMaker page and make the font size 48 point. Then move to *Actual size* so you can better see what you are doing. See Figures 69 through 72 for further instructions.

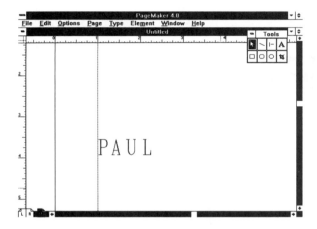

Figure 69. *The first step when rotating text is to make sure there is a text block on the page. So type in your name and make it at least 48-point.*

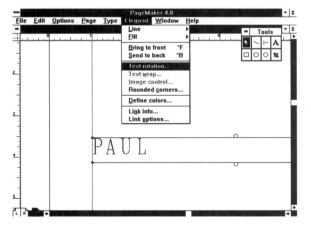

Figure 70. *Making sure your text block has been selected by the pointer tool, move to the* Text rotation *command in the* **Element** *menu.*

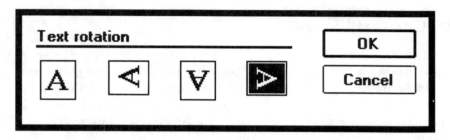

Figure 71. *The* Text rotation *dialog box will give you four choices, in 90 degree increments, of how you would like your text to be rotated. Select the angle by clicking on the icon that shows the direction you would like the text to rotate.*

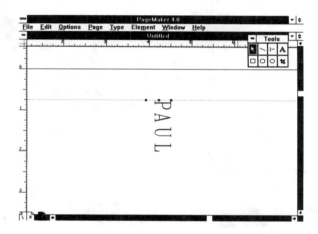

Figure 72. *After you click OK in the* Text rotation *dialog box, the text block will have been rotated in the direction selected.*

The rotated text will probably not appear back on the page in its original position. If you cannot see the text block, scan the screen using the scroll bars or move to *Fit in window* mode. Larger text blocks can just as easily be rotated by going over the same procedure (See Figures 73 and 74). All rotated text will immediately wrap around any graphics you have defined with text wrap attributes if they happen to clash.

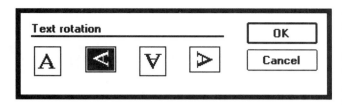

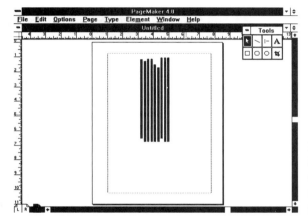

Figure 73. *With larger text blocks, you follow the same steps. After selecting a larger block with the pointer tool and choosing* Text rotation *from the* **Element** *menu, we clicked on the second rotation option. Figure 74 shows the result achieved after clicking on OK.*

Figure 74. *The whole text block has been rotated corresponding to the icon selected in the previous dialog box.*

Editing rotated text blocks can only be done through the *Edit story* command, which is fully explained in a later module. You can, however, use the pointer tool to change the layout and line breaks of rotated text. When selected with the pointer tool, the rotated text block will have eight handles around it, just like a graphic. Changing the layout of the text is done by holding the mouse button down on one of these handles and adjusting it to a new position and/or size (Figure 75).

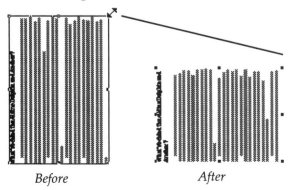

Before   *After*

Figure 75. The layout of this rotated text block has been changed by moving it with the top right handle.

EXERCISE: WORKING WITH TEXT BLOCKS

Working with Text Blocks

In this exercise you will be flowing text into columns and manipulating text files and blocks, once you have loaded them in. You will be resizing the columns, horizontally and vertically, and reflowing the text.

This training material is structured so that people of all levels of expertise with Page-Maker can use it to gain maximum benefit. In order to do this, we have structured the material so that the bare exercise is listed below this paragraph on just one page, with no hints. The following pages contain the steps needed to complete this exercise for those who need additional prompting. The **Working with Text Blocks** module should be referenced if you need further help or explanations.

Module 3 exercise steps

1.   *Create a PageMaker document consisting of four Letter pages, 0.75" margins all around, and three columns on each of the four pages.*

2.   *Load in the text file LEADSTRY.RTF from the lesson2 directory within the PageMaker tutorial directory and flow this file manually down the first column only of the first page.*

3.   *Resize the text block in the first column so that it only flows halfway down that column.*

4.   *Continue the text flow from halfway down the first column on the first page to the top of the first column on the second page.*

5.   *Move back to the first page and change the number of column guides to 2. Resize the existing text block so that it fills the first column entirely. Continue the flow from the first column to the second.*

The steps to complete this exercise are located on the following pages.

The steps in detail

1. Create a PageMaker document consisting of four Letter pages, 0.75" margins all around, and three columns on each of the four pages.

The PageMaker publication is created by selecting the *New* command from the **File** menu (Figure 1).

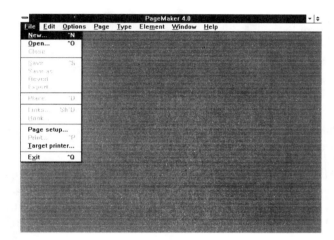

Figure 1. The New *command must be used to create a new PageMaker publication.*

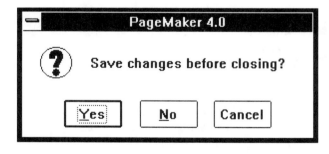

Figure 2. This message will appear if you choose New *with a currently open document, and you have modified your document since last saving. Choose* Yes *or* No, *as required in your circumstances.*

The Letter page size and the 0.75" margins are all set from the dialog box that appears upon selecting *New* (Figure 3). You should also set, within this dialog box, the number of pages to 4.

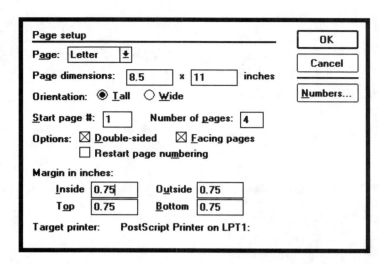

Figure 3. The New *dialog box should be set up like this — a Letter page four pages long with 0.75" margins all around.*

Once you have set up the box as in Figure 3, click on OK. The first page of the publication will then appear on screen (Figure 4).

To set the three column guides on the page you must use the *Column guides* command in the **Options** menu (Figure 4). In the dialog box that appears upon selecting this command (Figure 5), insert the number 3 for number of columns and click on OK. The space between columns can stay at the figure indicated (0.167").

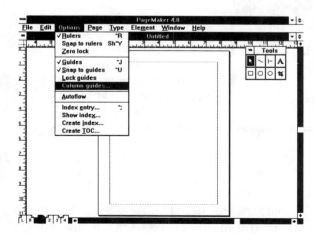

Figure 4. The Column guides *command from the* **Options** *menu must be used to create column guides for the page.*

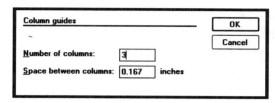

Figure 5. *Insert a 3 for the number of columns for the page and click on OK. The space between the columns, often called the "gutter," does not matter in this case.*

2. Load in the text file LEADSTRY.RTF from the lesson2 directory within the PageMaker 4 tutorial directory and flow this file manually down the first column only of the first page.

Before accessing this text file, make sure that the *Autoflow* command has not been left on. Have a look at the **Options** menu. If the *Autoflow* command has a check next to it, this means it is on. Select the command and it will then turn off. If it has no check next to it (as in Figure 6), just exit the menu.

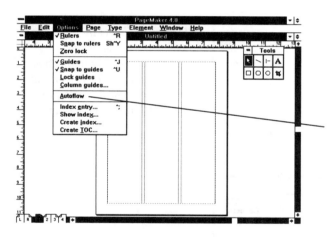

Figure 6. *Before you actually flow any text, make sure the* Autoflow *command in the* **Options** *menu has no check next to it. This will ensure that you are in manual mode and that the text only flows down one column at a time.*

To load in the file LEADSTRY.RTF you must use the *Place* command from the **File** menu (Figure 7). If, after using this command, you are unsure as to how to locate the directory lesson2, review the steps in detail for step 4 of the Module 2 Exercise. Figures 8 through 10, below, briefly summarize these steps.

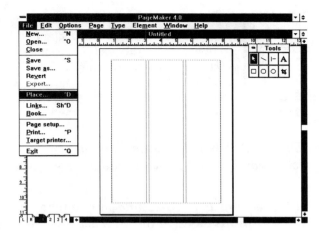

Figure 7. Choose the Place *command to load in any files.*

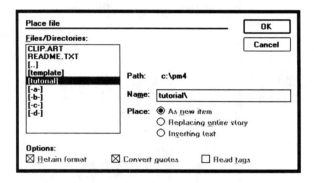

Figure 8. This is the sight that will greet you after selecting Place *and moving to the pm4 directory. Double-click on the directory name [tutorial] to access the file you are after.*

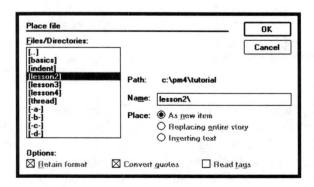

Figure 9. In this list of directories, double-click on lesson2.

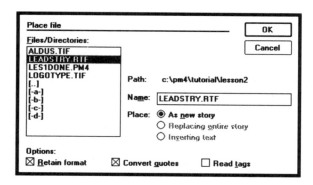

Figure 10. Then, from this list of files, double click on LEADSTRY.RTF.

Once the text file is ready to load into memory as in Figure 11, position the mouse cursor so that it appears in the very top left-hand corner of the first column of the page. From there, click the mouse button once. The text will flow down the first column and stop as shown in Figure 12.

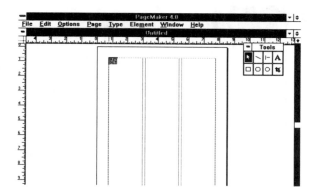

Figure 11. Position the mouse cursor at the very top left-hand corner of the first column and click the mouse button once.

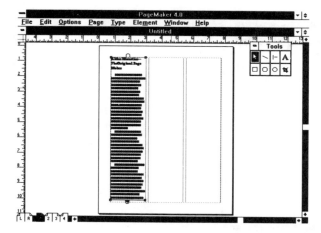

Figure 12. The text will flow down the first column and stop.

3. Resize the text block in the first column so that it only flows halfway down that column.

Before you resize this first text block, make sure that the pointer tool has been selected. This is the tool in the top left-hand corner of the Toolbox.

Click once anywhere inside this text block to select it. Once selected, a handle will appear at the bottom of the text with a small down arrow symbol in it. Move the mouse cursor over this handle and hold the mouse button down. (If all other handles of the text block suddenly disappear, it means that you were not quite on the bottom handle — reselect the text block and try again.) Once the mouse button is held down, move the mouse approximately halfway up the column (Figure 13) and release the mouse button (Figure 14). The text will now end exactly where you released the mouse.

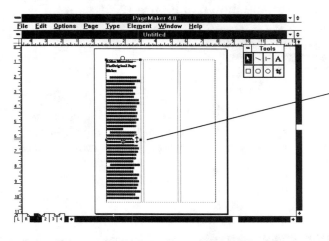

Figure 13. In this figure notice the position of the mouse cursor — which is actually a two-sided arrow now. We are in the process of resizing the column — achieved by holding the mouse button down on the bottom handle, and moving the mouse up the column.

Figure 14. Release the mouse button when you think you have resized it enough.

4. Continue the text flow from halfway down the first column on the first page to the top of the first column on the second page.

To continue text from one text block to another, regardless of where the second text block is going to flow, you must click once on the bottom handle of the existing text block (make sure this block is selected to make the handle visible). Once this is done, the mouse cursor will change appearance (Figure 15) — if it does not, try again until it does.

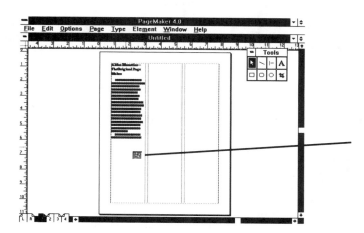

Figure 15. To continue text flow somewhere else, locate the same handle that you held the mouse button down on to resize the column, but this time click on it once — so that the paragraph mouse cursor comes back.

After you have obtained the new mouse cursor, click on the page 2 icon near the bottom left-hand corner of the page. You will move to page 2. Page 3 will also show on the screen (Figure 16), since we had *Double-sided* and *Facing pages* checked in the original dialog box of Figure 3.

Initially, pages 2 and 3 will not have three columns. To create three columns, use the *Column guides* command from the **Options** menu, as you did for page 1 earlier. You can set the column guides even while you have the special loaded text mouse cursor. (You can also choose, within the *Column guides* dialog box, to set page 2 on its own if you wish.)

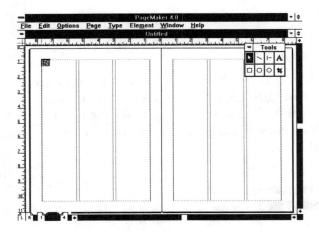

Figure 16. Click on the page 2 icon in the bottom left-hand corner of the screen. Because you are using the Facing pages selection, you will see page 3 as well. Also set three columns for these pages using the Column guides command from the **Options** menu.

Position the mouse cursor exactly as you did for page 1 — at the top left-hand corner of the first column (Figure 16) — and click the mouse button once. Text will flow down the first column of the second page (Figure 17).

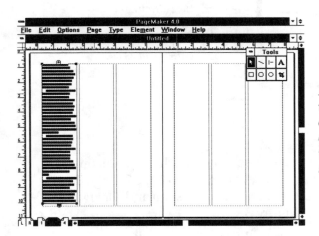

Figure 17. If the mouse cursor was positioned correctly at the top of the left-hand column and you click the mouse button once, text will flow down this column and stop.

5. *Move back to the first page and change the number of column guides to 2. Resize the existing text block so that it fills the first column entirely. Continue the flow from the first column to the second.*

Click on the page 1 icon to return to page 1.

To change the number of column guides on this page, use the *Column guides* command in the **Options** menu. Change the 3 in this dialog box to a 2 (see Figure 18).

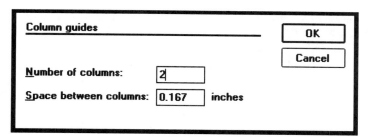

Figure 18. After clicking on the 1 icon in the bottom left-hand corner to return to page 1, use the Column guides *command from the* Options *menu to change the 3 columns to 2.*

When you return to the page, the text block will appear not to run into the newly created columns (Figure 19). You must now resize the block so that it does. Because the text block begins in the correct place (the top left-hand corner of the first column), you can resize it using one of its handles — in this case the bottom right-hand corner handle. These handles will appear after you select the text block with the pointer tool.

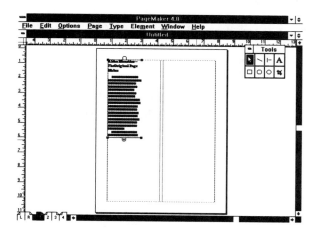

Figure 19. Because this text flowed when three column guides were on the page, it does not appear to fit the new two-column format. To resize it so that it does fit, you must first select the text block by clicking on it once with the pointer tool. Now move to Figure 20.

Make sure the text block is selected with the pointer tool and locate the bottom right handle (the small dot). Hold the mouse button down on this dot until the cursor changes to a two-sided diagonal arrow, then move the mouse until the box that is created fills the entire column (Figure 20). Release the mouse button and the text will reflow to fill the column (Figure 21).

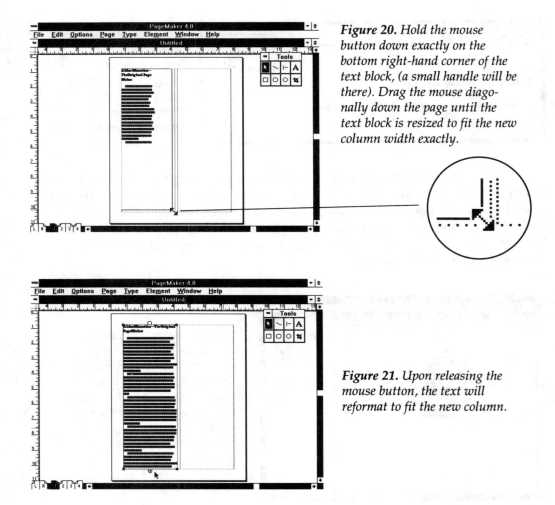

Figure 20. Hold the mouse button down exactly on the bottom right-hand corner of the text block, (a small handle will be there). Drag the mouse diagonally down the page until the text block is resized to fit the new column width exactly.

Figure 21. Upon releasing the mouse button, the text will reformat to fit the new column.

To continue the flow from the first column to the second column, make sure that the first column has been selected. Now, click once on the bottom handle of the first column where the plus sign is, so that the mouse cursor changes once again to the manual flow mode (Figure 22). Move the cursor to the top left-hand corner of the second column and click the mouse button (Figure 23). The text will not quite fill the second column as it runs out (Figure 24). The text that was put onto page 2 from step 4 will have disappeared, as all text has been reflowed onto page 1.

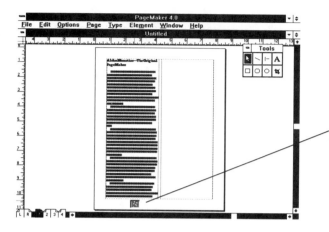

Figure 22. *To continue the text flow from the first column to the second, click on the bottom handle of the first text block. (Note the position of the mouse cursor in Figure 21.) The mouse cursor will then change to the manual flow mode as shown here.*

Figure 23. *Position the mouse cursor in the top left-hand corner of the second column and click once.*

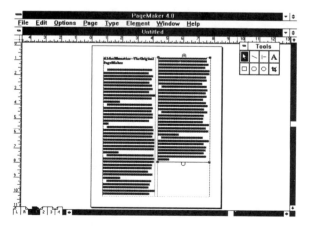

Figure 24. *Text will then flow down the text column to the end. In this case the text file ends before the column does. Any text that you flowed onto page 2 in step 4 has now moved back to page 1.*

EDITING TEXT

Editing Text

No text file that is imported into PageMaker is permanent — it can be deleted, edited, or added to, and can have its text attributes changed as well. Text can even be entered directly into Page-Maker. In this module we will be looking at editing PageMaker text in what is called the layout view. With PageMaker 4, it is now possible to edit and apply a number of useful word processing functions to text using the story editor. Details on the story editor are contained in Module 5.

Correcting errors

We will look first at how we can correct errors from any text on the PageMaker page or pasteboard area. This includes correcting simple errors, as well as deleting and adding a few words or lines to text. If you wish to follow our examples in this module, load the file LEADSTRY.RTF onto a three-column Letter page. Change to *Actual size* view and move to the top left-hand corner of the page (Figure 1). We will now make some corrections within this text.

Figures 2 through 6 show how to delete and add text directly on the PageMaker page.

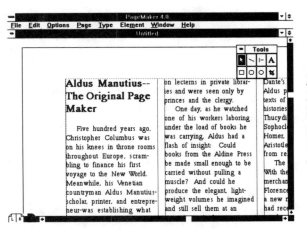

Figure 1. Load the file *LEADSTRY.RTF (from the lesson2 directory within the tutorial directory) into three columns to follow this section more clearly.*

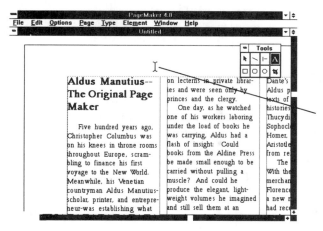

Figure 2. Select the A (text) tool from the Toolbox to do any text editing. The cursor changes to the text editing I-beam.

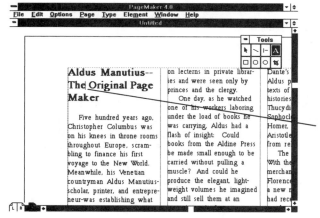

Figure 3. Move the mouse cursor to the right of the letter to delete, and click the mouse button once. A flashing text cursor will appear under the mouse cursor. Move the mouse cursor away.

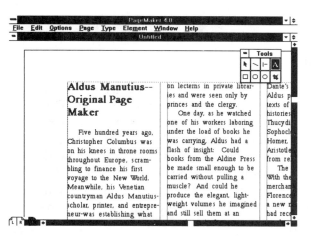

Figure 4. After the flashing text cursor has been inserted, pressing the Backspace key will remove the character to the left of the cursor. In this case, we have deleted the word "The."

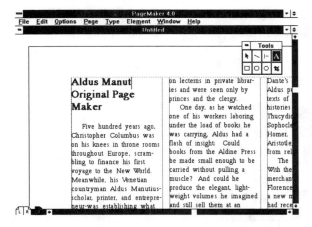

Figure 5. *Every time the Backspace key is hit, another character to the left is deleted.*

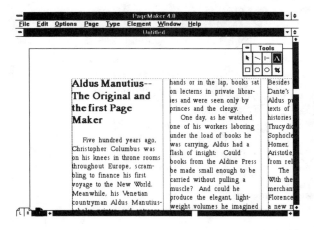

Figure 6. *The keyboard can also be used to add letters to any imported text. Here we have added some text to the first headline paragraph.*

Moving the flashing cursor

Obviously, the flashing text cursor has to move around from time to time to allow you to correct errors all over the page. This can be done two ways. The first method involves the keyboard and is best used when the distance to move the flashing cursor is not great. The directional keys on the keypad are functional with PageMaker, so hitting the right direction key will move the flashing cursor one letter space to the right. The up arrow key will move the mouse cursor one line up, the down arrow key one line down, and so on (see Figures 7 and 8).

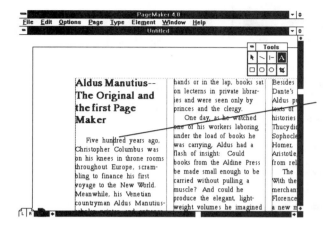

Figure 7. Note the position of the flashing text cursor now. We used the down arrow key on the keyboard to move the cursor down a line at a time from where it was in Figure 6.

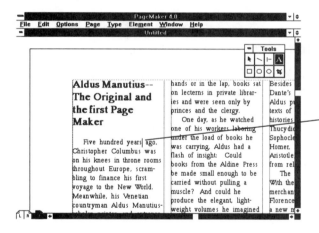

Figure 8. The text cursor has moved again from where it was in Figure 7, this time as a result of the right arrow key on the keyboard being tapped a number of times.

The second method of cursor movement involves the mouse. It is basically a repeat of how we inserted the text cursor in the text initially. Regardless of where the flashing text cursor appears in the text, you can still see the actual I-beam cursor on the page. Move the I-beam cursor where you would like to reinsert the flashing cursor and click the mouse button. The flashing cursor will become imbedded in this new position. (Figure 9).

Figure 9. The I-beam mouse cursor is still visible on the screen. It can be inserted anywhere else in the text in the same way it was inserted initially, as indicated in Figure 3.

Deleting more than one character at a time

Obviously, using the Backspace key to erase one character at a time is not a satisfactory way to delete any more than a couple of characters at once. There are other ways that words, paragraphs, and entire documents can be deleted and edited in one swift movement.

Before more than one character can be acted on, they must be selected. There are several selection techniques you can use, depending on exactly how much text you would like to delete. The first technique we will look at must be used when you want to select an irregular amount of text — that is, an amount of text that is not exactly one word, one paragraph, or one file.

Move the mouse cursor to the start of the text you would like to select. Now hold the mouse button down and move the mouse cursor to the end of the text you would like to select. As you move the mouse over the text, it will become highlighted in reverse video — indicating that this text is selected (see Figures 10 through 13).

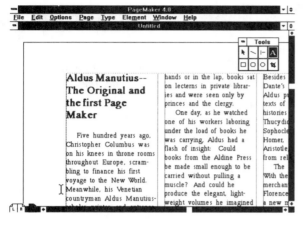

Figure 10. Here we are going to select the whole line that reads "Meanwhile, his Venetian" (seven lines down in the second paragraph). To do this, we move the mouse cursor so that it is positioned at the start of the first word we want to select. Hold the mouse button down here.

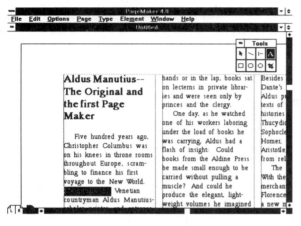

Figure 11. With the mouse button held down, move the mouse over the text. Everything the mouse passes is highlighted in reverse video. This indicates that the text is selected.

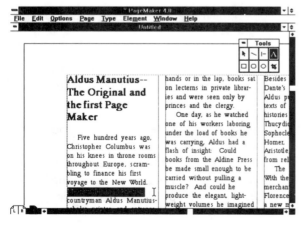

Figure 12. Release the mouse button when the desired text is selected.

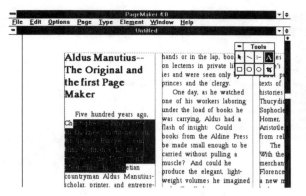

Figure 13. Any amount of text can be selected using the method shown in Figures 10 through 12 — not just full words, paragraphs, or lines.

There are several other methods which make it much quicker to select the text you are after. If, for example, you wanted to select one word, you may select that word by moving the mouse cursor anywhere over the word, and clicking twice. The entire word will become selected automatically (Figure 14).

Figure 14. To select a single word, move the mouse cursor over the desired word and double-click the mouse. The entire word will be selected automatically.

An entire paragraph can be selected in a similar method. Move the mouse cursor over the paragraph you would like to select, and triple-click the mouse. The entire paragraph will become selected (Figure 15).

If you select any text with the double or triple-click methods, you can still combine it with the original method of selection we talked about. After you double or triple-click, keep the mouse button held down and run it over the text. Words and paragraphs will be selected as you go, depending on whether you double or triple-clicked initially.

Figure 15. An entire paragraph can be selected in the same way as words — except a triple-click replaces the double-click.

Any text selected in the above methods will be acted on as a group. If you decide to bold text for example (which we will look at soon), all the selected text will become bold. If you press the Delete key on the keyboard, all the selected text will be deleted.

Another method for selecting irregular amounts of text is to insert the flashing text cursor at the start of the block, move to the end of the block, hold down the Shift key and insert the text cursor again. The entire block is selected. Finally, it is also possible to select, in one step, the entire text file loaded or being loaded. Simply place the cursor anywhere in the text and choose the *Select all* command from the **Edit** menu (Figure 16).

Figure 16. An entire text file can be selected by inserting the text cursor anywhere in the text and choosing the Select all command in the **Edit** menu. This selects an entire file — not just text on the screen, but even text that has not been laid out yet.

Once selected, text can then be cut, copied, or pasted elsewhere. All these commands are in the **Edit** menu. The *Cut* command deletes text from the screen, *Copy* copies it, and *Paste* will reinsert at the text cursor the last text block cut or copied.

The *Cut* and *Copy* commands store their text in a place called the *Clipboard*. The Clipboard only stores one block of text at a time. The last *Cut* or *Copy* command is the one that remains in the Clipboard, and it is from here that the *Paste* command will take its text. If you wish to delete text without changing the contents of the clipboard, then use the *Clear* command from the **Edit** menu.

Changing text attributes (Type menu)

In this module we will be showing you how to change text attributes using different commands within the **Type** menu. PageMaker 4 also offers a shortcut method for applying attributes to text using style sheets. The basic theory discussed in this module, however, is important to understanding the concept behind style sheets, which are discussed in Module 11.

All text in PageMaker can have certain styles applied to it, regardless of whether or not a font and size was applied to the text at the word processor stage. To effect any changes to text on the screen, the text must be selected using the techniques described above, and options from the **Type** menu must be applied to it.

Have a look now at the **Type** menu (Figure 17). We are going to look initially at the first six commands in this menu and how they relate to the text itself. (These commands are used in the **Type** menu a little differently from some of the others.)

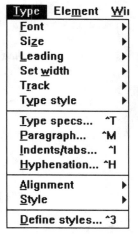

Figure 17. Commands in the Type menu will change the attributes of selected text.

Type menu — top six commands

First, make sure that you have some text selected on the page, say the first paragraph, so you can see how the changes you are about to make alter the text. The first six commands require that you keep the mouse button held down on the command you are after, and a sub-menu will appear to the right of the selected command (Figure 18). With the mouse button held down, run the mouse down the new menu. This may require honing your skills at first to actually use the new sub-menu.

Alternatively, click on the command, and the sub-menu will also pop up.

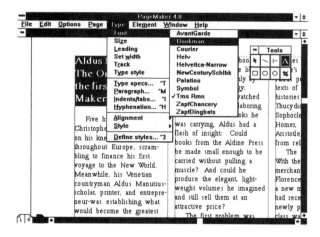

Figure 18. *Hold down the mouse button on the* Font *command and run the mouse down the sub-menu to select a font.*

Alternatively, you may click on Font *in the* **Type** *menu, and then click again on the particular font you wish to select from the sub-menu.*

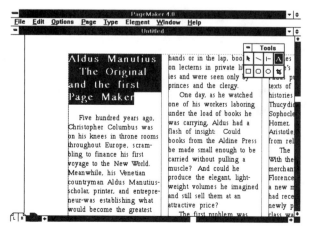

Figure 19. *The font Bookman, which we selected above, is reflected on the screen with a different screen font.*

Font command. Look first at the *Font* command (Figure 18). Listed in the sub-menu that appears in this figure is the selection of fonts available for use. The range of fonts will depend on how many are loaded into your system and the printer you use. Each one of these typefaces will have its own screen representation, which will change when another font is selected.

By choosing the Bookman font from Figure 18, we have changed the first paragraph to Bookman, as seen in Figure 19.

Size command. The *Size* command will allow you to manipulate the point size of the selected text, from 4 to 650 points in increments as small as 0.1 points. By choosing *Size*, a different sub-menu appears as shown in Figure 20. To access a point size not listed in this sub-menu, choose *Other* at the top of the sub-menu. Alternatively, a command further down the **Type** menu (*Type specs*) may be used. Select the type size that you would like to employ, in our case 8 points in Figure 20. Once again this will be reflected in the text selected (Figure 21).

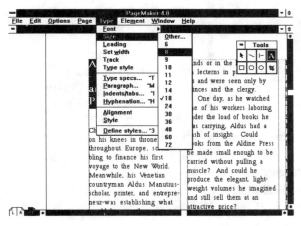

Figure 20. The Size *command is used in the same way as the* Font *command and Font sub-menu — run the mouse down the new* Size *sub-menu to select a size for the text. Alternatively, simply click on the* Size *command and then, in the sub-menu, click on the desired point size.*

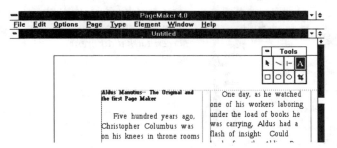

Figure 21. The size of text is then reflected on the screen. In our case, 8-point text for the first paragraph.

Leading command. The *Leading* sub-menu, accessed through the *Leading* command, is important, as it determines to a large degree exactly how the text is going to look. In the *Leading* sub-menu (Figure 22), you will see numerous values, in half-point increments, that you can set the leading to. Leading, by the way, is equivalent to line spacing.

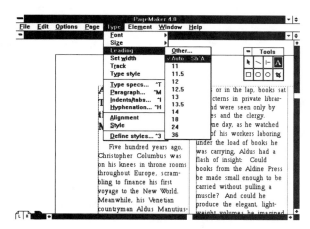

Figure 22. Once again, the Leading *command works like the commands above it — as it is selected, a sub-menu appears from which you must select a* Leading *value.*

You will also note a value that reads *Auto*. When *Auto* is selected as the leading value, it is set by default to twenty percent greater than the size of the text. The default value for *Auto* leading can be adjusted through the *Spacing* option in the *Paragraph specifications* dialog box (discussed later in this module). *Auto* leading automatically adjusts line spacing whenever the point size of the text is altered. This can be important: if your document uses ten point type with eleven point leading (commonly called ten on eleven, or 10/11) and you decide to change the point size to 12 points, the leading will remain at 11 points until you change it. If the leading were automatic, it would not necessarily need changing at all.

In the *Leading* sub-menu (Figure 22), you can therefore choose a predetermined size, *Auto* or *Other*. *Other* allows you to choose a leading value from 0 to 1300 points in 0.1 point increments. Leading can also be set in a similar way using the *Type Specs* command further down the **Type** menu.

Set width command. Below leading is the *Set width* command (Figure 23). This feature controls the width of the characters from 5% to 250% in 0.1% increments. *Normal* will be set by default in the sub-menu of Figure 23, or it will indicate whatever the selected text may have previously been altered to. To change to a different value, run down the sub-menu and make your selection. *Other* may be selected to choose a specific value within the available range indicated above.

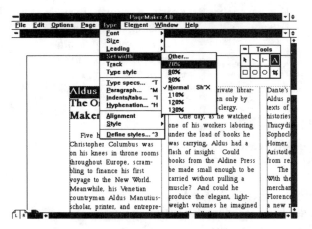

Figure 23. The Set width *command alters the width of your text characters. Here we are changing the word "Aldus" to 70% of its original width. Figure 24 shows the result.*

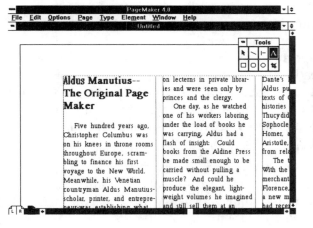

Figure 24. The result of what we did in the previous figure.

The width of the text ("Aldus") has been reduced.

Track command. The next command in the **Type** menu is the *Track* command. This refers to the amount of spacing between characters. The choices you have here, when the mouse is held down, will expand or decrease the space between the text based on the point size of the type. An example of this is shown in Figures 25 and 26.

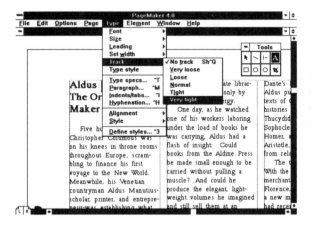

Figure 25. Here we are changing the inter-character spacing of the word "Manutius" using the Track command.

Figure 26. In moving to Actual size view, you will notice that the inter-character spacing of the word we selected is tighter than the other words.

Type style command. In this command, simple style changes are made to the text, including *Bold*, *Italic*, *Underline*, *Strikethru*, and *Reverse*. (Figure 27). These will be reflected on the screen, and different styles can be built on top of each other. To get a bold italic effect, for example, you must first select *Bold* and then reselect the command to choose *Italic*. In this way, multiple type style effects can be applied to any selected text (Figure 28).

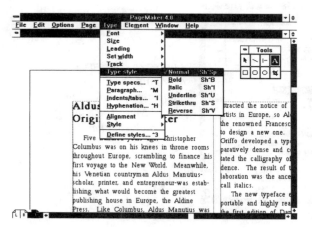

Figure 27. The type styles can only be applied one at a time, but multiple effects can be created by applying one style on top of another.

Figure 28. A number of the Style *commands have been applied to the first paragraph, including* Bold, Italic, *and* Underline.

Some font, size, and style examples:

Bookman 12 point italic

Times 14 point bold

Avant-Garde 10 point normal

Zapf Chancery 18 point italic

Helvetica 36 point

Type specs command

The commands described above — *Font, Size, Leading, Set width, Track, Type style* — are used as a kind of shortcut to changing text attributes. Although almost all type specifications can be changed using these commands, they can also be changed in one dialog box using the *Type specs* command. This command is located about halfway down the **Type** menu (Figure 29).

Within the dialog box that appears on choosing the *Type specs* command (Figure 30), there are several obvious choices which can be made, others not so obvious.

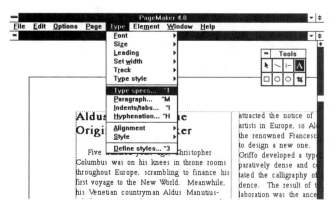

Figure 29. Selecting the Type specs *command will allow you to apply all the options found in the six commands above it, plus some additional ones — all as a group.*

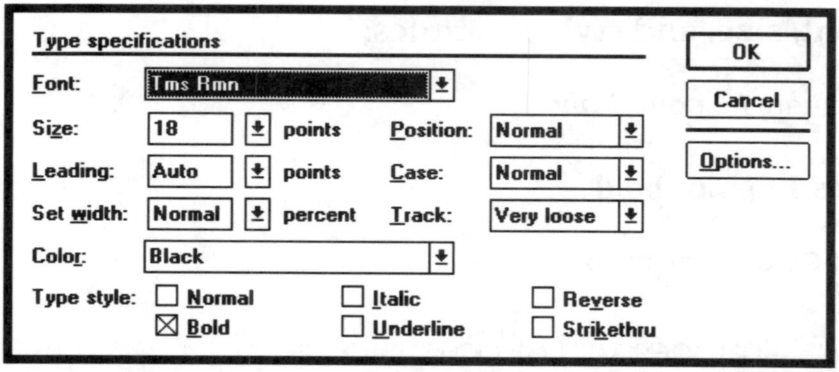

Type specifications

			OK
Font:	Tms Rmn	±	Cancel
Size:	18 ± points	Position: Normal ±	Options...
Leading:	Auto ± points	Case: Normal ±	
Set width:	Normal ± percent	Track: Very loose ±	
Color:	Black ±		

Type style: ☐ Normal ☐ Italic ☐ Reverse
             ☒ Bold   ☐ Underline ☐ Strikethru

Figure 30. This is the Type specifications *dialog box — reflecting all the current settings for the selected text.*

Font. The line at the top reads "Font: name of font . " Replacing *name of font* will be the actual font the selected text uses. In our case, Figure 30 indicates Times Roman (Tms Rmn). If you would like to change the font the selected text uses, hold down the mouse button on the arrow to the right of the box holding the font. A sub-menu appears which allows you to scroll down a list of available fonts. Use the scroll bar in conjunction with the mouse to locate the font you want and click on it. The *name of font* will be replaced with the new font.

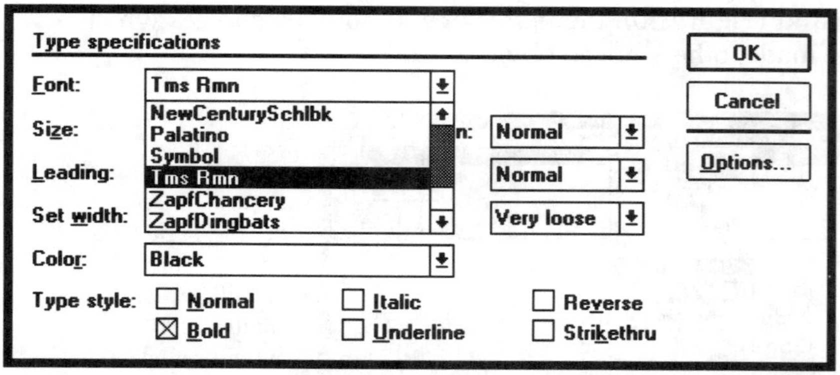

Type specifications

			OK
Font:	Tms Rmn	±	Cancel
Size:	NewCenturySchlbk ↑ Palatino Symbol	n: Normal ±	Options...
Leading:	Tms Rmn	Normal ±	
Set width:	ZapfChancery ZapfDingbats ↓	Very loose ±	
Color:	Black ±		

Type style: ☐ Normal ☐ Italic ☐ Reverse
             ☒ Bold   ☐ Underline ☐ Strikethru

Figure 31. When you hold down the mouse button on the arrow for the Font *selection, a sub-menu will appear from which you may select a new font.*

Size. Underneath the *Font* line is the *Size* line. Here, the size of the text can be easily altered in one of two ways. First, simply click on the *Size* box and the current setting will be highlighted in reverse video. Whenever a line is highlighted like this, the new selection can be typed straight in. Therefore, in this case you can simply type in the new size of the text, from 4 to 650 points. In Figure 32 we have typed in 14, for 14 points.

The other way to change the size is to click the mouse on the small arrow symbol just to the right of the *Size* box. The *Size* sub-menu will appear (Figure 33), and you can use the scroll bar to run up or down this sub-menu to select the size you are after. Once selected, this new figure will be reflected in the *Size* box.

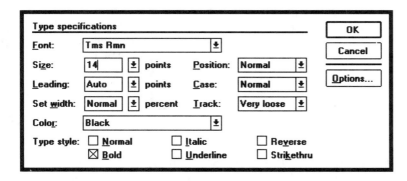

Figure 32. To change the Size *of the selected type, you can simply type a new size straight in. . .*

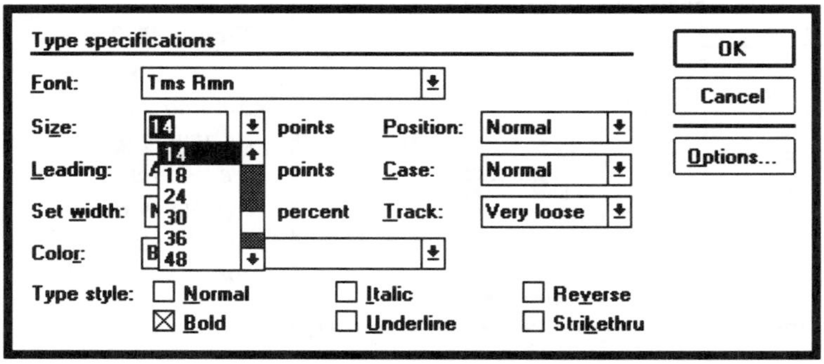

Figure 33. . . . or click the mouse button on the arrow to the right of the Size *box, and select a* Size *from the sub-menu that appears.*

Leading. The next command in the *Type specifications* dialog box is the *Leading* selection. This again will read whatever the selected text is set to at the moment. To change this figure, click the mouse button on the arrow just to the right. The *Leading* sub-menu will appear (Figure 34), from which you can highlight any new *Leading* figure for the selected text.

It is also possible (as for *Size*, discussed above) to key in your own figure over what is contained in the *Leading* box. Simply click in the box and it will change to reverse video. Key in your new figure at this time.

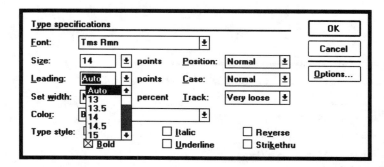

Figure 34. The Leading is altered in much the same way as the Size of the text.

Set width. Underneath *Leading* is the *Set width* option. The same procedure is used here to change the setting. The mouse is clicked over the down arrow and the sub-menu appears (Figure 35). Or you can click in the square and type in your own figure.

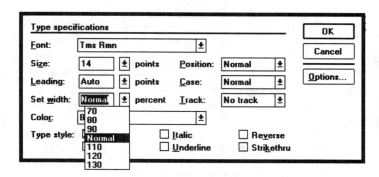

Figure 35. The Set width command has its own sub-menu, or a figure can be typed in the corresponding box.

Color. The *Color* choice will obviously only apply to those using either a color screen or a color printer. It also has a sub-menu that is activated by clicking the mouse button over the arrow to the right. Changing the color here will reflect in the selected text. For a more detailed description on color in PageMaker, please see Module 13 in this book.

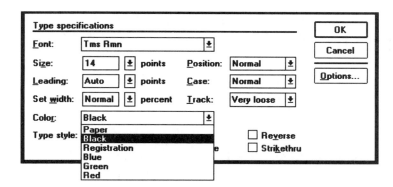

Figure 36. The Color command will affect selected text or text you are about to create.

Position. On the right side of this dialog box is the *Position* command. Once again, this will probably read *Normal*, but if you hold down the mouse button on the arrow, you may select either *Superscript* or *Subscript* text (Figure 37). These choices shift the text slightly higher or slightly lower than the baseline of the text, respectively.

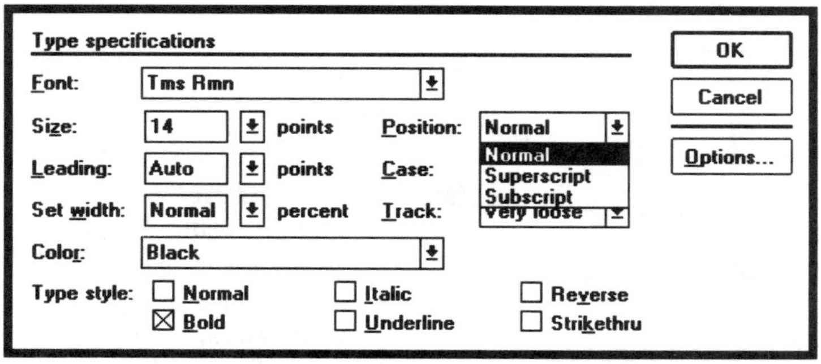

Figure 37. The position of the text, although generally set to Normal, *can be superscripted or subscripted for such things as footnotes, formulas, and so on.*

Case. Underneath *Position* is *Case*. At most times it will read *Normal*, but if you click the mouse button on the appropriate arrow, another sub-menu will appear, one that reads *Normal, All caps*, and *Small caps* (Figure 38).

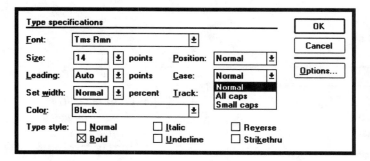

Figure 38. The Case *of the text can be adjusted automatically — a quite handy feature for converting lower case to upper case or vice versa.*

The *All caps* selection changes all letters to full-size capitals. The *Small caps* alternative changes lowercase letters to small capitals. The *Normal* selection reverts all text back to how it was originally placed or entered on the page.

Track. The *Track* command underneath *Case* gives you exactly the same choices as it does in the **Type** menu (Figure 39), and again is activated by clicking the mouse button down on the current selection.

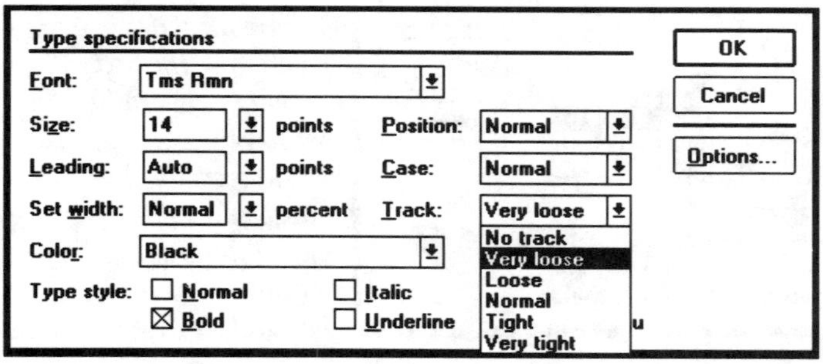

Figure 39. The Track *command controls the inter-character spacing. The choices here are the same as are available directly from the* **Type** *menu (Figure 25).*

Type style. At the bottom of the dialog box, you are given six different style changes you can make to your text. These are the same ones available in the *Type style* command previously indicated in Figure 27. Using the *Type style* selections of Figure 40, you are able to select multiple styles at one go. Simply click the mouse button in every box that you would like applied to your text.

Type style: ☐ **N**ormal   ☐ **I**talic   ☐ **R**e**v**erse
              ☒ **B**old   ☐ **U**nderline   ☐ Stri**k**ethru

Figure 40. The six choices available at the bottom of the Type specs *dialog box are selected by clicking the mouse inside the little squares. Multiple styles may be selected.*

Options. On the right-hand side of the *Type specifications* dialog box, under the OK and Cancel choices, is another selection. It is the *Options* command, that when clicked on reveals the *Type options* dialog box (Figure 41). This dialog box relates directly to the size of your small caps and superscript and subscript characters. Also, it controls the position of your superscript and subscript characters in relation to other text. All changes made here are done in percentages.

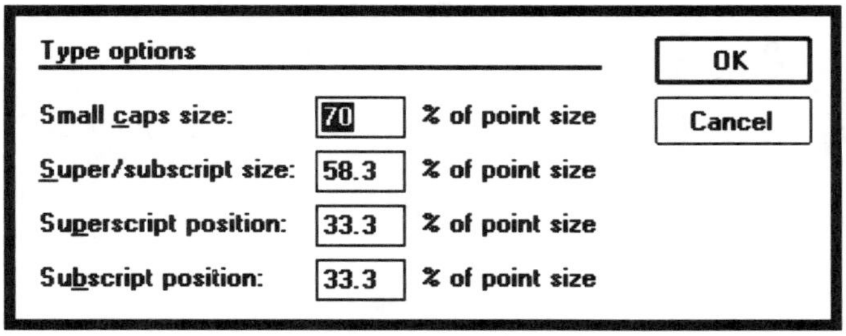

```
┌──────────────────────────────────────────────────┐
│  Type options _____  ┌──────┐ │
│                                           │  OK  │ │
│  Small caps size:      [70]  % of point size└──────┘│
│                                           ┌──────┐ │
│  Super/subscript size: [58.3] % of point size│Cancel││
│                                           └──────┘ │
│  Superscript position: [33.3] % of point size      │
│                                                    │
│  Subscript position:   [33.3] % of point size      │
└──────────────────────────────────────────────────┘
```

Figure 41. The Type options *dialog box. The choices here relate to small caps and superscript and subscript characters. To apply these options to your relevant text characters they must be first selected with the text tool.*

The *Small caps size* option changes the size of your small caps in relation to the current point size. For example, if you wanted the small caps of your selected text to appear larger or smaller compared to the full size capitals, they can be altered a specific percentage (Figure 42).

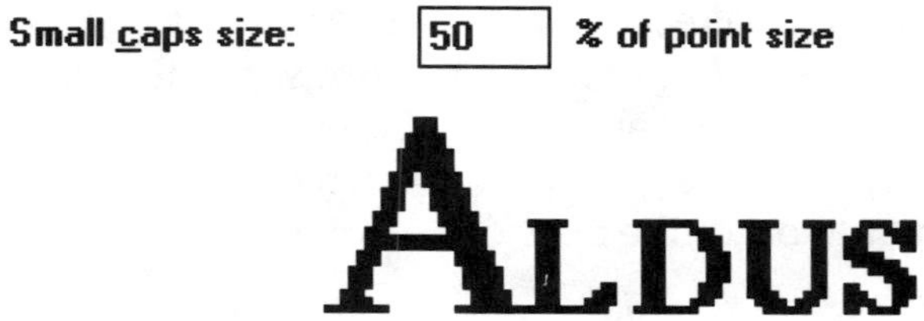

Small caps size: [50   ] % of point size

Figure 42. *Here we have adjusted the small caps to 50% the size of the larger caps.*

The same principle applies with the *Super/subscript size* option. The size of these characters can be set to your liking by double-clicking over the number already set in the box. It will now appear in reverse video and your own percentage can be typed in (Figures 43 and 44).

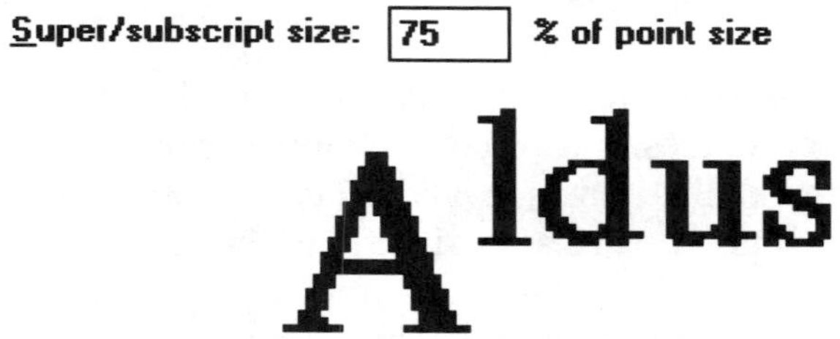

Super/subscript size: [75   ] % of point size

Figure 43. *The size of the superscript characters has been changed to 75% of the current point size.*

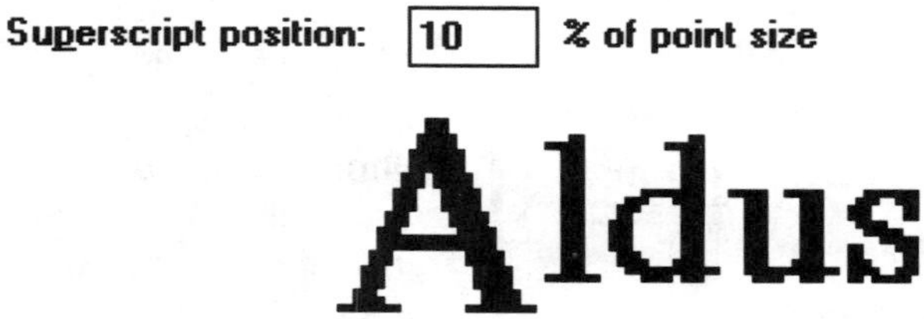

Superscript position: [10   ] % of point size

Figure 44. *The position of the superscript characters has been altered to 10%. The same rule applies when changing the position of subscript characters, only they are below the rest of the text.*

After changing everything you require about the text in the *Type specifications* dialog box, either click the OK button or hit Enter on the keypad. All set changes will be applied to selected text. If no text was selected and the pointer tool is active in the Toolbox, everything you set up will be new default values for all text entered into this particular PageMaker publication via the keyboard.

Paragraph command

All options in this command apply to entire paragraphs rather than just text. The entire paragraph does not have to be selected, as all paragraphs partially selected or the paragraph that contains the text cursor will be fully affected by this command.

Keep the first paragraph on the page highlighted and select the *Paragraph* command in the **Type** menu, just below the *Type specs* command (Figure 45). You will be presented with the dialog box shown in Figure 46.

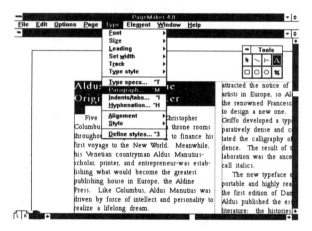

Figure 45. The Paragraph *command gives you access to a series of settings that apply to entire paragraphs rather than just selected text.*

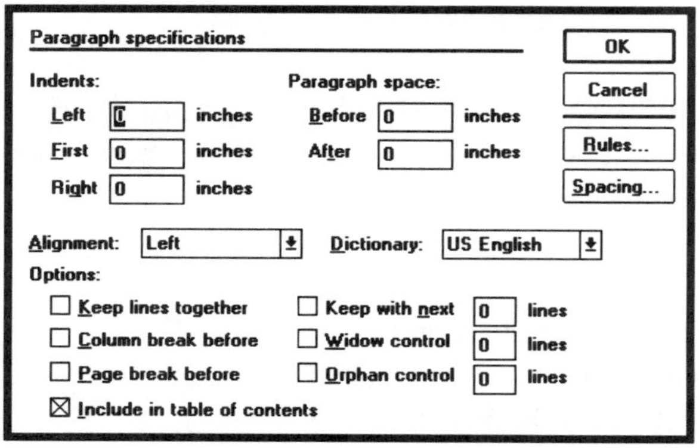

Figure 46. The dialog box that appears with the Paragraph *command shows the current settings for the selected text (in our case the first paragraph). If several paragraphs which use different settings are selected, some boxes in this dialog box may be empty.*

Indents. The first part of the *Paragraph specifications* dialog box is the *Indents* selections. Each of the three indents, *Left*, *First*, and *Right*, adjusts the text in a slightly different way. The figure in the rectangle next to the *Left* indent is the distance that the entire paragraph will be indented from the left of the margin. It must be zero or a positive number. White space will run down the left of the paragraph for whatever width is in this dialog box.

The *First* indent refers to how far the very first line in the paragraph is indented compared to the rest of the paragraph. A positive number here refers to a normal first line indent — a good way to denote the start of the paragraph. A negative number provides a hanging indent, where the first line is not indented, but all subsequent lines are.

The *Right* indent is the distance that the paragraph is indented from the right margin. This can only be set to zero or a positive number.

Indenting examples

> This paragraph has been indented three inches from the left. Note the strange word spacing that may occur, as this paragraph has the alignment set to *Justify* which is what we will be talking about next.

This paragraph is indented 1 inch from the left, .15 from the right. The word spacing that occurs over a large block of text should look better than the paragraph above.

This paragraph has a hanging indent in which the second and subsequent lines are indented from the first line. It also has 1 inch indent from the right, and a .50 inch indent from the left for the first line.

Alignment. From the *Paragraph specifications* dialog box, you may also select which way your paragraph(s) should be aligned. Different effects are created by selecting either *Left, Right, Center, Justify,* or *Force justify*. Run down the sub-menu of the *Alignment* selection (Figure 47) for the way you would like to align your text. Some examples follow:

This paragraph is centered

This paragraph is left justified

This paragraph is right justified

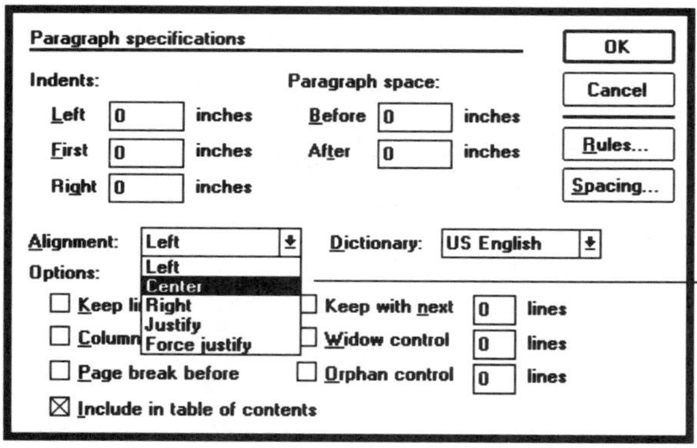

Figure 47. If you want to change the alignment of the text, click the mouse button over the arrow to the right of the word "Alignment" and run the mouse down the list. Choose either Left, Center, Right, Justify, *or* Force justify. *We have chosen* Center.

Paragraph Space. The *Paragraph space* selection (including *Before* and *After*) on the top right of the dialog box, inserts white space above and below the selected paragraph. Body text, for example, may have some space before (or after) every paragraph to make reading easier. Headings may have a quarter of an inch below them to break them from the rest of the text. Whatever the use, each figure inserted for *Before* and *After* will be the amount of white space above and/or below paragraphs. In Figure 48, we have inserted 1.180" *After* (below) our paragraph. Figure 49 shows the results of the Figure 48 settings.

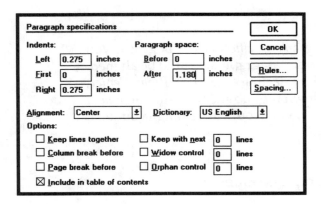

Figure 48. Here we have centered the paragraph, set indents to the left, to the right, and given 1.18" of space after the selected paragraph.

Figure 49. The results of our settings of Figure 48 applied to the heading. The text is centered, indented from either side, and has 1.18" of space after.

Alignment again. Shortcut paragraph alignment changes may be made using the *Alignment* command at the bottom of the **Type** menu. Holding the mouse button down (or clicking) on *Alignment* produces a sub-menu allowing you to choose among the five types of alignment already discussed and illustrated in Figure 47. As shown in Figure 50, however, the *Alignment* command can be a faster way of setting this paragraph function.

Dictionary. Now back to the *Paragraph specifications* dialog box. By holding the mouse down on the arrow to the right of the currently displayed dictionary within the *Dictionary* option

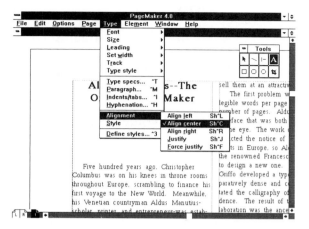

Figure 50. The Alignment *command can be used to set the justification of selected text quickly.*

(Figure 51), you can display all the installed language dictionaries. The language dictionary is used for both spelling and hyphenation, which is discussed later. PageMaker can support up to 10 installed hyphenation and spelling dictionaries, but using more than one dictionary in a publication can slow the text composition and spelling checker.

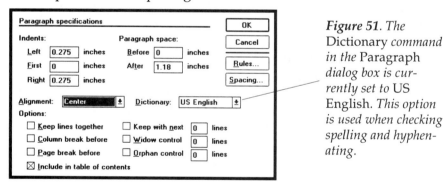

Figure 51. The Dictionary *command in the* Paragraph *dialog box is currently set to* US English. *This option is used when checking spelling and hyphenating.*

Options. The seven *Options* that appear in the bottom half of the *Paragraph* dialog box are activated by simply clicking inside the squares with your mouse. The first available option here is *Keep lines together*. Selecting this will ensure that an intended paragraph will not separate over columns, pages or graphics. Graphics with text-wrap attributes defined can sometimes split paragraphs because they are unusually shaped. This can be averted simply by choosing the *Keep lines together* option.

When *Column break before* is checked, the selected paragraph or the next one created will begin a new column. The same applies to the *Page break before* option, only the paragraph will start a new page.

If you have a heading or a paragraph that you want to be listed in the table of contents, select the intended text and click on the *Include in table of contents* option. PageMaker will automatically include this in your contents. Refer to Module 17, **Table of Contents,** to find out how to use this feature.

The *Keep with next* ☐ *lines* option gives you the choice of having a selected paragraph placed with 1 to 3 lines of the following paragraph. This option is useful for keeping titles and subtitles with their appropriate text, if they are likely to be separated by a column or page.

Widow control determines how many lines are left at the end of a paragraph at the start of a new column or page. This option is available so that one line does not have to be left on its own at the top of a column. PageMaker gives you a choice of 1 to 3 lines to be left alone. The same applies to *Orphan control*: a minimum number of lines, to be determined by you at the beginning of a paragraph, left alone at the bottom of a column or page. The widow and orphan control should be predetermined when auto-flowing longer documents. With smaller publications, these two functions aren't very useful, because the laying out of text can easily and quickly be changed manually.

Rules. Below the Cancel option in the *Paragraph specifications* dialog box is the *Rules* button. By clicking on this, the *Paragraph rules* dialog box (Figure 52) will appear. This dialog box specifies size, color, width, style, and placement of horizontal rules above and/or below a selected paragraph. These lines, once placed, cannot be moved separately with the pointer tool, as they will now be part of the text block. The only way they can be altered is through the *Paragraph rules* dialog box.

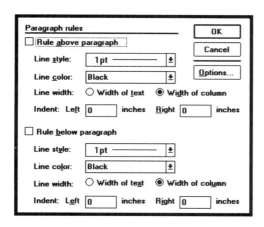

Figure 52. The Paragraph rules *dialog box is activated by clicking on the option* Rules *in the* Paragraph specifications *dialog box.*

By clicking inside the square to the left of the words *Rule above paragraph* and *Rule below paragraph,* you will place rules above and below your selected text. If you only want one of these rules, this is done simply by clicking in the corresponding box. Your above and below rules can be set up to have completely different attributes.

By clicking the mouse over the arrow to the right of the *Line style* and *Line color* rectangles, the attributes of the rule above or below your selected paragraph are determined. The *Line style* choices are identical to the choices available in the *Line* option under the **Element** menu. By clicking your mouse on the arrow to the right of the option *Line style* box, a sub-menu of choices will appear (Figure 53). Use the scroll bar to move up or down to view all available options.

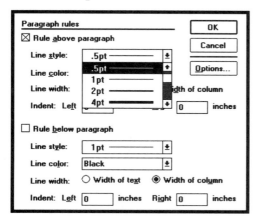

Figure 53. The Line style *for* Rule *above has been set to .5 pt.*

Line colors are also selected in the same way (Figure 54). The width of your rule can either be the width of your text or the width of your column. Click inside the circle for the width you want, as we have done in Figure 54.

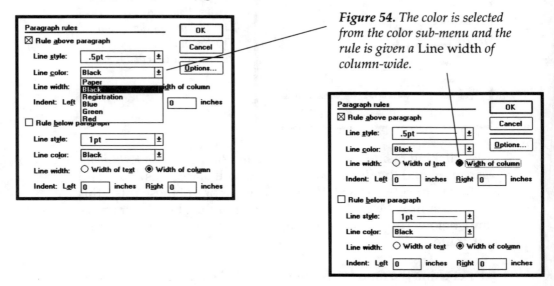

Figure 54. The color is selected from the color sub-menu and the rule is given a Line width of column-wide.

The rules can also be indented on both the right and left sides, so they can actually fall short of the text or column. The indents are set up by double-clicking inside the squares to the right of the words *Indent: Left//Right* and typing in the required measurements (Figure 55). Figure 56 shows the results of our settings for the first paragraph. Figures 57 and 58 show an example of the use of a rule below a paragraph.

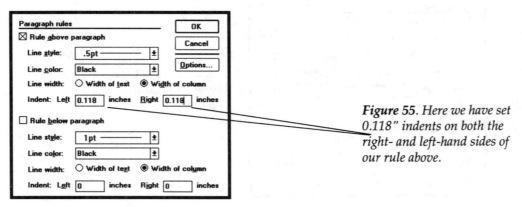

Figure 55. Here we have set 0.118" indents on both the right- and left-hand sides of our rule above.

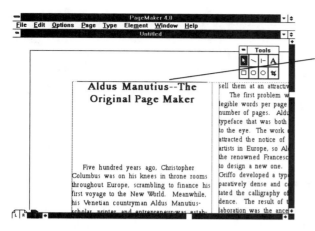

This is the rule inserted by PageMaker

Figure 56. *The final result of our settings for the rule above our selected paragraph (from Figures 53 through 55).*

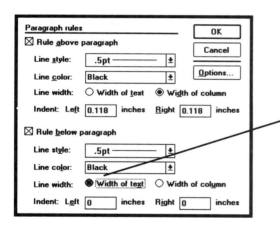

Figure 57. *The rule below the paragraph is set almost the same as the one above, but this time we choose* Width of text *as our line width.*

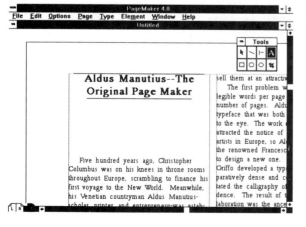

Figure 58. *The rule below the paragraph has the attributes we have just defined in the previous figure.*

The *Paragraph rules* dialog box of Figure 52 has an additional *Options* button on the right-hand side. This takes you into the *Paragraph rule options* dialog box of Figure 59. By default it should say "Auto" in the inches above and below baseline boxes for both the *Top* and the *Bottom* rules. If you double-click in these boxes, you can set your own measurement for spacing above and below the baseline for the rules we created in Figure 58.

See Figures 60 and 61 to see what happens when we change these figures.

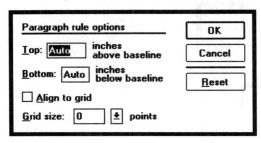

Figure 59. *The* Paragraph rule *options dialog box, which is accessed through the* Paragraph rules *dialog box of Figure 52.*

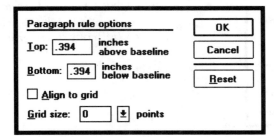

Figure 60. *We have selected the relevant paragraph and set the top rule to 0.394" above the baseline and the bottom rule to 0.394" below the baseline. Now see Figure 61.*

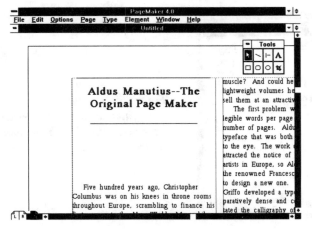

Figure 61. *The result of what we did in the previous figure.*

The *Align to grid* feature, also in the *Paragraph rule options* dialog box, is used when working with multiple text columns. When *Align to grid* is checked, the baselines of the body text will align horizontally. The grid size should be set the same as body text leading. See examples in Figures 62 through 64.

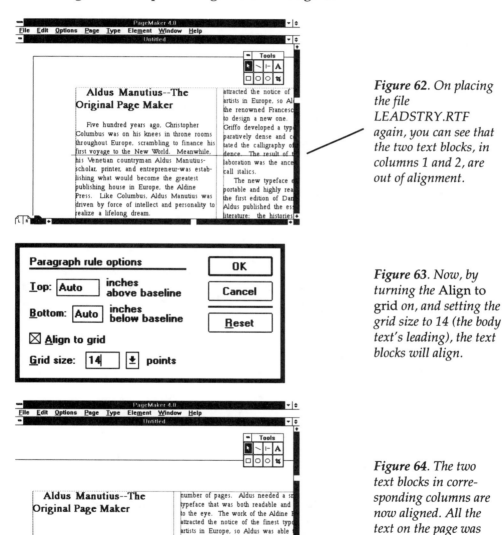

Figure 62. On placing the file LEADSTRY.RTF again, you can see that the two text blocks, in columns 1 and 2, are out of alignment.

Figure 63. Now, by turning the Align to grid on, and setting the grid size to 14 (the body text's leading), the text blocks will align.

Figure 64. The two text blocks in corresponding columns are now aligned. All the text on the page was selected to do this.

Spacing. On returning to the *Paragraph specifications* dialog box (Figure 65), you can see the *Spacing* option under the *Rules* option. When clicked, this will take you to the *Spacing attributes* dialog box (Figure 66).

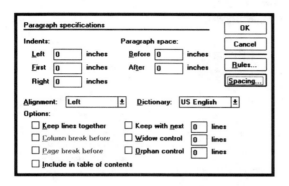

Figure 65. The Spacing attributes *box is accessed by clicking on the word "Spacing" in the* Paragraph specifications *dialog box.*

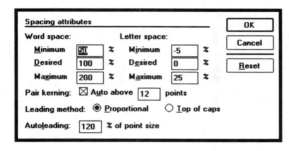

Figure 66. The Spacing attributes *dialog box. Many people may prefer to leave this command alone — unless they have very precise requirements for text spacing.*

The *Spacing attributes* dialog box is one that gives you a great deal of control over text spacing, but may not be required by all people. The default setting for text spacing is acceptable in the vast majority of cases.

Do not confuse this *Spacing* command, which adjusts the amount of horizontal spacing between letters and words, with the *Paragraph space* selection in the *Paragraph* command of Figure 46. This latter selection, as discussed previously, simply adjusts the amount of vertical spacing between paragraphs.

The *Spacing attributes* dialog box is used to adjust the amount of spacing between words and letters. *Word space*, the first selection, is used to set the space between words on the page. The designer of the font being used has set a value of 100% as the optimum space between words. The *Desired* space between words will be, by default, set at 100%. By decreasing this value, as well as the corresponding *Maximum* and *Minimum* values, the text will appear more tightly spaced. Increasing these values will cause the text to be more loosely spaced.

Word space works for both justified and unjustified text. You can change *Desired* to any figure between 0% and 500%. The limits for *Minimum* and *Maximum* are 0% and 500% of *Desired*.

Letter space, the next selection, is the amount of space that PageMaker is allowed to insert between letters in text when justifying. This selection does not apply to unjustified text. With *0* in all three boxes, PageMaker will not insert extra spaces between letters at all. By putting a figure of 25% in *Maximum*, you allow PageMaker to insert, at maximum, 25% of word space between letters, if necessary.

The range limits for *Minimum* and *Maximum* are -200% to +200%. *Desired* must be between *Minimum* and *Maximum*.

See the following examples of various word and letter spacing commands (Figures 67 through 71). These examples illustrate that text spacing can be modified many ways, some of which are unacceptable and some of which are useful for various applications. In many instances, the look of the text is up to the individual.

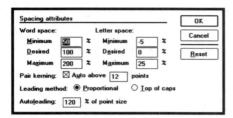

Figure 67. *The paragraph on the right shows the results of the PageMaker default settings on the left.*

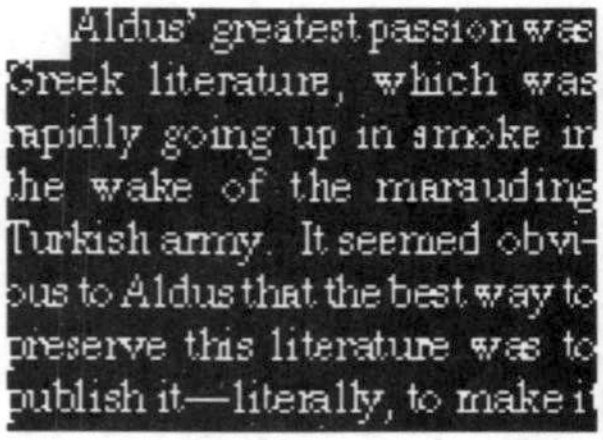

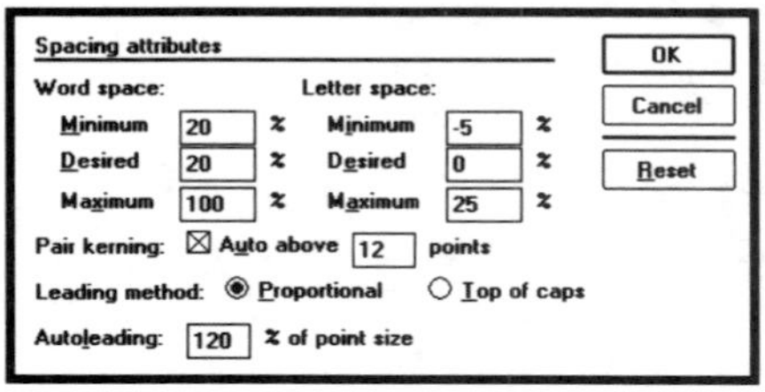

Figure 68. *We have tightened up on the word spacing settings on the left to give the results on the right.*

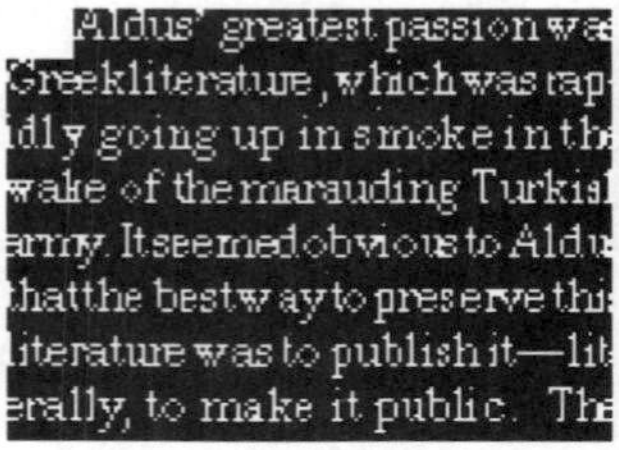

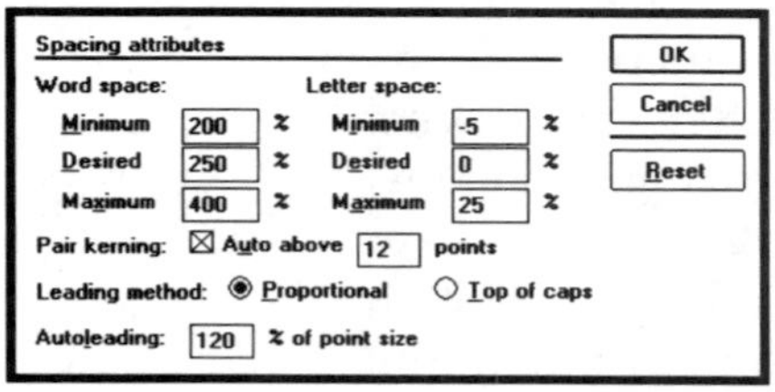

Figure 69. *We have now loosened the word spacing to produce the results on the right.*

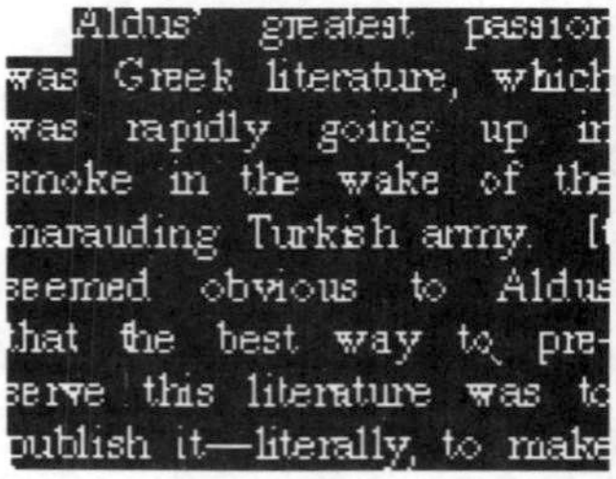

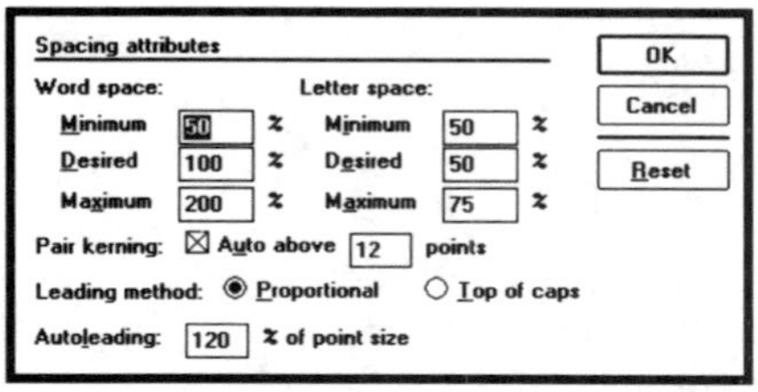

Figure 70. *Now we have adjusted the letter spacing by allowing more space between letters. Compare to Figure 67, which uses the same word spacing.*

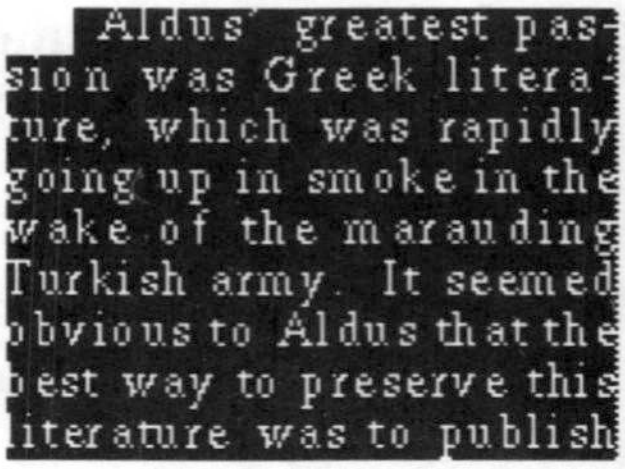

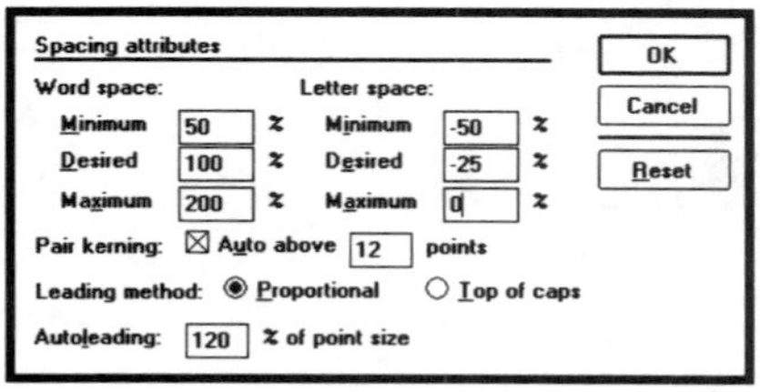

Figure 71. *Letter spacing has now been tightened to provide the results as shown.*

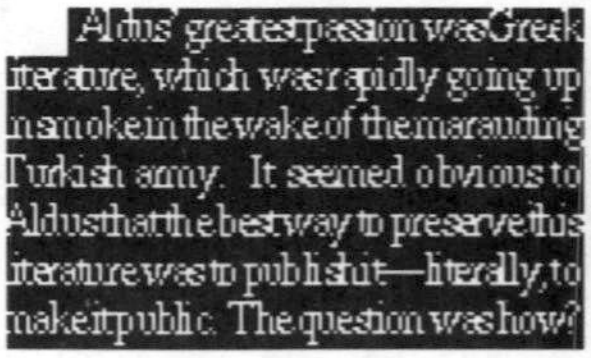

The final parts of the *Spacing* command dialog box of Figure 66 concern *Pair kerning* and *Leading method*.

Below word and letter spacing is the *Pair kerning* control. Kerning is the moving together of two very large letters that might otherwise appear too widely spaced. Generally, it is a good idea to leave kerning on (it is on if the check appears in the *Auto above* box next to *Pair kerning* in Figure 66). Being able to control the size above which text should be kerned may allow you to kern only your headings, which might be 36-point, and not your body text, which might be 12-point or less.

(These letters are not kerned)

(These letters are kerned)

The value set for *Autoleading* in Figure 66 is the amount Page-Maker uses by default (120%) when *Auto* leading is selected for text, either through the *Leading* or *Type specs* commands. The figure is taken as a proportion of the text size, so to achieve leading at around 10 % of the text size, you would insert the figure of 110% in this rectangle.

A *Leading method* must be selected — either *Proportional* or *Top of caps*. Both use different parameters to judge the leading distance. *Proportional* is generally easier to use and is the default method.

The *Top of caps* method is useful for special design effects and is not recommended for general use.

Indents/tabs command

As we discussed above, and as shown in Figure 48, it is possible to select *Left*, *First*, and *Right* indents of paragraphs using the *Paragraph* command in the **Type** menu. It is possible to do this as well, plus more, with the *Indents/tabs* command (Figure 72), also from the **Type** menu. The *Indents/tabs* dialog box, which results from selecting the command, is indicated in Figure 73.

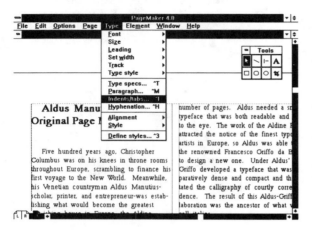

Figure 72. The Indents/tabs *command from the* **Type** *menu can be used for setting tabs and indents. The latter capability is similar to that available with the* Paragraph *command.*

Figure 73 shows the default tab settings of one tab every 0.5" (or 0.5 cm for international versions). Figure 74 expands upon this dialog box by showing the other user-settable tabs that are available. These include left justified, right justified, centered, and decimal tabs.

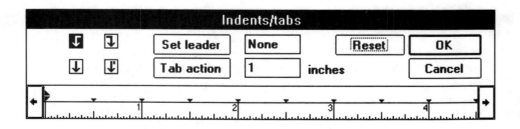

Figure 73. The Indents/tabs *dialog box. Note the tabs which are set by default to every 0.5".*

Changing the default settings of Figure 73 for a single publication, requires that the pointer tool in the Toolbox be selected. Once the pointer is selected, it is simply a matter of going to the dialog box of Figure 73 and adjusting indents and tabs to your requirements. Wherever you then click on the page to type text, it will automatically assume the new default values. You can change the indents and/or tabs of text already on the page by selecting it with the text tool and then changing the settings in the *Indents/tabs* dialog box.

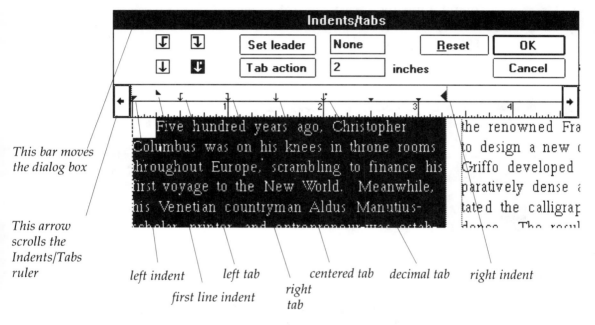

Figure 74. *The various components that make up the* Indents/tabs *dialog box are indicated. One of the important points to note in this figure is the way PageMaker has automatically aligned the zero point of the dialog box's ruler with the left-hand column guide for the left column. This makes it easier to set up indents and tabs for the column widths you may be working with.*

We will now provide some examples to illustrate the indents/tabs concept of PageMaker. Again, if you would like to follow this, you may wish to reload LEADSTRY.RTF into a single, two-column, A4 or Letter page. (It may be a little messy from some of the earlier experiments so far in this module.)

In Figure 75, we have selected the first body text paragraph with the text tool and then chosen the *Indents/tabs* command leading to the dialog box indicated in the figure. From this box you can see that there is a 0.25" first line indent and that the default tab settings of 0.5" apart are showing.

In Figure 76 we have set left, right, and (a new) first indents. Note the interrelationship between the *Indents/tabs* and *Paragraph* commands, which can be seen by comparing Figures 76 and 77. Figure 77 is the dialog box associated with the *Paragraph* command while the first paragraph of Figure 76 is still selected. The values given for first, left, and right indents correspond to the settings shown in the *Indents/tabs* dialog box of Figure 76.

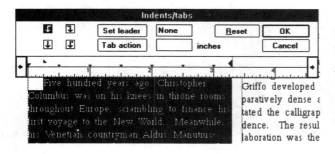

Figure 75. The initial paragraph we have selected has a first line indent of 0.25". Compare this to Figure 76 after we have made some adjustments.

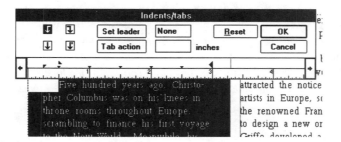

Figure 76. We have now set first, left, and right indents. Note that aligning the zero point of the ruler with the left margin allows you to view your settings pictorially and compare with the actual text. The tab ruler automatically aligns with the left-hand margin if text is selected when the Indents/tabs *command is chosen.*

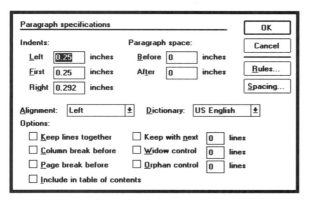

Figure 77. Compare the settings of this Paragraph *command dialog box with the same settings in the* Indents/tabs *dialog box of Figure 76. You'll see that the two lots of settings are identical showing the interrelationship between the two commands.*

In our final two examples, below, we have gone to the bottom of a three-column page (you can do this now by simply changing your columns from two to three) to an empty area, clicked on the text tool, and then typed the numbers 1 to 5 with a tab after each one. The result, as shown in Figure 78(a), is simply tabs every 0.5", which is the default setting. We then selected this text and changed the tab settings. The new tab settings (now spaced every inch) and the result, can be seen in Figure 78(b).

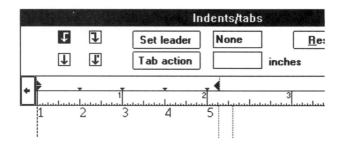

Figure 78(a). By clicking on the text tool and typing in the above numbers separated by tabs, we are using the default tab values of one every 0.5".

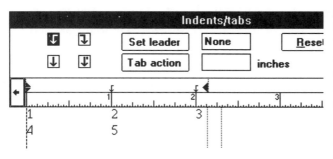

Figure 78(b). Here we have selected the numbers keyed in in Figure 78(a) and have changed the tab settings to one every inch. This results in the changed settings as shown.

See the following text for how to Add, Delete, Move, and Repeat tabs.

The *Set leader* choice from Figure 79, when turned on, places a repetitive line of characters on your page each time you select a tab. *Set leader* is set to *None* by default, and a leader must be selected before the tabs are set. The choices other than *None* can be seen when the mouse is clicked on the *Set leader* box (Figure 79).

If none of the choices available are what you want, you can select *Custom* and type your own character in the box that originally said *None*.

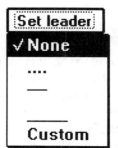

Figure 79. The Set leader *options include dots, dashes, and lines. Choosing* Custom *lets you type in your own choice of character for your leader. Below is an example using the dots as leaders. We set the tab for 1" and applied it to the text on the page.*

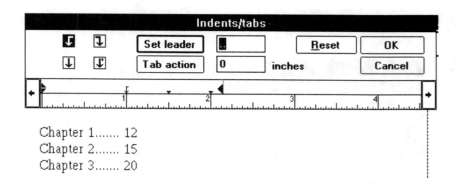

Chapter 1....... 12
Chapter 2....... 15
Chapter 3....... 20

Below the *Set leader* box is the *Tab action* box (Figure 80). This lets you *Add, Delete, Move,* and *Repeat* tabs more quickly, more easily, and more accurately. The *Add tab* choice will place a tab in whatever position you specify in the box to its right. For example, if you place a 2 in this box and highlight the *Add tab* choice from the *Tab action* sub-menu, PageMaker will put a tab at the 2" point. The *Delete tab* option simply removes a highlighted marker, or, if none is highlighted, it will remove the tab at the point you specify in the inches box.

Move tab will change the point of a highlighted tab to the setting requested in the inches box. For example, if you want your tab at 2" to be moved to 2.35", type this setting in the inches box and PageMaker will quickly and accurately change the position of the highlighted tab.

Repeat tab will speed up the process of multiple tabs at equal distances. You may want tabs set at every half inch. Instead of placing them there yourself, simply place one tab at the first half inch and, while this tab is still highlighted, select *Repeat tab* and tabs will be placed at every half inch point along your ruler.

Figure 80. The choices available in the Tab action sub-menu let you accurately Add, Delete, Move, and Repeat tabs. Below we typed 2 in the inches box and chose Add tab. PageMaker puts a tab at the 2" point on the ruler. We then applied this setting to the text on our page with the Set leader still on dots. As you can see, our second tab is exactly one inch away from our first.

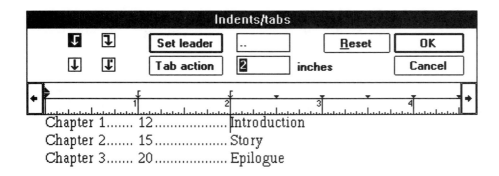

Hyphenation

The *Hyphenation* dialog box is available directly through the **Type** menu (Figures 81 and 82). It is also obtainable through the *Edit style* dialog box, which comes from the *Define styles* dialog box in the **Type** menu. The *Define styles* dialog box is explained in Module 11, **Style Sheets.**

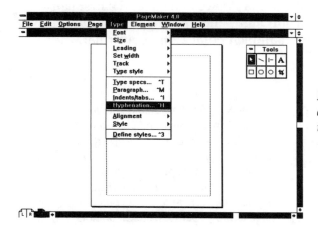

Figure 81. *The* Hyphenation *dialog box is accessed through the* **Type** *Menu.*

The *Hyphenation* command has to be turned "On" in this dialog box (Figure 82) before it can operate. By default, it will already be on. How PageMaker hyphenates depends upon the method you choose. Your first option is *Manual only*. On selecting this choice, PageMaker hyphenates only at the discretionary hyphens you place in the text yourself. A discretionary hyphen is activated by pressing the *Control + hyphen* keys. The discretionary hyphens placed in text are not seen until needed.

The *Manual plus dictionary* choice allows PageMaker to hyphenate words according to the dictionary, while still recognizing discretionary hyphens. The third choice is *Manual plus algorithm*. This has the features of the previous two in addition to a dictionary algorithm. PageMaker will determine the best places for hyphenating your words in a logical way. The layout of your work is a determining factor in the decision PageMaker makes on where to put hyphens. The *Manual plus algorithm* choice has an advantage over the *Manual plus dictionary* choice, as the latter will only hyphenate words it recognizes. The algorithm will hyphenate words that aren't recognized by the normal dictionary, as well as ones that are.

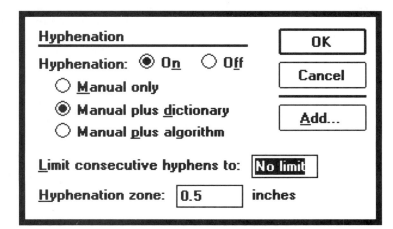

Figure 82. The Hyphenation *dialog box gives you three choices on how to hyphenate your text.* Manual plus dictionary *is selected by default.*

The total amount of hyphens appearing in one paragraph can also be determined. By double-clicking in the box after *Limit consecutive hyphens to*: you can put in your own figure from 1 to 255. By default it will say "No Limit". With this selected, there will be no limit to the number of hyphens PageMaker can place in your text. Depending on how long your paragraph is, it is recommended that a number no greater than 10 be used, as the paragraph may become too cluttered with hyphens.

Adjusting the *Hyphenation zone* command will change the amount of space at the end of a line for which hyphenation will occur. The larger the hyphenation zone, the fewer hyphens will occur and the smaller the zone, the more hyphens.

The *Add* word option lets you add an unlisted word to the dictionary. While adding this word to the dictionary you also insert discretionary hyphens. The number of discretionary hyphens you put together indicates your preference on how Page-Maker should hyphenate the word. Figure 83 gives an example of this.

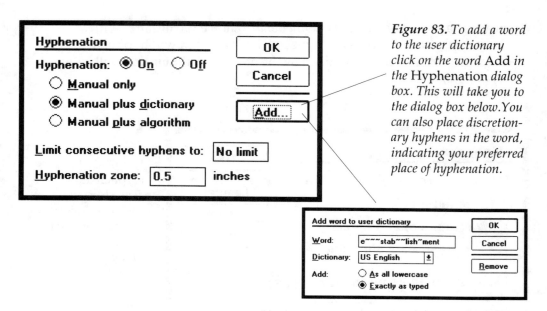

Figure 83. To add a word to the user dictionary click on the word Add in the Hyphenation dialog box. This will take you to the dialog box below. You can also place discretionary hyphens in the word, indicating your preferred place of hyphenation.

When adding discretionary hyphens to the words in this dialog box, one hyphen indicates the most preferable place for hyphenation. Two hyphens is your second choice, and three, the least preferable. You insert hyphens using tildes (~). If a word you add is already in the dictionary, the new discretionary hyphens you put in will replace the current settings. The *As all lowercase* option saves the word in the dictionary as lowercase characters and not necessarily as you typed it in. Whereas the *Exactly as typed* option will save the word exactly as you input it. Selecting *Remove* takes the displayed word out of the dictionary. If you have a word that you never want hyphenated, put a discretionary hyphen in front of the word in the *Add word to user dictionary* dialog box.

Alignment command

This sub-menu is a shortcut approach to paragraph alignment, outlined previously under the *Paragraph* command. See Figures 47 and 50 in this module for details.

Style and Define styles commands

These two commands are described in Module 11 — **Style Sheets.**

Creating new text files

Rather then creating your files wholly and solely from a word processor and then loading them into PageMaker, files of quite considerable length can be created totally from within PageMaker itself, in normal layout view. With PageMaker 4, it is also possible to do faster text entry and editing in the new story editor mode. Module 5 provides more details on story editor.

For simple headings and captions, however, it is sometimes easier to just create them in normal layout view. Figures 84 through 87 illustrate this approach.

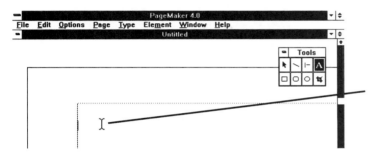

Figure 84. Choose the text tool, move to the area on the page you would like to start typing, and click the mouse button once. A flashing text cursor will appear, in this case at the left margin.

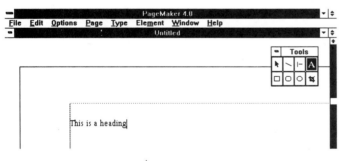

Figure 85. After the flashing text cursor has been inserted, you are free to add text as you see fit.

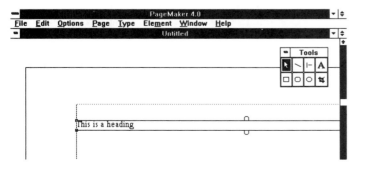

Figure 86. The new text file we have created occupies its own text block, as every new text file does (note the change of tool in the Toolbox).

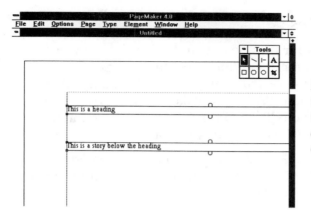

Figure 87. Every time the mouse cursor is clicked in a new position and text is entered, a new text block is created.

In entering text in layout view, the flashing cursor may not always be where you clicked the mouse cursor. Where it does end up depends on how the defaults for text are set. (Defaults are looked at in another module.) For example, if you tried to click the mouse cursor in the center of an empty page and the default text setting is left justified, the flashing cursor will appear to the left side of the page. If you want the text centered, type it in, select it, and center it. Alternatively, go to the **Type** menu, choose *Alignment*, and then *Align center*.

For these reasons it is often easier to move off to the side of the page to create smaller text files. Quite often, such things as headings, captions, footnotes, etc., are created in this way. After they have been formatted off the side of the page, move them into position on the page. Figures 88 through 91 illustrate this approach.

Figure 88. It is often easier to create small text blocks for such things as headings or captions off the actual page in the pasteboard area and move them onto the page later.

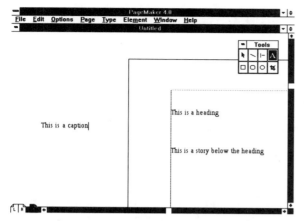

Figure 89. *The text we have added on the side of the page will now also occupy its own little text block. . .*

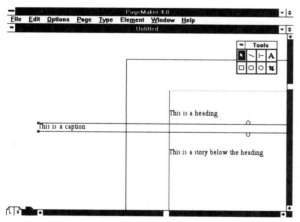

Figure 90. *. . . which can now be moved onto the page from the pasteboard area using the pointer tool. . .*

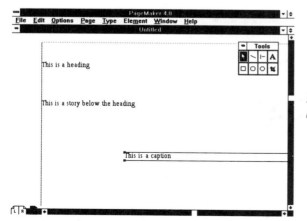

Figure 91. *. . . as we have done here.*

Exporting text

Text inside PageMaker, whether it was imported or created within PageMaker, can be exported in word processor format for use in a word processor or other such application.

The first step is to select the text you would like to export to a file. If you wish to export a whole file, insert your text cursor within the story and choose *Select all* from the **Edit** menu before you choose *Export.* Otherwise, simply select the text you would like to export (perhaps just a few words or paragraphs as shown in Figure 92).

After performing either of these steps, choose the *Export* command from the **File** menu (Figure 93). The Figure 94 dialog box will appear.

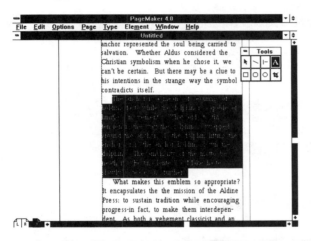

Figure 92. Here we have selected a single paragraph to export.

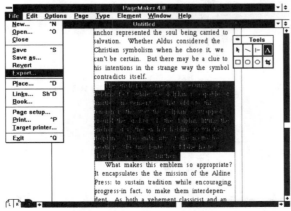

Figure 93. After selecting the text to export, choose the Export *command from the* File *menu.*

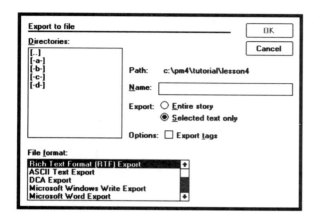

Figure 94. The Export *command dialog box.*

Insert the name of the word processor file you wish to create in the rectangle provided, and then select the format. The format you choose will depend on exactly what word processor you use, or what you want to use the file for. We have chosen "Example" in ASCII Text format; therefore, we gave the file a .txt extension (Figure 95).

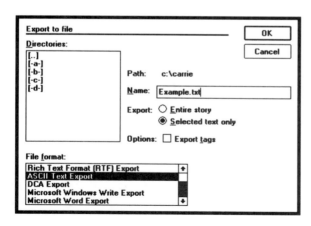

Figure 95. Insert the name of the file-to-be in the rectangle (we inserted the name Example.txt), and then choose the File format *type.*

After doing this, click on OK — in a few seconds a word processor file will be created and placed in the currently active directory (Figure 96).

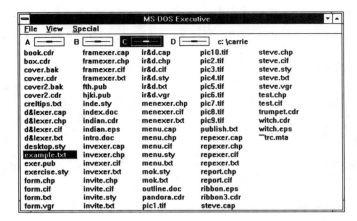

Figure 96. Looking at the C drive in the Carrie directory, we have highlighted the example.txt file we just created using the Export command.

EXERCISE: EDITING TEXT

Editing Text

In this exercise we will be editing text — moving through correcting simple errors, selecting text, and applying simple style and formatting information.

This training material is structured so that people of all levels of expertise with Page-Maker can use it to gain maximum benefit. In order to do this, we have structured the material so that the bare exercise is listed below this paragraph on just one page, with no hints. The following pages contain the steps needed to complete this exercise for those who need additional prompting. The **Editing Text** module should be referenced if you need further help or explanations.

Module 4 exercise steps

1. *Open up the template* NEWSLTR2.PT4 from the pscript sub-directory located in the template sub-directory.*

2. *At the top of the page is the major heading "Title," and directly below is the word "Head-line." You are going to rename these. First, change the word "Title" to "April News," and then the word "Headline" to "What's New?"*

3. *The two paragraphs below the heading "What's New?" have to be bolded. Next, move to the bottom half of the first column. The first two paragraphs under the word "Subhead" have to be italicized.*

4. *The subheading "What's New?" must now be centered. Next, change the font of the heading "April News" to Palatino, with a point size of 30, and then center this too.*

5. *Change the leading of the two paragraphs in the first column that were italicized in step 3 to 15 points.*

6. *Give these same two paragraphs a first line indent of 0.2", changing one paragraph at a time.*

*At this point, consider a template the same as a PageMaker publication. The special properties of templates are discussed in Module 10.

The details for completing these steps are found on the following pages.

The steps in detail

1. Open up the template NEWSLTR2.PT4 from the pscript sub-directory located in the template sub-directory.

Opening up an existing publication or template is a little different from starting a new one yourself. The command used to open a publication or template is the *Open* command from the **File** menu. (Templates are similar to publications. The different properties of templates are discussed in Module 10.)

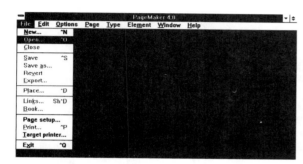

Figure 1. *The* Open *command must be used to access an existing publication or template.*

After selecting this command, you are presented with a dialog box similar to the one you get when you choose the *Place* command. However, this time only saved publications or templates are there for you to choose, whereas before, with the *Place* command, you were searching for text or graphics files. Locate the template sub-directory (Figure 2) and double-click on it. Then, double-click on the pscript sub-directory (Figure 2 again). Within this sub-directory is the NEWSLTR2.PT4 template (Figure 3). Double-click on its name to load it onto the page.

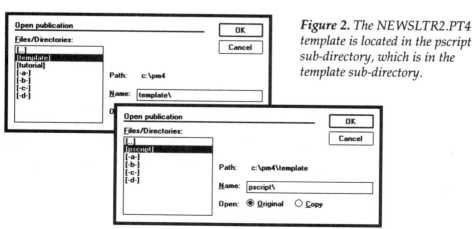

Figure 2. *The NEWSLTR2.PT4 template is located in the pscript sub-directory, which is in the template sub-directory.*

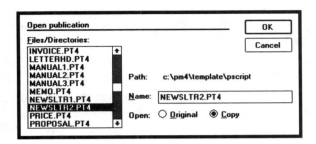

Figure 3. Locate the template titled NEWSLTR2.PT4 and double-click on it. This document will then open up on your page as an untitled publication (Figure 4).

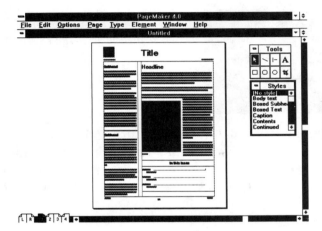

Figure 4. NEWSLTR2.PT4 will look like this when set to Fit in window *view.*

2. *At the top of the page is the major heading "Title," and directly below is the word "Headline." You are going to rename these. First, change the word "Title" to "April News," and then change the word "Headline" to "What's New?"*

There are several ways that you can delete these two words and replace them. First, however, change to *Actual size* view and use the scroll bars to move the page so that you can actually read this heading (Figures 5 and 6). Alternatively, just point your mouse cursor at the top of the page and click the right mouse button. This will move you to *Actual size* view from *Fit in window* view, with the page already positioned at the correct point.

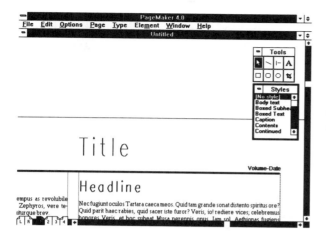

Figure 5. Change to Actual size *view so that the text can be read.*

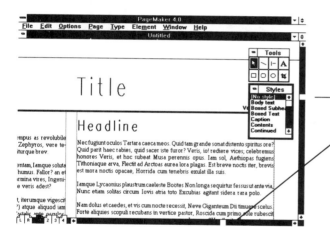

Figure 6. The scroll bars are used to move the page around so that you can read the heading. Alternatively, as mentioned in the text, clicking the right mouse button at the top of the page will move you to the correct position in Actual Size *view.*

Make sure the text cursor is selected before you start. When it is, move the mouse cursor over the first word you are going to replace — "Title." Now, double-click the mouse and the word will become selected (Figure 7). If it does not, wait a second or two and double-click the mouse again until the word is highlighted in reverse video.

Once the word "Title" is highlighted, you can type straight in with the replacement words — "April News." There is no need to delete the existing word first — just type the new words. As soon as you touch the first key on the keyboard, the highlighted word disappears — to be replaced by the new characters you are typing (Figure 8). This applies whenever a selection of text is highlighted within PageMaker. Any text keyed in simply replaces the highlighted text.

The method described above is now used to replace the word "Headline" (just below "Title"). The steps are detailed in Figures 10 through 12.

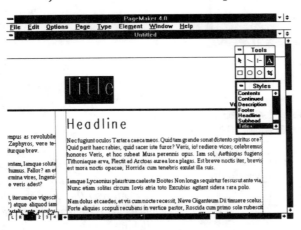

Figure 7. Making sure that the text cursor is selected (note the text tool selected in the Toolbox), move the mouse cursor over the word "Title" and click the mouse twice quickly. The word will become selected.

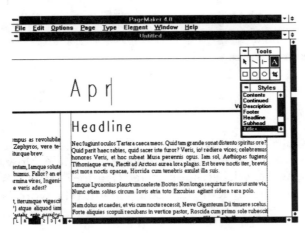

Figure 8. As soon as you start typing the new word in, the old word disappears. Continue typing until the new word or words have been entered.

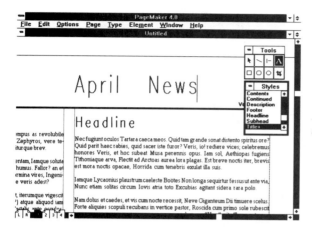

Figure 9. The new title completed.

Figure 10. The same steps can be followed to replace the word "Headline." Double-click on this word. . .

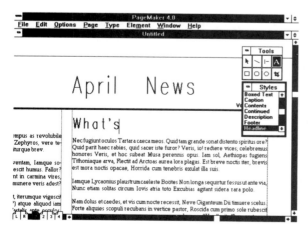

Figure 11. . . . and type in the new words.

Figure 12. Headline has now been reworded with "What's New?"

3. *The two paragraphs below the new heading "What's New?" have to be bolded. Next, move to the bottom half of the first column. The first two paragraphs under the word "Subhead" have to be italicized.*

Move the screen slightly down and across if necessary so that you can see fully the first lot of information you are going to edit (the two paragraphs under the sub-heading "What's New?"). Once again, there are several ways that you can select this text.

The most straightforward way to select the text is as follows. Making sure the text cursor is still selected, move the mouse cursor to the start of the text you would like to select. Hold the mouse button down and keep it down. Now run the mouse cursor over the text, releasing the mouse button only when it appears to the right of the very last letter you would like to select. The entire two paragraphs will be highlighted (Figures 14 and 15).

Figure 13. You are now to select the two paragraphs below the heading "What's New?"

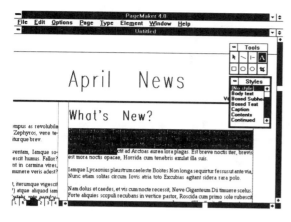

Figure 14. Run the mouse cursor over the text, keeping the mouse button held down, and all text will become highlighted as you go.

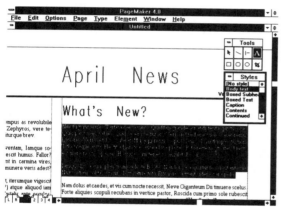

Figure 15. Release the mouse button when the mouse cursor is to the right of the very last letter you want to select. All letters between the start and end point will be selected.

If your hand slipped off the mouse, or for any other reason you were unsuccessful, click once and try again.

Two other methods could have been used to select the text. You could have clicked once to insert the text cursor at the start of the text to select, held down the Shift key, and clicked at the end of the text block. You may also have triple-clicked on the first paragraph, held the mouse button down on the third click, and moved the mouse anywhere into the second paragraph. If you are unsure of either of these latter methods, stick to the one described first.

Once the text is selected, move to the *Type style* command in the **Type** menu (Figure 16). Remember that this command is a little different from some others in that you must hold the mouse button down on the command and run the mouse down the resulting sub-menu (Figure 16). Select the style *Bold* from this sub-menu. Alternatively, you can click once on the *Type style* command, wait for the sub-menu to drop, and then click on *Bold*.

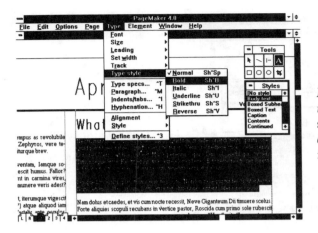

Figure 16. After selecting the text, choose the Bold *style from the* Type *style command in the* **Type** *menu.*

Figure 17. The two paragraphs that you selected now change to bold on the screen.

The two paragraphs have now changed to bold style (Figure 17). You could have also bolded these paragraphs in two other ways. The shortcut keyboard method could have used Control + Shift + B. Alternatively, you could have selected the *Type specs* command from the **Type** menu and chosen *Bold* from the subsequent dialog box.

After successfully completing this first part, move to the bottom left of the page to view the next two paragraphs you are about to change (underneath the word "Subhead" in the bottom half of the first column). Select these as well, using the methods described earlier in this step. Once selected, choose the style *Italic* from the *Type style* command. See Figures 18 through 20 for the steps involved.

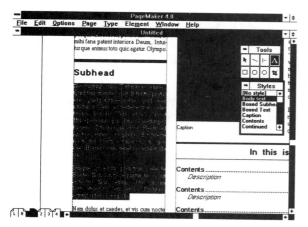

Figure 18. *Use the scroll bars to move yourself down to the bottom left of the page, enough to select the appropriate paragraphs under the word "Subhead." Use any one of the methods described earlier to select the text.*

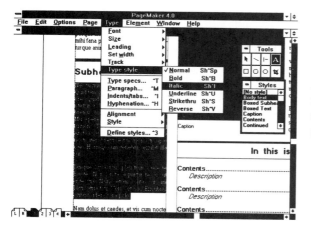

Figure 19. *After selecting the text, use the* Type *style command again to change the text, this time to italic.*

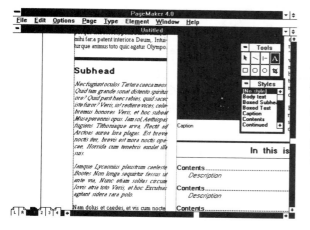

Figure 20. *The italicized text. As for bolding, you could have chosen one of the other two alternatives — shortcut keys of Control + Shift + I or the* Type specs *dialog box, also from the* Type *menu.*

191

4. The subheading "What's New?" must now be centered. Next change the font of the heading "April News" to Palatino, with a point size of 30, and then center this too.

Move the page back to the heading "What's New?" and select it. After selecting this (Figure 21), select the *Alignment* command in the **Type** menu, and choose *Align center* for alignment (Figure 22) from the associated submenu. The selected paragraph will be centered instantly (Figure 23).

Note that moving around the page can be done quickly using the right mouse button. This is often faster than using the scroll bars.

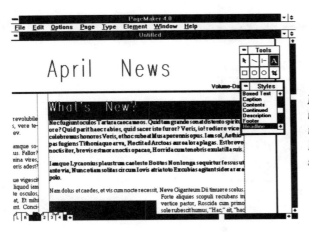

Figure 21. Our next task is to alter the justification of the heading "What's New?" Locate the heading and select it.

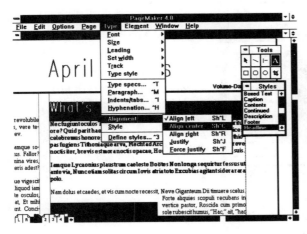

Figure 22. Use the Alignment command from the Type menu to center the selected text. The shortcut key method (Control Shift C) or the Paragraph command from the Type menu could also have been used.

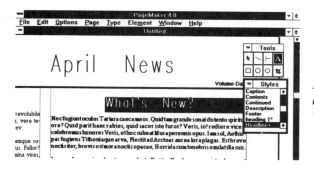

Figure 23. The result of centering the subheading "What's New?"

Move to the major heading that reads "April News" and select it (Figure 24). To change the size and font of the text, choose the *Type specs* command from the **Type** menu (Figure 25).

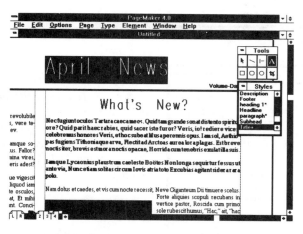

Figure 24. Use the scroll bars once again to move the page up a little so you can read the heading. Select the heading as shown.

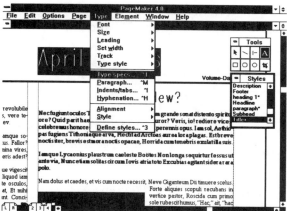

Figure 25. After selecting the heading, select the Type specs command from the Type menu.

Within the dialog box that appears when choosing the *Type specs* command (Figure 26), select the Palatino font by clicking and holding down the mouse button on the downwards arrow to the right of the current font name. Select Palatino from the sub-menu that appears (Figure 27). If Palatino is not available on your computer, choose Times Roman (Tms Rmn).

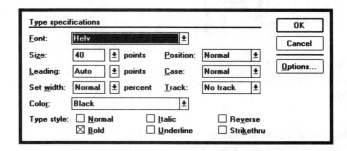

Figure 26. Initially, the Type specs *dialog box will display the current type face, size, etc. of the selected text.*

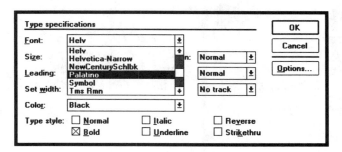

Figure 27. To change the font hold the mouse button down on the downwards arrow of the current font and select Palatino. If it is not available, choose Tms Rmn.

To change the size of the text, click in the *Size* box and type in the new value (Figure 28). Figure 29 shows the results of Figures 27 and 28.

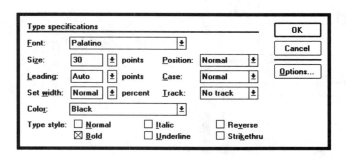

Figure 28. The text Size *has now been changed to 30 points.*

Changing the size and font of the text could have been achieved using the *Font* and *Size* commands from the **Type** menu. However, when more than one attribute of text has to be changed, it tends to be easier to change it via the *Type specs* command.

Figure 29. Here you see the result of the heading after the Type specs *command has been adjusted in Figures 27 and 28. You must center this heading next.*

To center the heading, make sure it is still selected, choose the *Alignment* command in the **Type** menu, and select *Align center* (Figure 30). The result is shown in Figure 31.

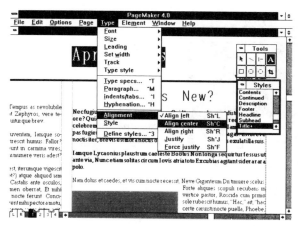

Figure 30. Centering the heading is achieved via the Alignment *command in the* **Type** *menu.*

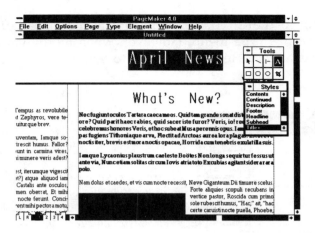

Figure 31. The result.

5. Change the leading of the two paragraphs in the first column that were italicized in step 3 to 15 points.

After scrolling to see these paragraphs, select both paragraphs using the text tool (Figure 32), and then choose the Type *specs* command (Figure 33). Within this *Type specs* command, select the current *Leading* figure and change it to 15 points (Figure 34). The space between the lines will change to reflect this new figure after you select OK (Figure 35).

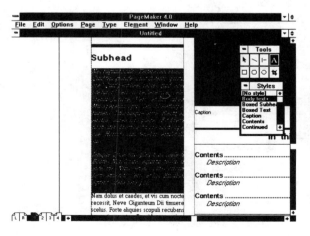

Figure 32. Select the two paragraphs in column 1 in order to change the interline spacing (leading).

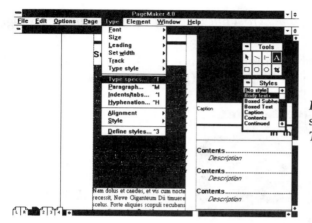

Figure 33. Select *the* Type specs *command from the* Type *menu.*

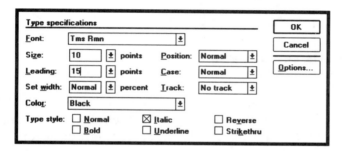

Figure 34. In the Type specs *dialog box, change the leading by entering the number 15 in the* Leading *box.*

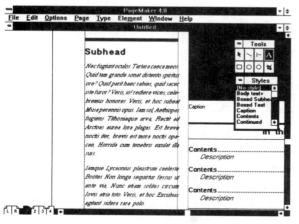

Figure 35. The change of leading in these paragraphs makes them stand out from the rest of the body text.

6. Give these same two paragraphs a first line indent of 0.2", changing one paragraph at a time.

Select the first paragraph mentioned (Figure 36). After doing this, select the *Paragraph* command from the **Type** menu (Figure 37).

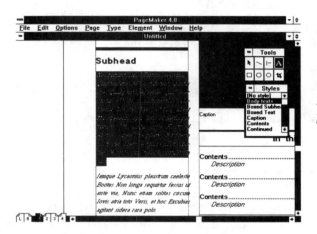

Figure 36. *Select the first paragraph under the word "Subhead."*

Within this command, you must alter the number for *First*, which at the moment should read *0*. Change this figure to *0.2* (if in inches) — see Figure 38. If using another measurement unit, insert *0.2i*. The first paragraph now reflects the 0.2" first line indent (see Figure 39).

Repeat these steps for yourself after selecting the second paragraph.

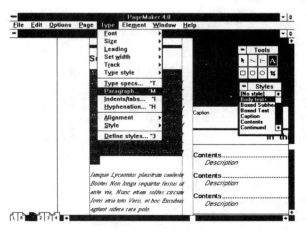

Figure 37. *Now select the* Paragraph *command in the* **Type** *menu in order to change the indents.*

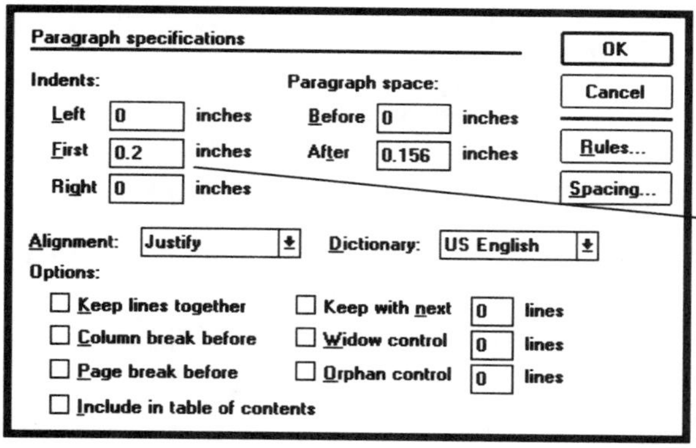

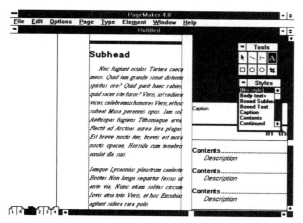

Paragraph specifications

Indents:			Paragraph space:			OK
Left	0	inches	Before	0	inches	Cancel
First	0.2	inches	After	0.156	inches	Rules...
Right	0	inches				Spacing...

Alignment: Justify   Dictionary: US English

Options:
- ☐ Keep lines together   ☐ Keep with next   0 lines
- ☐ Column break before   ☐ Widow control   0 lines
- ☐ Page break before   ☐ Orphan control   0 lines
- ☐ Include in table of contents

Figure 38. *Change the* First *rectangle to 0.2 (inches). This will cause the first line of the selected paragraph to be indented this amount.*

Figure 39. *The paragraph that was selected now reflects the first line indent you set. Repeat the last few steps yourself (Figures 36 through 38) after selecting the second paragraph. Alternatively, you could try setting this indent using the* Indent/tabs *command from the* **Type** *menu.*

THE STORY EDITOR

Module 5

The Story Editor

The story editor feature in PageMaker gives you many of the important capabilities of a stand-alone word processor. Story editor displays a separate text window on top of the normal publication layout view. It can be used in three ways: (1) to open a text view of a currently placed PageMaker story; (2) to open an empty story window for adding new text; and (3) to import and edit a new word processor file before it is placed into PageMaker.

Each story view opened contains a single PageMaker story file. Multiple stories within a single PageMaker publication can open separate story editor views.

Entering story editor view

By triple-clicking on your text with the pointer tool, you can call up the story editor screen, which is similar in format to that of a word processor. From here, you are able to add, delete, or edit text, as well as use the spell checker and the search/replace facilities — just like an external word processor. PageMaker even displays the styles of each paragraph to the left of the text (Figure 1). Notice, in Figure 1, the different menu items available in story view.

As an alternative to triple-clicking on text with the pointer tool , you can invoke the story editor by clicking an insertion point with the text tool and choose *Edit story* from the **Edit** menu. Two other methods may also be employed: if a story editor window is already open but behind the normal publication window, click on an exposed part; or choose, from the **Window** menu, the story window's name. The **Window** menu allows you to move between story editor and publication layout views, at will.

It is also possible to open up a new, empty, story editor window for adding more text within PageMaker. This is done by choosing *Edit story* from the **Edit** menu without any text selected.

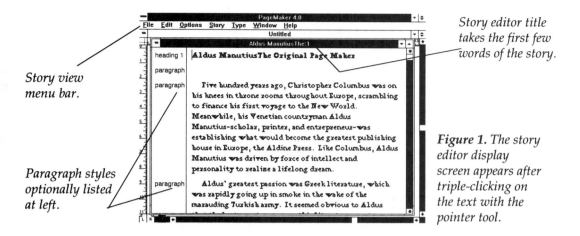

Story view menu bar.

Paragraph styles optionally listed at left.

Story editor title takes the first few words of the story.

Figure 1. The story editor display screen appears after triple-clicking on the text with the pointer tool.

Once a story window is open, you can edit, delete, or type in text, and use the spell check and search/replace features. To move up or down in the text file, use the scroll bar to the right of the screen in the same way you would on the publication layout screen.

You can even use this view to change paragraph styles. (Refer to Module 11, **Style Sheets,** for more details on style sheets.) Paragraph styles are displayed to the left of the text. A paragraph may be selected in story view by clicking on these style names.

Story view differences

In Figure 1, you can see some of the differences available with the new story view. The menus are slightly different. All text is shown in the font and size selected in the *Preferences* command from the **Edit** menu. Text styles are shown, but page or line breaks are not displayed. Graphic tools are not available. Story windows are automatically named with the first few words of the actual story.

Color and *Style* palettes may be displayed and utilized. Most changes will become apparent only on return to layout view. The style names listed at left in Figure 1 can be optionally shown or hidden using the *Display style names* command in the **Options** menu.

Style sheets and color details are discussed in a later module. Understanding them is not necessary at this point in order to understand the story editor.

Spell checking

To activate this function select the *Spelling* option in the **Edit** menu, once in story view (Figure 2). The dialog box of Figure 3 will appear. Spell checking is only possible in story view. Note that in layout view, the *Spelling* command is gray and cannot be selected.

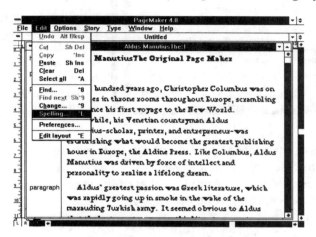

Figure 2. Select the Spelling *option in the* **Edit** *menu. Don't worry about which part of the document is displayed on your screen — PageMaker can check through the entire document regardless.*

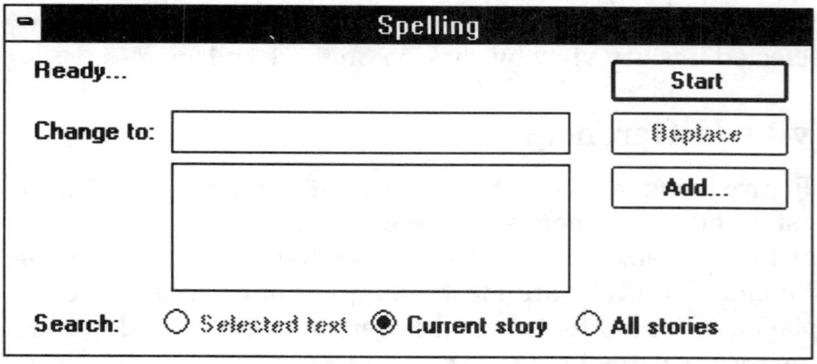

Figure 3. If an insertion point is clicked in the story view, then you can choose Current story *or* All stories *at the bottom of the dialog box. If a paragraph or portion of text is highlighted,* Selected text *can also be chosen.*

Clicking on the *Start* button of Figure 3 causes spell checking to begin. Once checking is underway, the *Start* button of Figure 3 is replaced with the *Ignore* button of Figure 4.

As each misspelled word is detected, it is displayed at the top of the dialog box and also in the *Change to*: box (Figure 4). You then have the opportunity to replace the word with the correct spelling, ignore it, or add it to the dictionary. PageMaker will also prompt you, in the large bottom rectangle, with alternative, correctly spelled words to choose from (Figure 4). The *Add* command, to the right of the Figures 3 and 4 dialog boxes allows you to add words to PageMaker's dictionary (initially 100,000 words for US English and 80,000 words for International English).

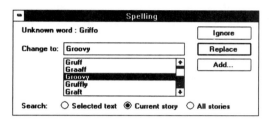

Figure 4. PageMaker has found an unknown word. We have highlighted one of the suggested alternatives which is then automatically placed in the Change to: *box. The next step is to click on the* Replace, Ignore, *or* Add *command so that PageMaker can continue its search through the document.*

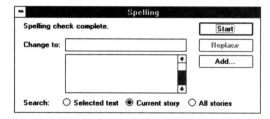

Figure 5. When the spell checker has reached the end, it will display this message in the dialog box.

To remove the *Spelling* dialog box when you have finished with the spell check, double-click on its close button in the top left-hand corner.

Search and replace

PageMaker allows you to search for, and optionally replace, text, text attributes, and nonprinting characters. The *Find* command from the **Edit** menu (in story view) produces the dialog box in Figure 6. Enter the text you wish to find and click the *Find* button. Once PageMaker finds the text, it replaces *Find* with *Find Next*. You then have the option of continuing or clicking the close button and exiting. It is possible to search *Selected text, Current story*, or *All stories* in a publication.

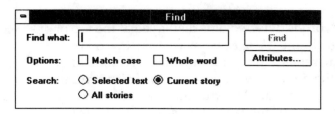

Figure 6. The Find
command dialog box
appears on choosing Find
from the **Edit** *menu in*
story view.

Clicking on the *Attributes* button of the *Find* command, causes
the *Attributes* dialog box to appear (Figure 7). This allows you to
search for a range of attributes, rather than just text. Figure 7, for
example, shows the sub-menu for paragraph styles. Any style
name in your current style sheet can be selected and searched for.

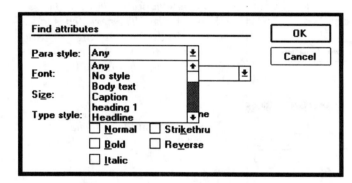

Figure 7. The Find
attributes *dialog box.*
Holding the mouse on the
arrow to the right of the
Para style *dialog box will*
display a sub-menu
containing all the available
styles that also appear in the
Style palette. (*See Module*
11 for information on
Styles.)

The *Change* command (in the **Edit** menu) searches for a selected
item and changes this item to whatever you have specified. If, for
example, you wish to change every occurrence of the word Griffo
to Groovy throughout the text, you would do this by setting up the
Change command dialog box as shown in Figure 8.

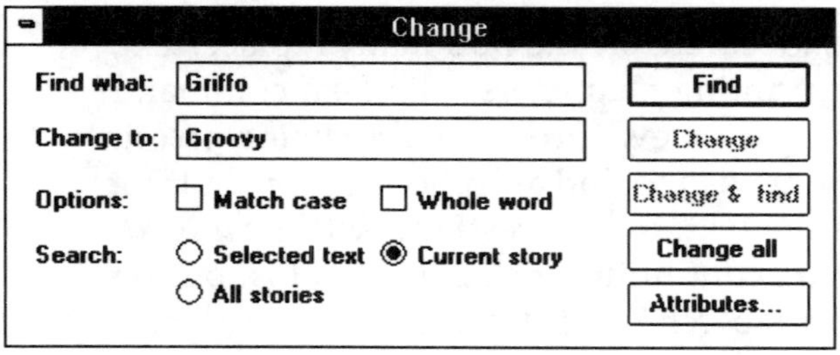

Figure 8. *Click inside*
the Find what: *and*
Change to: *boxes with*
the mouse and then type
in these entries.

206

Initially, you would have the choice of *Find* (find first occurrence) or *Change all* (change all occurrences). If you choose *Find*, once the first occurrence is found you have the option of *Change*, *Change & find* or *Change all*. The *Attributes* button of Figure 8 gives both a *Find* and a *Change* attributes dialog box. Its operation is similar to the one in Figure 7, but change attributes are also included.

Importing files to a story window

It is possible to import word-processed text, in-line graphics, and PageMaker text into story view using the *Import* command from the **Story** menu (Figure 9). This command only operates in story editor mode.

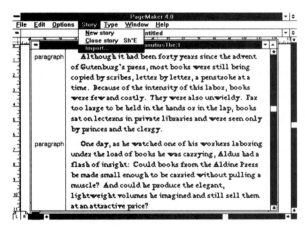

Figure 9. To import text and in-line graphics while in story view, choose the Import *command from the* **Story** *menu.*

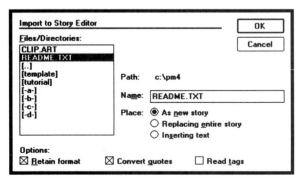

Figure 10. The Import to Story Editor *dialog box will appear upon selecting* Import *from the menu in Figure 9.*

Using the *Import* command you can load the following:

• **Word processor files**. If you select *As new story* in the Figure 10 dialog box, the text will be placed into a new story window. If you select *Inserting text*, it will go into the current active window at the text cursor location. If you select *Replacing entire story*, it goes into the currently active window, completely replacing the original story.

• *PageMaker 4 files*. A similar set of circumstances applies. A PageMaker 4 document can, however, include more than one story. You have the option, therefore, through the *Place PageMaker stories* dialog box (Figure 11), of choosing one or more stories to import. Multiple stories are imported as a single story with carriage returns between.

Figure 11. This is the Place PageMaker stories *dialog box from the* Import command. *We have decided to load the LES3DONE.PM4 PageMaker publication from the lesson4 directory within the tutorial directory. This box is telling us there are three different stories we can load. We can choose one, two, or all three. The* View *command gives you a small window to view the story contents.*

• *Inline Graphics*. These files will load into the currently open story window with a small graphics marker (■) showing the insertion point.

Exiting story view

When you have finished with story view, simply double-click on the *System* menu in the top left-hand corner (Figure 12), or choose *Close story* from the **Story** menu. If your story is new, PageMaker will alert you to either *Place* or *Discard* the story (Figure 13).

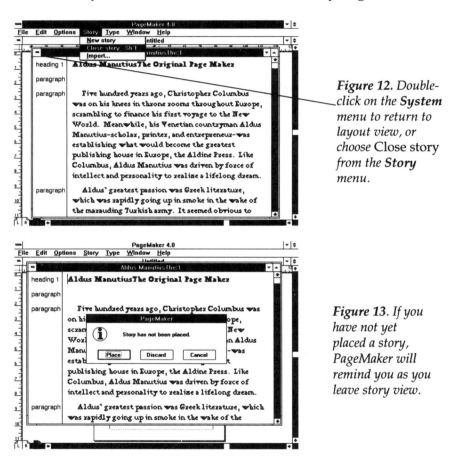

Figure 12. *Double-click on the **System** menu to return to layout view, or choose* Close story *from the **Story** menu.*

Figure 13. If you have not yet placed a story, PageMaker will remind you as you leave story view.

You may also return to layout view by clicking on an exposed part of the publication, or by choosing *Edit layout* from the **Edit** menu. Any changes made to text in story view will be automatically included in layout view. Selecting the publication name from the **Window** menu will also allow you to move between the two (or more) open windows in your document, but this method keeps the story editor window open.

EXERCISE:
THE STORY
EDITOR

The Story Editor

In this exercise, you will be utilizing story editor functions.

This training material is structured so that people of all levels of expertise with Page-Maker can use it to gain maximum benefit. In order to do this, we have structured the material so that the bare exercise is listed below this paragraph on just one page, with no hints. The following pages contain the steps needed to complete this exercise for those who need additional prompting. **The Story Editor** module should be referenced if you need further help or explanations.

Module 5 exercise steps

1.   *Place the text file STORY2.RTF (in the lesson4 directory within the tutorial sub-directory) into a new PageMaker document.*

2.   *Activate the story editor screen.*

3.   *Change the heading "What's behind the Aldine Dolphin and Anchor?" to "The Real Story of Aldine Dolphin."*

4.   *Activate the* Change *command and replace every carriage return with three carriage returns.*

The steps to completing this exercise are on the following pages.

The steps in detail

1. Place the text file STORY2.RTF (in the lesson4 directory within the tutorial directory) into a new PageMaker document.

Start a new PageMaker publication, Letter size, of one page in length. If you have trouble with this initial step, please review the first few steps of the Module 3 exercise (**Working with Text Blocks**). Go to the *Place* command in the **File** menu, locate STORY2.RTF in the lesson4 directory (inside the tutorial directory), and load the file onto your page in one or two columns (your choice).

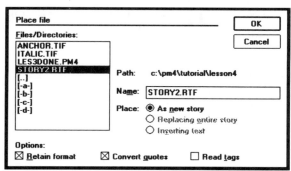

Figure 1. Place the file STORY2.RTF (located in the lesson4 directory). Load it onto a blank page.

2. Activate the story editor screen.

Triple-click in the text block with the pointer tool to activate the story editor screen. Alternatively, you can place the text cursor anywhere in the text and choose *Edit story* from the **Edit** menu.

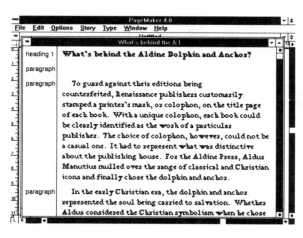

Figure 2. Triple-click in the text block with the mouse. This ensures that the story editor screen will open with the text you clicked on in layout view.

3. *Change the heading "What's behind the Aldine Dolphin and Anchor?" to "The Real Story of Aldine Dolphin."*

Select the text tool and highlight the heading (Figure 3). Type in the new heading (Figure 4).

Figure 3. Highlight the heading with the text tool and simply retype the new heading.

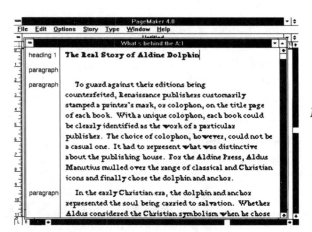

Figure 4. The new heading.

4. *Activate the* Change *command and replace every carriage return with three carriage returns.*

Go to the **Edit** menu and select *Change* (Figure 5). Now, follow the instructions given in the caption of Figure 6. The result is shown in Figure 7.

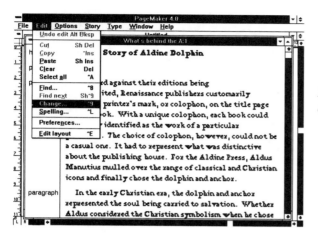

Figure 5. Select the Change *command from the* **Edit** *Menu.*

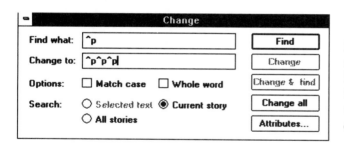

Figure 6. Enter one carriage return symbol (^p) in the Find what: *rectangle and three in the* Change to: *rectangle. Then select the option* Change all.

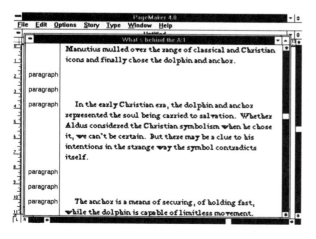

Figure 7. The result should look something like this. If you choose Display ¶ *in the* **Options** *menu, the screen will display three carriage return symbols after each paragraph throughout the text.*

CREATING GRAPHICS

Module 6

Creating Graphics

Most of the time, third-party packages will be used to create the complex and professional quality graphics that can be used within PageMaker. There are countless packages available for the PC that make incredible graphics a reality for all types of users— a reality that usually cannot be achieved with PageMaker alone.

This is not to say that PageMaker can't create a large array of graphics internally — because it can. When it comes to preparing simple graphics, such as borders, underlines, boxes, circles, simple graphs, and charts, you may not need to look any further than PageMaker itself.

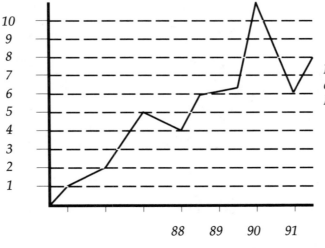

Figure 1. A simple graph created using the Page-Maker graphic tools.

Figure 1 is an example of how graphics can be created within PageMaker in very little time.

All of the PageMaker graphics tools are found in the Toolbox (Figure 2). They include two straight line drawing tools, two rectangular drawing tools, and the oval drawing tool. The way these tools are used is quite simple.

The diagonal-line drawing tool

The perpendicular-line drawing tool

The square-corner drawing tool

The rounded-corner drawing tool

The oval drawing tool

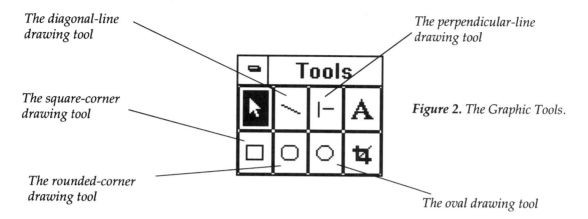

Figure 2. The Graphic Tools.

Simply select the tool you would like to use from the Toolbox. Let's say you select the square-corner drawing tool first (Figure 3). The mouse cursor changes to a crosshair.

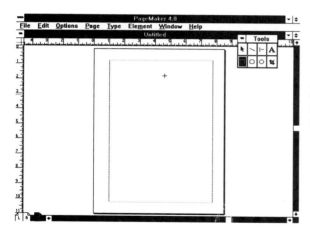

Figure 3. As soon as any graphic tool is selected, the mouse cursor becomes a crosshair.

Hold down the mouse cursor where you would like to start drawing the graphic. Dragging the mouse in any direction will cause a box to appear which will become set, or fixed, when the mouse button is released (Figures 4 and 5). All other graphics can be created in exactly this manner — by selecting the appropriate tool and dragging the mouse along the page. Experiment with all the graphic drawing tools to see the results you get, as we have done in Figure 6.

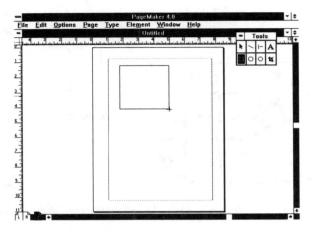

Figure 4. To create a graphic once you have selected a tool (in this case the square-corner drawing tool), hold the mouse button down and drag the mouse across the page. In this example, a rectangle is created.

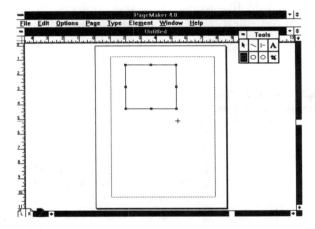

Figure 5. Release the mouse button when the graphic is the correct size. It will then become selected. Note the small square dots (called handles) around the edge of the graphic.

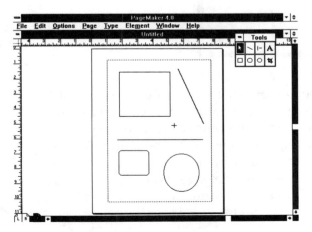

Figure 6. Here is an example of a graphic from each of the graphic drawing tools.

Altering graphics

As soon as you draw a graphic, you will notice that the graphic is selected (Figure 5) — that is to say, it has several small square dots, or handles, around its edge. However, when you create another graphic, the new object becomes selected and the previously selected graphic is deselected.

To manipulate a graphic on the page, it must first be selected. This is done by activating the pointer tool in the Toolbox and clicking with the arrow on the border of the graphic. Once selected, a graphic will display the handles around its border (Figure 7). Alternate graphics can be selected simply by clicking anywhere on their border.

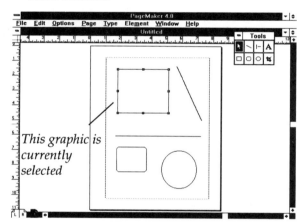

Figure 7. To select a graphic, you must first make sure the pointer tool is active (note the Toolbox), then click on the border of the graphic you would like to select.

Changing borders and fills

After selecting a graphic, there are several things that you can do with it. First, you can change the border and/or the fill for that graphic. If you have created a graphic using either of the line drawing tools, you will only be able to adjust the line thickness because a line has no fill at all.

Make sure a rectangular graphic is selected on screen, similar to Figure 8, and study the *Line* and *Fill* sub-menus under the **Element** menu. Most of the choices in these menus are self-explanatory — line thickness and patterns can be set by selecting the ones that appeal to you, as can the shade and pattern to fill a selected graphic. Figures 8 through 14 illustrate some examples.

221

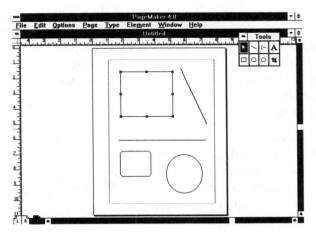

Figure 8. The process of changing the appearance of a graphic begins by selecting the graphic you would like to change.

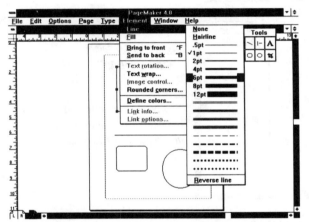

Figure 9. After selecting the graphic, move to the Line command under the **Element** menu and select the desired line thickness from the sub-menu that appears.

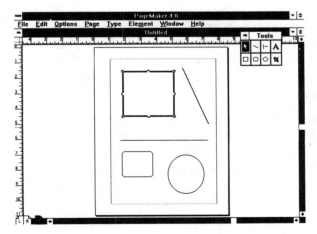

Figure 10. On screen, the graphic will reflect the new line thickness. A small change may sometimes not look like a change due to the resolution of the screen.

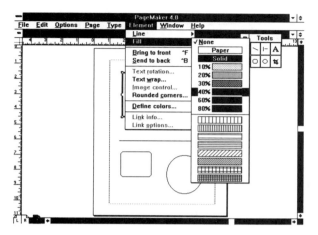

Figure 11. *The same procedure works when changing the fill pattern of a graphic. Make sure the graphic is selected, then move to the* Fill *command under the* **Element** *menu.*

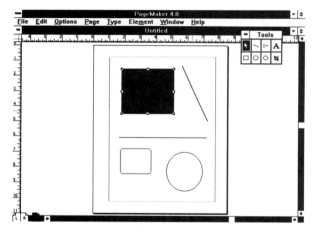

Figure 12. *The selected graphic will reflect the new pattern or shade on screen.*

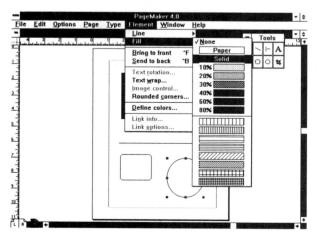

Figure 13. *Here we have selected the ellipse near the bottom of the screen and are in the process of choosing the* Solid *option, which will be black.*

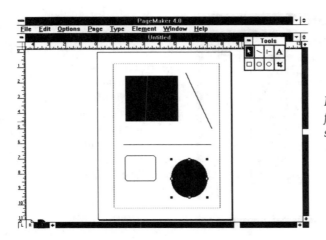

Figure 14. The color black fills the selected ellipse on screen.

Moving

Any graphic can be moved in exactly the same way as a text block. Select the pointer tool, hold down the mouse button on the border of the graphic if it is hollow, or anywhere in the graphic if it has a fill pattern, and move the mouse. The graphic will be dragged along with the mouse and will move to the point where the mouse button is released (Figure 15).

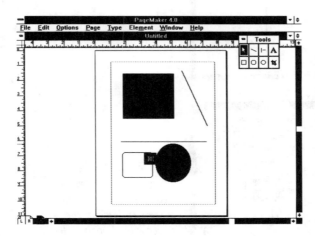

Figure 15. The ellipse has been selected and is now being moved. Note the shape of the mouse. Where the mouse cursor is released will determine the new position for the graphic.

Resizing

Any graphic can be resized in any direction, much the same way as a text block can. Only, in the case of a graphic, there are more dots around the edge, giving more flexibility. To resize, first select the graphic using the pointer tool, hold down the mouse button on any handle around the edge of the graphic, and drag it in any direction you like. Release the mouse button when the graphic has been sized correctly.

You will notice, as you experiment with the resizing of graphics, that the handle you grab will determine the direction in which the graphic can be resized — horizontally, vertically, or diagonally. See Figures 16 through 18, illustrating this point.

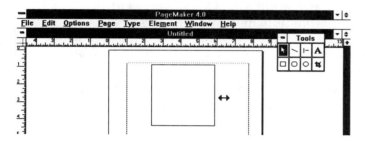

Figure 16. Holding the mouse button down on a side handle means that the graphic can only be resized in that direction (in this case the width of the graphic can be shortened or lengthened, depending on the movement of the mouse).

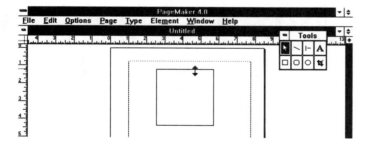

Figure 17. Here we have selected a top handle — allowing us to size the graphic vertically.

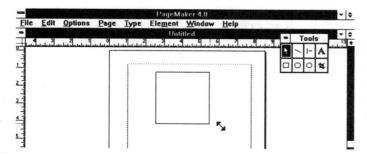

Figure 18. We have now selected a corner handle to size the rectangle diagonally (i.e. both horizontally and vertically).

Editing

Any selected graphic can be deleted, copied, cleared, or pasted to and from the PageMaker screen with the editing commands in the **Edit** menu. *Cut* will remove the selected graphic from the screen and keep it in a temporary memory (the Windows Clipboard). The graphic is not yet lost, although it is not visible. *Copy* will put a copy of the selected graphic into the Clipboard, removing it from the screen.

Paste will transfer the graphic from the Clipboard back to the screen. It will paste the new graphic at a slight offset to its original position. Once the graphic is in the Clipboard, it can be pasted any number of times back onto the page. This has several advantages, one of which is in duplicating a selected graphic repeatedly. A graphic can be cleared from the screen, without being transferred to the Clipboard with the *Clear* command from the **Edit** menu. The *Clear* command operates identically to the Delete key.

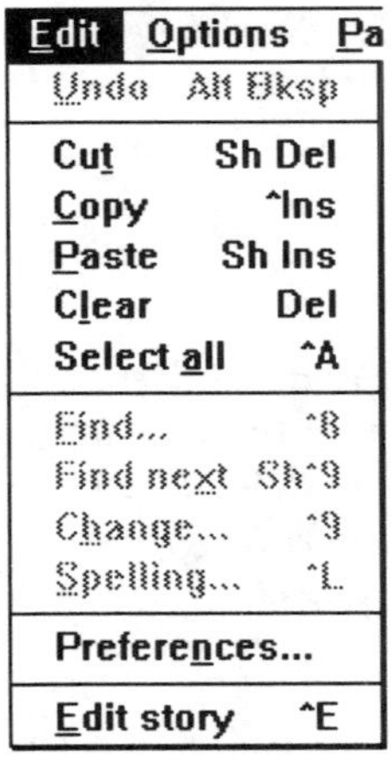

Figure 19. Cut *removes a selected graphic from the screen and puts it into memory (the Clipboard).* Copy *copies the selected graphic from screen to the Clipboard (the screen graphic is not altered in any way).* Paste *transfers whatever is in the Clipboard back to the middle of the screen, and* Clear *removes a graphic from the screen without putting it into the Clipboard.*

Be cautious when using the Clipboard: it will hold only one element at a time. Every time you cut or copy something to this temporary memory, the previous element in that memory is lost.

You can view the contents of the Clipboard any time by accessing it from the Windows Program Manager.

Figures 20 through 22 provide examples of using the *Copy* command with graphics.

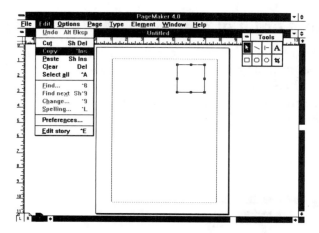

Figure 20. *The graphic on this page has been selected. Let's now select the* Copy *command. The graphic is copied to the Clipboard.*

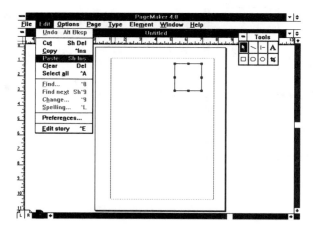

Figure 21. *Immediately after choosing* Copy *we can choose the* Paste *command. (It does not have to be immediately after, but it does have to be before something else is cut or copied or your computer is turned off.)*

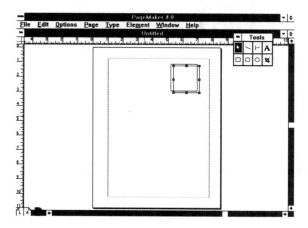

Figure 22. *After choosing* Paste, *what was in the Clipboard is pasted back at a slightly offset position to the original graphic. This process can be repeated to obtain multiple copies of any graphic.*

Changing the printing order of graphics

It's very easy to create graphics that either overlap each other or overlap text on the page. Using two other commands in the **Element** menu, *Send to back* and *Bring to front*, the order of the graphics overlap can be changed. Study Figures 23 through 28 for examples of this technique.

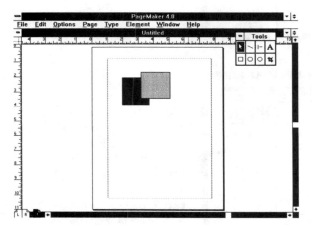

Figure 23. *Here we have two graphics that overlap each other. Let's say you want to change the order of the overlap so that the black graphic is on top.*

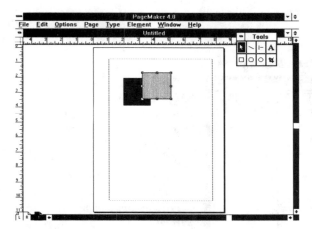

Figure 24. *You could actually select either graphic here, but we will start with the graphic on the top.*

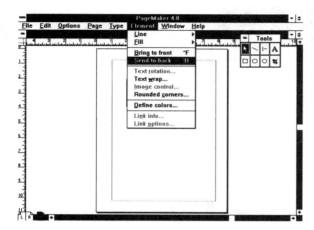

Figure 25. *After the top graphic is selected, choose the* Send to back *command from the* **Element** *menu (because the graphic we have selected is on the top).*

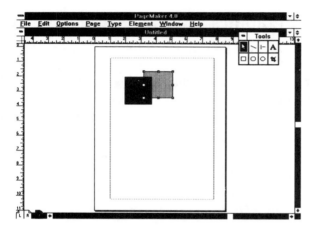

Figure 26. *The change can be seen immediately — the black graphic is now on the top.*

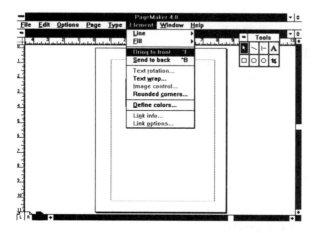

Figure 27. *If you wanted to bring the shaded graphic back to the top, you would need to select the* Bring to front *command (because the shaded graphic is still the selected object).*

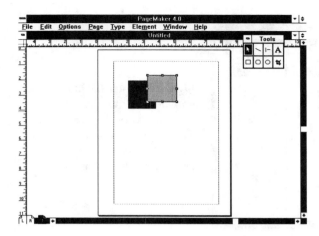

Figure 28. After selecting the command in Figure 27, the shaded graphic sits back on top.

Transparent and solid graphics

Graphics can be filled with transparent and solid selections from the *Fill* sub-menu (Figure 13), as well as a with range of shaded options. It is important when using the *None* and *Paper* selections to understand the difference between *None*, which is hollow, and *Paper*, which is usually white. Both look white on the screen.

Note the two overlapping diagrams in Figure 29. In both cases the white rectangle is on the top. In the example towards the top of the page, the white rectangle has a shade of *None* selected from the *Fill* sub-menu, while in the bottom example, the white rectangle has a fill selection of *Paper*.

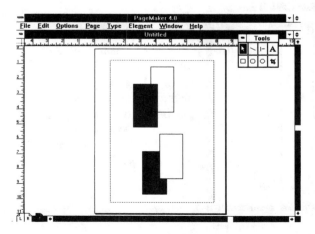

Figure 29. The white rectangle at the top of the page has a fill selection of None. *It is hollow, and the black rectangle underneath can be seen unobscured. The bottom rectangle has a fill selection of* Paper, *which is usually white and therefore covers the black rectangle underneath it.*

Rounded-corner drawing tool

It is possible to draw both squares and rectangles with rounded corners as well as square corners. This is done by selecting the rounded-corner drawing tool from the Toolbox (see Figure 2).

This tool is used in exactly the same manner as the square-corner tool. The one additional thing to remember is the *Rounded corners* command available in the **Element** menu. This command offers a choice of radius for the rounded corners of the rectangle or square. Figure 30 shows an example of the rounded-corner tool and Figure 31 illustrates the dialog box activated with the *Rounded corners* command.

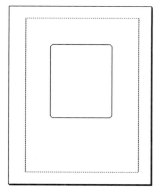

Figure 30. This rectangle was drawn using the rounded-corner drawing tool. The actual radius of the corners can be set using the dialog box of Figure 31.

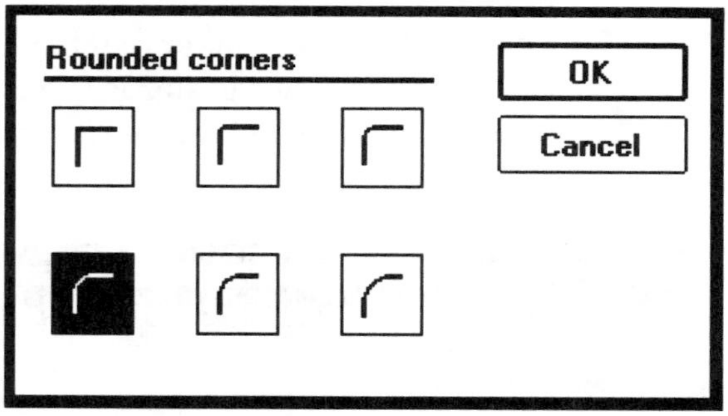

Figure 31. This is the Rounded corners *dialog box associated with the* Rounded corners *command from the* **Element** *menu. You simply choose the radius that suits you.*

Line drawing tools

The diagonal and perpendicular line drawing tools are indicated in the Toolbox diagram of Figure 2. The perpendicular tool draws lines at 45 degree increments, while the diagonal tool creates straight lines at any angle. The diagonal tool acts like the perpendicular one when the Shift key is held down.

The thickness of the lines can be set using the *Line* sub-menu from the **Element** menu (see Figure 9). Some examples are shown in Figure 32.

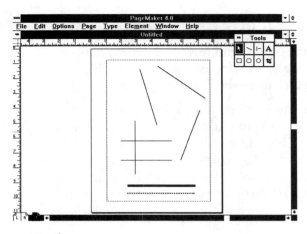

Figure 32. Examples of the two different line drawing tools are shown. All lines drawn are 1 point in thickness except for the bottom two. The second line from the bottom is 12 points thick, and the bottom line represents one of the pattern selections from the Line *command in the* **Element** *menu.*

Rulers

One element of PageMaker that makes the creation and manipulation of graphics a lot easier is the PageMaker rulers. These are activated by the *Rulers* command in the **Options** menu (Figure 33).

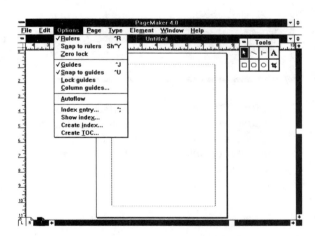

Figure 33. Selecting the Rulers *command from the* **Options** *menu will cause rulers to appear down the left and across the top of the page (see Figure 34).*

When you select this command, you will notice a ruler appear down the left and across the top of the page (Figure 34). These rulers are measured in units controlled by the *Preferences* command in the **Edit** menu. The rulers will always reformat to give accurate measurements on the screen irrespective of the current PageMaker view. The increments in these rulers change depending on the current page view.

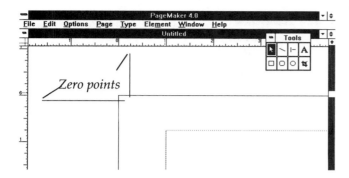

Figure 34. Note that the zero point of the ruler, both vertically and horizontally, is aligned with the top left-hand corner of the page. If the increments on your ruler look a little different from this figure, you may have millimeters or other units set up in the Preferences *command in the **Edit** menu. We currently have inches selected.*

We can also change exactly where the zero points of both the horizontal and vertical rulers start. By default, the zero point of both these rulers starts at the top left corner of the actual page for single page views. *Facing pages* view puts the zero point midway between the two pages. Move to *Actual size* view through the **Page** menu and look at the top left corner of the page to check this (Figure 34).

To change the zero point of the ruler, move the mouse to the top left corner where the two rulers intersect (see Figure 35) and hold the mouse button down. Keep this button held down and slowly move the mouse cursor back onto the page. A crosshair will follow the mouse cursor back down the page (Figure 35). Where the mouse button is released will determine the new zero point of the ruler, both horizontally and vertically. The rulers will reformat to show this when the mouse button is released (Figure 36).

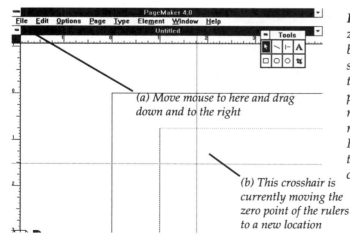

Figure 35. To change the ruler's zero point, hold the mouse button down in the intersecting square of both rulers and pull the mouse back out onto the page. A crosshair indicating the new zero point of the rulers replaces the mouse cursor. Release the mouse button when the crosshair is positioned correctly.

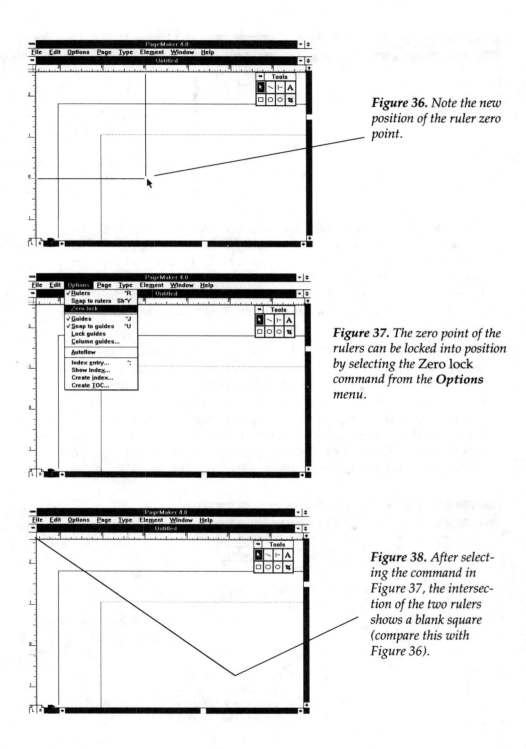

Figure 36. Note the new position of the ruler zero point.

Figure 37. The zero point of the rulers can be locked into position by selecting the Zero lock command from the **Options** menu.

Figure 38. After selecting the command in Figure 37, the intersection of the two rulers shows a blank square (compare this with Figure 36).

Additional features are available with the rulers. Ruler guides can be "pulled" from the rulers, horizontally and vertically, allowing a form of grid to be set up — a grid that graphics can snap to and precisely align themselves very easily.

To use these ruler guides, hold the mouse button down in either ruler and pull the mouse cursor back down onto the page. As long as the mouse cursor is released on the page, rather than in the pasteboard area that surrounds it, a dotted line parallel to the ruler will be visible on the page from where this guide originated (Figure 39).

Multiple guides can be pulled from either ruler (Figures 40 through 42), and it is quite easy to set up a grid with these guides. All guides can be positioned precisely by aligning them with the measurements of the rulers. More exact alignment is possible at larger page views. Any ruler guide can be moved around on the screen by holding the mouse button down on it and dragging it to a new position (Figure 41). If you want to get rid of one or more ruler guides, simply pull them right off the page (Figure 42) and they will disappear.

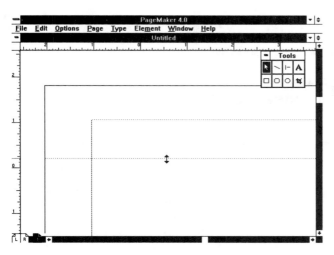

Figure 39. Ruler guides can be pulled from the rulers onto the page by holding the mouse button down inside a ruler and dragging down onto the page.

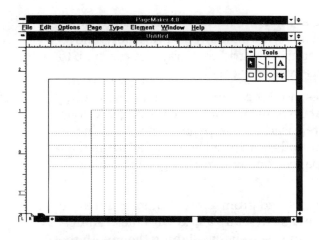

Figure 40. Here we have built up quite a few guides, from both the vertical and horizontal rulers, creating a grid.

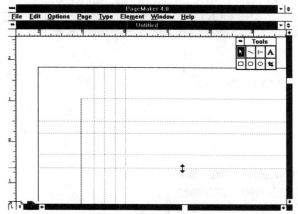

Figure 41. Any guide can be repositioned by holding the mouse button down on it and moving it to a new position.

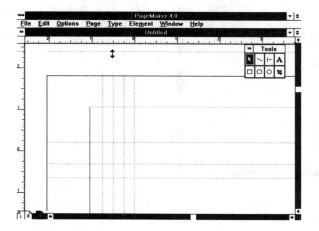

Figure 42. To remove a ruler guide from the page, simply move it so that it is no longer on the page. It will not remain on the pasteboard area when the mouse is released.

Multiple selections

So far we have talked only about selecting one graphic at a time. It is possible, however, to select multiple graphics in a number of different ways. The easiest way to select all graphics on a page is to choose the *Select all* command in the **Edit** menu (Figures 43 and 44). Any operation, whether it be editing, line changes, or fill changes, will then affect all selected graphics.

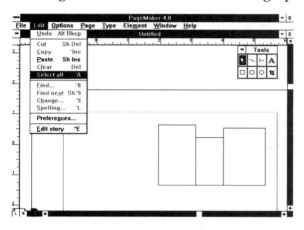

Figure 43. The Select all *command can be used to select all the graphics on a page — but remember that this command will also select any text blocks that may be on the screen.*

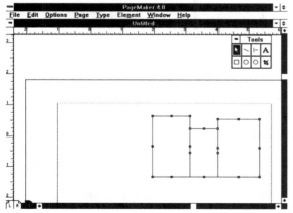

Figure 44. Here are all the graphics selected from Figure 43 using the Select all *command. These graphics can now be deleted, moved, copied, and modified, all as a group.*

Generally, when you select a graphic, the graphic previously selected becomes deselected. However, if you hold down the Shift key on the keyboard as you select other graphics, all graphics will remain selected. Once again, any future operations will then apply to all selected graphics. This is an alternative way of selecting multiple graphics.

Yet another way to select a group of graphics is to draw an imaginary box around them with the pointer tool. Pretend that you are drawing a box around a group of graphics, but make sure that the pointer tool is active. A dotted box will be drawn as the mouse button is held down (Figure 45), and once released, any graphics that are entirely enclosed by this imaginary box will be selected.

If you ever have trouble selecting a graphic because it is behind a guide (ruler, margin, or column) or a block of text, try holding down the Control key as you attempt to select the graphic. This often allows hidden or hard-to-get-at graphics to be selected.

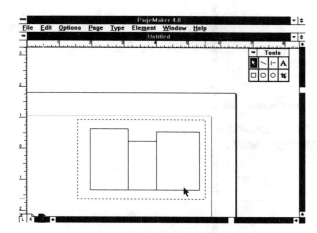

Figure 45. Drawing an imaginary box around a set of graphics will also select multiple graphics. Make sure the pointer tool is selected and draw a border around the graphics you would like to select. Upon releasing the mouse, all the graphics within the border will be selected.

Setting the graphic default

Initially, every graphic you create has a line thickness setting and a fill setting. It would be a nuisance to have to change every graphic you create to the line thickness you want, rather than the one that is set.

Setting the default line and fill values for graphics is achieved by making sure that no graphic is currently selected and choosing the required values from the *Line* and *Fill* sub-menus. Although you will see no immediate change on screen, every graphic that is created from now on will use the *Line* and *Fill* values you have just set by default.

Maintaining aspect ratio

When you create a rectangle, an ellipse, or a line, you will find it extremely difficult to create a square, a circle, or in some cases a straight line. Combine the use of the mouse with the aspect ratio of the screen, and this is almost impossible. PageMaker, however, allows you to use a technique that automatically maintains the correct aspect ratio.

When creating a graphic, or even resizing a graphic, hold down the Shift key as you do so. The graphic will snap to its correct shape (square or circle) immediately. Make sure that you release the mouse button before you release the Shift key; otherwise the aspect ratio may be lost.

Using all these features of PageMaker together means that fairly complex graphics are quite easy to create. Since no freehand drawing is possible, any freehand drawings must be created in other packages. Try not to get too involved, however, in very complex graphic creations in PageMaker. Many graphics, although possible to create in PageMaker, may be created much more easily, and perhaps a little better, in third-party packages.

Bar charts are a good example of this. Although possible to draw in PageMaker, a number of graphing programs produce such charts automatically when you enter the actual data. The Table Editor program which is included with PageMaker 4 can also be used for this purpose. This is discussed in Module 19.

Wraparounds

All internally created PageMaker graphics can be set up as regular or irregular wraparounds. The method by which this is done is identical to the way it is done with imported graphics — and for this reason is explained in detail in Modules 7 and 14 (regular wraparounds in Module 7, and irregular wraparounds in Module 14). All facets of wraparounds described in these modules can be applied identically to internally created graphics.

EXERCISE: CREATING GRAPHICS

Creating Graphics

In this exercise we will be creating simple graphics from within PageMaker.

This training material is structured so that people of all levels of expertise with Page-Maker can use it to gain maximum benefit. In order to do this, we have structured the material so that the bare exercise is listed below this paragraph on just one page, with no hints. The following pages contain the steps needed to complete this exercise, for those who need additional prompting. The **Creating Graphics** module should be referenced if you need further help or explanations.

Module 6 exercise steps

1.   *Create a new one page publication using a Letter page with 0.75" (or 20 mm) margins.*

2.   *Assign three columns to the first page.*

3.   *Load in the text file LEADSTRY.RTF using the Autoflow method.*

4.   *Insert a border of 2 points thickness around the outside of the page, with a spacing of approximately 5 mm (or 0.2"), horizontally and vertically, between the margins and the border.*

5.   *Insert intercolumn rules of 2 points thickness.*

6.   *Change the first paragraph heading to 24-point bold Palatino.*

7.   *Create a box behind the heading using a 2-point outline and a 10% fill background.*

8.   *Draw a box in the bottom right-hand corner of the third column, 1.5" high, with a 2-point thick border.*

9.   *Load in the PRACTICE.TIF graphic file from the basics directory (within the tutorial directory), and place it into the Pasteboard area to the right of the page. Proportionally reduce its size to fit into the box of step 8 with white space all around, and then move it into this box.*

10.   *Select the box and the graphic from steps 8 and 9, delete from page 1, and place them into the top left-hand corner of page 2.*

The steps to completing this exercise are on the following pages.

The steps in detail

1. Create a new one page publication using a Letter page with 0.75" (or 20 mm) margins.

The new publication is created using the *New* command (Figure 1). Set up the associated dialog box as shown in Figure 2.

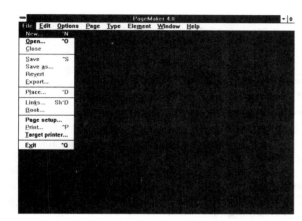

Figure 1. Use the New *command to open a new PageMaker document.*

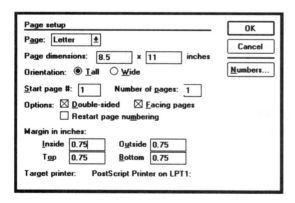

Figure 2. Set the page size to Letter in the New *dialog box, one page long, and 0.75" margins all around.*

2. Assign three columns to the first page.

The page is assigned columns using the *Column guides* command from the **Options** menu (Figure 3). Insert *3* in the *Column guides* dialog box (Figure 4).

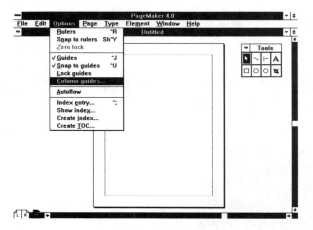

Figure 3. The Column guides *command from the* **Options** *menu allows you to set columns on the page.*

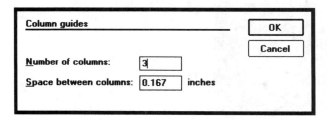

Figure 4. Set three columns for the page within the Column guides *dialog box.*

3. Load in the text file LEADSTRY.RTF using the Autoflow *method.*

Use the *Place* command to load in the LEADSTRY.RTF file from the lesson2 directory (within the tutorial directory) inside the pm4 directory. Locate the lesson2 directory and the LEADSTRY.RTF file within it, and double-click on them (Figures 5 through 8).

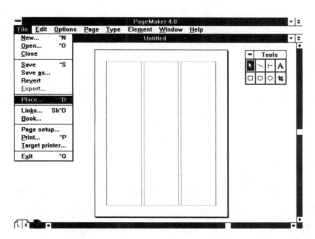

Figure 5. The now familiar Place *command is used to insert text into PageMaker.*

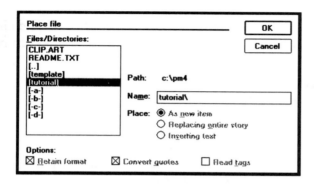

Figure 6. Lesson2 is located in the tutorial directory.

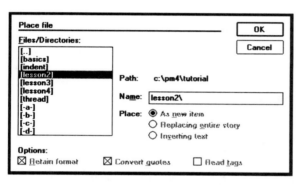

Figure 7. Double-click on the directory lesson2.

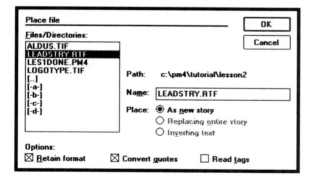

Figure 8. Now double-click on the file LEADSTRY.RTF.

To use the *Autoflow* method to flow the text, make sure this option is selected within the **Options** menu (Figure 9). It is selected when a check mark appears next to the command. If it doesn't have a check beside it, select it. The mouse cursor will then appear as in Figure 10.

Position the mouse cursor at the top of the first column (Figure 10) and click once. After a few seconds, text will have flowed into all three of the columns (Figure 11).

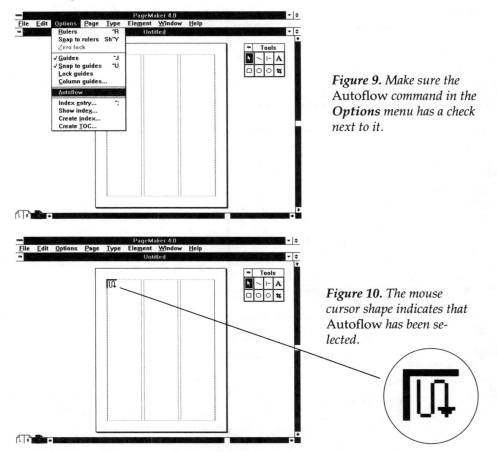

Figure 9. Make sure the Autoflow *command in the* **Options** *menu has a check next to it.*

Figure 10. The mouse cursor shape indicates that Autoflow *has been selected.*

4. Insert a border of 2 points thickness around the outside of the page, with a spacing of approximately 5 mm (0.2"), horizontally and vertically, between the margins and the border.

A border around a page is best created using either the square-corner or rounded-corner drawing tool. Select either of these two tools from the Toolbox. We have chosen the square-corner tool in Figure 11.

Position the mouse cursor (which will now look like a crosshair) just above the top left-hand margin (Figure 11). Hold down the mouse cursor and move it to below the bottom right-hand margin. Release the mouse button (see Figure 12).

In our example, we aligned this border by eye, approximately 5 mm (or 0.2") outside of all margins. To be more exact, you could display the rulers and adjust the settings more precisely.

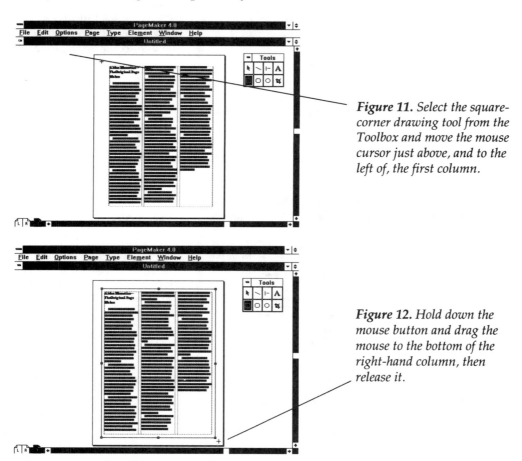

Figure 11. Select the square-corner drawing tool from the Toolbox and move the mouse cursor just above, and to the left of, the first column.

Figure 12. Hold down the mouse button and drag the mouse to the bottom of the right-hand column, then release it.

What the rectangle looks like now depends on how the default was set. However, there are two commands that should be chosen to ensure that the graphic is set correctly. The first command makes sure that the graphic has no fill whatsoever (Figure 13).

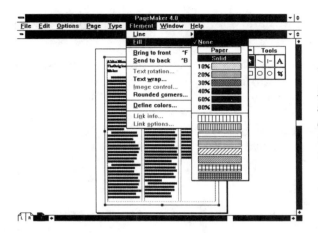

Figure 13. *To make sure the setting for the shading is correct, use the* Fill *sub-menu under the* **Element** *menu to set the fill to* None.

The second command makes sure that the border of the graphic is set at 2 points thickness (Figure 14).

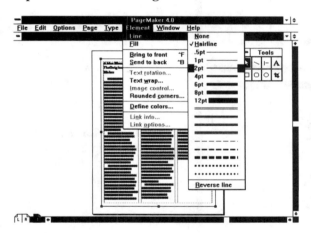

Figure 14. *Again, under the* **Element** *menu, use the* Line *sub-menu to set the thickness of the outline to 2 points.*

After using these two commands, the border of the page will be set correctly.

5. Insert intercolumn rules of 2 points thickness.

Intercolumn rules are inserted using the perpendicular line drawing tool. Select this tool now from the Toolbox (Figure 15).

Before creating the intercolumn guides, try this helper. Turn the *Snap to guides* command from the **Options** menu off. It is off when there is no check mark alongside it. This ensures that the line drawn does not snap to either side of the column guides, but is drawn down the middle. Move the mouse cursor to the top, between the first set of column guides (Figure 15), hold the mouse button down, drag the mouse to the bottom of this column, and release the button (Figure 16). Repeat this operation for the second set of column guides.

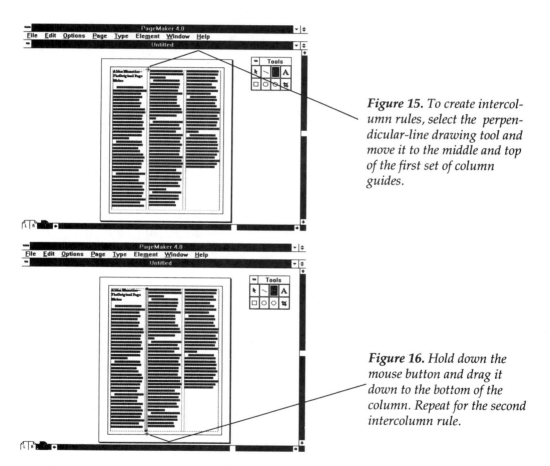

Figure 15. To create intercolumn rules, select the perpendicular-line drawing tool and move it to the middle and top of the first set of column guides.

Figure 16. Hold down the mouse button and drag it down to the bottom of the column. Repeat for the second intercolumn rule.

Set the line thickness for the intercolumn rules to 2 points as shown in Figure 17. Make sure the lines are selected when you do this.

After performing this step, re-select the *Snap to guides* command from the **Options** menu.

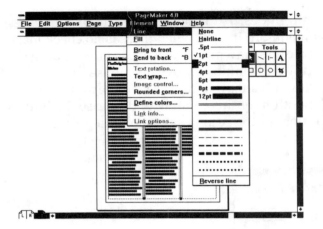

Figure 17. *Set the line thickness for the intercolumn rules to 2 points.*

6. Change the first paragraph heading to 24-point bold Palatino.

This step has to be achieved with the text cursor selected. Select this tool from the Toolbox (Figure 18). Next, move to *Actual size* view by clicking the right mouse button on the top left of the page.

To select the first paragraph heading, use the triple-click method. Move the mouse cursor anywhere over the heading and click the mouse button three times in succession. The paragraph will be highlighted in reverse video (Figure 18).

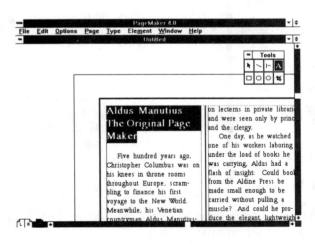

Figure 18. *Select the heading to change its specifications.*

Select the *Type specs* command from the **Type** menu to set the specifications for this paragraph (Figure 19). Set up the dialog box that appears on selecting this command as shown in Figure 20. The new heading is shown in Figure 21.

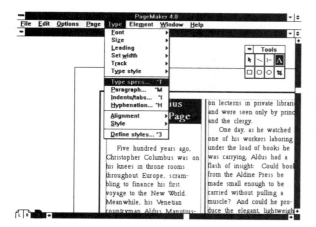

Figure 19. The Type specs command can change the specs for the text.

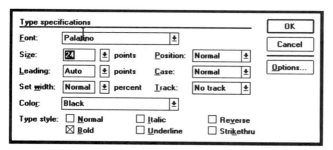

Figure 20. Set up the Type specifications dialog box as illustrated (Palatino font, bold and 24 points in size). If you don't have Palatino, use Tms Rmn.

Figure 21. The new heading resulting from the settings of Figure 20.

7. Create a box behind the heading using a 2-point outline and a 10% fill background.

Select the square-corner drawing tool from the Toolbox and draw a rectangle to completely cover the first paragraph, as shown in Figure 22. Use the *Line* sub-menu from the **Element** menu to set the outline at 2 points (Figure 23), and the *Fill* sub-menu to set the background to 10% (Figure 24).

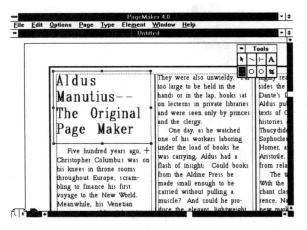

Figure 22. Select the square-corner drawing tool, hold the mouse button down above and to the left of the heading, and drag it to the bottom right of the heading.

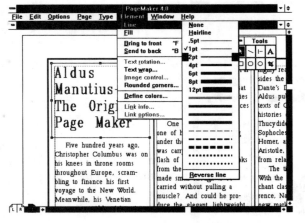

Figure 23. Set the thickness of the box outline to 2 points.

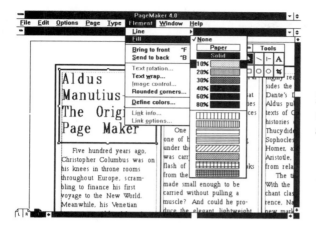

Figure 24. Also make sure that the shade for the rectangle is set to 10%.

At this stage, the rectangle will be sitting on top of the text, so that the text is unreadable (Figure 25). Make sure the rectangle is selected and choose the *Send to back* command from the **Element** menu (Figure 26). The text will immediately appear over the graphic (Figure 27).

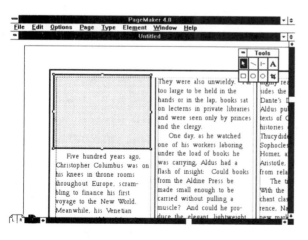

Figure 25. Don't panic if your heading disappears. See Figure 26 for details.

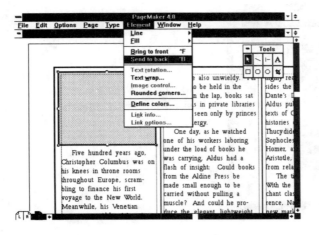

Figure 26. Make sure the rectangle is still selected, and choose the Send to back *command from the* Element *menu.*

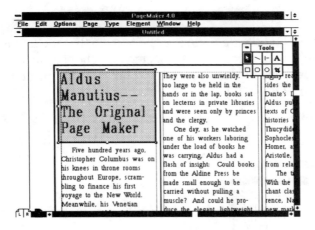

Figure 27. The heading reappears when the shaded rectangle is sent behind the text.

8. Draw a box in the bottom right-hand corner of the third column, 1.5" high, with a 2-point thick border.

To ensure that you get the vertical dimension of 1.5" correctly placed, display your rulers through the *Rulers* command in the **Options** menu. Then move in *Actual size* view to the bottom right-hand column and set up two ruler guides, as shown in Figure 28. A horizontal guide is set at 10", and another at 8.5" for the 1.5" box height. See the Figure 29 caption for the next step.

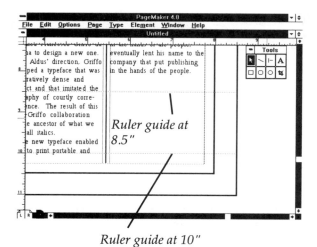

Figure 28. We are now posi-
tioned in Actual size *view at the*
bottom right-hand corner of the
page. Two ruler guides are set up
at 10" and 8.5"to help draw the
1.5" high box at the bottom of
this last column.

Ruler guide at 10"

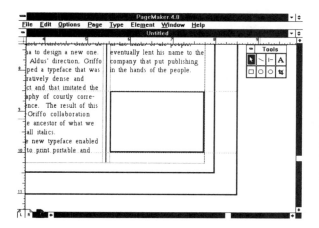

Figure 29. Draw the box using the
rulers and column guides as align-
ment tools. If the Snap to guides
command was on, the box outlines
would have automatically snapped to
the correct positions. The border was
set to 2 points thickness using the
Line *sub-menu under the* **Element**
menu.

9. *Load in the PRACTICE.TIF graphic file from the basics directory within the tutorial*
   directory and place it into the Pasteboard area to the right of the page. Proportionally
   reduce its size to fit into the box of step 8 with white space all around, and then move
   it into this box.

   In Figure 30, we have changed back to *Fit in window* view through the **Page**
menu and shifted the page to the left by moving the white horizontal scroll
bar to the right. Through the *Place* command, select the PRACTICE.TIF
graphic picture from the basics directory (within the tutorial directory), and
position the cursor as shown in Figure 30. At this point all you need to do is
click the mouse to get the result in Figure 31.

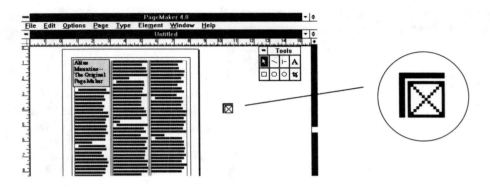

Figure 30. This is Fit in window *view with the page moved to the left. PRACTICE.TIF graphic has been selected from the basics directory using the* Place *command, and the mouse cursor is positioned at a convenient location to load the picture onto the Pasteboard.*

Figure 31. The mouse has been clicked and the picture is loaded onto the Pasteboard area.

The picture now needs to be reduced proportionately to fit into the box. This is accomplished by selecting the picture (it is normally selected after loading), holding down the Shift key, grabbing the bottom right handle with the mouse button down, and dragging upwards diagonally and to the left. The result of this operation is indicated in Figure 32.

Now place the mouse in the middle of the picture. Hold down the button, and move it into the box as shown in Figure 33. We are back to *Actual size* view for a better look in this figure.

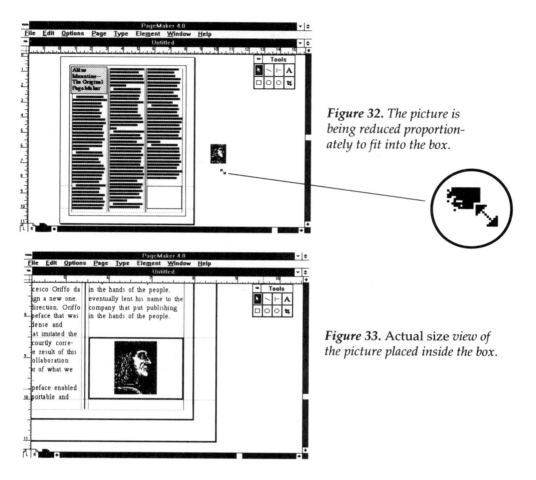

Figure 32. *The picture is being reduced proportionately to fit into the box.*

Figure 33. Actual size *view of the picture placed inside the box.*

10. *Select the box and the graphic from steps 8 and 9, delete from page 1, and place them into the top left-hand corner of page 2.*

To achieve this last operation, you need to go through the following steps:

- Insert a new page, since the publication is only one page long.
- Select and cut the picture and the box from page 1.
- Move to the new page 2.
- Paste the picture into page 2. Initially, it will be pasted into the center of the page.
- Move the picture to the top of the first column.

Figures 34 through 39 show the steps that are required.

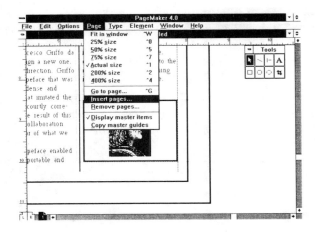

Figure 34. The Insert pages *command is selected from the* **Page** *menu.*

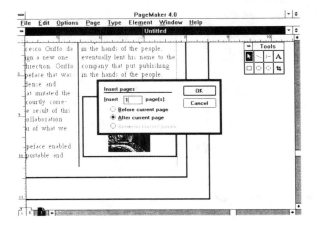

Figure 35. The Insert pages *dialog box is then filled out as shown. This will move you to page 2. Click on the page 1 icon to return to page 1.*

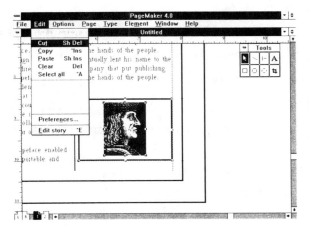

Figure 36. The picture and box are both selected and the **Cut** *command is chosen from the* **Edit** *menu. The simplest way to select both items together is to hold down the Shift key to select the second item. If you have trouble selecting the box because it is aligned with ruler and margin guides, hold down the Control key as you select.*

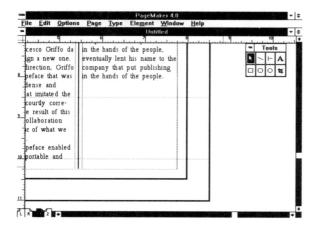

Figure 37. After the operation of Figure 36, the picture and the box are both deleted from page 1.

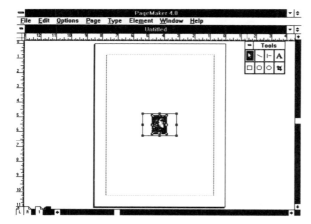

Figure 38. Move to page 2 and choose the Paste *command from the **Edit** menu. The result of this operation is that the picture and box are pasted into the middle of the page.*

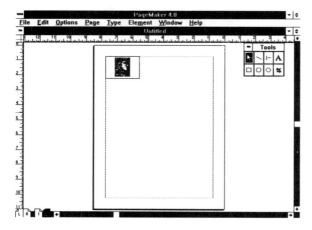

Figure 39. To finish this final step, grab the picture with the mouse, hold the button down, and move it to its required position in the top left-hand corner. Then release the mouse.

IMPORTING GRAPHICS

Importing Graphics

A large variety of graphics programs can be used in conjunction with PageMaker to create very professional presentations with your PC. This module looks at the types of graphics you can import, how to import them, how to size them, crop them, move them, and generally alter them. A later module looks at the more complex things that can be done with imported graphics — dealing with irregular wraparounds and shading.

There are four different types of graphics that can be imported into PageMaker. The type of graphic that you import depends generally on the type of graphics package that was used to create it.

Paint-type or *bit-map* graphics are the pictures that come from Paint-like packages. They are generally of a much lower resolution than other types of drawings, usually with a maximum resolution of 72 to 300 dpi. These pictures are made up of a rectangular array of dots. PageMaker can read any documents saved in this format.

Draw-type or object-oriented graphics are based on the sequence of drawing commands that describe the graphic. Programs that produce these types of graphics include Windows Draw, AutoCAD, and .PIC files from Lotus 1-2-3. These graphics are output device resolution dependent — meaning that the print resolution depends on the output device. These are generally much higher quality pictures than can be achieved with Paint-type programs.

Figure 1. This graphic has been imported from PC Paintbrush.

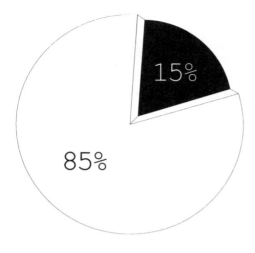

Figure 2. This graphic, in PICT format, has been created in CA Cricket Graph. This image can be resized and still maintain crystal clear resolution.

EPS graphics are quite possibly the highest quality graphics of the lot — produced at the moment by graphics programs such as CorelDRAW! and Adobe Illustrator. These types of graphics use PostScript code to create the pictures — so that unless a screen image is created when the actual graphic is created (in TIFF or PICT format), only a box will appear on screen. Most packages do, however, create a screen image to match the PostScript code. These graphics are limited in resolution only by the output device.

Figure 3. Both text and graphics can be manipulated and created in EPS format graphics. This image has been imported from CorelDRAW!

Scanned images are usually those in the TIFF format — although they can be imported in other formats. These images usually print at a maximum resolution of 300 dpi, and are normally created with the specialized programs that come with the many scanners available in halftone, grayscale, or color formats.

Importing graphics

Figure 4. *A TIFF image.*

Before you can import any graphics into PageMaker, you must make sure that the graphics are in the correct format for importation. Using a program like CorelDRAW! does not automatically mean that the graphic will slip directly into PageMaker. By default, the image will be saved in the CorelDRAW! format — not the EPS format required (Figure 5). Most other programs also offer a choice of formats to save the graphic under.

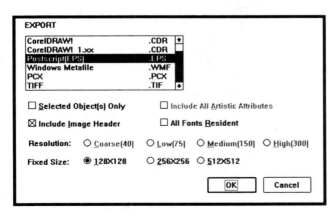

Figure 5. *This is the CorelDRAW! Export dialog box. If you wanted to use a CorelDRAW! file in PageMaker, you would have to export it in a different format — such as EPS.*

All graphics are imported into PageMaker in exactly the same way as text files are — via the *Place* command in the **File** menu. Once imported, however, the mouse cursor takes on a different appearance — depending on the type of graphic that has been imported. Figures 7 through 10 illustrate the various mouse icons that might result from importing graphics.

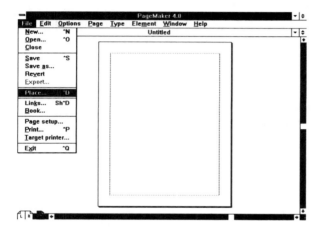

Figure 6. The Place *command is used to import all files into PageMaker — all varieties of graphics as well as text.*

Figure 7. An imported Paint-type graphic will cause the mouse cursor to take on this appearance.

Figure 8. A Draw-type graphic causes this. . .

Figure 9. . . . an EPS format file this. . .

Figure 10. . . . and a TIFF scanned image this.

Once the mouse cursor has changed to indicate a graphics file has been loaded into memory, as shown in Figure 11, there are two ways to place it — just as there are with text. The first way, preferable for text files but definitely not for graphics, is simply to click the mouse button where you want the graphic to load. Although the graphic will certainly load, it could be very large and probably nowhere near the size that you want it to be. Extra time must then be spent to resize the picture.

In Figures 11 and 12, we are loading in the PRACTICE.TIF graphic from the basics directory, within the tutorial directory, using the method outlined above. Figures 13 and 14 illustrate a different method, described on the following page.

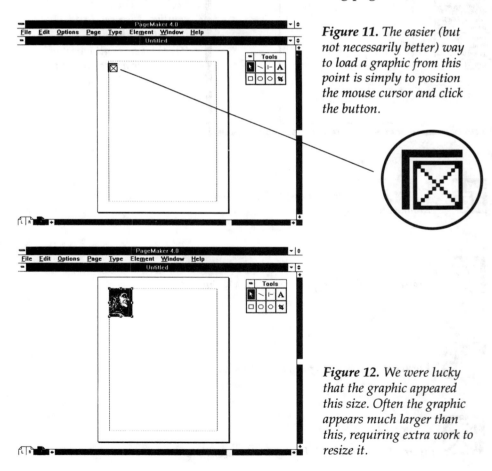

Figure 11. The easier (but not necessarily better) way to load a graphic from this point is simply to position the mouse cursor and click the button.

Figure 12. We were lucky that the graphic appeared this size. Often the graphic appears much larger than this, requiring extra work to resize it.

A better way to load a graphic file onto the page is to pretend that you are working with the square-corner drawing tool, even though the mouse cursor is loaded with one of the graphic options shown in Figures 7 through 10. Then draw a box exactly the size you would like the picture to be. Depress the mouse button and drag the mouse down and across the screen (Figure 13), releasing it only when the box is big enough. A temporary box will appear as the mouse button is held down. When the mouse button is released, the graphic will appear in that box (Figure 14).

With this approach, the graphic may not initially be in the correct proportion. See the section later in this module entitled **Proportional resizing** to return it to the correct aspect ratio.

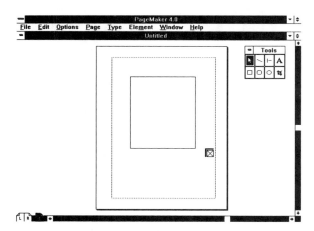

Figure 13. *A better way to load the graphic is to draw an imaginary box the size you would like the graphic to be. This is done by holding down the mouse button and drawing a box.*

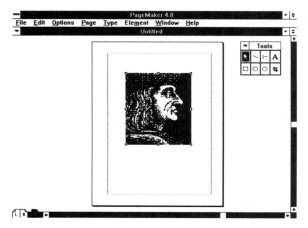

Figure 14. *Once the mouse button has been released, the graphic will be loaded at exactly the same size as the box you drew.*

Moving graphics

Once the graphic has been placed on the screen, chances are it may have to be moved from one area of the screen to another. To do this, hold the mouse button down inside the graphic and move the mouse to the new position. If you move the mouse immediately after holding the button down, only a box representing the graphic outline will be moved with the mouse (Figure 15). However, if you keep the mouse still for a few seconds before moving it, the entire picture will move with the mouse (Figure 16).

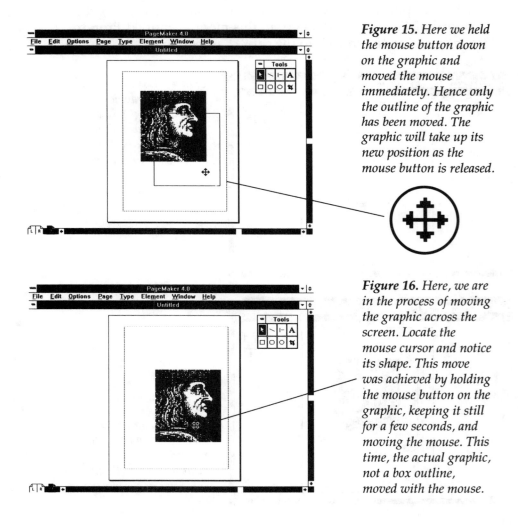

Figure 15. Here we held the mouse button down on the graphic and moved the mouse immediately. Hence only the outline of the graphic has been moved. The graphic will take up its new position as the mouse button is released.

Figure 16. Here, we are in the process of moving the graphic across the screen. Locate the mouse cursor and notice its shape. This move was achieved by holding the mouse button on the graphic, keeping it still for a few seconds, and moving the mouse. This time, the actual graphic, not a box outline, moved with the mouse.

Simple wraparounds

Before discussing resizing and cropping imported images, we will look at the options for setting the wraparound for this graphic — that is, controlling how the text flows around this picture. This is achieved with the *Text wrap* command in the **Element** menu (Figure 17). This command also works in exactly the same way for graphics created within PageMaker.

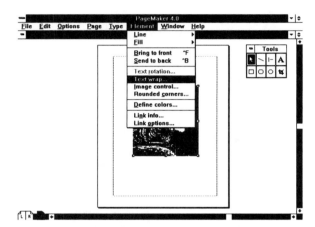

Figure 17. Simple text wrap-around control is achieved using the Text wrap *command. Choosing this command causes the dialog box of Figure 18 to appear. Ensure that you still have the graphic selected.*

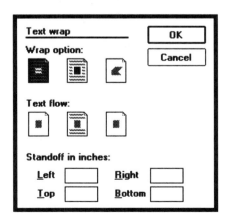

Figure 18. The Text wrap *dialog box.*

The commands in the Figure 18 dialog box are visually straightforward. You make the decision as to how the text will flow around your graphic — and how far the text must stay away from the graphic.

Your first decision falls under the *Wrap option* heading, where you have three choices. Within this dialog box, you may only choose between the first two. This choice is simple — do you want the text to flow around the graphic or not? If the answer is no, then select the first box (Figure 19). When this is done, all other commands in this dialog box become unusable and you are finished with this command. However, if your answer is yes, select the second box (Figures 20 and 21). The third box on the top line is explained in the **Advanced Picture Formatting** Module.

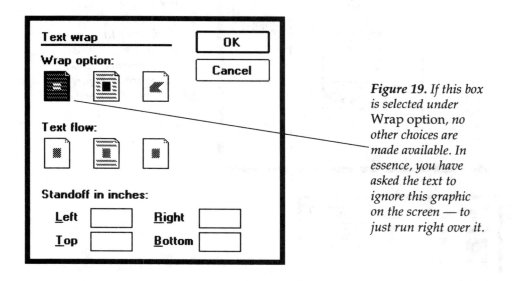

Figure 19. If this box is selected under Wrap option, *no other choices are made available. In essence, you have asked the text to ignore this graphic on the screen — to just run right over it.*

When the middle *Wrap option* box is selected, you must make a choice as to the *Text flow* (i.e., the three page icons in the middle of the dialog box). The first choice causes text to stop flowing when it reaches a graphic and not continue unless manually. The second choice causes the text to jump the graphic completely — i.e., stop when it reaches it, yet continue underneath (Figure 20). The third box will cause the text to flow as best it can around the graphic — not irregularly, but straight up and down the outsides of the graphic (Figure 21).

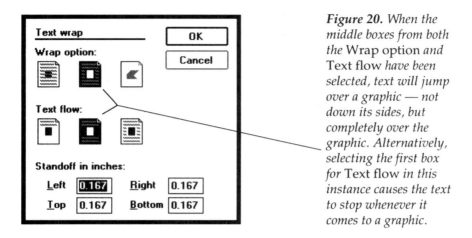

Figure 20. When the middle boxes from both the Wrap option *and* Text flow *have been selected, text will jump over a graphic — not down its sides, but completely over the graphic. Alternatively, selecting the first box for* Text flow *in this instance causes the text to stop whenever it comes to a graphic.*

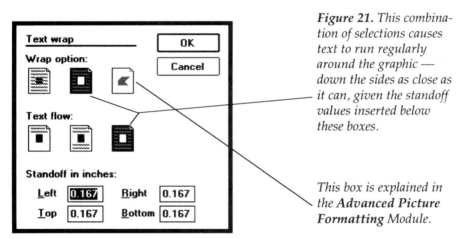

Figure 21. This combination of selections causes text to run regularly around the graphic — down the sides as close as it can, given the standoff values inserted below these boxes.

This box is explained in the **Advanced Picture Formatting** *Module.*

If you choose the middle *Wrap option* (Figures 20 and 21), you must also define a *Standoff* for this graphic. This is the area around the graphic that the text cannot flow into — in effect a margin for the graphic. Insert your own figures here or keep the default values.

If you chose this command without having a graphic selected, then everything you set up in that command will become the default settings. If, however, a graphic was selected, the settings will only apply to that particular graphic .

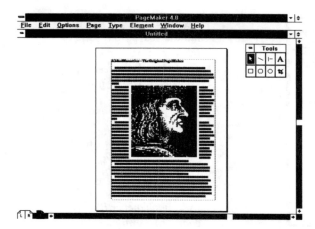

Figure 22. Here you see the practical result of a graphic wrap-around. This graphic was set up as in the dialog box of Figure 21.

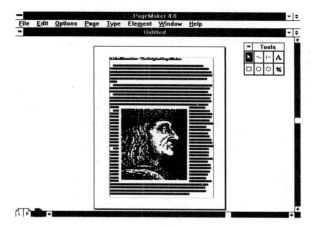

Figure 23. Once the wrap-around has been set up, the graphic can be moved around and the text will still reflow around it.

Graphic resizing

All imported graphics are resized in exactly the same way as graphics created in PageMaker. Each graphic contains six handles around its edge, which are used to resize that graphic in the direction of the handle. However, you must be careful when doing this.

Depending on the *Wrap option* you set for the graphic in the *Text wrap* command, you may have two sets of handles around the graphic. The inner handles are the normal graphic selection handles, while the outer handles are associated with the middle

Text wrap option of Figures 20 and 21. These outer handles, connected by a dotted line, indicate the *Wrap option* selected, as well as the standoff. In the module, **Advanced Picture Formatting**, you will be looking at the use of these outer handles, so make sure that you select the inner ones (these will, quite likely, be a little harder to see). If you would like to get rid of the outer handles altogether, move to the *Text wrap* command and click on the first *Wrap option*, as for Figure 19. The outside handles for that graphic will then disappear.

Figures 24 through 26 give examples of graphic resizing.

Figure 24. Resizing a graphic is done using the handles that appear around the selected graphic. The pointer tool must also be selected.

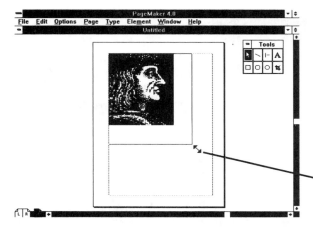

Figure 25. Hold the mouse button down on any handle until the mouse cursor changes to a two-sided arrow. Whichever directions the arrows are pointing are the directions that the graphic can be resized. Here we are resizing it diagonally.

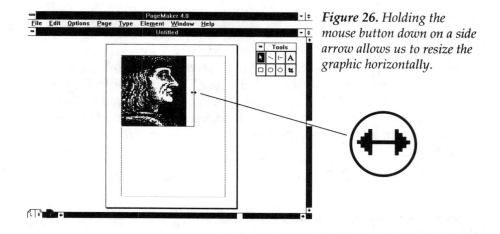

Figure 26. Holding the mouse button down on a side arrow allows us to resize the graphic horizontally.

Proportional resizing

If the Shift key is held down as the graphic is resized, the graphic will snap to the correct aspect ratio from which it was created. Make sure you release the mouse button before the Shift key. If you hold down the Control key as well as the Shift key, the graphic will be resized according to your printer's resolution, so that it will look better when printed. You will notice the graphic snapping to certain size increments when the Control key is held down.

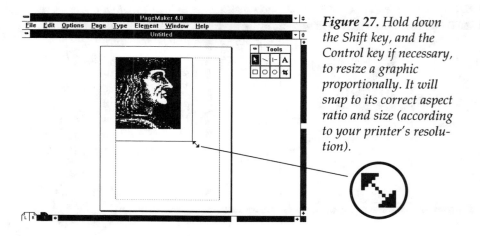

Figure 27. Hold down the Shift key, and the Control key if necessary, to resize a graphic proportionally. It will snap to its correct aspect ratio and size (according to your printer's resolution).

Figure 28. After Figure 27, release the mouse button first, and the graphic will snap to the correct size.

Graphics cropping

Graphics are cropped (you may find it easier to think of it as chopped) in almost exactly the same way they are resized, except that a different tool is used. The cropping tool is located in the bottom right-hand corner of the Toolbox (Figure 29).

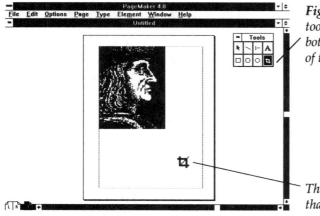

Figure 29. The cropping tool is selected from the bottom right-hand corner of the Toolbox.

The cursor changes to that of the cropping tool.

Once this tool is selected, locate the graphic you would like to crop. Don't worry— the removal of parts of graphics is never permanent using this method — any hidden part of the graphic can be recovered at any later stage. Click once on the graphic to be cropped, this time using the cropping tool, rather than the pointer tool, to make sure it is selected. Now decide from which side you would like to start cropping.

Locate one handle on the side of the graphic, position the cropping tool over it with the handle showing through, and hold the mouse button down. Keep the mouse still for a few seconds until the cursor turns into a two-headed arrow, and then move the mouse button towards the center of the graphic. This is much the same approach as in resizing the graphic — yet you will note that there is a dramatic difference as the mouse is moved. Depending on which handle of the graphic you selected, you will be able to chop off different parts of the graphic with ease.

In Figure 30, we have selected the middle handle on the right-hand side and are in the process of cropping towards the center of the graphic. Figure 31 shows the result of cropping, both from the top and the right.

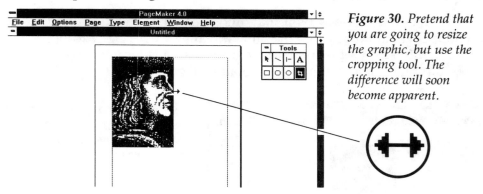

Figure 30. Pretend that you are going to resize the graphic, but use the cropping tool. The difference will soon become apparent.

To reverse the crop at a later stage, reselect the cropping tool, and select the cropped side's handle, and move the mouse away from the graphic.

Once a graphic has been cropped, another technique can be used to alter what has been cropped. This is particularly effective if the graphic has been cropped considerably. Position the cropping tool in the center of a cropped graphic, hold down the mouse button, and move it around. The cursor changes to a hand (Figure 32). Rather than the entire graphic, the image itself is moved, as if behind a window — you are merely altering which part of the graphic is showing and which is hidden.

Any cropped graphic can still be moved, resized, and have the text wrap altered.

Figure 31. We have cropped this graphic from both the top and the right-hand side.

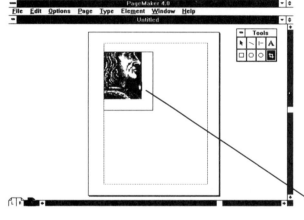

Figure 32. We can move the cropped graphic around, as if behind a window, by holding down the cropping tool positioned in the middle of a cropped graphic and moving the mouse around.

Note that the cursor changes to a hand.

Figure 33. After a graphic has been cropped, it can still be resized, moved, and have wraparounds applied to it.

EXERCISE: IMPORTING GRAPHICS

Importing Graphics

In this exercise you are going to import a graphic, then manipulate it by resizing, moving, and cropping it. You will also load some text to automatically wrap around the graphic.

This training material is structured so that people of all levels of expertise with Page-Maker can use it to gain maximum benefit. In order to do this, we have structured the material so that the bare exercise is listed below this paragraph on just one page, with no hints. The following pages contain the steps needed to complete this exercise, for those who need additional prompting. The **Importing Graphics** module should be referenced if you need further help or explanations.

Module 7 exercise steps

1. *Load the picture PRACTICE.TIF graphic onto an A4 or Letter page (your choice), flush with the top left margin.*

2. *Resize this picture so that it measures 2.5" wide by 3.25" high exactly.*

3. *Resize the picture proportionally so that it stays 2.5" wide.*

4. *Crop the picture so that only the face is showing.*

5. *Load the text file LEADSTRY.RTF into two columns on the page.*

6. *Move the graphic into the middle of the screen.*

7. *Make LEADSTRY.RTF wrap around all sides of the graphic.*

8. *Make space for a border around the graphic, and then create a border.*

The steps for completing this exercise are on the following pages.

The steps in detail

1. Load the picture PRACTICE.TIF graphic onto an A4 or Letter page (your choice), flush with the top left margin.

The PRACTICE.TIF graphic is located in the basics directory within the tutorial directory. Locate and load this picture through the *Place* command in the **File** menu. Load this file onto the page, flush with the top left margin, by either clicking the mouse button once, or holding the mouse button down and drawing an imaginary square.

See Figures 1, 2, and 3 to perform these steps.

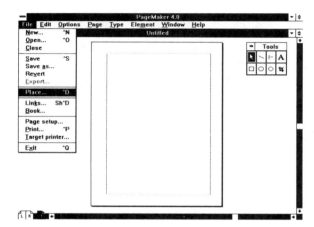

Figure 1. Select the Place *command from the* **File** *menu to load the PRACTICE.TIF graphic.*

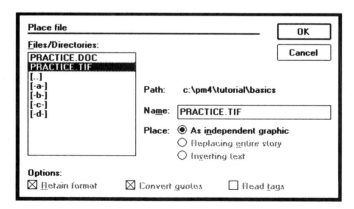

Figure 2. Select the PRACTICE.TIF graphic from the basics directory.

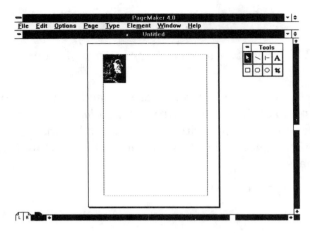

Figure 3. The file PRACTICE.TIF graphic is now loaded on the page — the actual size that it appears on the page depends on the method you used to load it. In this case we clicked the mouse once.

2. Resize this picture so that it measures 2.5" wide by 3.25" high exactly.

To make sure the graphic is the correct size, you should first display the PageMaker rulers. Using these rulers and the accompanying guides, create a grid on the page of 2.5" by 3.25". Figures 4 through 6 provide explanations.

Figure 4. In order to create the grid to contain the file, you must first perform a few steps — use the Rulers *command from the* **Options** *menu to display the rulers (the* Preferences *command in the* **Edit** *menu can be used to ensure inches are used in the ruler), and then move the zero point of the ruler to the top left margin of the page. The zero point of the ruler is moved by holding down the mouse button in the area where the two rulers intersect, and dragging the mouse to the spot on the screen where the new zero point will be. We have also moved to* Actual size *view in order to see the graphic better.*

Now, grab the bottom right-hand handle and resize the image (Figure 7) so that the bottom right-hand corner snaps to the bottom right-hand corner of the grid (Figure 8). The picture is now exactly 2.5" by 3.25". For this step to work correctly you must have the *Snap to guides* command from the **Options** menu activated.

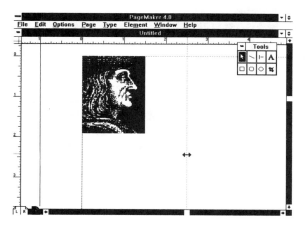

Figure 5. After the zero point of the ruler is in the correct spot, you must pull ruler guides from both the vertical and horizontal rulers to align with the desired measurement. Here we have just pulled a ruler guide from the vertical ruler to align with the 2.5" horizontal ruler mark. Hold the mouse button down in a ruler to first obtain a guide.

Figure 6. Here we have added a horizontal ruler guide, at the 3.25" mark. (Make sure your zero point in the ruler is at the same place as ours.) Note your picture may be bigger or smaller than ours, depending upon how you loaded it.

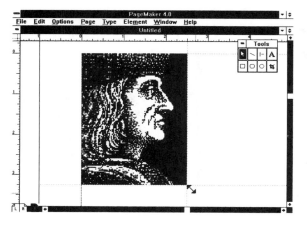

Figure 7. You can now resize the picture (make it smaller or bigger — depending on its original size) to fit it into the grid you defined. Begin resizing by holding the mouse button down on the bottom right-hand handle and move this corner up or down to the intersection of the two ruler guides.

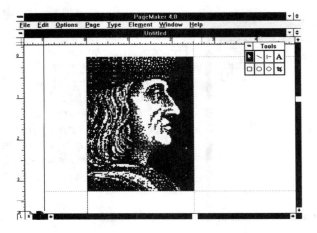

Figure 8. *We have now reached the intersection of the two ruler guides. The picture has now been resized to exactly 2.5" by 3.25".*

3. Resize the picture proportionally so that it stays 2.5" wide.

Although you have resized the picture so that it is exactly 2.5" by 3.25", it is not necessarily in its correct proportion. To make sure that it is, you must resize the picture with the Shift key held down. Once the picture is in the grid, hold the mouse button on the bottom right-hand corner of the picture, as though you were about to resize it. Now, with the mouse button down, hold down the Shift key.

The picture moves to its true proportion as shown in Figure 9. Note the slight gap now showing above our 3.25" horizontal ruler.

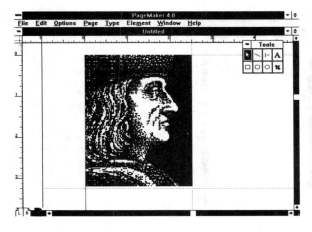

Figure 9. *The true proportion of the picture at 2.5" wide. Although similar to what it was before, this is the result of holding down the mouse button on the bottom right-hand corner handle of Figure 8 and holding down the Shift key. The mouse was not moved at all, and was released before the Shift key.*

4. Crop the picture so that only the face is showing.

Before you can crop the picture, you must select the cropping tool from the Toolbox. This is the tool in the bottom right corner of the Toolbox (Figure 10).

Figure 10. *Select the cropping tool from the bottom right-hand corner of the Toolbox, and start cropping from the top.*

Select the picture by clicking on it once with the cropping tool. From this point, act as if you are going to resize the picture. Hold down the cropping tool so that the middle of the tool is over the top middle handle (Figure 10). You may have to wait a second or two before you can do anything while PageMaker readies itself for the crop. After the double-arrowed vertical mouse cursor appears (Figure 10), keep the mouse button held down and move towards the center of the picture. The picture itself will not be resized, but cropped.

Figure 11. *We have now cropped from the top and the right.*

After cropping from one side, move to the other handles and cut additional sides off the picture. Continue cropping the picture from all four sides until only the man's face is visible (Figure 12).

Figure 12. Here we have cropped the picture from all sides — leaving only the man's face.

5. *Load the text file LEADSTRY.RTF into two columns on the page.*

The first step is to make sure that you have two columns on the page. This is achieved using the *Column guides* command from the **Options** menu. Select the command and, from the resulting dialog box, specify two columns. Change to *Fit in window* view as shown in Figure 13.

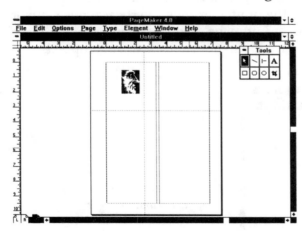

Figure 13. Move back to Fit in window view to load the text file. Add two columns to the page via the Column guides command in the Options menu.

Use the *Place* command from the **File** menu to locate the tutorial directory and then the LEADSTRY.RTF file in the lesson2 directory (Figure 14). Select this file and flow it into the two columns on the page (Figure 15). Choose either the manual or the *Autoflow* method.

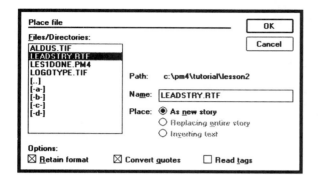

Figure 14. The LEADSTRY.RTF text file is located in the lesson2 directory within the tutorial directory.

How the text reacts when it comes to the picture will depend on how the picture wraparound was set before starting this exercise. So far, however, it doesn't really matter. In our case in Figure 15, the text has run through the graphic.

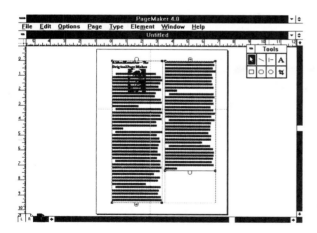

Figure 15. In our example, after loading the file, the text has run all over the graphic. Whether or not yours does this does not really matter at this stage — although it does mean that the Control key should be held down in order to select the graphic for step 6.

6. Move the graphic into the middle of the screen.

Select the picture with the pointer tool and move it into the middle of the screen (Figure 16). The text may reflow around the picture. If the text flows over the picture as it has in our example, you will have to hold down the Control key as you attempt to select the graphic.

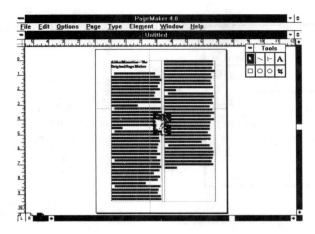

Figure 16. Here we have moved the graphic down to the middle of the page. Remember, if the text is over the graphic, you will have to hold down the Control key as you select the graphic.

7. Make LEADSTRY.RTF wrap around all sides of the graphic.

To do this, you must first make sure that the picture remains selected (if it is not, simply click on it using the Control key as well, if necessary). Next, move to the *Text wrap* command in the **Element** menu (Figure 17).

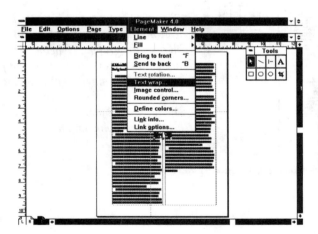

Figure 17. Making sure the graphic is still selected, choose the Text wrap *command from the* Element *menu.*

Within the dialog box that appears (Figure 18), set up the wraparound so that the text will wrap around all sides of the picture regularly. Check the settings of Figure 18 if you are unsure of how this is done.

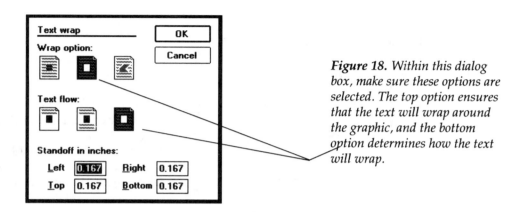

Figure 18. *Within this dialog box, make sure these options are selected. The top option ensures that the text will wrap around the graphic, and the bottom option determines how the text will wrap.*

After setting up the dialog box as in Figure 18, your page will look similar to Figure 19 (in *Actual size* view).

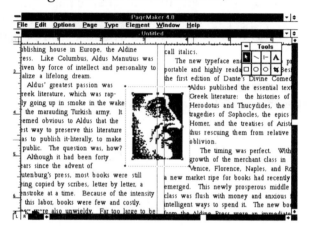

Figure 19. *Here you can see the graphic at Actual view. Note that the text has indeed wrapped around the graphic.*

8. Make space for a border around the graphic, and then create a border.

To make space for a border around the picture, move once again to the *Text wrap* command in the **Element** menu. It is likely that a space for the border has already been created, so we will look at how to alter the space around the picture. Figure 20 shows the *Text wrap* dialog box again with the graphic still selected.

Notice the space above, below, and around the picture in Figure 19. This will be the forced white area around the graphic. Increase this space slightly to provide a larger area around the picture for your border. Change the settings for Standoff in inches from the Figure 18 dialog box to those shown in Figure 20 (.4" in all cases).

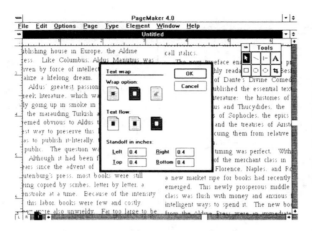

Figure 20. Note the figures at the bottom of this dialog box that determine how close the text can flow to all sides of the graphic. Increase these figures slightly from those of Figure 18, to push the text further away from the graphic. Figure 21 shows the result.

Once you OK these changes, you will be returned back to the page. Move to *Actual size* view so that you can see the picture and the text (Figure 21). You will now see an increased amount of white space around the picture (compare this with Figure 19).

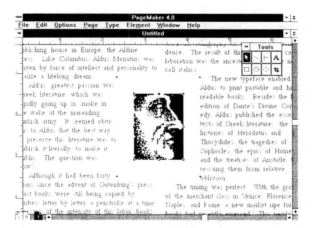

Figure 21. The result — a distinct white space between the photo and the text — equal in size to the measurements you entered in Figure 20.

Now grab the rectangle drawing tool from the toolbox, and draw a rectangle around the picture (Figure 22). If the rectangle has a shade or a color, it will overlay the picture. If this happens and you cannot see the picture, choose the *Send to back* command from the **Element** menu. After choosing this command, you might like to apply a shade, color, and/or line thickness to the outline. The result is shown in Figure 23.

Figure 22. *Select one of the graphics tools from the Toolbox (in this case the rectangle), and draw a box around the picture. If the box you create sits on top of the graphic and you cannot see it, immediately choose the* Send to back *command from the* **Element** *menu.*

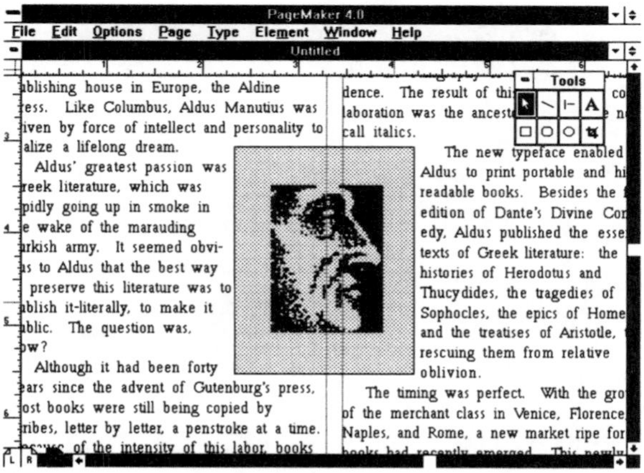

Figure 23. *We increased the thickness of the line using the* Line *sub-menu and gave the box a background shade using the* Fill *sub-menu (and sent it to the back) to make it look a little different.*

MASTER
PAGES

Module 8

Master Pages

Master Pages are used when text, graphics, page numbers, headers, footers, and whatever else, must be repeated on many pages throughout the document. They save having to repaste or recreate the same item on multiple pages.

Master page icons

Along the bottom left-hand corner of the screen are the page number icons. We have looked at these icons before when you changed, created, and deleted pages. However, there are two extra icons that read L and R. There will only be an R icon if your document is not set up as a *Double-sided* publication in the *Page setup* command from the **File** menu. These icons represent the left and right master pages. When you click on either of these icons, you will be presented with either one or two blank pages; for two pages to show, the *Facing pages* option must be selected from the *Page setup* command. These are the master pages and on the screen they look like any others (Figure 1).

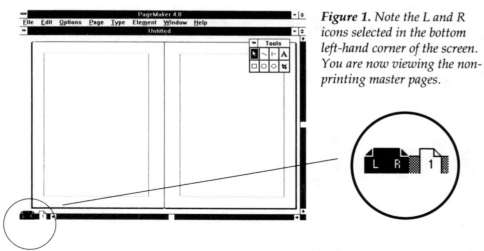

Figure 1. Note the L and R icons selected in the bottom left-hand corner of the screen. You are now viewing the non-printing master pages.

These master pages are exactly like any others in the way graphics, text, columns, etc., are applied to them. Anything you place on these pages, however, will repeat on all pages throughout

294

the publication. These pages do not print. To print the contents of a master page, you must first display them on a standard page and print from there.

Master page guides

These master pages are much like any others — they can have columns set up, ruler guides inserted, and margins altered, either as individual left or right pages, or together. If you apply three columns to the right master page, all right-hand pages in the publication, already created or not, will have these three columns. The same applies to the left-hand page. Consequently, if every page in your 100-page book needs three columns, you only need define these columns on the master pages. You can change these column guides individually on each page after the master pages have been set. This flexibility allows you to change any specific page to look a little different from all the others.

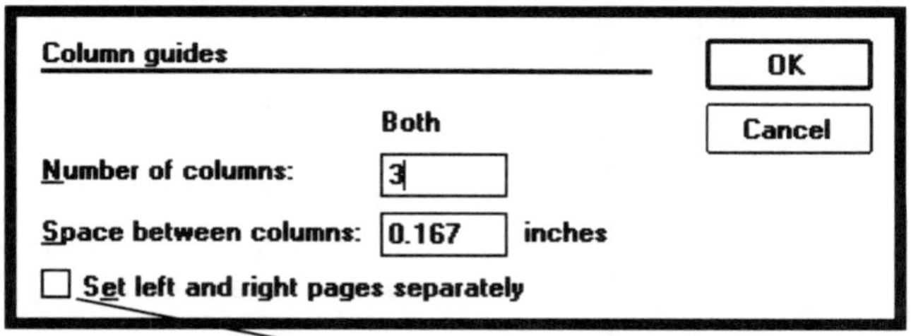

Figure 2. Here we are defining the number of column guides for both left and right master pages. This dialog box allows both left and right to be defined in one operation.

If you click the bottom left-hand square, you get the slightly different dialog box of Figure 3.

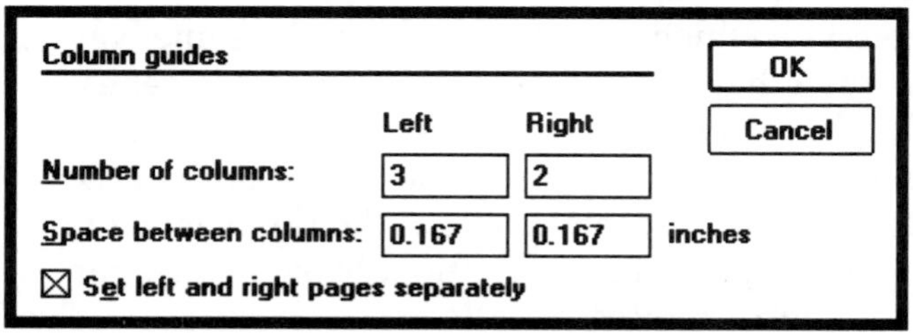

Figure 3. In this instance, it is possible to set different columns for left and right pages. For example, we have selected three columns for the left pages and two columns for the right pages.

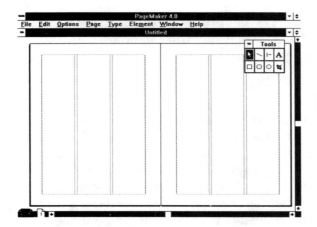

Figure 4. These column guides are a result of the operation of Figure 2. Three columns were defined for both left and right pages.

Any non-printing margin guides and/or ruler guides added to these pages will also be seen on all corresponding pages in the publication (Figure 5).

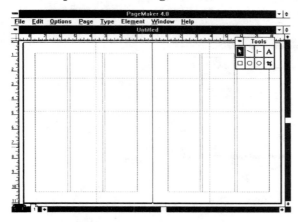

Figure 5. Two horizontal and one vertical ruler guides have been included on the master pages. These will now, like the column guides, appear on each page.

Text and graphics additions

As you might have guessed, any text or graphics that are placed on the master page(s) — which is done in exactly the same way they are placed on any other page in the document — will repeat on every page. In this way, a company logo, motto, and/or address and phone number, can be placed on one or both of the master pages. These will then repeat, exactly as they appear on the master pages, on every page in the publication. Master pages can also be used to create borders effectively.

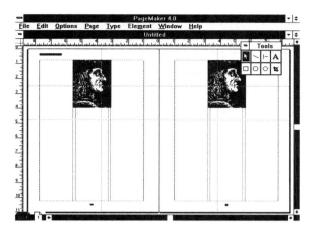

Figure 6. We have just placed a graphic onto both master pages and sized it as shown. This graphic will now repeat on all pages of the document.

Headers, footers, and page numbers

Headers and footers are the repeating bits of information that appear at the top and bottom of every page in a book or magazine. This often includes such items as the book name, chapter name, chapter number, date, and/or the page number. To define these for a publication, simply create them any way you like on the master page(s).

In Figure 7, we are positioned in *Actual size* view at the top left corner of the left master page. A heading that we want repeated on each page has been keyed in. This will now appear on all pages.

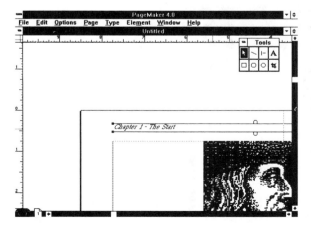

Figure 7. A header — "Chapter 1 — The Start" — has been keyed in and placed just above the border on the top left-hand corner of the left master page.

We have also keyed in the same header on the top right-hand corner of the right master page.

Page numbers, however, require a slightly different technique. This is because they need to be updated on every page throughout the publication. Putting a number on the master page will result in that same number being literally copies on every page.

To achieve an automatically updated page number, instead of typing the actual number, hold down the Control and Shift keys and type a 3 (you must first select the text tool from the Toolbox and place it on the page where you want the page number to appear). On the master page, this will appear as LM on the left master and RM on the right master (Figure 8), but will appear as the correct number on all other pages (Figure 9). The correct number is the number that appears on that page's icon box. To alter the number that this uses, select the *Page setup* command in the **File** menu and see the instructions given in Figure 10.

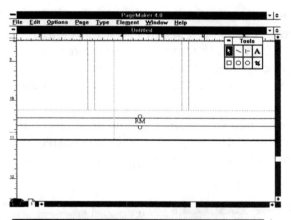

Figure 8. An automatic page number has been added to the bottom of a master page. It always shows as LM on the left page and RM on the right page.

Figure 9. Page 1 is now displayed and includes all the master items from the master page — column guides, ruler guides, graphics, headers, and footers.
As page 1 is a right-hand page the header is shown on the right-hand side.

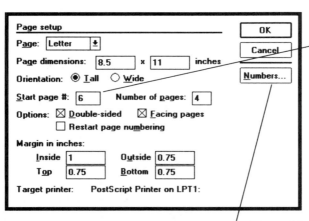

Figure 10. It is possible, through the Page setup *command in the* **File** *menu, to alter the starting page number of any publication. We are just adjusting the* Start page # *of a four-page publication to 6.*

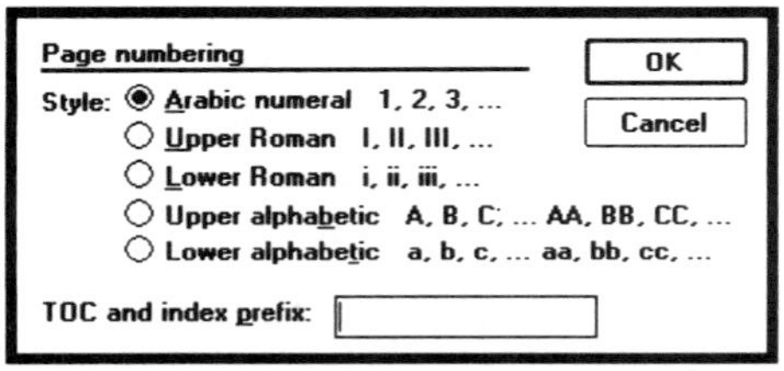

Figure 11. Another option for numbering pages is available through the Page Numbering *dialog box. This lets you choose between Arabic numeral, Upper Roman, Lower Roman, Upper and Lower alphabetic. The preference you select will appear automatically as your page numbering system. To get to this dialog box, click on the* Numbers. . . *button in the* Page setup *dialog box.*

Composite page numbers, whereby additional information is included with the basic page number, are possible. These can include such items as the word "page" or chapter numbering, such as 4-1, 8-7, etc. In Figure 12 a composite page number is being added to a master page.

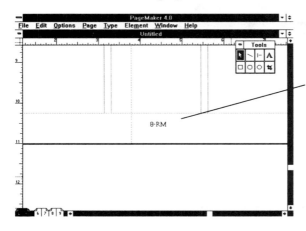

Figure 12. In this example, we would like to preface all page numbers with the chapter number 8. This is done by typing 8- in front of the Control-Shift-3 (auto page number) combination on the master pages. If we moved to the second page, which is now page 7 (see Figure 10), this page would display the number 8-7.

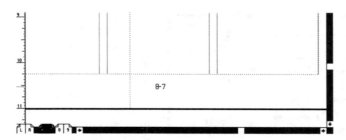

Figure 13. A close-up view of the second page of the publication showing that the operations of Figures 10 through 12 worked correctly.

Removing master items

There will, of course, always be pages where master items, such as logos, headers, and footers, will not be needed. The first page in a book, for example, rarely uses a header or footer.

If you move to a normal page where you do not want master items to appear, you will notice that text or graphic items cannot be deleted simply by selecting and deleting them. As a matter of fact, you will notice they cannot be selected at all.

There are three ways to remove master items from a particular page. Any guides, whether column, ruler, or margin guides, can be moved out of the way as if they were created on that page. Unlike text or graphics, these can be changed or moved.

One or more master elements can be hidden from view by drawing a pure white box over them (this is particularly useful when you wish to remove some master elements from a page but not all). This is illustrated in Figure 14.

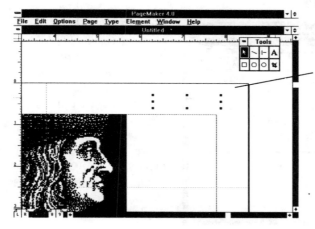

Figure 14. This is a white graphics box (only the selection handles are shown) which has been drawn over the master page header. This item is thus removed from the page without upsetting any other master items. The white box is achieved by choosing None from the Line sub-menu and Paper from the Fill sub-menu.

Finally, if you wish to remove all master items from a particular page, you must deselect the *Display master items* command in the **Page** menu (Figure 15). The result of this is shown in Figure 16.

Any pages that do not use the master items will still be included in the page number count.

As indicated above, it is possible to readjust non-printing master guides (column, ruler guides) on any actual page. If you wish to revert back to the guides from the master page, select the *Copy master guides* command from the **Page** menu. All relevant non-printing guides will then reappear on your page.

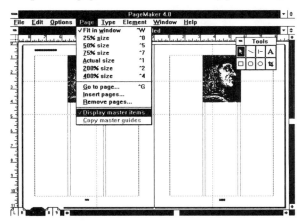

Figure 15. The Display master items *command removes all master items from your page. The result is shown in Figure 16.*

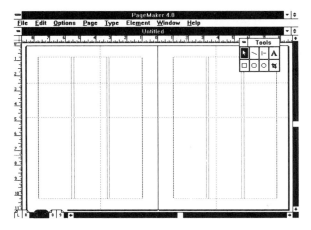

Figure 16. The result of using the command of Figure 15. All master items are deleted. They can be brought back by simply reselecting the same command.

EXERCISE: MASTER PAGES

Master Pages

In this exercise we are going to utilize master pages to set up headers, footers, and column guides. We will then remove master items from selected pages and also change column guides. This is an involved exercise which combines techniques from many of the modules we have already looked at.

This training material is structured so that people of all levels of expertise with Page-Maker can use it to gain maximum benefit. In order to do this, we have structured the material so that the bare exercise is listed below this paragraph on just one page, with no hints. The following pages contain the steps needed to complete this exercise for those who need additional prompting. The **Master Pages** module should be referenced if you need further help or explanations.

Module 8 exercise steps

1. *Set up a four page publication with the following specifications: Letter size, Tall, four pages, Double-sided, Facing pages, and .75" margins all around.*

2. *Go to master pages to setup left page headers and footers as follows: (a) April 1991, flush left header; (b) DTP Newsletter, flush right header; (c) page number, centered footer. All this text to be Times, 10 point, italic.*

3. *Set right master page in mirror image format to that of step 2.*

4. *Set left and right master page in two column format with 1-point intercolumn rules.*

5. *Go to page 1 and load PRACTICE.TIF graphic (basics directory) into bottom half of page.*

6. *Load LEADSTRY.RTF (lesson2 directory) using* Autoflow *method onto pages 1 and 2. Make sure it jumps over the graphic.*

7. *Load LEADSTRY.RTF again using* Autoflow *method starting from top of column 2 on page 2.*

8. *Remove master item headers from page 1 (but not footer).*

9. *Change column guides on page 3 from 2 to 3 columns, and adjust text to fit.*

10. *Remove master items from pages 2 and 3.*

11. *Change column guides on page 3 back to 2 columns without using the* Column guides *command.*

The steps for completing this exercise are on the following pages.

The steps in detail

1. Set up a four page publication with the following specifications: Letter size, Tall, four pages, Double-sided, Facing pages, and .75" margins all around.

After choosing *New* from the **File** menu, set up the publication details in the *Page setup* dialog box as shown in Figure 1. Click on OK once you have performed this step.

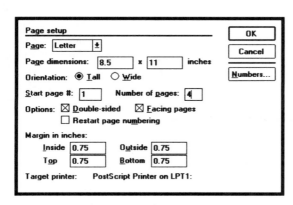

Figure 1. The initial Page setup dialog box should be filled in to these exact specifications.

2. Go to master pages to setup left page headers and footers as follows: (a) April 1991, flush left header; (b) DTP Newsletter, flush right header; (c) page number, centered footer. All this text to be Times, 10 point, italic.

Master Pages are displayed by clicking on the L and R page icons. Figure 2 shows the left-hand master page with the flush left and flush right headers in place. They were simply created with the text tool and placed 0.5" below the top of the page.

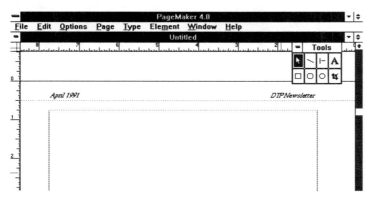

Figure 2. The top of the left-hand master page is displayed in 75% view showing the two headers.

The page number was then inserted in the middle of the left master page as a footer using the Control-Shift-3 special combination. Figure 3 shows the result. This special page number key combination always appears as either LM or RM on the master pages.

Select each block of header and footer text with the text tool, and use the *Type specs* command in the **Type** menu to set these headers and footers in Times, 10 point, italic.

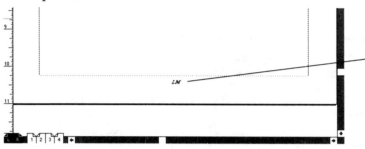

Figure 3. The Control-Shift-3 automatic page number combination always shows up on the master pages as either LM or RM, which stands for Left Master or Right Master.

3. Set right master page in mirror image format to that of step 2.

On the right master page, "April 1991" should be flush right, and DTP Newsletter flush left. Figure 4 shows the result. The page number footer should still be in the middle of the page, as for Figure 3.

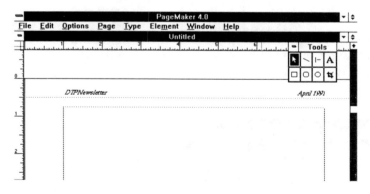

Figure 4. The right master page is now set up with mirror image headers. Compare this with Figure 2.

4. Set left and right master pages in two column format with 1-point intercolumn rules.

To set two columns, go to the *Column guides* command in the **Options** menu and select 2 columns. The intercolumn guides are drawn using the perpendicular line drawing tool selected from the Toolbox. It is wise to turn off the

Snap to guides option in the **Options** menu when drawing the intercolumn rules (Figure 5). This allows the vertical line to be drawn between the columns without its snapping to either of the column guides. The line thickness of 1 point is chosen from the *Line* sub-menu in the **Element** menu. Figure 6 shows the final results for both master pages in *Fit in window* view.

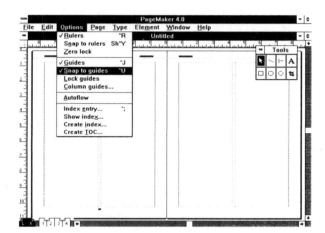

Figure 5. Turn off the Snap to guides *feature to more easily draw the intercolumn rules. This feature is on when a check mark is next to it and off when there is no check.*

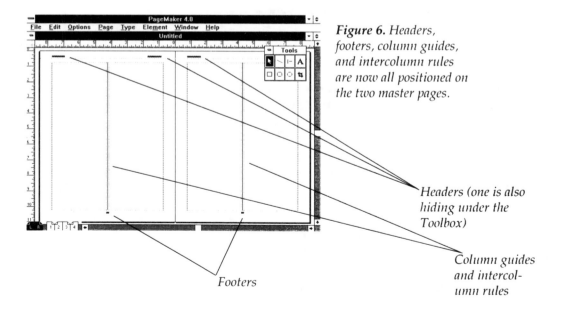

Figure 6. Headers, footers, column guides, and intercolumn rules are now all positioned on the two master pages.

Headers (one is also hiding under the Toolbox)

Footers

Column guides and intercolumn rules

5. Go to page 1 and load PRACTICE.TIF graphic (basics directory) into bottom half of page.

Click on 1 on the page icons in the bottom left-hand corner of the screen. Choose the *Place* command from the **File** menu and select the PRACTICE.TIF graphic from within the basics directory (Figure 7). Place this picture into page 1 by drawing an imaginary box with your cursor before releasing the mouse button. Position it at approximately the same position and size as shown in Figure 8.

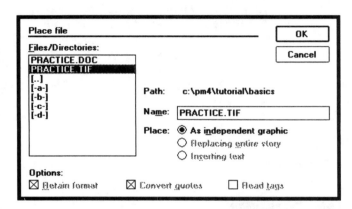

Figure 7. By selecting the Place *command from the* **File** *menu, you are provided with this dialog box. Choose the PRACTICE.TIF graphic from the basics directory.*

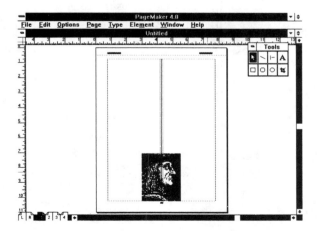

Figure 8. Put the PRACTICE.TIF graphic on page 1 at approximately this size and position.

6. Load LEADSTRY.RTF (lesson2 directory) using Autoflow *method onto pages 1 and 2. Make sure it jumps over the graphic.*

Before you select LEADSTRY.RTF, select the picture on page 1 and adjust the picture wrap to that required. Since you want the text to jump right over the graphic, choose the options as shown in Figure 9. This dialog box is accessed through the *Text wrap* command in the **Element** menu.

Now choose the *Place* command from the **File** menu, and from the associated dialog box (Figure 10) select LEADSTRY.RTF from the lesson2 directory. Flow this text onto pages 1 and 2 using the *Autoflow* command (make sure the *Autoflow* command has a check next to it in the **Options** menu). The results of this autoflow are shown in Figures 11 and 12.

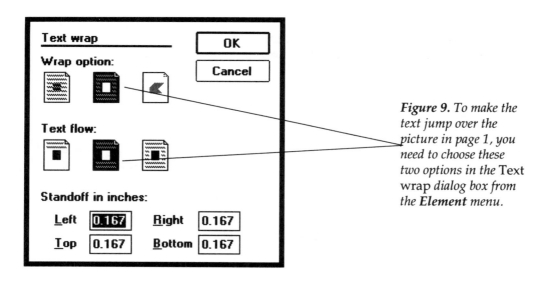

Figure 9. *To make the text jump over the picture in page 1, you need to choose these two options in the* Text wrap *dialog box from the* **Element** *menu.*

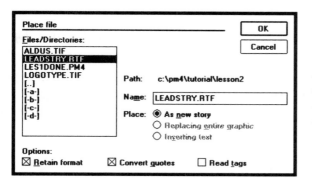

Figure 10. *This is the* Place *dialog box again. Choose LEADSTRY.RTF from the lesson2 directory.*

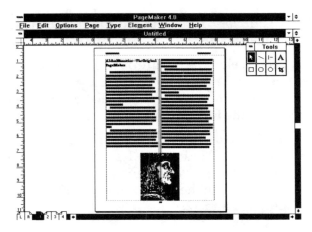

Figure 11. LEADSTRY.RTF has flowed onto page 1 and has completely jumped over the picture. This is because of the Figure 9 settings. Remember you are using the Autoflow text method.

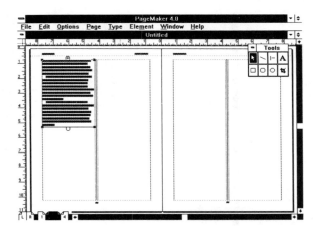

Figure 12. As you used the Autoflow method to flow the text, LEADSTRY.RTF has flowed automatically onto page 2. Note from the page icons that we are now displaying pages 2 and 3.

7. *Load LEADSTRY.RTF again using* Autoflow *method starting from top of col umn 2 on page 2.*

Figure 13 shows the reselection of LEADSTRY.RTF for placement onto page 2. Figure 14 indicates the position at the top of column 2 of page 2 to start flowing this new text file. Note the *Autoflow* cursor at the top of the column. Figure 15 shows the results of flowing the text.

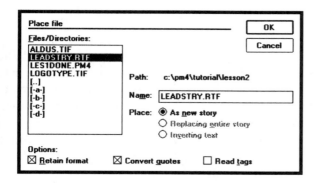

Figure 13. LEADSTRY.RTF *is being loaded again because it is a suitable size for this exercise.*

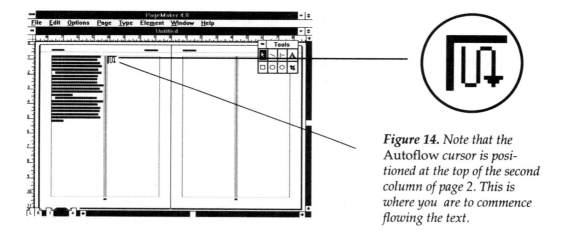

Figure 14. Note that the Autoflow *cursor is positioned at the top of the second column of page 2. This is where you are to commence flowing the text.*

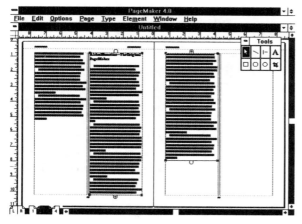

Figure 15. This is how your pages 2 and 3 should look after flowing the LEADSTRY.RTF text file again.

8. Remove master item headers from page 1 (but not footer).

Under the **Page** menu, there is a command called *Display master items*. When this is selected (has a check alongside it), all master items are displayed on the page currently being viewed. When it is not selected, no master items are displayed. In this step, you have been asked to remove only some of the master items. This command cannot be used, therefore, since it hides or shows all master items. The simple way to perform this step is to draw boxes around the flush left and right headers, and give them a *Paper* fill (through the *Fill* sub-menu) and a line thickness of *None* (through the *Line* sub-menu).

This is shown in Figures 16 and 17, where you can see box selection handles, but no box. This *Paper* (color white) box completely covers the two headers. As these boxes are white and have no lines, they will not appear on the printout, but will still cover the two headers.

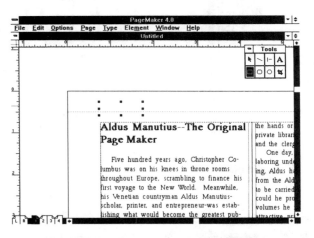

Figure 16. We have moved back to page 1 and are looking at the top left-hand corner where the flush left header should be. It cannot be seen because we have drawn a box over it and shaded the box Paper from the Fill sub-menu and made its lines None from the Line sub-menu. The selection handles, however, can still be seen.

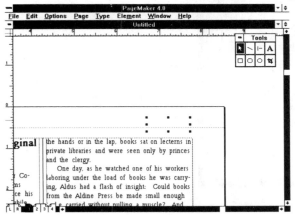

Figure 17. Similarly to Figure 16, we have drawn the same sort of box around the right header on page 1. The selection handles can be plainly seen.

Perform the steps from Figures 16 and 1 for your page 1.

9. Change column guides on page 3 from 2 to 3 columns and adjust text to fit.

This step is best explained in pictures. Please read the captions associated with Figures 18 through 21. Also make sure you have turned to pages 2 and 3. Note from Figure 21, that there will be more text that could be placed in column 2 of page 3 (as indicated by the down arrow in the bottom selection handle). For this exercise, we won't place the rest of the text and will leave the file as is (Figure 21).

Column guides				
	Left	**Right**		**OK**
Number of columns:	2	3		**Cancel**
Space between columns:	0.25	0.25	inches	
☒ **Set left and right pages separately**				

Figure 18. This is the dialog box that results from choosing the Column guides *command in the* Options *menu. Change the right page figure (page 3) from 2 to 3 columns. Make sure that the* Set left and right pages separately *box is checked at the bottom left of this figure.*

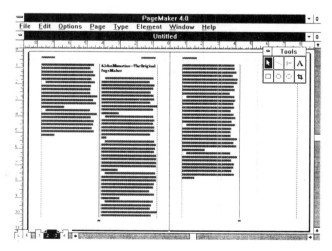

Figure 19. Note that page 3 is now showing column guides for three columns in the background of the text. If column guides are changed, as you have just done, the original text still remains in its old format. You need to change it manually, as shown in the following figures.

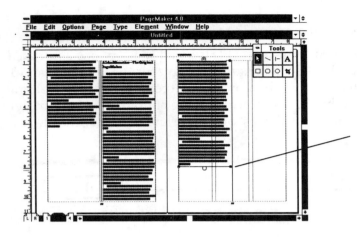

Figure 20. Select the text in column 1 of page 3 with the pointer tool. Next, grab the bottom right-hand corner handle and drag the text to the left to align with the new column guides (Figure 21).

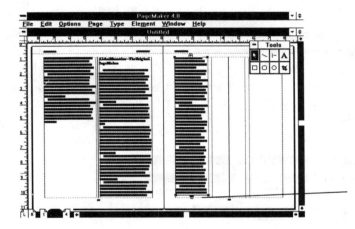

Figure 21. The left column of the right-hand page is now aligned. Note the problem however — the intercolumn rule drawn for two columns per page on the master page is still showing down the middle of the second column. This is fixed in the next step.

The down facing arrow in the bottom selection handle indicates there is more text that can be placed.

10. Remove master items from pages 2 and 3.

As mentioned in step 8 above, the *Display master items* command from the **Page** menu can be used to show or hide (as a group) all master items on any page. Select that command now (Figure 22); it shows as a check in this figure indicating that it was already selected. You are currently deselecting it.

The result is indicated in Figure 23. Note that not only have you removed the intercolumn rule showing in Figure 21, but you also have removed the headers and footers on both pages.

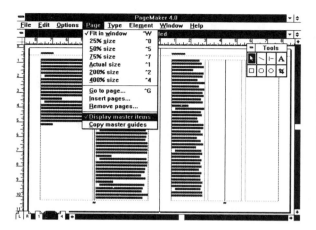

*Figure 22. This is the Dis-*play master items *command which allows you to show or hide items from master pages.*

Figure 23. Here are pages 2 and 3 without master items showing. Note the headers and footers are missing, as well as the intercolumn rules. This figure is a result of choosing the command in Figure 22.

11. *Change column guides on page 3 back to 2 columns without using the* Column guides *command.*

This step reverses what you were doing in step 9. Again, it is better described in pictures. Please refer to Figures 24 through 28 for details.

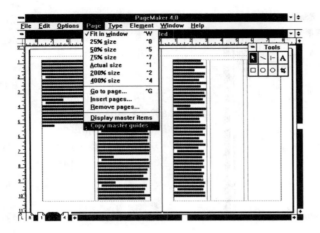

Figure 24. *As the master pages were set up with two columns, it is possible to restore those column guides to your page 3 without going through the* Column guides *command. Just choose, as shown here, the* Copy master guides *command from the* Page *menu.*

Figure 25. *Column guides have now changed back to 2 after the procedure of Figure 24.*

Figure 26. Now select the first column of page 3 with the pointer tool. Grab the bottom right-hand handle and pull the text column to the right to widen it to the full width of the first column.

Figure 27. The first column on page 3 is now fixed.

PRINTING

Module 9

Printing

Your PageMaker publication is ready to print at any time. There is no need to save before printing, and certainly no need to have completed your publication. In fact, the more often you get a chance to print your publication, the better it will probably turn out. The printer always gives a clearer indication of what the document is going to look like than does the screen, thanks to the printer's higher resolution.

Several printers are available for use with PageMaker, most using the printer language PostScript. LaserWriters, QMS, Varityper, AST, Dataproducts, and others can be used with the PC.

Before you actually print your document, you must select a printer. If you have only one printer which is always connected, this step will not need to be taken, since that printer will always be used. However, if you have several printers loaded, you must select the printer you wish to use from the *Printers'* option in the **Control Panel** (Figure 1). Double-click on the **Control Panel** icon and then on the *Printers'* option and you will be presented with the window of Figure 2.

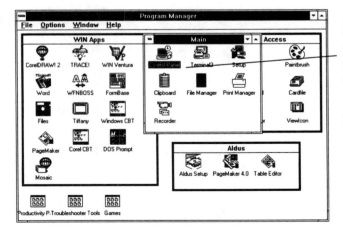

*Figure 1. Double-click on the **Control Panel** icon from the Program Manager, and then double-click again on the* Printers' *icon, to get the window of Figure 2.*

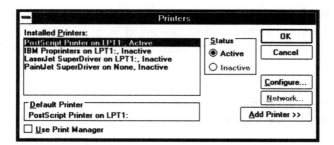

Figure 2. *A printer is selected from this dialog box.*

From the dialog box of Figure 2, select the printer you wish to use — this is the printer the PC will talk to. If a printer is not listed when it should be, make sure it is turned on, connected correctly, and has the correct settings. See Figures 3(a) and 3(b) for more details.

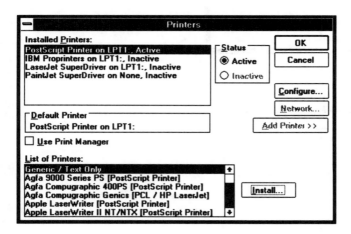

Figure 3(a). *From the main* Printers *dialog box you can add extra printers to the* Installed Printers *list. This is done by selecting the* Add Printer *button.*

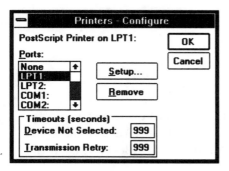

Figure 3(b). *The* Configure *dialog box is activated by selecting the* Configure *button in the Figure 3(a) dialog box. Here you can include extra details for printing. Refer to the Windows User manual for more information.*

The Print Command

To print your document, select the *Print* command from the **File** menu (Figure 4). After selecting this command, you will be presented with the dialog box of Figure 5.

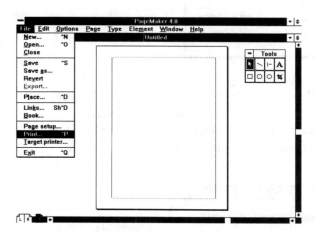

Figure 4. The Print *command from the* **File** *menu can be selected at any time — even, as you can see, when nothing appears on the page.*

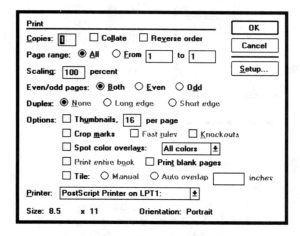

Figure 5. The Print *command dialog box.*

As you can see from Figure 5, printing is not quite as simple as just saying "print." There are a variety of options available to control the output of your publication. We will look at each of these options now in more detail.

Your first selection in Figure 5 is how many copies of the publication to print. This can be any figure up to 100. (If you have a fairly low throughput printer, don't try to use it as a printing press — a photocopier or instant printer may work out much faster and more economical.)

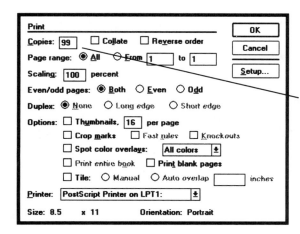

Figure 6. Here we have entered 99 as the number of copies we would like of our publication.

Next to the number of copies is the *Collate* square. If this square is selected, all copies printed will be collated as they are printed. (Obviously, this will only work if multiple copies of multiple pages are being printed.) Although this sounds like an attractive proposition, it will take much longer to print when this option is selected, as each page has to be processed individually rather than just once for multiple copies of the same page.

Alongside the *Collate* option is the *Reverse order* option. Depending on the output tray of your printer (some flip the pages as they are coming out), you may prefer to print first page to last, or the other way around, so that when the pages are picked up they do not have to be resorted into the correct order. PageMaker will try to determine which way your printer sorts its output and then print so that the pages are in the correct order.

The *Page range* line is used to select the actual pages that are to be printed. Choose *All* to print the entire publication, or insert figures after *From* into the page range boxes to print specified pages (Figure 7). If you wish to print just one page, put that same page number in both the *From* and the *to* boxes.

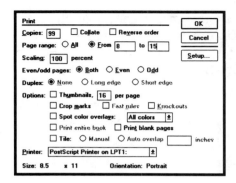

Figure 7. Here we have opted to print 99 copies of pages 8 to 15 inclusive.

The *Scaling* option allows you to scale the print of your document from 25 percent to 1,000 percent (Figure 8) at full PostScript resolution. In this way, larger point sizes than can be accessed through the PageMaker dialog boxes can be achieved by scaling the publication as it is printed. PageMaker centers reduced and enlarged pages on the paper.

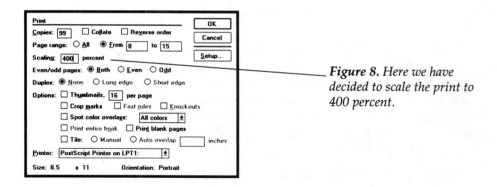

Figure 8. Here we have decided to scale the print to 400 percent.

Underneath the *Scaling* option is the *Even/odd pages* selection. This is used when you are doing double-sided printing. You can print either even or odd pages at a time, and then reverse the pages in the printer so it will print on both sides of the page.

The *Duplex* option is only available for a limited number of printers. It lets you print on both sides of the page. The *Long edge* option is selected if you are using a *Portrait* page and you want the pages to turn in the printer on a vertical axis. If you want the pages to turn along a horizontal axis and you are using a *Portrait* page, you should select *Short edge*.

Thumbnails is a very useful PageMaker feature that allows you to print a wide range of publication pages shrunken down to fit onto one page. This is especially useful for keeping on file exactly what is in every publication, rather than spending the time and money to print them out in full. Up to 64 thumbnails can be printed per page.

Crop marks can be added to a printed page, so that printers can align pages together correctly and see exactly what page size they are working with. They appear as not quite joined crosshairs in every corner of the page. This feature is used when printing spot color overlays (see below) to ensure correct registration of each page.

The *Fast rules* option will quicken the printing time of rules and boxes created with PageMaker drawing tools. The dimensions of these rules are sent to the printer instead of a bitmap image. When printing spot color overlays with knockouts, do not select this option.

Knockouts is only available when *Spot color overlays* is selected. This option is used so that different color graphics are printed separately on each overlay in the order they were created. A blank spot will appear where the colors overlap.

Spot color overlays is a choice that is used when preparing color work to be taken to a printer for finishing. When you select this option, every new color is printed on a page by itself, as this is what the printer requires. The box to the right of *Spot color overlays* provides a pop-up sub-menu where you can choose to print color overlays for one color only, or for all colors.

The *Print entire book* option in this dialog box is only available when the current publication contains a book list (see Module 16, **Long Document Capabilities**). If the current publication is contained in a book list, it is possible to print just that publication or all publications contained in the book list.

When the *Print blank pages* box is checked, PageMaker prints all blank pages in your publication until you deselect it.

The *Tile* option lets you print oversize pages, so that you are not limited to the page size supported by your printer (Figures 9 and 10). To print a Tabloid page size from a Letter size printer, you can select tiling so it will print out as several Letter pages all overlapped (to whatever degree you like in manual tiling, or whatever overlap you specify in automatic tiling). These can be pasted back together after printing. The *Tile* option can also be used when scaling A4 or Letter pages larger than normal.

Automatic tiling will cause PageMaker to determine the starting point of each tile, based on the specified overlap. PageMaker will start at the upper left-hand corner of a page and print all of one page's tiles before moving on to another. Automatic tiling should be used when there is no need to control what is printed (i.e., preventing a complex image from printing twice, too many tiles per page, etc.).

Manual tiling is achieved by repositioning the zero point on the ruler to specify where the tile is to start. After the starting point for a tile has been specified, PageMaker prints that tile for every page in the range of pages you are printing. You then set the zero point for the second tile, and PageMaker prints that tile for all pages that are printed again. In this way, if your publication consists of ten pages, manual tiling will first cause ten tiles to print (one per page), then another ten (one per page again), and so on.

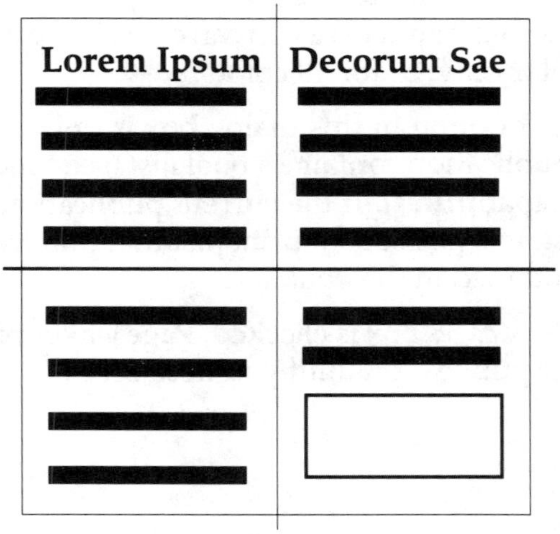

Figure 9. A page divided into four tiling segments.

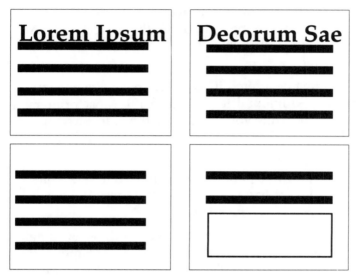

Figure 10. *The four tiles each appear on separate pages.*

Printing parameters

Underneath the print options of Figure 8 are the *Printer* type, paper *Size*, and paper *Orientation*. The first choice is the *Printer* type. Click on the relevant box, then run down the menu to select your brand and model of printer (Figure 11).

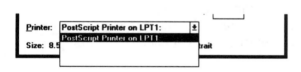

Figure 11. *This menu will appear after holding the mouse down on the printer type. We have only one printer installed at the moment.*

To change the other settings, select the *Setup* button in the *Print* dialog box of Figure 8 to activate the dialog box of Figure 12.

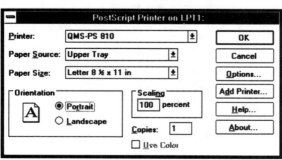

Figure 12. *To change the* Printer, Paper Source, Paper Size, *and* Orientation, *select the* Setup *button (under Cancel) in Figure 8. You will see this dialog box.*

The first option in this dialog box is activated by holding the mouse on the down arrow to the right of the *Printer* rectangle. A list of available printers will appear. To select the one you want, click on it with the mouse.

The *Paper source* must be altered if you wish to change printing from the paper tray to manual feed (Figure 13). Most printers support this feature, allowing you to insert a letterhead, envelope, certificate, or slightly thicker piece of paper that would not be suitable for the paper tray.

If your printer has multiple paper trays, you need to select one. Note that in Figure 11, we have chosen the PostScript Printer on LPT1 and the *Paper Source* is *Upper Tray*.

Next, you must select the paper size that your printer is using (Figure 12). If you specify a Letter size for your laser printer and it is using an A4 paper tray, PageMaker will prompt you, once given the command to print, to remove the A4 tray and insert the Letter tray. The page size and print area on that page are automatically indicated as you select *Paper Size* in Figure 12. If the print area is larger than the page area, you need to select the *Tile* option as discussed earlier in this module. Also ensure that you have chosen the correct *Orientation*.

The remaining options in this dialog box refer to printer setup. Consult your Windows User manual for more information on the setting up and installing of printers. Once you have set up the options in this dialog box, select OK to get back to the first print dialog box.

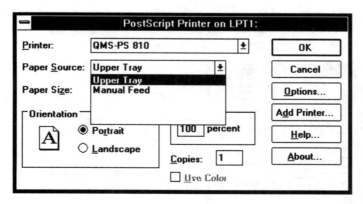

Figure 13. The QMS-PS 810 has two options available for the Paper Source.

Errors

Several errors may occur during the print process (Figure 14). Nearly all of these relate to the connection between the PC and the printer. Make sure they are connected securely with cables, as well as through the *Control Panel*, and that the printer is switched on and selected for the PC.

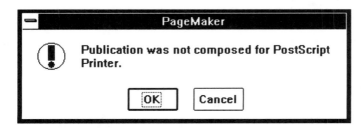

Figure 14. This is one of the error commands that could occur when printing from PageMaker.

Creating PostScript print files

Most of the time when you print, your output goes directly to a printer. There exists, however, an option that allows you to create a PostScript print file — one that can be used in a variety of ways. This print file can be used as a way to transmit to a service bureau, but can also serve as an EPS file that can be placed in other PageMaker documents and other applications.

The first step is to select the *Print* command (Figure 15) to activate the *Print* dialog box, as you would when printing any PageMaker file. Go about the print process in the usual way, selecting the page numbers, the quantity, tiling, and crop mark options as explained earlier in this module (Figure 16).

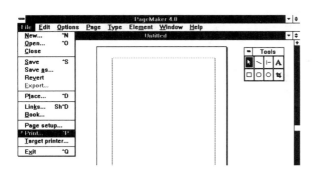

Figure 15. To create a PostScript print file you must first select the Print command.

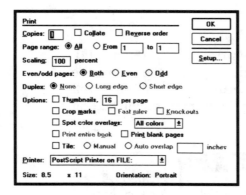

Figure 16. *Set up your print options as usual, keeping in mind exactly what you would like to do with the print file.*

After selecting your print preferences, click the mouse on the *Setup* button to get the dialog box of Figure 17. Then, from this dialog box, click on the *Options* button to get the dialog box of Figure 18.

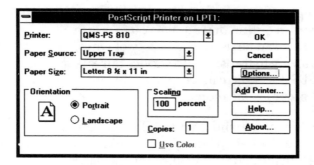

Figure 17. *From this dialog box, click on the* Options *button to get the dialog box of Figure 18.*

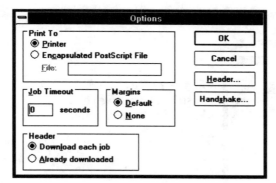

Figure 18. *The options in this dialog box let you create a print file.*

In the *Print To* section, select the *Encapsulated PostScript File* option by clicking inside the circle (Figure 19). Then key in the output path (where you would like the file to be saved) and the name of the file. For this example, we called the file "test" and saved it in the Paul directory on the C drive. Give the file a .PRN extension (Figure 19). If you don't key in an output path, the file will be saved on the current directory.

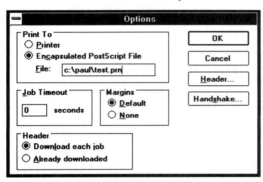

Figure 19. To create a print file, first select the Encapsulated PostScript File *option. Then key in the output path and name the file.*

Once you have set up the *Print To File* options, select OK to return to the Figure 17 dialog box. Select OK again and then once more in the first print dialog box. The file will now print directly to the disk.

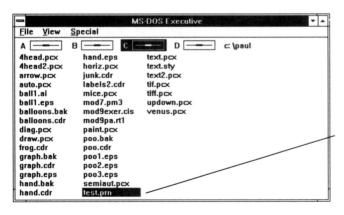

Figure 20. If we look in the Windows MS-DOS executive program, we can see the print file that we created.

Next time you print, make sure you change the *Print To* section in the *Options* dialog box of Figure 19 back to *Printer*; otherwise, every time you print in future you will create print files again. This, of course, can be changed at any time to suit your printing needs.

EXERCISE:
PRINTING

Printing

In this exercise you will look at some of the printing options available with PageMaker — although for this exercise to be completed a printer is not necessary.

This training material is structured so that people of all levels of expertise with Page-Maker can use it to gain maximum benefit. In order to do this, we have structured the material so that the bare exercise is listed below this paragraph on just one page, with no hints. The following pages contain the steps needed to complete this exercise, for those who need additional prompting. The **Printing** module should be referenced if you need further help or explanations.

Because printing itself is a fairly straightforward exercise (it will either work or it won't, and if it doesn't, it is probably a connection problem anyway), we will not be printing directly to a printer in this exercise. We will, however, be looking at the print procedures as well as printing to disk.

Module 9 exercise steps

1. *Set up the print dialog box to print the first page of the template* NEWSLTR2.PT4 three times. This document is found in the pscript directory (located in the template directory). Enlarge the print by 200%, and tile the print with a 1" overlap. Check your dialog boxes with Figure 5 of this exercise.*

2. *Print the same file (page 1 only) to disk as an EPS file, and name the print file EXER10PS.EPS. After printing the file to disk, start a new publication and load in the EPS file EXER10PS.EPS.*

   *Templates are similar to publications. See Module 10 for details on templates.

The details for completing this exercise are on the following pages.

The steps in detail

1. *Set up the print dialog box to print the first page of the template NEWSLTR2.PT4 three times. This document is found in the pscript directory (located in the template directory). Enlarge the print by 200%, and tile the print with a 1" overlap. Check your dialog boxes with Figure 5 of this exercise.*

The first step in this exercise is to open a copy of the PageMaker template NEWSLTR2.PT4, located in the pscript directory within the template directory (Figure 1). If you are already in PageMaker, choose *Open* to select this template.

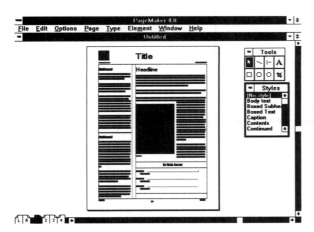

Figure 1. *Make sure this NEWSLTR2.PT4 file is opened as a copy of the original template. (In the* Open publication *dialog box you have a choice to check either* **Original** *or* **Copy***. Please choose* **Copy***.) Your title bar should read "Untitled," as ours does here.*

After opening this template, your next step is to select the *Print* command from the **File** menu (Figure 2).

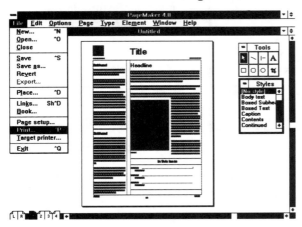

Figure 2. *After opening the file, select the* Print *command from the* **File** *menu.*

335

To print the publication three times, make sure you alter the number in the *Copies* box to 3. Set *Page range* from 1 to 1. See Figure 3 for both these adjustments.

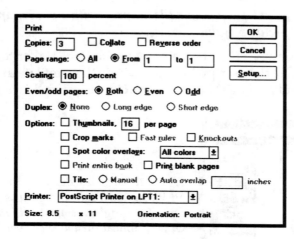

Figure 3. Change the figure in the top left-hand corner of the dialog box (Copies) to 3. This ensures three copies of the publication will be printed. The Page range should be set from 1 to 1, because you only need to print the first page.

To scale the print to 200 %, alter the *Scaling* figure to 200 (Figure 4).

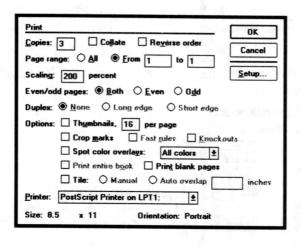

Figure 4. Change the figure for Scaling to 200 to double the print size.

Now make sure the *Tile* command has been checked to ensure tiling is used. Select *Auto overlap* and change the figure in the overlap box to 1" (Figure 5).

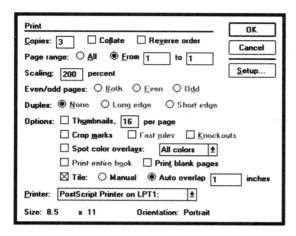

Figure 5. Select the Tile *box, and set the* Auto overlap *to 1".*
Choose Cancel from here unless you have a printer connected and would like to see the output.

Choose Cancel at this time, unless you wish to try out these print options.

2. *Print the same file (page 1 only) to disk as an EPS file and name the print file EXER10PS.EPS. After printing the file to disk, start a new publication and load in the EPS file EXER10PS.EPS.*

    With the same publication open, select the *Print* command again. However, make sure that you are only printing one copy and that the print is not scaled or tiled (Figure 6).

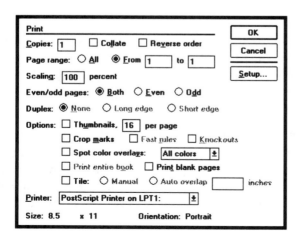

Figure 6. Set up the first Print *dialog box as we have done here.*

From the *Print* dialog box of Figure 6, click on the *Setup* button (below *Cancel*) to activate the dialog box of Figure 7. From this dialog box, another one must be activated to create an EPS print file. To do this, click the mouse on the *Options* button of Figure 7.

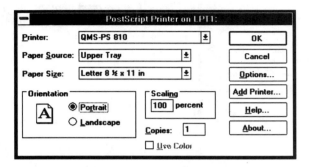

Figure 7. From this dialog box click on the Options *button to activate the* Options *dialog box of Figure 8.*

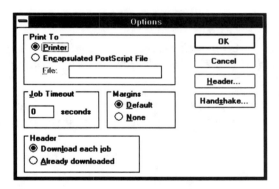

Figure 9. Clicking on the Options *button in the Figure 7 dialog box will activate this* Options *dialog box. Here you can set up the current file to print to the disk as an EPS file.*

The first section in the *Options* dialog box is the *Print To* section. This is where you make the changes so that the file will print to the disk as an EPS file. The first thing to do is to select the *Encapsulated PostScript File* option. Then you must key in the output path of the file and name it. This is done in the rectangle to the right of the word "*File.*"

If you do not put in the output path (where you want the file to be saved), the EPS file will be placed in the current directory (which will be the pscript directory). For this exercise, you are not going to key in the output path, which means the file will be saved in the pscript directory. Key in the name of the file, which is EXER10PS, and give the name a .EPS extension (Figure 10).

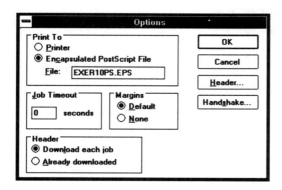

Figure 10. In this dialog box, select the Encapsulated PostScript File *option and name the file. Once you have done this, select OK.*

Once you have set up your dialog box as shown in Figure 10, select OK, and then select OK again in the print dialog box currently on the screen. This will get you to the first *Print* dialog box. If all the settings are correct here, select OK, and the file will print to the disk as an EPS file (Figure 11).

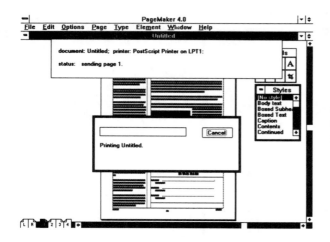

Figure 11. The file is now printing to disk as an EPS file.

When the file has finished printing, close it, but do not save any changes. Again select the **File** menu and execute the *New* command. Select OK from the *Page setup* dialog box to start a new publication (Figure 12).

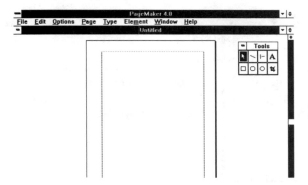

Figure 12. Close the file that was open, and select New *from the* **File** *menu to create a new publication.*

After creating a new publication, use the *Place* command from the **File** menu (Figure 13) to insert the EPS file you just created. From the list of files displayed (Figure 14), choose EXER10PS.EPS and flow it onto the page (Figure 15). It will appear on the page as a gray box, but will still print out exactly as page one of the NEWSLTR2.PT4. The gray box contains information about the file, such as where and when the file was created, in the top left corner.

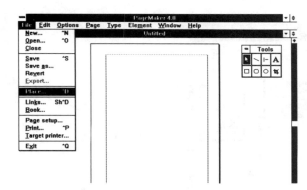

Figure 13. Choose the Place *command to gain access to* EXER10PS — *the PostScript file you just created.*

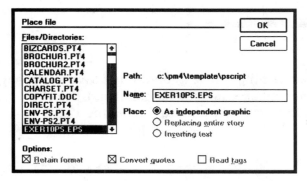

Figure 14. Select EXER10PS *from the list of files presented from the* Place *command.*

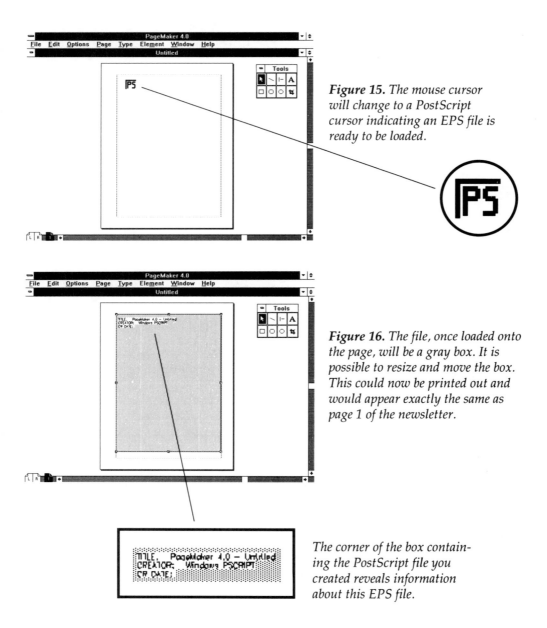

Figure 15. *The mouse cursor will change to a PostScript cursor indicating an EPS file is ready to be loaded.*

Figure 16. *The file, once loaded onto the page, will be a gray box. It is possible to resize and move the box. This could now be printed out and would appear exactly the same as page 1 of the newsletter.*

The corner of the box containing the PostScript file you created reveals information about this EPS file.

341

TEMPLATES

Module 10

Templates

The purpose of PageMaker templates is to save you time and effort in creating new publications. You do not have to recreate the format of a document if that format exists elsewhere. The way this works is quite simple.

Templates are like partially created publications — publications that can be used over and over again without destroying the original. Let's say, for example, that every month you create a company newsletter. The specifications for this newsletter might be: eight pages, Letter page, two columns on pages 1-6, three columns on pages 7 and 8, a border around all pages, vertical rules between all columns, headers, footers, numbered pages, etc.

Initially, this would be set up from scratch in the normal way, and would take a little time. Once done, however, with all these attributes saved as a template, this template could be used as the starting point for the next month's newsletter. By using this approach, you could spend more time concentrating on the content of the newsletter rather than the format, since the format has already been created.

PageMaker 4.0 contains a library of templates covering a wide range of publication types to be used as starting points for documents. You can either use these templates as they are, modify them to meet your needs, or create your own. Two types of templates are included — grid templates and placeholder templates. The former are general purpose templates that consist of a variety of document sizes with different column and grid (ruler guide) settings. The placeholder templates are specially designed for a particular type of publication, and include text and graphics within them. Either type of publication can be created as discussed in this module. We will mainly be talking about placeholder templates.

Creating templates

Initially, creating templates is done in exactly the same way as creating a typical publication. The *New* command is selected, as many pages as necessary are added, the margins and columns are defined, and text and graphics inserted where necessary. These steps are briefly summarized in Figures 1 through 5. The difference comes when the document is saved.

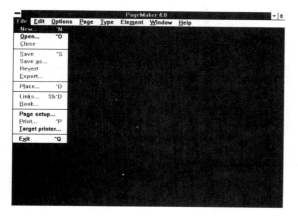

Figure 1. *We are going to look at the steps in creating a simple template. Start off as you normally would — by selecting the* New *command from the* **File** *menu.*

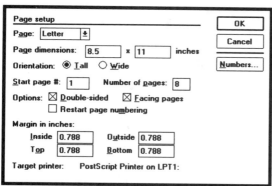

Figure 2. *Define the page in the* Page setup *command as you need. In this case we have set the number of pages, new margins, etc.*

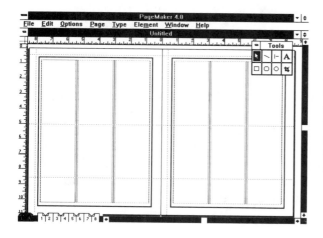

Figure 3. Once the document opens, set up all the document formatting — number of columns, borders, intercolumn rules, etc. — in the master pages.

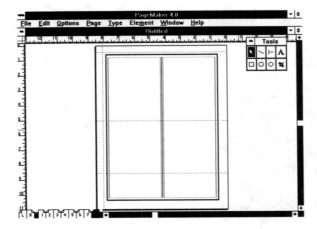

Figure 4. Any page in the document can be set up independently of the others — as always. Here, page 8 has two columns, while all others have three.

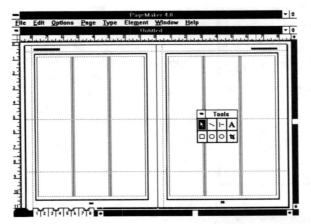

Figure 5. Text information such as headers, footers, and page numbers can also be set up in the master pages of a template.

*Additionally, text and graphics could have been added to this original set-up. See the later section on **Text and Graphics Placeholders** to see how to take advantage of this option.*

Whenever you choose the *Save* command for the first time (Figure 6) or the *Save as* command from the **File** menu, you are presented with the dialog box of Figure 7. The name is entered as usual (in our case Temp1), but the difference comes in the option in the right-hand side of the dialog box. Here you have a choice as to how to save the document — either as a traditional *Publication* (this will be selected by default) or as a *Template*. If you choose *Template*, this file will take on special qualities.

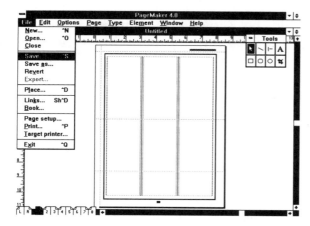

Figure 6. Up until now, the creation of the template has been exactly the same as the creation of a publication — the difference comes during the Save command.

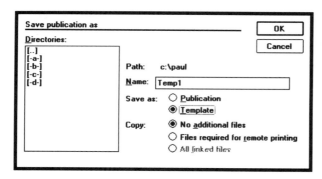

Figure 7. Give the document a name, as you normally would, but click on Template below the Publication option. Then click on OK.

PageMaker publications and PageMaker templates can be distinguished quite easily — publications have an extension of .PM4 while templates have a .PT4 extension.

The main difference between publications and templates appears when the PageMaker file is opened. When a publication is opened, the original file is opened and any changes saved affect the file permanently. However, if a template is selected, then, by default, an unnamed original (a copy) is opened. The named original remains untouched on disk to be used another time. The template copy that was opened can be added to, modified, etc., and saved as a new publication. Because this template opens up without a name, there is no chance of saving over the original template and destroying its contents by mistake.

In Figure 8, the *Open* dialog box shows, in the bottom right section, the options of *Original* or *Copy*. A template always defaults to the *Copy* option, whereas a publication defaults to *Original*. Figure 9 gives further examples.

Opening copies or originals of either publications or templates can be manually overridden through the *Open* command in Figure 8. Whenever you select a PageMaker file to be opened from within this dialog box, the default conditions of *Original* or *Copy* will occur as indicated above. When you select a template, however, you can override this and select *Original*. This is necessary, of course, if you wish to modify the original template. In the same way, you can override the *Original* default for a publication and open up a *Copy*.

An example of opening up a copy of the Temp1 template, which we saved in Figure 7 as a template, is shown in Figure 10.

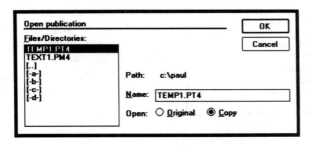

Figure 8. Here we have used the Open *command to gain access to this list of PageMaker files. As we select a template to open (this was the template we just created), note how the option in the bottom right-hand switches to* Copy *rather than* Original.

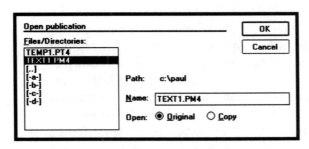

Figure 9. However, when you select a normal publication to open, the option switches back to Original. *This can be manually overridden if need be.*

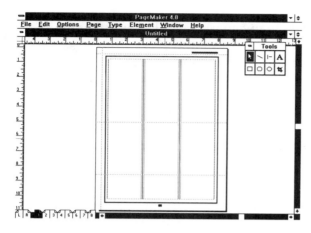

Figure 10. Here we have opened up a copy of the template we just created (Temp1). Note how it looks exactly the same as the right master page of Figure 5, yet is untitled.

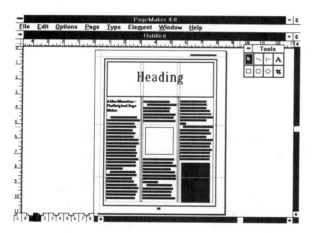

Figure 11. Once the copy of the template has been opened, you are free to add this month's text and graphics without having to redefine page parameters.

Text and graphic placeholders

We have mentioned that a template can contain any quantity of graphics or text you like. If you consider a monthly newsletter, the actual content of this newsletter will change from month to month. One might think, therefore, that you cannot include much text in the template, as it will have to be updated anyway. However, by using text and graphics as "placeholders," you can include as much text and graphics in your template as you need, without having to worry about this text being removed or updated. Using text and graphic placeholders in templates makes creating a publication a much easier task.

Let's say that you loaded in one major text file, several graphics files, and several headings throughout a previously saved monthly newsletter template. When you open up the template next month, the graphics, text, and headings will all be there, but you will have new text, graphics, and headings that have replaced those of the current month. Replacing the old files with the new ones becomes very easy, and this process helps you to format and position the new elements in your newsletter precisely.

Graphic placeholders

In a simple copy of a newsletter template (Figure 12), let's choose to first replace one of the graphics on the first page with a new graphic. (See the caption of Figure 12 if you wish to work through this example with us.) Select the old graphic that is to be replaced immediately before selecting the *Place* command (Figures 13 and 14). When you choose the *Place* command, locate the new graphic as in Figure 15 and select it, but do not yet click on OK.

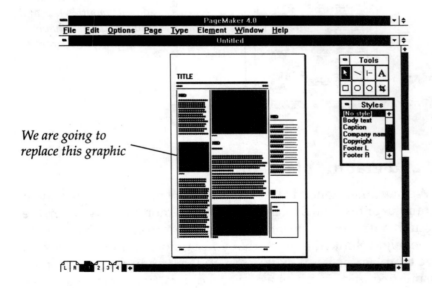

Figure 12. *To work through with us in this section of the module, load the TABLOID.PT4 template contained in the PageMaker pscript sub-directory in the template sub-directory. As shown in this figure, it contains various text and graphics placeholders on page 1. We are going to replace the graphic in the middle of the first column.*

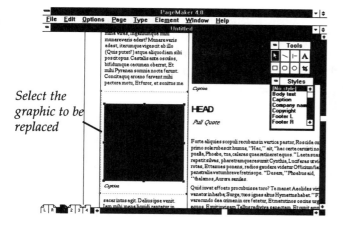

Select the graphic to be replaced

Figure 13. We have changed to 75% size view so that you can see how the graphic we have selected will be replaced

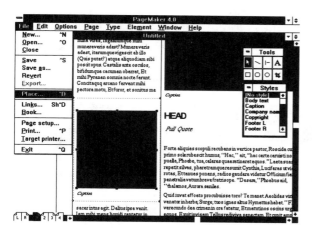

Figure 14. With the graphic still selected, choose the Place command from the **File** menu to locate the new graphic.

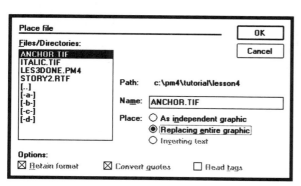

Figure 15. The graphic you are using to replace the old graphic is ANCHOR.TIF from the lesson4 sub-directory (within the tutorial sub-directory). Note that you also must select the option to the right — Replacing entire graphic (*see the explanation on the next page*).

There are several options within the Figure 15 dialog box that may be active depending on the steps that were taken before choosing this command. The one that should be active now, located in the right of the dialog box, gives you the choice between two ways to load the graphic — either *As independent graphic*, which is selected by default, or *Replacing entire graphic*. *As independent graphic* is a picture loaded in the traditional way — the mouse cursor will change appearance and you may choose where to load the graphic on the page.

Replacing entire graphic will insert the new graphic not only in the same area as the existing graphic, but also using the same sizing, cropping, and wraparound attributes as the previous graphic. This can, of course, be modified after the graphic has been replaced. (This option cannot be selected unless a graphic is selected on screen before choosing the *Place* command, as in Figure 13.) On clicking OK in Figure 15, the new graphic totally replaces the old (Figure 16).

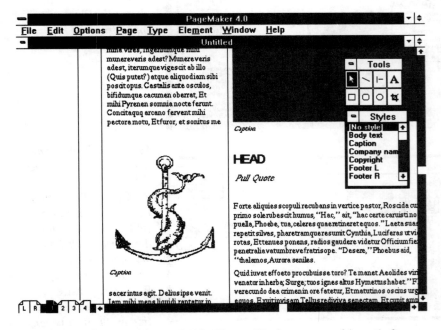

Figure 16. *When you choose OK in Figure 15, the new graphic entirely replaces the old, taking on all its attributes.*

Text placeholders

The same theory applies to text replacement as it does to graphics. Select any part of the text file that you would like to replace with a new file (use either the pointer tool or make an insertion point with the text tool) and choose the *Place* command. Locate the new text file and note the new option to the right of the list of files. It will read *As new story* and *Replacing entire story*. As with graphics, if you select *Replacing entire story*, the new text file will completely overlay the previous file — following its exact path. If the files are of different lengths, there will either be a blank space following the file (if it is shorter), or more text to flow (if it is longer).

See Figures 17 through 19 for examples of this approach.

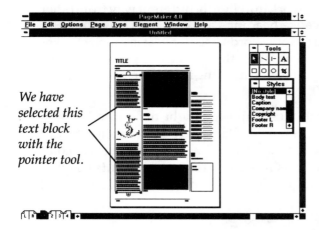

We have selected this text block with the pointer tool.

Figure 17. The procedure for replacing existing text files with other text files works in the same way as the graphics example. First, select any text block with the pointer tool or create an insertion point within a story with the text tool. These two options will cause the total text file to be replaced. If you wish to replace only a portion of a text file, then select part of that file using the text tool.

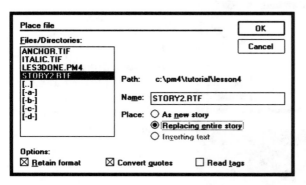

Figure 18. After choosing the Place command, select the new text file and the Replacing entire story option. If you have selected only a portion of your text with the text tool, then the bottom option (which would read Replacing selected text) would have been available for selection as well.

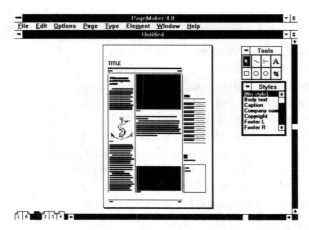

Figure 19. When OK is selected, the new text file completely replaces the old — flowing in exactly the same pattern. The procedure replaces the entire story associated with the text block initially selected (Figure 17). Because the file just flowed is shorter than the original file, the space that was filled with the original story will be blank.

Heading placeholders

Heading placeholders work in a slightly different way from other text placeholders. Because headings are generally much shorter than text files — three or four words usually — it is much quicker to type them in PageMaker rather than in a word processor. Let's say, for example, that you have a heading in place in your template as shown in Figure 20.

Simply select the text cursor and highlight the entire heading (Figure 20). Without pressing the Backspace key or using the *Cut* command, type in the new heading. The new heading will completely overwrite the old, using exactly the same attributes (Figure 21). The same type style, justification, and spacing will be applied to the new text.

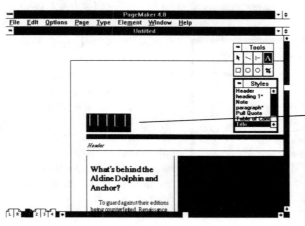

Figure 20. Replacing headings while keeping their formatting is very simple. Using the text cursor, select the old heading, but do not cut or delete the text.

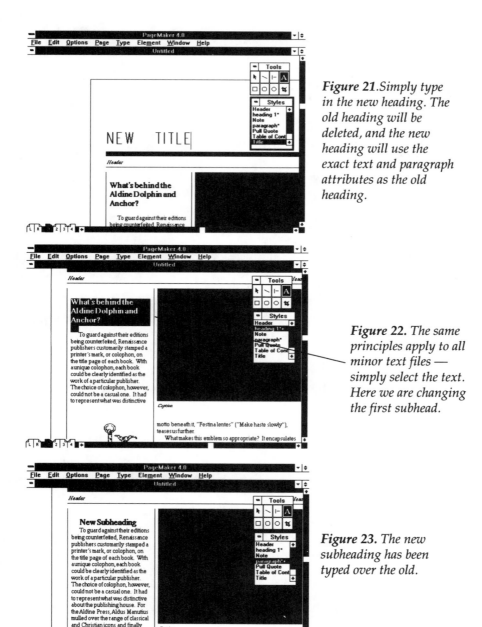

Figure 21.*Simply type in the new heading. The old heading will be deleted, and the new heading will use the exact text and paragraph attributes as the old heading.*

Figure 22. The same principles apply to all minor text files — simply select the text. Here we are changing the first subhead.

Figure 23. The new subheading has been typed over the old.

All text and graphics placeholders can be regular or simulated. Provided with PageMaker are several "dummy" files that can be used to create a template, so that real files do not have to be created and used.

EXERCISE:
TEMPLATES

Templates

In this exercise we are illustrating the use of templates and showing how to work effectively with them.

This training material is structured so that people of all levels of expertise with Page-Maker can use it to gain maximum benefit. In order to do this, we have structured the material so that the bare exercise is listed below this paragraph on just one page, with no hints. The following pages contain the steps needed to complete this exercise, for those who need additional prompting. The **Templates** module should be referenced if you need further help or explanations.

Module 10 exercise steps

1.   *Load the template TABLOID.PT4 from the pscript sub-directory located in the template sub-directory.*

2.   *On page 1 of this template, you are going to replace four major sections — the graphic in the first column, the title, the text of column 1, page 1, and the graphic at the top of the middle column. Make sure you understand which parts of page 1 we are talking about when we refer to them (see Figure 1 to get a better idea).*

3.   *Replace the graphic in column 1 with the file PRACTICE.TIF from the basics sub-directory within the tutorial sub-directory.*

4.   *Replace the column 1, page 1 text with the file STORY2 from the lesson4 sub-directory.*

5.   *Replace the graphic at the top of the middle column with the file ANCHOR.TIF from the lesson4 sub-directory.*

6.   *Replace the title with a title of your own choosing.*

7.   *Save the template as a publication called TEMPEXE.*

The steps to completing this exercise are on the following pages.

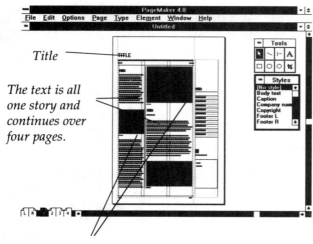

Title

The text is all one story and continues over four pages.

Figure 1. *The Tabloid template. This figure indicates the different graphic and text sections we will be replacing.*

Graphics we will be replacing

The steps in detail

1. *Load the template TABLOID.PT4 from the pscript sub-directory located in the template sub-directory.*

   Make sure PageMaker is open and then select the *Open* command from the **File** menu to access this template from the pscript sub-directory (see Figures 2 and 3).

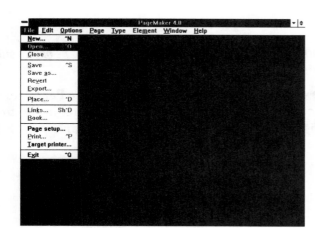

Figure 2. *The* Open *command from the* **File** *menu is the way to get access to both publications and templates.*

Locate the template sub-directory and double-click on it. Inside will be the pscript sub-directory. Double-click on this, and locate the TABLOID.PT4 file (Figure 3). Load this file by double-clicking on it, or clicking on it once and selecting OK.

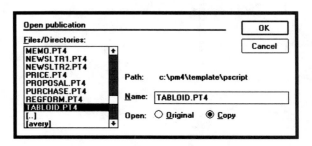

Figure 3. The TABLOID.PT4 template is located in the pscript sub-directory in the template sub-directory, which is inside the pm4 sub-directory. Note we are opening a copy of this template.

2. *On page 1 of this template, you are going to replace four major sections — the graphic in the first column, the title, the text of column 1, page 1, and the graphic at the top of the middle column. Make sure you understand which parts of page 1 we are talking about when we refer to them (see Figure 1 to get a better idea).*

See Figure 1 to make sure you understand what we refer to as the title, the page 1 text, and the graphics.

3. *Replace the graphic in column 1 with the file PRACTICE.TIF from the basics sub-directory (within the tutorial sub-directory).*

If you are not in *75% size* view, change to this view through the **Page** menu. Select the existing graphic, or in this case a gray shaded square, in the first column by clicking on it (Figure 5). Now move to the *Place* command in the **File** menu (Figure 6).

Select this graphic

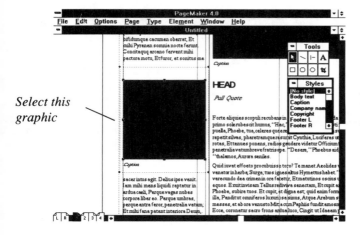

Figure 5. *The first step in replacing a graphic is to select it with the pointer tool.*

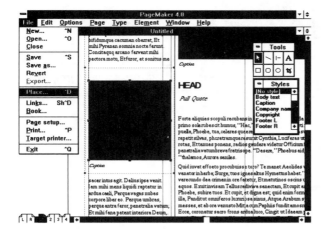

Figure 6. *After Figure 5, move to the* Place *command in the* **File** *menu to choose the graphic to replace the selected one with.*

Locate the file PRACTICE.TIF in the basics sub-directory (Figure 7). After selecting it in this dialog box (by clicking on it once, not twice) check the option *Replacing entire graphic* to the right of the list of files. This will make sure that the currently selected graphic is deleted and replaced with the new one at exactly the same place and size. Click on OK. The new graphic replaces the old (Figure 8).

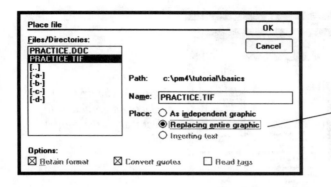

Figure 7. Select the file PRACTICE.TIF to replace the graphic you had originally selected in Figure 5. Make sure you also choose Replacing entire graphic.

Figure 8. After clicking on OK in Figure 7, the new graphic will, after a few seconds, replace the old.

4. Replace the text of column 1, page 1, with the file STORY2 from the lesson4 sub-directory.

The same steps are used to replace one story with another as are used to replace graphics. In this case you are only replacing column 1, page 1 text, not the entire story. In this template, the text is basically one whole story. Therefore, you need to select just the first column of the page 1 text with the text tool (Figure 9). (We have returned to *Fit in window* view for Figure 9.)

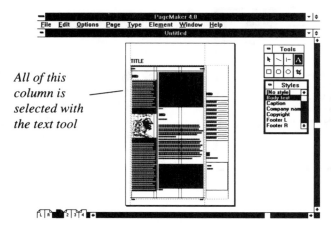

All of this column is selected with the text tool

Figure 9. To replace part of a text file, select the desired portion (in our case, column 1 of page 1) with the text tool.

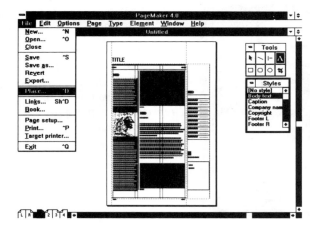

Figure 10. Once again, after selecting the section to be replaced using the text tool, move directly to the Place *command in the* **File** *menu.*

Locate the file STORY2 from the lesson4 sub-directory (Figure 11). You will notice that *Replacing entire story* as well as *Replacing selected text* can be selected while the file STORY2 is highlighted in the list of files. Check *Replacing selected text* (Figure 11) and click on OK. By selecting *Replacing selected text*, STORY2 will replace all text in column 1 and continue through the publication until it runs out. STORY2 is only a small file and it finishes halfway down the middle column. The rest of the original text in this template will remain. If you selected *Replacing entire story*, STORY2 would fill the same amount of space, and the rest of the text belonging to this story would disappear from this template.

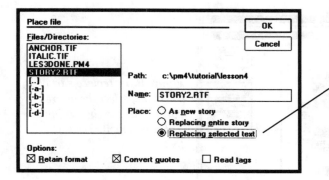

Figure 11. Select the file STORY2 *to replace the text in column 1, page 1. Make sure you also choose* Replacing selected text *and then click on OK.*

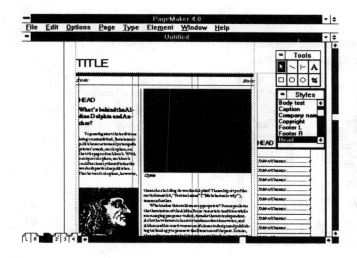

Figure 12. The new file will replace the old column 1 text and continue until it runs out. Sometimes, however, this replacement may require a little tidying up.

5. Replace the graphic at the top of the middle column with the file ANCHOR.TIF from the lesson4 sub-directory.

The graphic we refer to here is actually the gray square at the top of the middle column. See Figure 1 again if in doubt. Move across the page so that you can see this graphic (Figure 13).

After locating the space set aside for a graphic and selecting it with the pointer tool, move to the *Place* command (Figure 14), select the file ANCHOR.TIF, and check the *Replacing entire graphic* option (Figure 15). The result is shown in Figure 16.

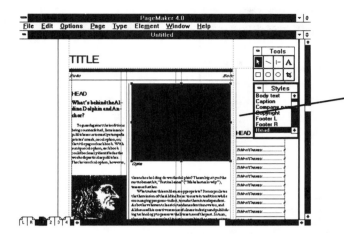

Figure 13. *Locate the graphic placeholder at the top of the middle column and select it.*

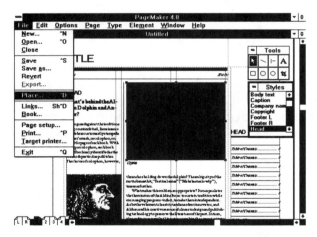

Figure 14. *After selecting the space set aside for the graphic, move directly to the* Place *command in the* **File** *menu.*

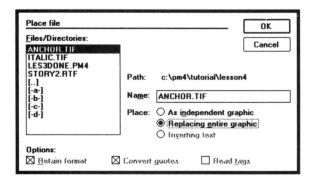

Figure 15. *Choose the file ANCHOR.TIF, and check the* Replacing entire graphic *option. Click on OK.*

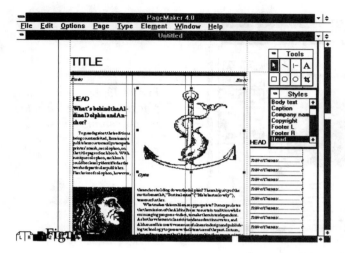

Figure 16. *The file ANCHOR.TIF will entirely replace the graphic placeholder and take up no extra room.*

6. Replace the title with a title of your own choosing.

Move to the top of the screen and locate the title at the top of the page. This is the title placeholder — it has defined the position as well as the type specifications of the title. In fact, you could replace this in either of two ways — by selecting it using the pointer or text tool and loading a new text file to replace this one; or by selecting the title with the text tool and simply typing in the new text. Because the title is short, the latter method is generally the easier of the two.

Select the title in text mode and type in your new one — anything you like (Figures 17 and 18).

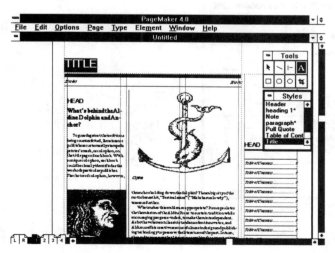

Figure 17. *For this step, select the title using the text editing mode.*

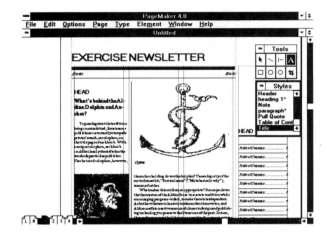

Figure 18. Type in what you want the new title to say.

7. Save the template as a publication called TEMPEXE.

You should note that the template you are working with is actually called "Untitled," indicating that you are working on a copy of the original. You must now save it as a new publication. Use the *Save* command in the **File** menu (Figure 19) and insert the name TEMPEXE in the name rectangle (Figures 20 and 21).

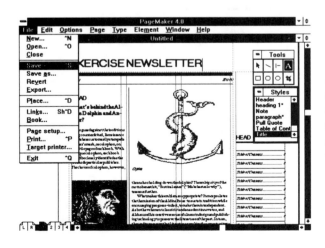

*Figure 19. It is a good idea to save before you finish. You can save your work at any stage by choosing the Save command from the **File** menu.*

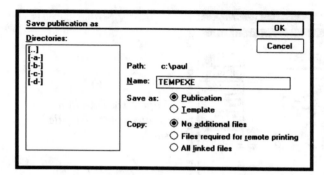

Figure 20. Insert the name in the name rectangle as shown. Here we have called the publication TEMPEXE.

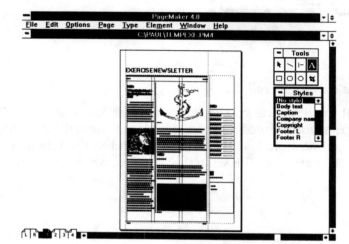

Figure 21. The name of the publication replaces "Untitled" in the menu bar at the top of the screen.

STYLE SHEETS

Style Sheets

A PageMaker style sheet comes with every template or publication that you open. A style sheet contains several different groups of text characteristics, identified by style names, that can be applied to text. For example, a style sheet may contain four different style types — **Heading**, **Body text**, **Subheading**, and **Caption**. (These style names can be absolutely anything you want them to be.) **Heading** may be defined as Bookman, 24 point, bold, centered, 1" of space below, indented 0.5" from the left and right, etc. All other style names are defined differently again. You decide what attributes are saved under what name.

Once you load in text and are ready to format, previously you would have had to move through a lot of menus and commands to format such things as headings. However, with style sheets, you can apply the style name **Heading** to a paragraph on the page and all attributes defined for this style are applied immediately. This is a much quicker way to format text than using the **Type** menu.

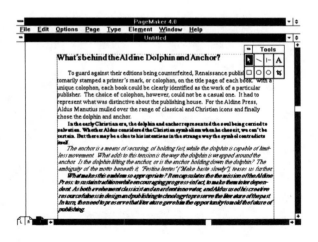

Figure 1. All the paragraphs on this page were formatted in a matter of seconds using style sheets — not minutes using the **Type** menu.

The benefits of style sheets do not end here. Let's say, for example, that you have applied the style **Heading** to a hundred or so paragraphs throughout a very large publication. This **Heading** style might be defined as Palatino 24-point bold, yet you decide that it would look better if it were Bookman 24-point bold. Instead of having to find every single paragraph and alter its appearance, all you have to do is alter the attributes of the style named **Heading**. Every time this style occurs in the text it will be altered automatically.

Style sheets can be copied from publications and templates to other publications or templates. Style sheets can also link up to word processors, like Microsoft Word, that use style sheets.

Don't get style sheets confused with type styles — which include bold, italic, underline, and so forth. When we talk about applying a style, we mean applying one of the style names in a style sheet to text.

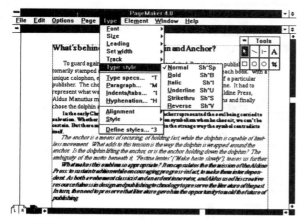

Figure 2. Don't get the type styles shown here confused with styles from the style sheet — they are two separate things.

Adding new styles to a style sheet

You can add new styles to a publication's style sheet by (1) defining styles from scratch, (2) basing a new style's definition on one of the current publication's existing styles, (3) copying an existing style sheet from another publication, (4) importing styles with imported word-processed documents, or (5) importing style names from a word processing program.

We will look at each of these methods soon, but first we will look at the default styles in every style sheet.

As already mentioned, every template or publication contains a style sheet, even if you are not really aware of it. To see the styles that are used in your current document, choose the *Style palette* command from the **Window** menu (Figure 3). Just below the Toolbox a small window will appear as shown in Figure 4.

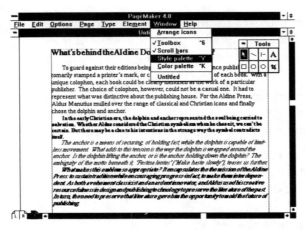

Figure 3. *When using style sheets, make sure that the* Style palette *is shown by choosing the* Style palette *command in the* **Window** *menu.*

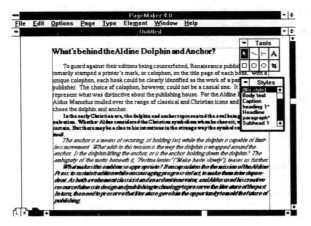

Figure 4. The Style palette *will appear somewhere below the Toolbox and can be moved around similarly to the Toolbox.*

Inside this *Style palette*, there may be listed several different names. However, if this is a new publication (i.e., it contains no imported text), it will contain several style names by default— **No style** and **Body text**, as well as **Caption**, **Headline**, **Subhead 1**, and **Subhead 2**.

No style is exactly as it sounds — it indicates those paragraphs that do not use a specific style. Consequently, it contains no specific text attributes — it will change all the time.

Body text, by default, includes such attributes as Times 12-point, auto leading, flush left paragraphs, first indent and hyphenation on. We will show you in this module how to modify all default styles, as well as how to create your own, among other things.

Defining styles from scratch

Once you become familiar with PageMaker's style sheets, you will continue to add new styles — maybe some to represent headings, others for footnotes, formulas, headers, footers, etc. The alternative method that you can also use to format text, involves selecting text, moving through the commands in the **Type** menu, and applying characteristics one at a time. We covered this in detail in Module 4. This latter method can still be used in conjunction with style sheets — so that you can phase in the use of style sheets if they are a little confusing at first.

Before we start looking at creating new styles, load some text onto the page to see the effect of creating these new styles. We have loaded the STORY2 file from the lesson4 folder in the tutorial subdirectory into a single column. If, upon loading the text, new styles appear in the style sheet, ignore them for now. We will look at those a little later on. Don't worry if the formatting of your STORY2 file looks different from our Figure 5; you can adjust this later on in Figure 16.

New styles are created using the *Define styles* command in the **Type** menu (Figure 5). Select this command now and the dialog box of Figure 6 appears.

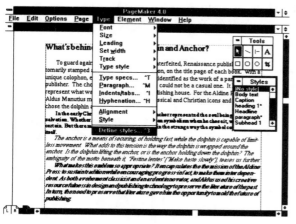

Figure 5. The Define styles *command is used to create new styles to add to the style sheet.*

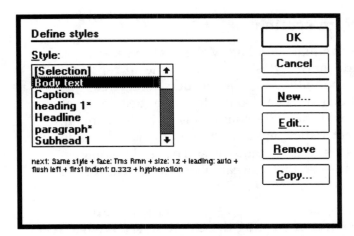

Figure 6. The Define styles *dialog box. Don't worry if your dialog box has some different styles from ours — it doesn't matter.*

At the left of this dialog box is the list of all the styles in this publication's style sheet. It should include **Selection** and **Body text**. Listed below these names there may well be other styles that are different from Figure 6. This does not matter. Next to these styles are several commands you will be using to create and edit new styles.

Click the mouse on the word **Selection** at the top (Figure 7). Below the list of names will appear a list of type specifications. This list reflects the attributes of the selected text (if any is selected). If you click on the words **Body text** (Figure 6), the text specifications will reflect exactly how the style **Body text** is set up. It is possible that **Body text** and **Selection** are set up to be exactly the same, or they may differ.

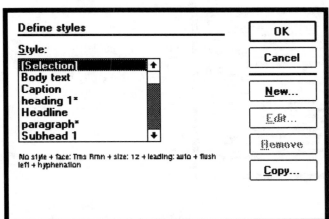

Figure 7. Compare Figures 6 and 7 to see the type specifications defined below the list of styles.

To create a new style, you must click on the command *New* within the Figures 6 or 7 dialog box. The *New* dialog box of Figure 8 will appear. This relates to having the word **Selection** actually highlighted, as shown in Figure 7. If **Body text** or another style had been selected, then this selected style would appear in the *Based on:* rectangle in Figure 8.

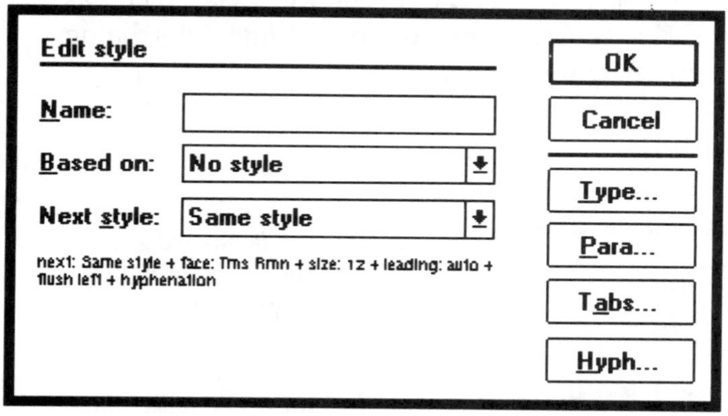

Edit style	OK
Name:	Cancel
Based on: No style ±	**T**ype...
Next **s**tyle: Same style ±	**P**ara...
next: Same style + face: Tms Rmn + size: 12 + leading: auto + flush left + hyphenation	T**a**bs...
	Hyph...

Figure 8. Upon selecting the New *command from the dialog box in Figure 7, you will be presented with this dialog box.*

The first thing to do in the Figure 8 dialog box is to insert the name that you would like to give this style. You can call it anything you like, but make it meaningful so that it can be recognized later on. We called ours "Title" in Figure 9.

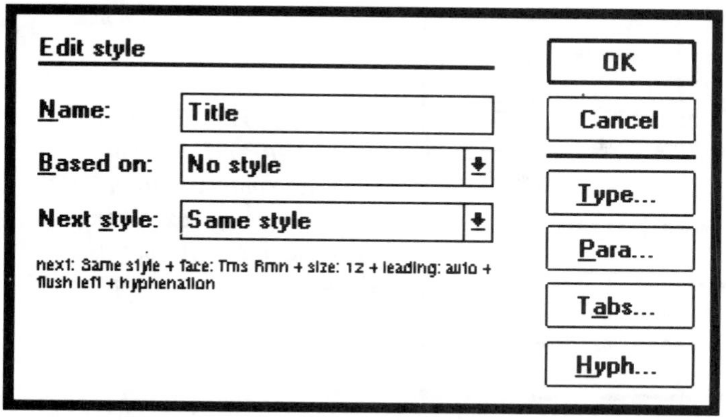

Edit style	OK
Name: Title	Cancel
Based on: No style ±	**T**ype...
Next **s**tyle: Same style ±	**P**ara...
next: Same style + face: Tms Rmn + size: 12 + leading: auto + flush left + hyphenation	T**a**bs...
	Hyph...

Figure 9. Your first step in this dialog box is to name the style you are about to create. Try to name it something meaningful — it will make things a lot easier later on.

To the right of the Figures 8 and 9 dialog box are four commands — *Type, Para, Tabs,* and *Hyphenation.* When you click on any one of these, the appropriate dialog box relating to these commands will be presented (Figures 10 through 13). In these dialog boxes, adjust the style you have just created so that it is a larger point size — or at least a little different from **Body text**. Every time you use one of these commands in Figures 10 through 13 and click on OK, you are returned back to the dialog box of Figure 9 to select another command. When you have finished defining the style exactly as you want it, click OK to return to the previous *Define styles* dialog box of Figure 7, shown again in Figure 14.

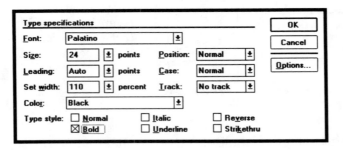

Figure 10. This dialog box is invoked after clicking once on the Type *command in the dialog box of Figure 9. Change the value inside the box to reflect these selections and click on OK. If Palatino is not available, choose Tms Rmn.*

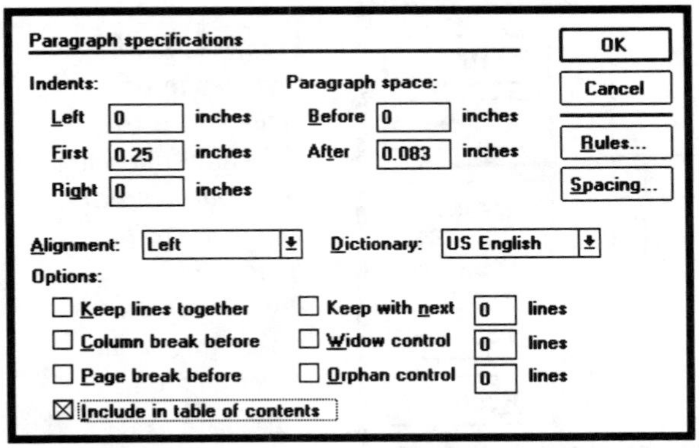

Figure 11. This dialog box is accessed by clicking on the Para *command from the Figure 9 dialog box. Change the value inside the box as shown here and click on OK.*

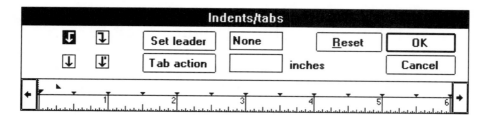

Figure 12. This box comes from selecting the Tabs *command in Figure 9. Keep as is and click on OK.*

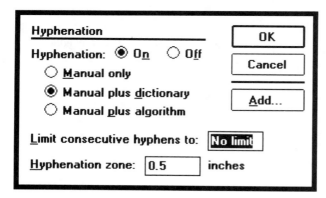

Figure 13. And this box comes from selecting the Hyphenation *command. Keep as is and click on OK.*

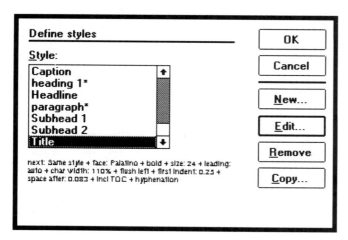

Figure 14. Note the new attributes of the style we have just created. With **Title** *highlighted, the attributes for this style are listed at the bottom of the dialog box.*

In Figure 14, the new style name (**Title**) joins the list of styles. Underneath the list, the type specifications for this new style are listed. Click OK again to return to the page. Joining the *Style palette* is the new **Title** style you created (Figure 15). The *Define styles* command can be used as many times as necessary to create all the styles you need.

For example, in Figure 14, after defining the **Title** style, you could have chosen *New* again to create more styles if you wished.

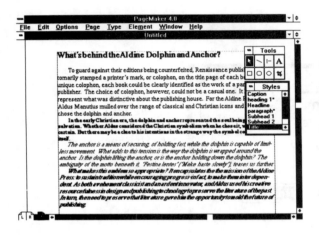

Figure 15. The *style you created,* **Title,** *has been added to the list of styles in the* Style palette.

Applying styles

Styles are very simple to apply to paragraphs on the page. If you want one paragraph alone to use the new style you created, change to the text cursor. Insert the text cursor inside the paragraph, or simply select the entire paragraph if that's easier. Now move back to the *Style palette* and click on the style you would like to apply to the paragraph. Instantly, any attributes you created with that style are applied to the paragraph on screen. Whatever attributes it had previously have been totally overwritten.

Read carefully the captions of Figures 16 and 17 illustrating this operation. Several paragraphs in sequence can be applied a style at once simply by selecting more than one paragraph before you select the style.

Styles can also be applied through the *Style* command in the **Type** menu (Figure 18).

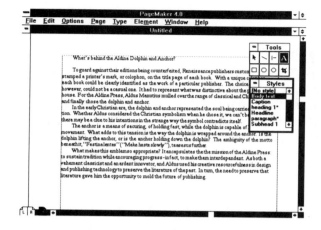

Figure 16. *To illustrate how you can apply styles to unformatted text, we have changed all the paragraphs of our STORY2 text file to look the same. We applied the* **Body text** *style to every-thing by simply selecting all text and clicking on* **Body text** *in the Style palette.*

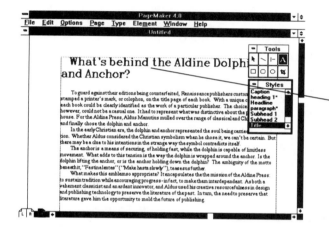

Figure 17. *To apply styles to single or multiple paragraphs of text, you insert the text cursor in the first paragraph (or whatever paragraph(s) you like), and click on the required style (in this case,* **Title**) *in the Style palette. The attributes defined in creating the* **Title** *style (Figure 14) are instantly applied to that paragraph.*

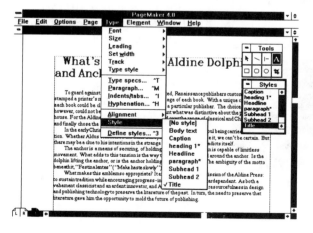

Figure 18. *Apart from clicking on the style name in the Style palette, styles can also be applied through the Style command in the* **Type** *menu. Simply insert the text cursor in the paragraph(s) concerned, choose the Style command, and then the style name of your choice.*

Editing styles

Let's say you have applied the style **Body text** to most of your publication and now decide that it must be changed. As we mentioned when looking at the benefits of style sheets, there is no need to find all the paragraphs that use the **Body text** style. Simply edit the **Body text** style itself and all paragraphs using this style will change. To perform this procedure, first of all change all text back to **Body text**, as shown in Figure 19, except for the first paragraph (**Heading**).

Select once again the *Define styles* command from the **Type** menu. From the list of styles presented (Figure 20), select the style you would like to edit (**Body text**) and choose the *Edit* command to the right of this box. You will then get the Figure 21 *Edit style* dialog box.

Alternatively, you can click on the name of the style you would like to edit in the *Style palette* with the Control key depressed to go immediately to Figure 21.

In either case, you will be presented with the dialog box of Figure 21 that was also used to create a new style. You can edit the style in exactly the same way you created a new style. When editing styles, the name comes up automatically in the *Name* rectangle at the top of the dialog box (in our case, **Body text**).

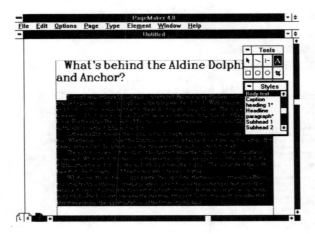

*Figure 19. Every paragraph in this document has been applied the **Body text** style (apart from the first paragraph). We now want to change the look of **Body text**, without having to select every paragraph before we do it. To work through this, first change back to **Body text** style, as we have done here, if you have been experimenting with other styles in the Style palette. Simply select the whole page (except for the first paragraph) with the text tool and click on **Body text** in the Style palette.*

Select the four commands one at a time from Figure 21 — *Type, Para, Tabs,* and *Hyphenation,* and edit the style as you see fit. Choose OK twice when you are happy with the newly-edited style.

See Figures 22 and 23 for some editing changes we have made to the **Body text** style.

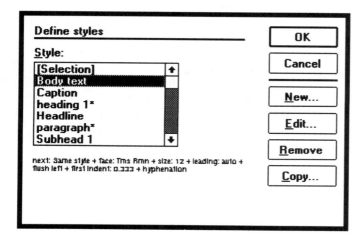

Figure 20. Your first step in editing **Body text** *is to select the* Define styles *command again. From the dialog box that appears, select* **Body text** *(or whatever style you would like to edit), and choose the* Edit *command.*

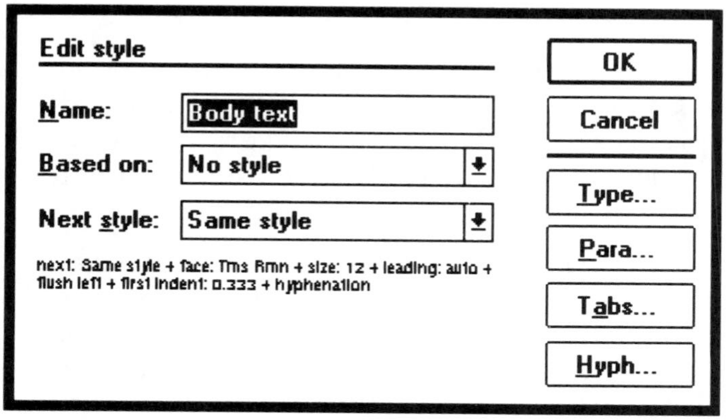

Figure 21. After selecting Edit *from Figure 20, this dialog box will appear. Note that the name* **Body text** *already appears next to* Name.

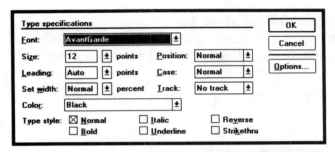

Figure 22. We chose the Type *command from Figure 21, and were presented with this dialog box. We changed the font from Times Roman (Tms Rmn) to Avant Garde.*

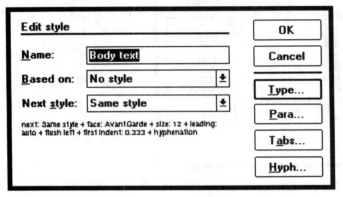

Figure 23. Note how the definition of **Body text** has changed to reflect the new attributes. Compare with Figure 20 — Avant Garde has replaced Times as the font.*

In Figures 20 through 23, we have only changed the type specifications to Avant Garde. *Para, Tabs,* and *Hyphenation* commands were not changed. The result is shown in Figure 24. All the paragraphs throughout the document that use the **Body text** style will be updated with its new characteristics.

One other option in the *Edit style* dialog box of Figure 21 is *Next style*. This allows you to set the style of the following paragraph. For example, a paragraph defined as **Heading** and a *Next style* as **Body text** — every time you start a new paragraph after a **Heading**, it will be **Body text** (Figure 25).

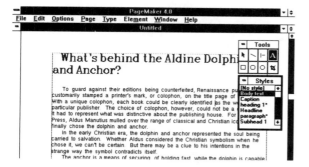

Figure 24. All paragraphs that use the **Body text** *style have changed, while all paragraphs that use other styles remain as they were. Compare this* **Body text** *style with that of Figure 16.*

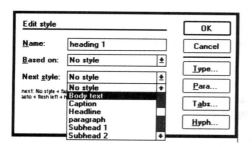

Figure 25. The Next style *option lets you establish what attributes a following paragraph will have. This is helpful when you want a certain style of paragraph to always follow a specific style.*

Removing styles

Removing a style is even easier than creating or editing a style. Choose *Define styles*, select the style you would like to remove, and choose the *Remove* command (Figures 26 through 28).

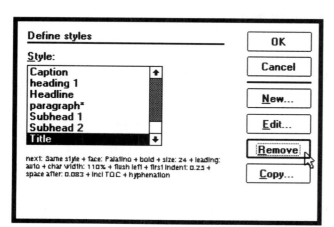

Figure 26. Removing a style is as simple as selecting it from within the Define styles *dialog box and clicking on* Remove.

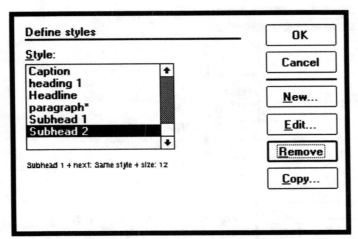

Figure 27. The style name is immediately dropped from the style sheet.

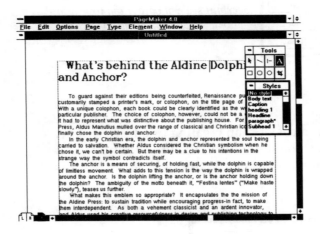

Figure 28. All paragraphs that use the style just deleted remain as they were, but they now use the style name No style.

Basing a new style's definition on one of the current publication's existing styles

Let's say that you have now created several styles in this style sheet, one of which may be a **Heading** style. What you want to do now is to create another **Heading** style, which is quite similar to the existing **Heading** style but with minor changes. Instead of creating the new style from scratch, it would be nice to start with the old **Heading** attributes and modify them to create the new style. This is quite straightforward.

We have a *Style* name in our style sheet called **Heading 1** (see Figure 29). We are now going to use it to produce a new style. You can follow on with us, if you wish, using any style name of your choice. The principle is the same.

When you choose the *Define styles* command from the **Type** menu, you would normally go straight to the *New* command to create the new **Heading** style. However, before you do this, click in the list of styles on the original **Heading** style before choosing *New* (Figure 29). Upon choosing this style first, the *Based on* box in the *Edit style* dialog box of Figure 30 will display the name of that style. Insert the name of the new style (in our case, **Heading 2**) and change what you have to. In this way, new styles can be created with a minimum of fuss (Figures 30 through 33).

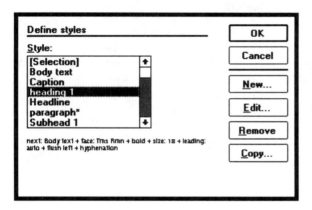

Figure 29. To create a style similar to another style, select that style in the Define styles *dialog box before selecting the* New *command.*

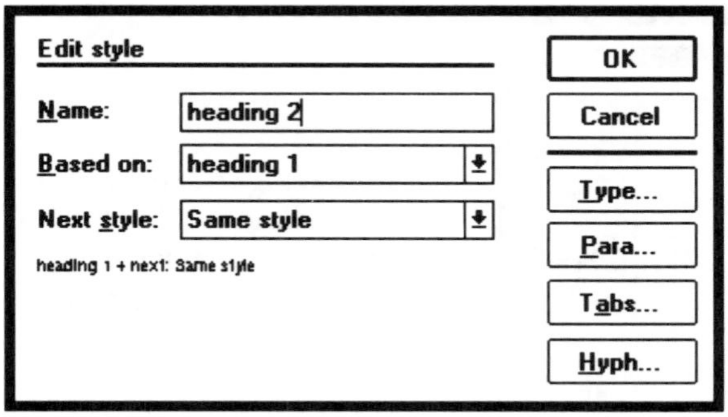

Figure 30. In the Edit style *dialog box that appears, a name will be listed in the* Based on *box. This will be the name of the style selected before choosing* New (*Heading 1*). *Enter the name of the new style above this name (*Heading 2*).*

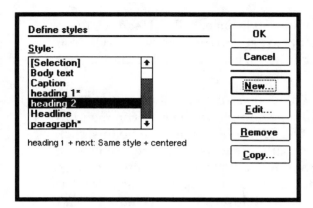

Figure 31. We used the Para *command from the dialog box in Figure 30 to alter the appearance of the new style. Note, however, that the description of the new style below the list tells us that* **Heading 2** *is exactly the same as* **Heading** *except that it is centered. Note that in Figure 29 one of the attributes of a* **Heading 1** *paragraph was that it was flush left.*

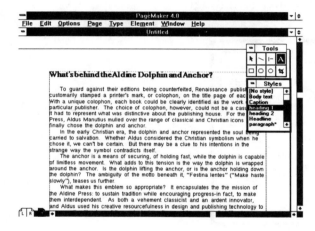

Figure 32. To see the difference between the styles of **Heading 1** *and* **Heading 2** *(note how* **Heading** 2 *has been added to the Style palette), we selected the first paragraph and tagged it with our original* **Heading 1** *style. Note how this paragraph is left justified. Now ensure the text cursor is still in this first paragraph. . .*

Figure 33. . . . and click on the style **Heading 2** *in the Style palette. The paragraph now looks basically the same as the* **Heading 1** *style, yet is centered.*

Renaming styles

The easiest way to rename a style is to create an identical one with the new name (using the method described above), and then remove the one with the old name. Effectively, you have renamed the style.

Copying an existing style sheet from another publication

Copying a style sheet from a separate publication or template into another document will combine the two style sheets together. Once again, to use this function, you must choose the *Define styles* command from the *Type* menu. This time, however, select the *Copy* command (Figure 34).

You must know which document you want to copy a style sheet from. When the *Copy* command is chosen, you are presented with a list of publications (you can move to other directories) from which you must select a publication or template (Figure 35). As you select the new document (Figure 36), PageMaker spends a few seconds combining the two style sheets together and you are returned to the new *Define styles* dialog box. It now contains a list of styles from both style sheets (Figure 37).

The *Style palette* will then also reflect the new list of styles that have been added (Figure 38).

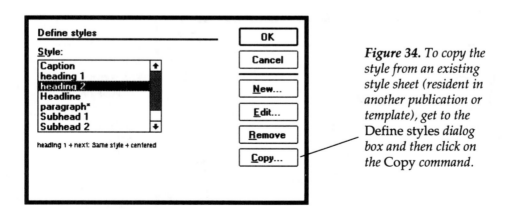

Figure 34. To copy the style from an existing style sheet (resident in another publication or template), get to the Define styles *dialog box and then click on the* Copy *command.*

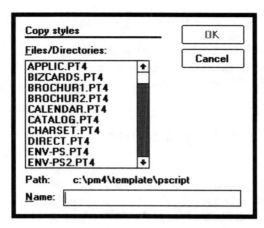

Figure 35. You will instantly be presented with the list of publications and templates in the currently open sub-directory. Locate the publication or template that you know has the other styles in it, and click OK.

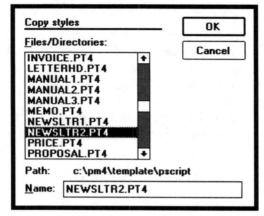

Figure 36. We are going to copy the styles from a file called NEWSLTR2 from the pscript sub-directory.

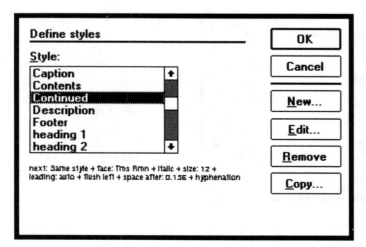

Figure 37. After a few seconds, the styles from NEWSLTR2 are combined with the styles already existing in this publication. Note the new styles listed in this dialog box, as compared to Figure 31.

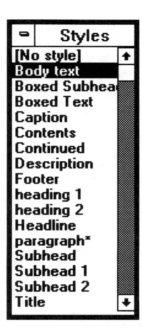

Figure 38. Here we have extended the Style palette *box from its bottom right-hand corner to show all the styles now contained in this style sheet. Compare this with Figure 31.*

In copying styles, you may get a message which asks if you wish to copy over existing styles. You have the option, at this point, of clicking on OK or Cancel.

Importing styles or style names with an imported word-processed document

This can be achieved in two different ways. First, if your word processor uses style sheets, they can be applied and created with all style names being carried through into PageMaker. If the style names already exist in PageMaker, then the imported paragraphs that use that style are applied the attributes of PageMaker's style. Don't forget to ensure that *Retain format* is checked in the *Place* dialog box (Figure 39).

If your word processing document does not support style sheets, it is still possible to have the imported text formatted to a pre-defined PageMaker style. All you need to do is type style name tags in angle brackets (<>) at the beginning of each paragraph, making sure that these tags match the style names in your publication's style sheet.

Figure 39, which shows the *Place* command dialog box, indicates the different options to choose from in deciding how to import text with styles intact. The *Retain format* option brings in all the style information intact from word processors that support style sheets. The *Read tags* option reads the tag names you have physically typed into your word-processed document using angle brackets.

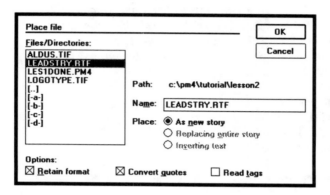

Figure 39. The Place *command dialog box. Note the* Retain format *and* Read tags *options at the bottom of the dialog box.*

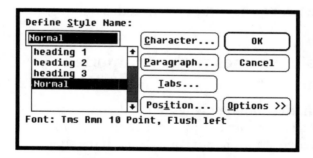

Figure 40. Styles are recognized from word processing packages such as Microsoft Word. Here we are looking at the dialog box for the Define Styles command within Microsoft Word.

Overriding styles

Any style can be overridden by selecting the text and applying any type specifications from the **Type** menu. If you apply a new style altogether to a paragraph that currently uses an overridden style, only type style changes (such as italic or bold) will survive the style change.

Changing styles from story editor view

To change a style from story editor view, you must first activate the *Style palette* from the **Window** menu so it appears on screen. Let's say, for example, you wanted to change the highlighted paragraph style of Figure 41 from **Paragraph** to **Caption**. You can either highlight a paragraph by dragging the text tool over the text, or by simply clicking on the paragraph style name in the left-hand column. Then go to the *Style palette* and select **Caption**. This paragraph will assume the new style and the new name will appear at the left (Figure 42).

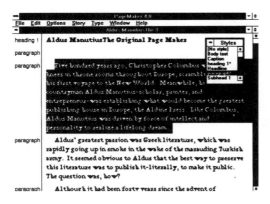

Figure 41. In story editor view, the paragraph styles appear in the left margin. The style of a selected paragraph will also be highlighted in the Style palette. *To change the style of a paragraph in story editor view, highlight the paragraph and select the new style from the* Style palette.

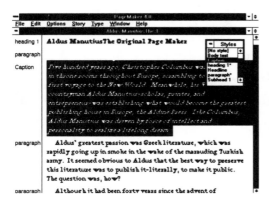

Figure 42. We have changed the style of the selected paragraph to **Caption**. *The new style name also appears in the left margin at the beginning of the paragraph.*

EXERCISE:
STYLE SHEETS

Style Sheets

In this exercise you will be working with style sheets and seeing how quickly you can format text using this method.

This training material is structured so that people of all levels of expertise with Page-Maker can use it to gain maximum benefit. In order to do this, we have structured the material so that the bare exercise is listed below this paragraph on just one page, with no hints. The following pages contain the steps needed to complete this exercise, for those who need additional prompting. The **Style Sheets** module should be referenced if you need further help or explanations.

Module 11 exercise steps

1. *Create a new document, using one Letter size vertical page with margins of your choice.*

2. *Create and/or modify three styles using these names and parameters:*

   (a) Body text
   10-point Helvetica
   Left justified
   Automatic leading
   0.1" paragraph spacing
   0.1" first line indent
   2" left indent

   (b) Heading
   24-point Times Bold
   Centered
   Automatic leading
   0.2" Before and After paragraph spacing

   (c) Introduction
   14-point Times Italic
   Centered
   15-point line spacing (Leading)
   .12" Before and After paragraph spacing

3. *Load the file LEADSTRY.RTF from the lesson2 sub-directory.*

4. *Apply the **Heading** style to the first paragraph of the text file, the style **Introduction** to the second paragraph, and make sure that the rest of the paragraphs in the text file use the style **Body text**.*

5. *Change the **Body text** style so that it uses the font Times Roman and is 12-point.*

The steps to completing this exercise are found on the following pages.

The steps in detail

1. Create a new document, using one Letter size vertical page with margins of your choice.

This is achieved by starting PageMaker and using the *New* command from the **File** menu. In the *New* dialog box, make sure that a Letter page is selected and that only one page is in the publication.

See Figures 1 and 2 for this first step.

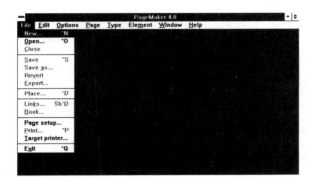

Figure 1. Select the New *command from the **File** menu to create a new publication.*

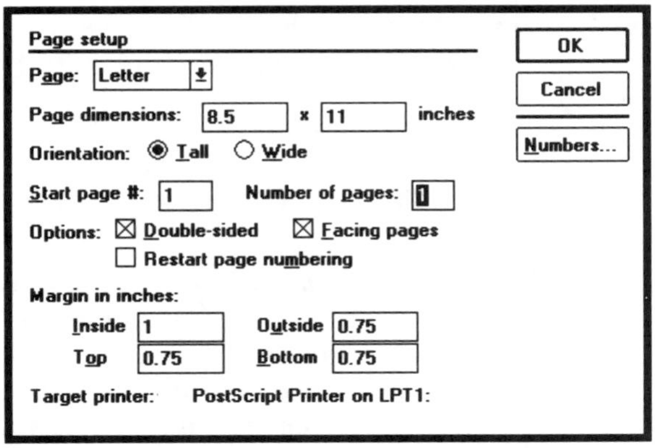

Figure 2. Set up a single vertical Letter page (the other settings do not matter for this exercise).

2. Create and/or modify three styles using these names and parameters:

(a) Body text
10-point Helvetica
Left justified
Automatic leading
0.1" paragraph spacing
0.1" first line indent
2" left indent

Body text is a style that will have to be modified rather than created, as it always exists by default in every publication. In order to modify its settings, first choose the *Define styles* command in the **Type** menu (Figure 3).

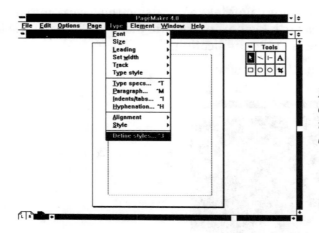

Figure 3. The Define styles *command from the* **Type** *menu is used to alter and create styles.*

In the dialog box that then appears (Figure 4), you must click on the line that reads **Body text**. When you do this, the bottom of this dialog box will list all the attributes currently assigned to **Body text** — these are the ones you will be changing. Some may be set up already — it depends on how **Body text** is currently set for your publication.

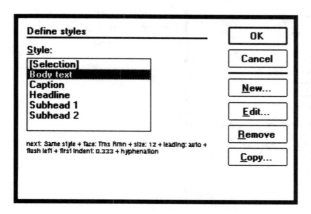

Figure 4. The Define styles *dialog box — note how we have clicked on* **Body text** *to select it. The current attributes for* **Body text** *are then shown in the bottom of this dialog box. Your settings may differ — it really doesn't matter at this moment.*

To alter the settings for **Body text**, you must click on the *Edit* command within the Figure 4 dialog box. Upon doing this, you will be presented with the additional dialog box of Figure 5.

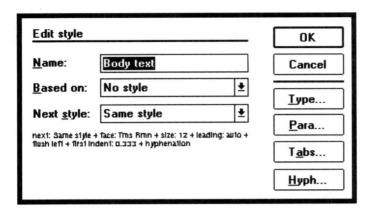

Figure 5. After clicking on the Edit *command in Figure 4, you will be presented with the* Edit style *dialog box.*

This *Edit style* dialog box will have the name of the style you are editing at the top of its dialog box against *Name* (in this case **Body text**), as well as the current attributes of this style at the bottom. To the right of this box are four commands — *Type, Para, Tabs,* and *Hyphenation.* Each one of these commands allows you to alter a different part of the style. The two commands you will use to change the style according to the step 2 (a) specifications for **Body text** are the *Type* and *Para* commands. Click first on the *Type* command.

Yet another dialog box will appear (Figure 6) — this one is concerned with the type specifications of the style Body text. Part of the specifications for step 2 require that you change Body text to 10-point Helvetica. Just change the *Font* and *Size* commands in the normal way, to that shown in Figure 7. Also check that *Leading* is set to *Auto.*

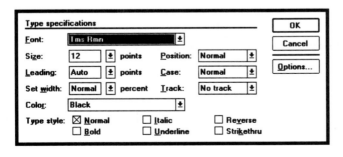

Figure 6. After selecting the Type *command from Figure 5, you will be presented with this dialog box, but don't worry if it contains different values from these. It depends on the defaults currently set for your copy of PageMaker.*

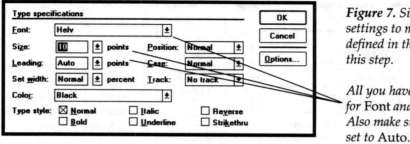

Figure 7. Simply change your settings to match these — as defined in the specifications for this step.

All you have to adjust is Helvetic for Font *and 10 points for* Size. *Also make sure that* Leading *is set to* Auto.

Click on OK when you have set the text attributes correctly in Figure 7 to return you to the Figure 8 *Edit style* dialog box.

You will notice back in the dialog box of Figure 8, that the settings for **Body text** have been altered. Compare Figure 8 with the earlier settings of Figure 5.

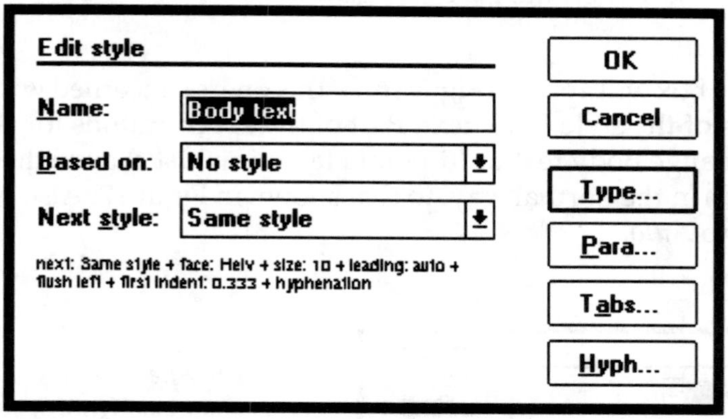

Figure 8. Read the attributes fo Body text now in this dialog bo: — they have altered to reflect th changes you just made. Compar with Figure 5.

You must now click on the *Para* command in the Figure 8 dialog box to adjust the other settings for **Body text**. Once again, you will be greeted with a new dialog box, this time that of Figure 9.

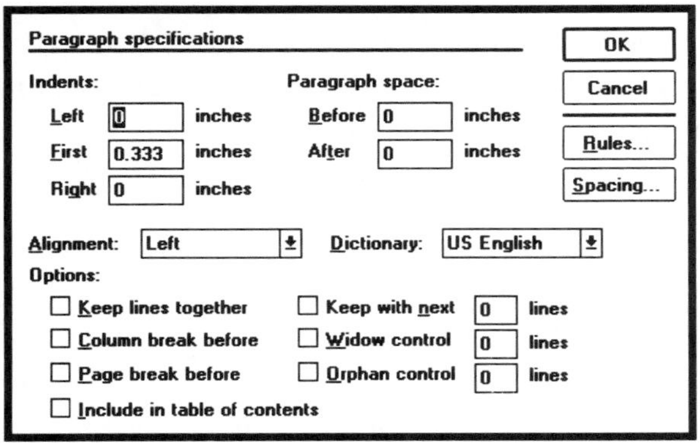

Figure 9. *The* Para *dialog box is identical to the* Paragraph *command in the* **Type** *menu —although this time it applies to a style rather than simply selected text.*

Here you must set 0.1" paragraph spacing, a 0.1" first line indent, a 2" global left indent, and left justify. If you find that you are working in millimeters, don't worry — or change to inches using the *Preferences* command from the **Edit** menu. Remember, you can still set measures in inches even if millimeters are selected (just put an "i" after your value).

To set the paragraph spacing, we have chosen to put 0.1" in the *After* rectangle (Figure 10). You could have put it in the *Before* rectangle if you wished. It is entirely up to you.

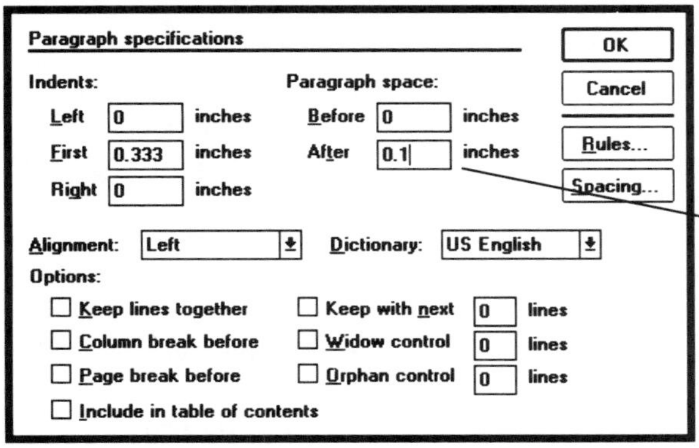

Figure 10. *Here we have inserted 0.1" of paragraph space in the* After *rectangle.*

The first line indent is set using the *First* rectangle. Insert 0.1" in this box also (Figure 11). To set a global left indent of 2", you must use the *Left* rectangle. Insert a 2 in this box (Figure 11).

Finally, make sure that the setting for *Alignment* is *Left* in order to achieve left justification (Figure 11).

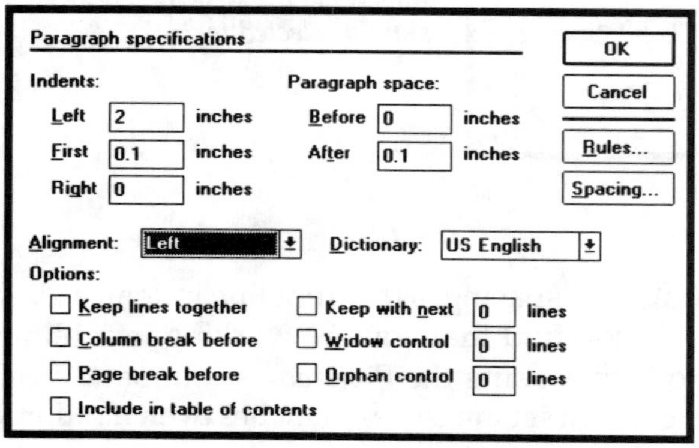

Paragraph specifications

Indents:	Paragraph space:	OK
Left 2 inches	Before 0 inches	Cancel
First 0.1 inches	After 0.1 inches	Rules...
Right 0 inches		Spacing...

Alignment: Left   Dictionary: US English

Options:
- ☐ Keep lines together   ☐ Keep with next 0 lines
- ☐ Column break before   ☐ Widow control 0 lines
- ☐ Page break before   ☐ Orphan control 0 lines
- ☐ Include in table of contents

Figure 11. In this dialog box, set a global left indent of 2" and a first line indent of 0.1".

Also select Left *as the preferred* Alignment.

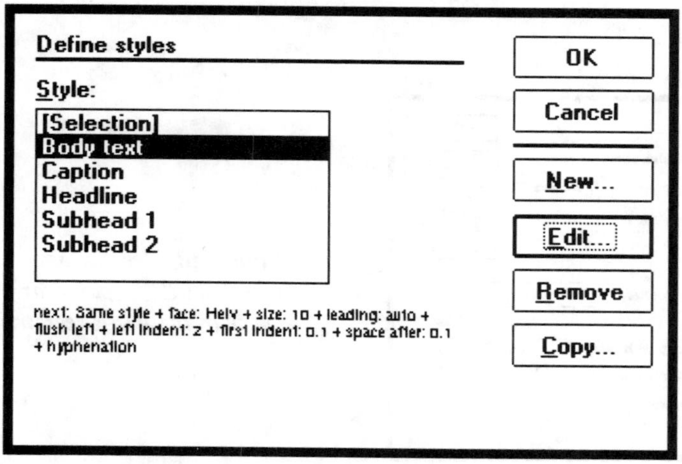

Define styles

Style:
- [Selection]
- **Body text**
- Caption
- Headline
- Subhead 1
- Subhead 2

next: Same style + face: Helv + size: 10 + leading: auto + flush left + left indent: 2 + first indent: 0.1 + space after: 0.1 + hyphenation

OK | Cancel | New... | Edit... | Remove | Copy...

Figure 12. After clicking OK in the dialog box of Figure 11, and then OK again in the Edit style *dialog box that appeared after doing that, you are returned to the original* Define styles *dialog box. Note all the new settings for* **Body text***.*

(b) Heading
24-point Times Bold
Centered
Automatic leading
0.2" Before and After para spacing

To create any new style, click on the *New* command from the *Define styles* dialog box of Figure 12. The *Edit style* dialog box will be presented yet again (Figure 13), although this time it will be slightly different. It initially has no name in the *Name* box. Notice that the *Based on:* box includes the name **Body text**. This is because we had **Body text** selected in the *Define styles* box before clicking on *New*. This doesn't matter since you can still base the new **Heading** style on any other style you like.

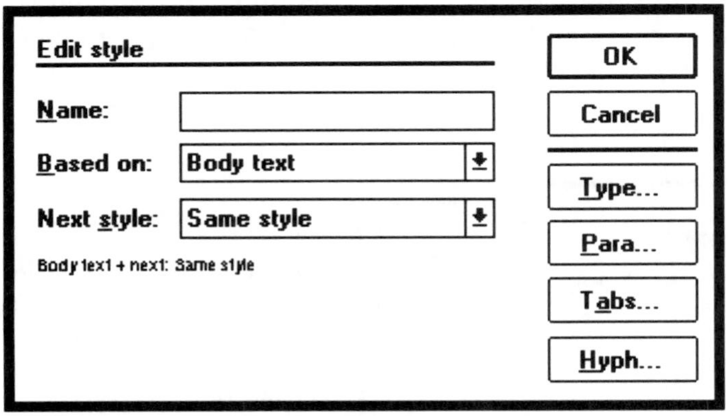

Figure 13. The New *dialog box is very similar to the* Edit style *dialog box — but this time you must insert a name for the new style (Figure 14).*

This time, in creating a new style, you must name the style before you create it. Simply type the name of the style — the mouse cursor is correctly positioned to receive the name, which in this case is **Heading** (Figure 14).

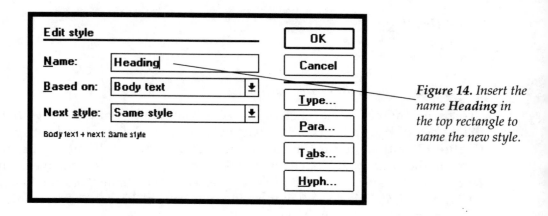

*Figure 14. Insert the name **Heading** in the top rectangle to name the new style.*

After naming the new style, it is once again a case of using the four commands in this dialog box to alter the settings for the **Heading** style; although once again the *Type* and *Para* commands are the main ones. Select *Type* first of all to get to Figure 15.

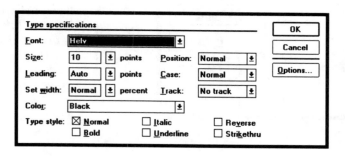

Figure 15. This is the dialog box you get after selecting the Type *command from Figure 14. This needs to be altered to that of Figure 16.*

Within this command you must make the *Size* 24 points, the *Font* Times, and the *Type style* Bold. You must also make sure the *Leading* is set at Automatic. Perform these steps as you would normally, as shown in Figure 16, then click OK. You will be returned to the Figure 14 dialog box. Click on the *Para* command to get to Figure 17.

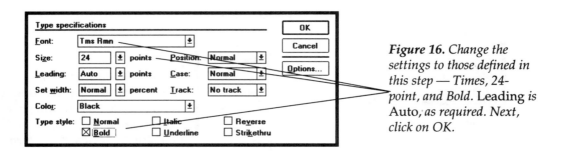

Figure 16. Change the settings to those defined in this step — Times, 24-point, and Bold. Leading is Auto, as required. Next, click on OK.

Use the Figure 17 dialog box to center the paragraph, and also to put 0.2" of space *Before* and *After* it (Figure 18). Click OK twice to return to the *Define styles* dialog box of Figure 19.

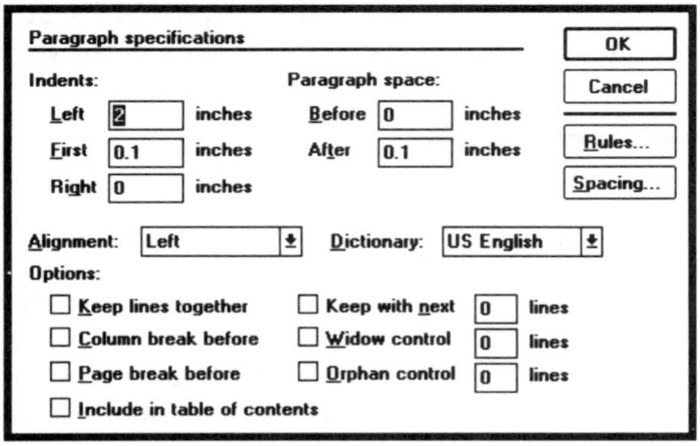

Figure 17. The dialog box for the Para *command may initially look like this. However, all you want for* **Heading** *is space* Before *and* After *— not left, first, or right. Note the modifications performed in Figure 18.*

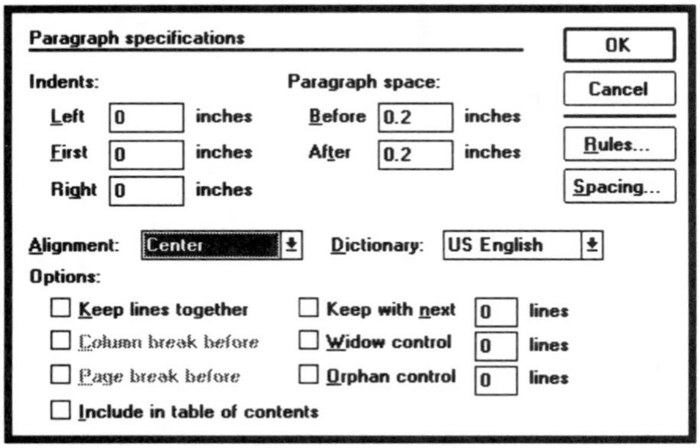

Figure 18. You must change to 0 all the Indents *rectangles on the left, and insert 0.2" of space in the* Before *and* After Spacing *rectangles. Also change the* Alignment *to Center.*

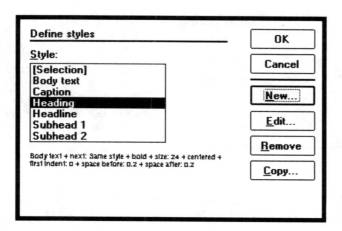

Figure 19. *After returning once again to the* Define styles *dialog box, you will find* **Heading** *has been added to the list of styles. If selected, its attributes will then be listed at the bottom of the dialog box as shown here.*

Within the Figure 19 dialog box, you will now find added to the list the **Heading** style you just created with its attributes at the bottom of the screen. Click on the name **Body text** in the list and the attributes will change again, as shown in Figure 20.

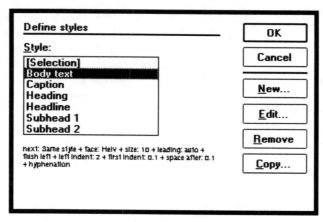

Figure 20. *When* **Body text** *is selected within this dialog box, its settings are immediately reflected beneath the list of styles.*

You must create one more style from within this dialog box.

(c) Introduction
14-point Times Italic
Centered
15-point line spacing (Leading)
.12" Before and After para spacing

Following the steps you used above for **Heading**, trying to create this style on your own.

3. Load the file LEADSTRY.RTF from the lesson2 sub-directory.

This file exists in the lesson2 sub-directory, within the tutorial sub-directory, and is loaded via the *Place* command in the **File** Menu and (Figure 21).

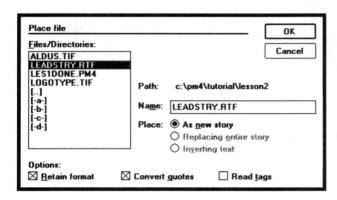

Figure 21. Select and load in the file LEADSTRY.RTF

Once a file is loaded, flow it onto the first page as indicated in Figure 22 (this should only have one column in it).

Figure 22. LEADSTRY.RTF loaded onto the page.

*4. Apply the **Heading** style to the first paragraph of the text file, the style **Introduction** to the second paragraph, and make sure that the rest of the paragraphs in the text file use the style **Body text**.*

After the text has been loaded onto the page, applying styles is simple. You must, however, first make sure that the *Style palette* is visible — through the *Style palette* command in the **Window** menu (Figures 23 and 24).

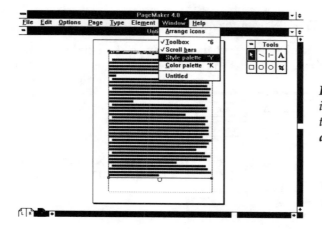

Figure 23. *The* Style palette *is accessed via the command of the same name in the* **Window** *menu.*

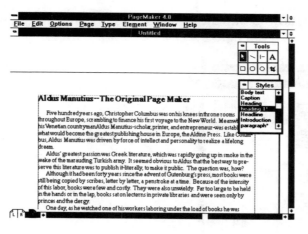

Figure 24. *The* Style palette *is now visible complete with default styles, the styles you created, and any styles that may have been carried through from the word processor that created the text.*

You have been asked to apply the style **Heading** to the first paragraph in the text file. This is achieved by simply inserting the text cursor (make sure this is selected in the Toolbox) somewhere in this first paragraph. The whole paragraph need not be selected. From here, move to the *Style palette* and click on the style **Heading** (Figures 25 and 26). All the attributes you gave to **Heading** will be instantly applied to this paragraph.

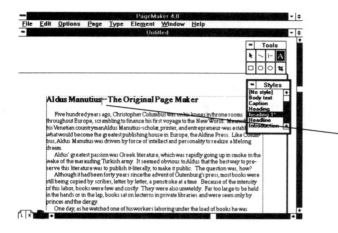

Figure 25. Insert the cursor in, or select, the paragraph where you would like to apply a new style. . .

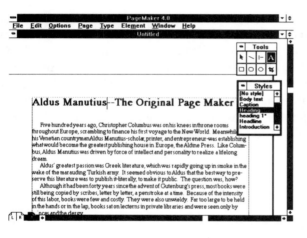

Figure 26. . . . and click on the name of the style (**Heading**, in this case) in the Style palette. *This paragraph now takes on all the text attributes of the chosen style.*

To apply the style **Introduction** to the second paragraph, the steps are exactly the same — insert the text cursor in this paragraph, and click on the style **Introduction** in the *Style palette*. Once again, everything that was set up for **Introduction** is applied to the paragraph with the text cursor in it.

Figure 27 illustrates the result.

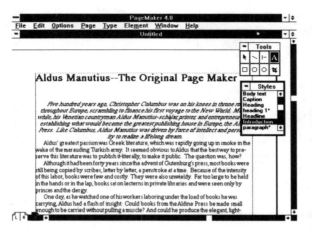

Figure 27. Insert the text cursor in the second paragraph on the page and click on the style Introduction. Immediately, the text will be altered to reflect this new style (italic, centered, etc.).

Finally, to make sure that all other paragraphs are using the style **Body text**, select the rest of the page using the text editing tool and click on the style **Body text** in the *Style palette* (Figure 28). All the text will change to **Body text** if it was not already using it. For example, note the 2" left indent in Figure 29 which was part of the **Body text** definition. Don't worry about the extra styles that may have entered the *Style palette* — these are merely carried through from the word processor. You do not need to use them.

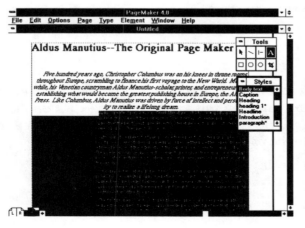

Figure 28. All other paragraphs were selected and applied the style Body text in one operation. Remember, when applying a style to more than one paragraph, to select these paragraphs in the normal fashion before clicking on the style in the Style palette.

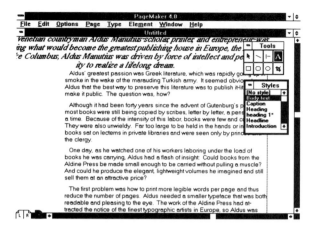

Figure 29. Here you see in Actual size *view the look of* **Body text** *at 10-point Helvetica. You will now change all* **Body text** *to 12-point Times by making one simple change.*

5. Change the **Body text** *style so that it uses the font Times Roman and is 12-point.*

The style **Body text** can be altered without having to select any text. Merely move to the *Define styles* command in the **Type** menu and select **Body text** from the list (Figures 30 and 31).

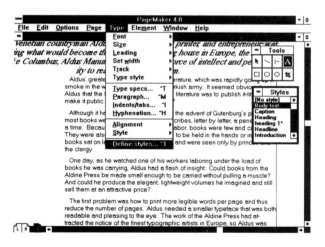

Figure 30. Move to the Define styles *command in the* **Type** *menu to change the attributes of the* **Body text** *style.*

From the *Define styles* dialog box of Figure 31, choose the *Edit* command (Figure 31), and from within the *Edit* style dialog box, choose the *Type* command (Figure 32).

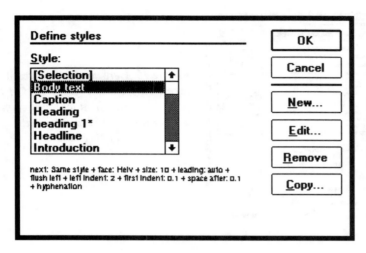

Figure 31. *From the* Define styles *dialog box, select the style* **Body text** *and choose the* Edit *command.*

Figure 32. *Once in the* Edit style *dialog box, choose the* Type *command. Note that the name* **Body text** *is already included since it was selected in Figure 31. Now move to Figure 33.*

From within the *Type* dialog box of Figure 33, alter **Body text** to use the *Font* Times at 12 points *Size*. Once you return to the page from here, all paragraphs using the style **Body text** will have been altered and will display the new attributes you just set (Figures 34 and 35).

Compare Figure 35 to that of Figure 29.

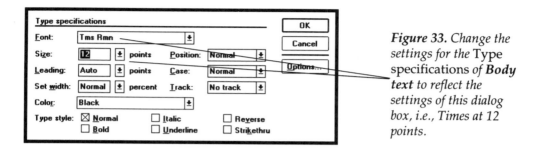

Type specifications

Font:	Tms Rmn				OK
Size:	12	points	Position:	Normal	Cancel
Leading:	Auto	points	Case:	Normal	Options...
Set width:	Normal	percent	Track:	No track	
Color:	Black				

Type style: ☒ Normal ☐ Italic ☐ Reverse
☐ Bold ☐ Underline ☐ Strikethru

*Figure 33. Change the settings for the Type specifications of **Body text** to reflect the settings of this dialog box, i.e., Times at 12 points.*

Define styles

OK

Style:

[Selection]
Body text
Caption
Heading
heading 1*
Headline
Introduction

Cancel

New...

Edit...

Remove

Copy...

next: Same style + face: Tms Rmn + size: 12 + leading: auto + flush left + left indent: 2 + first indent: 0.1 + space after: 0.1 + hyphenation

*Figure 34. When you return to the Define styles dialog box, the attributes for **Body text** listed along the bottom of this box have changed to reflect the new settings.*

PageMaker 4.0

File Edit Options Page Type Element Window Help

Untitled

Venetian countryman Aldus Manutius-scholar, printer, and entrepreneur-was
ing what would become the greatest publishing house in Europe, the
e Columbus, Aldus Manutius was driven by force of intellect and pe
ity to realize a lifelong dream.

Aldus' greatest passion was Greek literature, which was rapidly
going up in smoke in the wake of the marauding Turkish army
seemed obvious to Aldus that the best way to preserve this liter
was to publish it-literally, to make it public. The question was,

Although it had been forty years since the advent of Gutenbu
press, most books were still being copied by scribes, letter by l
penstroke at a time. Because of the intensity of this labor, bool
few and costly. They were also unwieldy. Far too large to be held in
the hands or in the lap, books sat on lecterns in private libraries and
were seen only by princes and the clergy.

One day, as he watched one of his workers laboring under the load of
books he was carrying, Aldus had a flash of insight: Could books
from the Aldine Press be made small enough to be carried without
pulling a muscle? And could he produce the elegant, lightweight
volumes he imagined and still sell them at an attractive price?

The first problem was how to print more legible words per page and

Tools

Styles
[No style]
Body text
Caption
Heading
heading 1*
Headline
Introduction

*Figure 35. Back on the page, all **Body text** paragraphs have been altered to reflect the new settings for **Body text**. Compare to Figure 29.*

SETTING
DEFAULTS

Setting Defaults

It is useful, at times, to be able to utilize certain preset options within PageMaker, without having to readjust them each time PageMaker is opened or used to create new publications. Of course, you could set up a template to do this (one that uses all the settings you want to), but there are times when you just don't need to use a template.

So far we have looked at many options that can be invoked from within PageMaker, such as *rulers, Column guides,* and *Style palette.* Suppose, however, that for all your publications you wanted the *Style* and *Color palettes, Rulers,* four columns, and a Letter page with pre-defined margins all around (Figure 1). Setting this up each time you opened PageMaker would not be very productive.

Application defaults

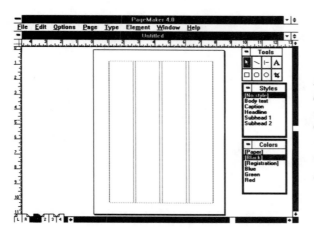

Figure 1. If all of your documents start off like this (Rulers, Style palette, Color palette, *four columns, Letter page size), it would take a fair amount of setting up each time.*

PageMaker is normally shipped with pre-defined options for many of its settings. These are referred to as the default settings and may differ for the US and International versions. The settings for all standard defaults are listed in the Appendix of the Page-Maker Reference Manual.

What you might like to do sometimes, for ease of operation, is to change these defaults to those of your own choosing. This can be done in two ways — through what are called Application defaults or Publication defaults.

To customize the use of PageMaker with Application defaults, you must have no publications open. This will involve either using the *Close* command to get rid of the current document, or simply restarting PageMaker.

You may have noticed that even with no publication open, all the menus appear at the top of the screen and can be invoked (Figures 2 and 3). Further, many of the commands within these menus can be selected.

The long and short of it is that most commands that can be selected while no publication is open can be set up as defaults. For example, you could select the *Rulers* command and, although no rulers would show, you would see that the option has a check alongside it. This indicates that its default status is on (Figure 3). If you prefer that the rulers do not come up automatically in any of your publications, select this command again to uncheck it. Now, whenever a new publication is opened, the rulers will not be displayed. In this way, you can set up defaults in the following areas:

Type Size, Face, Leading, Style, *and other commands in the* **Type** *menu;*

Page size, margins, and number of pages;

Rulers *and other commands in the* **Options** *menu, including text flow method;*

All guide commands;

Line *and* Fill;

Preferences;

Palettes;

Colors; and so on.

Remember that any of these commands, if altered while no publication is opened, will become the new default. Any time a new publication is opened, it will use these settings. These defaults can be changed, if desired, for a single publication. This method is described below.

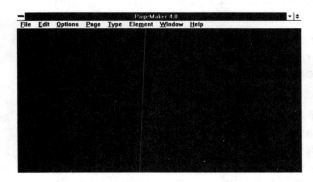

Figure 2. PageMaker opened with all publications closed will look exactly like this.

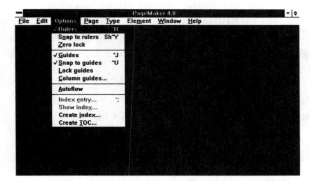

Figure 3. All menus and many commands can be used even though no publication has been opened.

Publication defaults

Publication defaults differ from Application defaults in that Publication defaults are set up inside a publication and are only defaults for that particular document. For instance, you may decide that in one publication you wish to draw lines of 8-point thickness. Before you draw any lines, you would move to the *Line* command in the **Element** menu, and select an 8-point thickness line (Figure 4). Any line now drawn within this publication will automatically be of 8-point thickness (Figure 5).

To create these Publication defaults, it is important that the pointer tool be chosen and no text or graphics be selected.

As another example, if you want the *Style palette* to always appear on screen for a particular publication, turn it on in the **Window** menu and it will appear on screen every time this publication is opened.

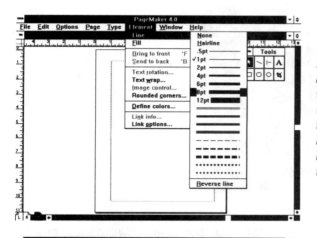

Figure 4. Publication defaults are set up within a publication. In this case, because a line is not selected as we set a line thickness, all future lines will be of 8-point thickness.

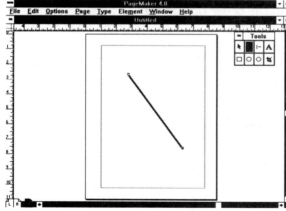

Figure 5. Any line drawn now is of 8-point thickness.

More default settings

Most likely, you will not set up defaults for every single Page-Maker option or command, but only for the most frequently used functions. We will go through some of the more common ones and show you how to set up or change the defaults to suit your needs.

Open PageMaker 4, or if you are already in it, close your current document. For the rest of this module we will be setting Publication defaults, which will only apply to the current document.

First, select *New* from the **File** menu.

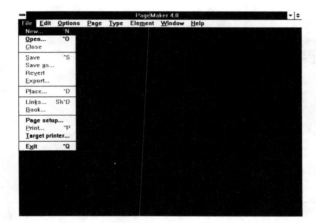

Figure 6. *Choose* New *to start up a completely new PageMaker document.*

You will now be confronted with the *Page Setup* dialog box (Figure 7). Here, stay with the *Letter* option for the page size, and keep this document in portrait format (select *Tall* for *Page orientation*). Next give yourself five pages. Both *Double-sided* and *Facing pages* should be set already by default, so leave them as they are. Lastly, give your page a 1" margin around the whole page.

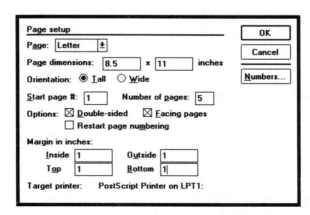

Figure 7. *These are the defaults to be set in the* Page setup *dialog box, as discussed above.*

After clicking on OK, your document will open to the specified defaults. Now that you have your document opened, you can set up some more defaults before doing anything. First, select the *Column guides* command under the **Options** menu (Figure 8).

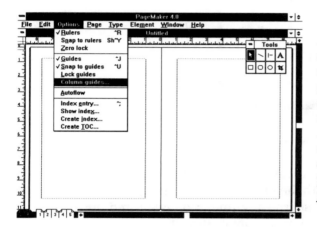

Figure 8. To set up your columns for this publication, go to the Column guides *command under the* **Options** *menu. Note that we are on the master L and R pages to set the column guides. This ensures all pages of your publication will have four columns.*

Here, give yourself four columns and leave the 0.167" spacing (Figure 9). Click on OK, and now the page will have four columns.

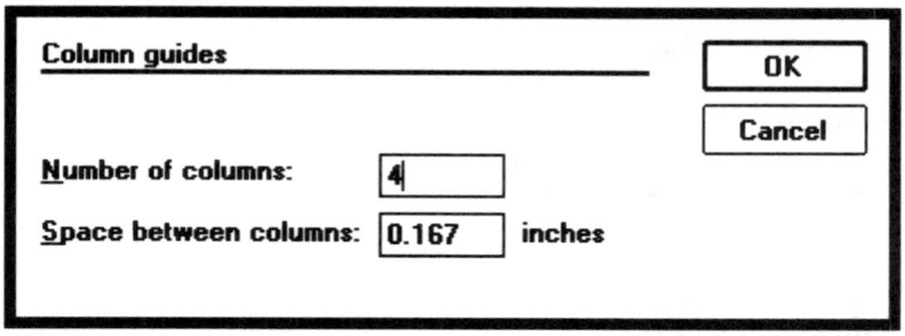

Figure 9. The Column guides *dialog box. Give your document four columns here.*

Now, select the *Paragraph* command in the **Type** menu (as in Figure 10).

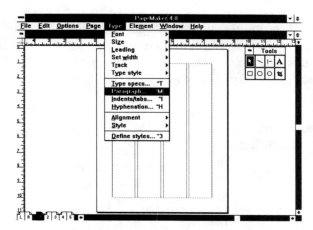

Figure 10. *The next step is to set the defaults in the* Paragraph specifications *dialog box with the pointer tool selected.*

In the *Paragraph* specifications dialog box (Figure 11), set a first line indent of 0.25" with the same amount of space before and after each paragraph. Also set the alignment to *Justify* and put *Widow* and *Orphan control* on a minimum of three lines.

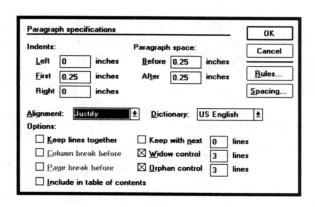

Figure 11. *The new default settings for the* Paragraph specifications *dialog box.*

Under the **Edit** menu is the *Preferences* command. In this dialog box (Figure 12), change the *Measurement system* to millimeters and the *Vertical ruler* to millimeters. There are other options here to change, but keep them at their original default values. After clicking on OK, you will notice the measurement units of the rulers change from inches to millimeters.

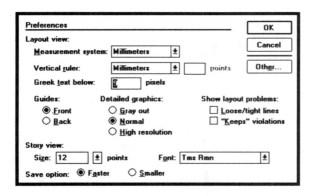

Figure 12. *The* Measurement system *in this dialog box is the one that controls all measurements in PageMaker. Choose millimeters for general measurements as well as for the* Vertical ruler.

Quickly looking under the **Options** menu (Figure 13), you can see there are a few more choices here that can be altered for this publication. There's the *Rulers* command, which gives you the choice of having your rulers on or off, and the *Snap to rulers, Guides, Snap to guides* and *Lock guides* commands, that you can also have on or off in your document. The choice is up to you.

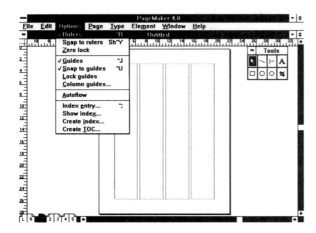

Figure 13. *The* **Options** *menu has a number of choices that you can set at the beginning of your document so that they stay in use the whole time. Another choice here is the* Autoflow *command that can be set so that text automatically flows onto your page.*

Under the **Type** menu (Figure 14), go into the *Type specifications* dialog box and set up defaults for the text.

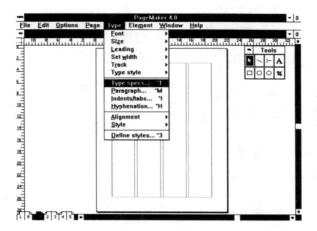

Figure 14. The Type specifications *dialog box is accessed through* the **Type** *menu.*

In Figure 15's *Type specifications* dialog box, change the *Font* to Palatino, with 11 as the new point size. Then change the *Leading* to 13, which works well with 11 point text. The only other change to make here is the *Type style* to *Italic*.

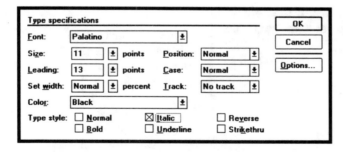

Figure 15. The Type specs *dialog box showing the new defaults.*

The finished result of all these default changes can't really be observed until you start putting text onto the page.

Figure 16. *This figure shows some of the defaults we have set. For example, Palatino 11-point italic text, justified, on a four column page, with a 0.25" first line indent.*

The defaults you set for *Type* and *Paragraph*, as shown in Figure 16, all worked correctly. If you now saved this as a new publication and re-opened it, you would find that all the new defaults set in this module would still apply. Try it if you wish. If all your future documents were to be the same, or very similar to this document, you could have set all these defaults as Application defaults before the document had been opened.

Many more defaults can be set in PageMaker. For a comprehensive list of all US and International defaults see the Appendix of your PageMaker Reference Manual. The procedure for setting all other defaults, whether they be Application or Publication defaults, is as simple as selecting them and adjusting them to meet your own requirements.

EXERCISE: SETTING DEFAULTS

Setting Defaults

In this exercise you are going to set different defaults, both Application and Publication, to see how easy this is to do within PageMaker.

This training material is structured so that people of all levels of expertise with Page-Maker can use it to gain maximum benefit. In order to do this, we have structured the material so that the bare exercise is listed below this paragraph on just one page, with no hints. The following pages contain the steps needed to complete this exercise, for those who need additional prompting. The **Setting Defaults** module should be referenced if you need further help or explanations.

Module 12 exercise steps

1. *Set the Application defaults for PageMaker as follows:*
    Letter size page
    Two columns
    20 mm (0.8") margins top, bottom, left, and right
    Style *and* **Color palettes** *showing*

2. *Start a new publication to see if the new defaults have worked.*

3. *Once you have started the new publication, set new Publication defaults as follows:*
    Lines at 2-point thickness
    Shades at 10% black
    Text of 14-point Helvetica, bold, justified

4. *Test both graphics and text to determine if you were successful.*

The steps to completing this exercise are found on the following pages.

The steps in detail

1. Set the Application defaults for PageMaker as follows:
Letter size page
Two columns
20 mm (0.8") margins top, bottom, left, and right
Style *and* **Color palettes** *showing.*

Application defaults are the defaults that are set when no publication is open. These will apply to all publications that are created subsequently. So, to set these defaults, make sure that only PageMaker (and not a publication or template) is open. By double-clicking on the PageMaker 4 option at the Windows Program Manager or from DOS, you will activate the screen shown in Figure 1.

If you are in an existing PageMaker publication, even if it's a blank page, you must choose *Close* from the **File** menu (not *Exit*). Your screen will then look like Figure 1, as well.

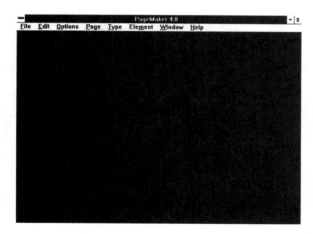

Figure 1. PageMaker without a publication open will look like this.

To set the page size and margin defaults, you must choose the *Page setup* command in the **File** menu, as shown in Figure 2 (remember — do not open or create a new publication). In the dialog box that appears (Figure 3), set up Letter page size and change all four margins to 20 mm (0.8").

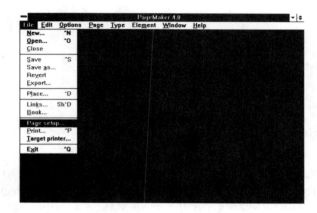

Figure 2. Select the Page setup *command in the* **File** *menu.*

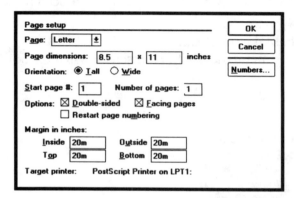

Figure 3. Change the page size to Letter *(it may already be there), and change all margins to 20 mm (0.8"). Click on OK. In this dialog box, you could just enter 0.8, as the* Margin *dimensions are already in inches. We have chosen to enter the metric equivalent and needed to include the "m" after the 20. (If we did not include the "m" the margin would be 20".)*

The columns default figure must be set using the *Column guides* command in the **Options** menu (Figure 4). Set the number to 2 in the ensuing dialog box (Figure 5).

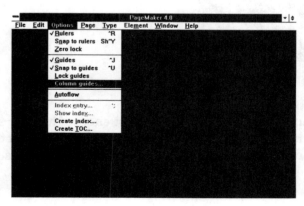

Figure 4. Select the Column guides *command from the* **Options** *menu to get the Figure 5 dialog box.*

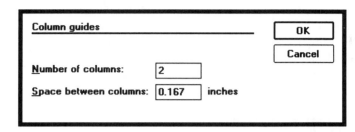

Figure 5. In the Column guides *dialog box, insert 2 for the number of columns. Once again, this number of columns will become the default.*

Finally, to make sure that the *Style* and *Color palettes* are showing, select these options from the **Window** menu (Figures 6 and 7). Although once again you will not see anything happen, you know these palettes will show if the options are checked in this menu.

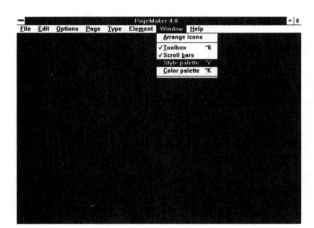

Figure 6. Select the Style palette *command from the* **Window** *menu.*

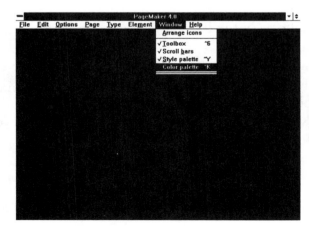

Figure 7. Also select the Color palette *command from the same menu.*

2. Start a new publication to see if the new defaults have worked.

Select *New* from the **File** menu — all the options you set in step 1 should be visible on the page. See Figure 8 for what to expect. The *Page setup* dialog box will also have appeared before the Figure 8 screen, allowing you to check that margins were 20 mm (or 0.8"), and the page was of Letter size.

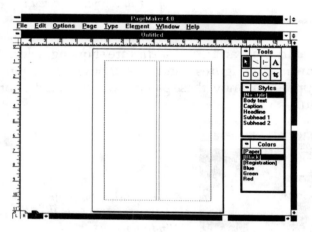

Figure 8. Your PageMaker publication, opened using the New *command from the* **File** *menu, now shows the options displayed in this figure — including both palettes and two columns.*

3. Once you have started the new publication, set new Publication defaults as follows:
   Lines at 2-point thickness
   Shades at 10% black
   Text of 14-point Helvetica, bold, justified

Publication defaults are set when a publication is opened. These defaults will not affect any other publications, but will affect the future operation of this publication.

To set the line thickness default, make sure that the pointer tool is highlighted and there are no selected lines on the page. To make sure, do not draw any lines or select the line drawing tool. Move to the *Line* sub-menu in the **Element** menu and select the 2-point thick line (Figure 9). As with Application defaults, you will not see anything happen immediately.

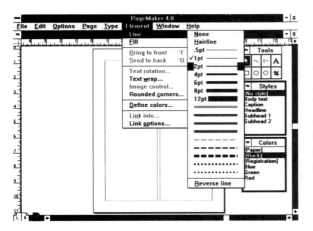

Figure 9. *Select the* 2 *pt option in the* Line *sub-menu to ensure that the default for all lines drawn in this publication is 2 points. Make sure before you do this that NO lines are selected on the page, because if they are, only these lines will be affected by this command.*

The same procedure is followed to set the graphic fill pattern — make sure your pointer tool is selected and there are no selected graphics on the page; then move to the *Fill* sub-menu under the **Element** menu. Within this menu, select 10% as the fill pattern (Figure 10).

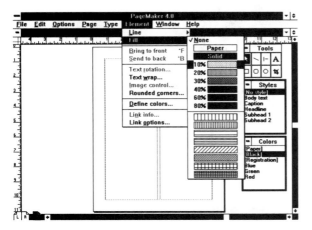

Figure 10. *Select the* 10% *command from the* Fill *sub-menu to set this graphic default.*

The text default setting also works in a similar way. Make sure the pointer tool is selected, move to the **Type** menu, and select the *Font* command. From the associated sub-menu, select Helvetica (Figure 11).

Figure 11. Set the Font default to Helvetica.

Next, select the *Size* command from the **Type** menu and choose 14-point (Figure 12).

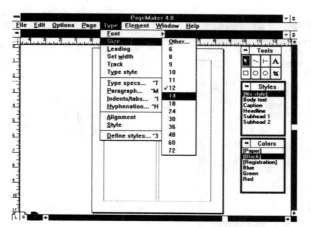

Figure 12. Set the size default to 14-point.

The next step is to select the *Type style* command and choose *Bold* from the sub-menu (Figure 13).

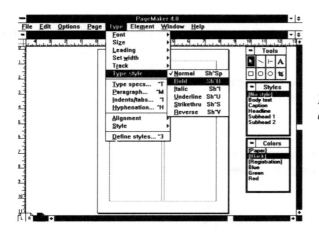

Figure 13. *The type style default is set to* Bold.

Finally, select *Justify* from the *Alignment* command towards the bottom of the **Type** menu. All of the settings we have just modified, except for *Alignment*, could have been selected at one time through the *Type specs* command and its associated dialog box.

4. Test both graphics and text to determine if you were successful.

To test whether the Publication defaults you set were successful, the first step is to draw a rectangle on the page. It should look like it has a 2-point outline and a 10% shade. Go to *Actual size* view and compare your graphic to Figure 14. Test both line thickness and fill shade settings through the *Line* and *Fill* sub-menus.

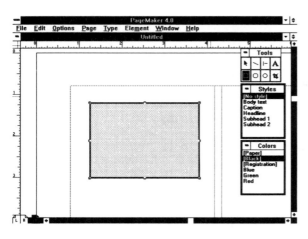

Figure 14. *Select the rectangle tool and draw a rectangle on the page to test the default settings. Go to the* Line *and* Fill *sub-menus to check that 2-point thickness and 10% fill actually apply to this box.*
Unless you have made an error in step 3 (Figures 9 and 10), this will be the case.

To test the type specification defaults, we must type some text onto the screen. Make sure you are in a view that allows you to read the text, select the text tool, click on the page, and tap on the keyboard. Although you may not immediately be able to tell how the text is set up (Figure 15), select the text and move through the **Type** menu to see exactly what its attributes are.

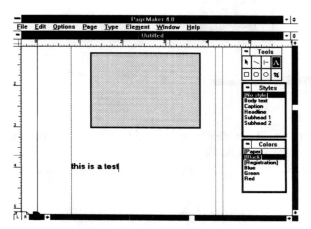

Figure 15. Now select the text tool and type some text on the page. Once again, it appears as though the default settings you created have worked. However, to make sure, select the text and check its attributes through the **Type** *menu.*

COLOR

Color

PageMaker 4 supports color operation on both screen and output devices. Lower-cost laser printers are becoming available for use with color, and there are many ongoing developments in this area. A color publication may be printed directly on a color laser printer, or sent to a commercial printer for spot or process color printing.

To see PageMaker in color, you need a PC with the appropriate color monitor and Windows drivers. With the right equipment, a PC monitor can display up to 16 million colors, with 256 showing at any one time. All the features of PageMaker involving color can also be run on monochrome monitors, although, obviously, it becomes a little more difficult to follow, define, and apply colors when working in monochrome.

Color can be set using the PC control panel, where menus, commands, and background shades are set for all applications, regardless of whether or not the individual publications themselves support color.

On a monochrome monitor, the PageMaker page appears as a black outline, with a dotted line representing the margin inside that page. On a color monitor, all guides appear as solid colors, making them easy to see and identify as printing or non-printing guides.

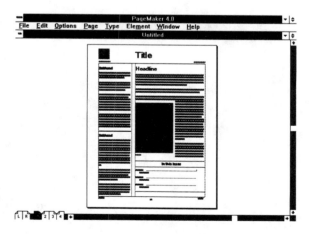

Figure 1. PageMaker still works with color on monochrome monitors. This colored page, with the appropriate printer, will print in full color.

Using color

Two commands, *Define colors* from the **Element** menu and the *Color palette* from the **Window** menu, need to be invoked to see how color works within PageMaker. First, invoke the *Color palette* command as shown in Figure 2.

The *Color palette* which appears (Figure 3) looks very similar to the *Style palette*, and in fact works in a similar way. Colors, which are defined much as styles are, can be applied to any selected portion of the page simply by clicking on the color you want from the palette. This process is virtually identical to that of applying styles as discussed in Module 11.

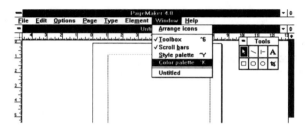

Figure 2. *Choosing the* Color palette *command in the* **Window** *menu will make visible the* Color palette *as shown in Figure 3 (assuming that it is not already visible).*

Numerous colors are pre-defined within the *Color palette* (Figure 3) by default. These include *Paper, Black,* and *Registration.* We will look quickly at what each of these is before we start creating and applying other colors. Your palette will also include Red, Blue, and Green.

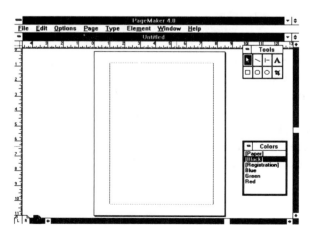

Figure 3. *The* Color palette *looks very similar to the* Style palette *used by Page-Maker. Your* Color palette *will include, by default, all colors shown here.*

Paper, Black, and Registration

Paper is set to white by default — you can change it, however, to any color you wish.

Black is the tone black and cannot be altered. It is more or less the normal color — the color you apply to an element on the page in the absence of any other color. Black initially applies to all text.

Registration is not really a color — but it can be applied to any element of the page. It is used when spot color overlays are to be created directly from PageMaker. Normally, for color overlays, every new color is printed on a page by itself. Any page element that uses the color Registration, however, will be printed on every page in the document.

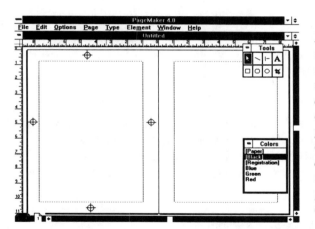

Figure 4. The color Registration is applied to Registration marks placed on the master pages of your document. Registration-colored markers help a printer align spot color overlays much more accurately. These Registration markers print on every page when using color overlays.

Registration marks are added manually to a publication when that publication occupies an entire page. You produce them on any blank area on the master pages (Figure 4) and they will then be replicated throughout the document. The color Registration is then assigned to these marks, allowing them to print on every page irrespective of the overlay's color. Registration marks are created so that the page can be aligned perfectly when color printing is being done.

If your publication's page is smaller than the printed page, PageMaker can then automatically add the Registration marks. This is done by checking *Spot color overlays* and *Crop marks* in the *Print* dialog box.

Other default colors

Red, Blue, and Green are the other default colors that will be defined and included in your *Color palette*.

Creating new colors

To create a new color, you must select the *Define colors* command in the **Element** menu (Figure 5). The dialog box of Figure 6 then appears.

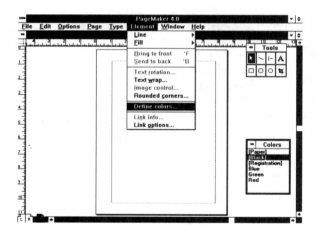

Figure 5. The Define colors *command is used to create your own colors. It causes the dialog box of Figure 6 to appear.*

As you can see, the process of creating new colors is almost identical to creating new styles — up to this point at least. Select *New* in the dialog box of Figure 6 to define a new color.

After selecting *New*, you will be presented with the additional dialog box of Figure 7.

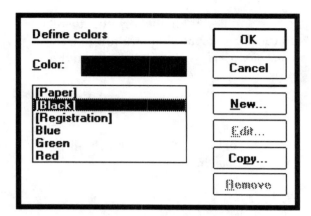

Define colors

Color: ████████████

[Paper]
[Black]
[Registration]
Blue
Green
Red

OK
Cancel
New...
Edit...
Copy...
Remove

Figure 6. The Define colors *dialog box looks like this — much like the* Define styles *dialog box.*

Edit color

Name:

Model: ○ **RGB**   ○ **HLS**   ● **CMYK**

Cyan: `100` %
Magenta: `100` %
Yellow: `100` %
Black: `0`   %

OK
Cancel
PANTONE®...

Figure 7. After selecting New *from the dialog box in Figure 6, this additional dialog box appears.*

Figure 8. Enter a name for your color in the rectangle towards the top of the dialog box — in exactly the same way as you would name a new style.

Edit color

Name: `Devils red`

Model: ○ **RGB**   ○ **HLS**   ● **CMYK**

Cyan: `0`   %
Magenta: `100` %
Yellow: `50`   %
Black: `0`   %

OK
Cancel
PANTONE®...

This box is actually in two parts. The top half reflects the color as it is edited by you. On a color monitor, it constantly changes to reflect any changes made to the percentages to the left. The bottom half of the box will reflect the color as it was originally defined.

From here, there are several ways to create the new color. The first step you must take is to give the color its name, in much the same way you would name styles. In Figure 8, we called our color "Devils red."

Your next choice is the *Model* to be used to create the color. The reason that you can select between four models, *RGB, HLS, CMYK,* and *Pantone®* is that traditionally these are the four ways in which colors can be defined. Depending on your background, your available information, and the output device you are using, you can choose any one of the four.

Process and spot colors

PageMaker gives you the choice of using either process or spot color for your publication. Process coloring is the blending of four separate colors to create the colors for your publication. For process colors to work, four color separations are needed. The CMYK color model defines process colors and is used for things such as photographs, where colors are required to blend. Spot colors are generally defined in the Pantone® section. Only one spot color can be applied to an object at a time, and this concept is generally used for logos and the like, when one solid color is needed.

It is possible to separate a spot color into process colors when such a color is used on a page in conjunction with four-color photographs. Alternatively, the photograph can be separated into its four-color CMYK model, and a fifth spot-color printing plate produced for the fifth spot color.

RGB

The *Red, Green,* and *Blue* method is perhaps the easiest and most common of the three methods for defining colors. It relies on the defining of a percentage of each of the three colors (Figure 9) — which gives a wide range of possibilities as to actual colors, although not quite as many as the other methods. Use the horizontal scroll bars (Figure 9) to adjust the percentage of each color.

This is much like mixing red, green, and blue paint in different proportions to create a new color.

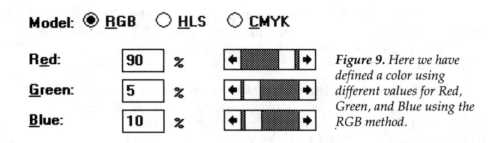

Figure 9. Here we have defined a color using different values for Red, Green, and Blue using the RGB method.

At the extreme right of the Figure 8 dialog box, a small rectangle showing the current color will constantly update, giving you some idea of what color you have created (this is assuming that you have a color screen — you are working blind with a monochrome monitor). With a monochrome monitor, you must have some idea beforehand as to what percentage makeup you require for your color(s).

HLS

The *Hue, Lightness,* and *Saturation* method (Figure 10) works in a very similar way to the RGB method, except Hue is defined from 0 to 360 degrees, while Lightness and Saturation are defined as percentages. Once again, the color being created will constantly update next to the percentage bars on color monitors.

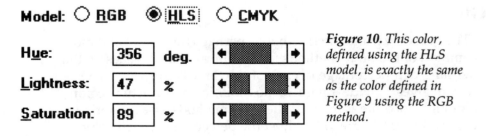

Figure 10. This color, defined using the HLS model, is exactly the same as the color defined in Figure 9 using the RGB method.

CMYK

The *Cyan, Magenta, Yellow,* and *Black* method is the most precise of all — each of these four colors and tones can be defined in percentages. Otherwise, it works in exactly the same way as the two methods described above. The CMYK model is commonly used in four-color printing. It is the method to use for defining process colors.

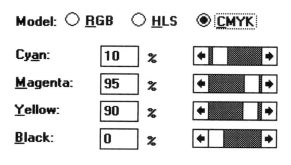

Figure 11. Once again, we have the same color defined as in the last two figures, yet this time we used the CMYK model.

Note that with any of the three methods above which you use to describe a color, selecting a new method will cause the percentage bars to display that color in the new method (see examples in Figures 9 through 11).

After defining the required color, selecting a name (Devils red in our case), and selecting OK from Figure 12, the new color has been created. It will appear in the *Define colors* dialog box of Figure 13 and in the *Color palette* of Figure 14. It is then available for selection when needed.

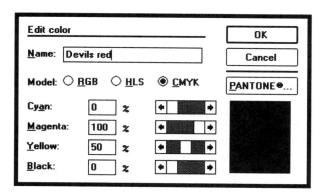

Figure 12. After having gone this far — naming the color, and defining the color using any of the three models so far discussed, you are ready to click on OK. We have called our new color Devils red.

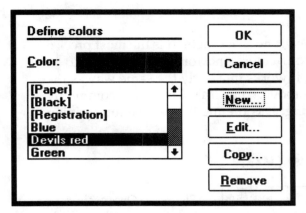

Figure 13. After clicking OK in the previous dialog box (Figure 12), you will be returned to this dialog box. The new color is now listed with the default colors, and, on a color monitor, will be displayed in the rectangle next to the word "Color."

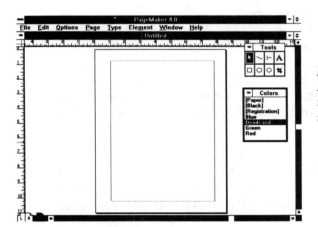

Figure 14. After exiting the Figure 13 dialog box, the new color will also be listed in the Color *palette.*

Pantone®

The fourth color option is based on Pantone® colors. The Pantone® Color system is a library of standard industry colors used by printers and graphic designers. PageMaker now contains this library of colors in the *Pantone Color* dialog box, accessible through the *Edit color* dialog box (Figure 15(a)). The Pantone® color library is well suited to defining spot colors. (As a reminder on how to get to Figure 15(a), please refer to Figures 5, 6, and 7.)

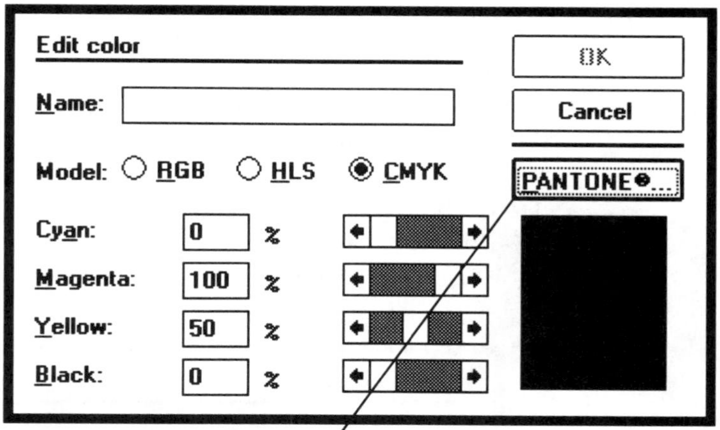

(a) Edit color *dialog box*

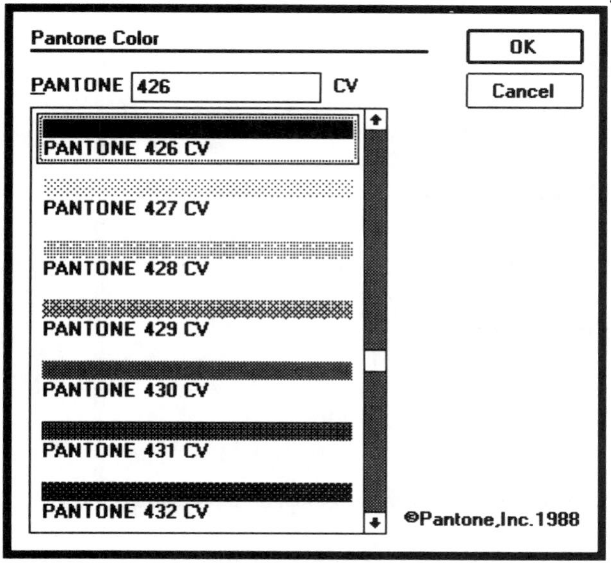

Figure 15. The Pantone
Color *dialog box is accessed
through the* Edit color *dialog
box. It is a library of standard
industry colors where each
color is represented by a
number.*

(b) Pantone Color *dialog box*

The vertical scroll bar to the right of the colors in the *Pantone Color*
dialog box is used like any other scroll bar in PageMaker. By
holding the mouse down on either the up or down arrow, all color
possibilities can be viewed. When you've found the color you
want, you click on it once and then click on OK.

Because Pantone® colors are recognized by number, if you know the number of the color you want, you can key it directly into the box above the colors. On returning to the *Define colors* dialog box, you will see the Pantone® color you selected in the list of colors. After leaving this dialog box, you will also see the new Pantone® color in the *Color palette*. This new color is applied to text and graphics the same way all other colors are. See Figures 16 through 18 for more details.

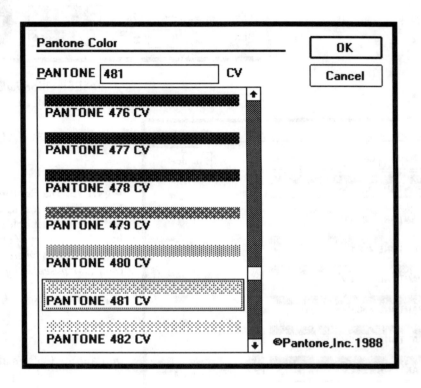

Figure 16. *We selected Pantone 481 by simply clicking over it. A box appears around the color to indicate it is selected, and the number appears in the rectangle above the colors. Now see Figures 17 and 18.*

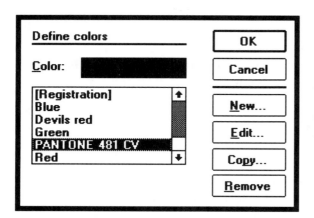

Figure 17. On returning to the Define colors *dialog box, the selected Pantone® color is shown in the list of colors.*

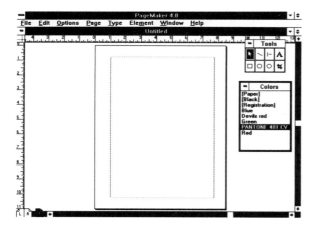

Figure 18. The Pantone® color is also displayed in the Color *palette.*

Editing colors

Any color besides Black and Registration can be edited using the *Edit* command in the Figures 6 or 17 *Define colors* dialog box. Select the color you would like to edit — note that the defined color is displayed above the list of colors for color monitors. Now select the *Edit* command from this dialog box. The same dialog box used in creating a new color is displayed (Figure 12), but this time there's a name already included in the *Name* rectangle. From here you can simply change the percentages for the color, using any of the four models, and then click on OK.

The only difference in editing, versus creating, a new color is that with editing you do not have to type in a new name as we did in Figure 8 for color creation. The name of the color to be edited will already appear in the *Name* section of the dialog box.

Removing colors

Colors are also removed using the *Define colors* dialog box shown again in Figure 19. Select the color you would like to remove from this list, and then choose the *Remove* command. The color is then permanently removed from the *Color palette*. See further notes on this subject in the Figure 19 caption.

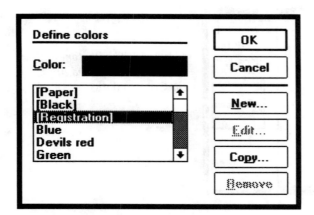

Figure 19. The colors Paper, Black, and Registration cannot be removed. Black and Registration cannot be edited either. Note in this figure that the Edit and Remove commands are grayed and are not available when Registration is selected.

Copying colors

Copying colors into your publication is also a simple process. After choosing *Define colors* from the **Element** menu to get the Figure 19 dialog box, you choose the *Copy* command near the bottom of the box. The *Copy colors* dialog box (Figure 20) will appear. This provides a list of publications from which it is possible to copy color descriptions.

Select the publication (or template) whose colors you wish to copy into your current publication, and click on OK in Figure 20. Any new colors will be added to your *Define colors* box and *Color palette*, as shown in Figures 21 and 22.

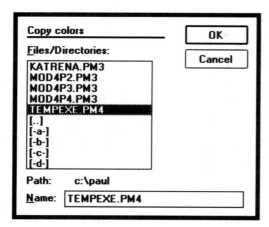

Figure 20. The Copy colors *dialog box lists publications and templates that can be used to copy color descriptions into your currently opened document.*

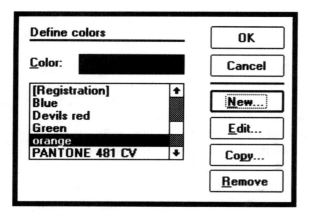

Figure 21. Using the Copy *procedure of Figure 20, we have added orange to our list of colors. This now appears in the* Define colors *dialog box. See also Figure 22.*

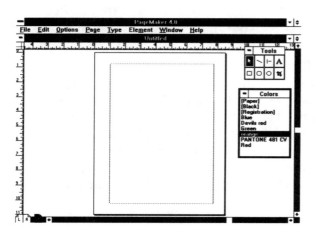

Figure 22. The new color, orange, added through the Copy *process, also appears in the* Color palette *as well as in the* Define colors *dialog box of Figure 21.*

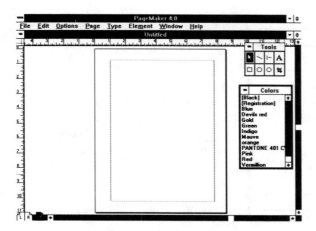

Figure 23. Here we have created a wider range of colors we can use — the number of colors that can be created is virtually unlimited.

Applying colors

Colors are applied exactly the way styles are. If a dialog box is still showing, click OK to remove it from the screen. Any printing element on the screen can be applied a color — whether it be text, graphics created in PageMaker, or imported graphics. Simply select the element you would like to color — text, using the text cursor (Figure 24), other elements, using the pointer tool.

As the object is selected, move to the *Color palette* (if this is not showing, choose the command *Color palette* from the **Window** menu) and click on the color you want to use. On color monitors this becomes apparent immediately, and on color output devices the color will be matched as closely as the output device can manage.

EPS, Windows metafiles, and TIFF graphics which have been imported into PageMaker can also have colors applied to them, but these colors will not appear until the publication has printed. A selected object's color will be highlighted in both the *Color palette* and the *Define colors* dialog box. Any text or graphic not assigned a color will be black by default. Color can be applied to individual text characters, lines, and all graphics created in PageMaker. However, only one color can be applied to an element at a time.

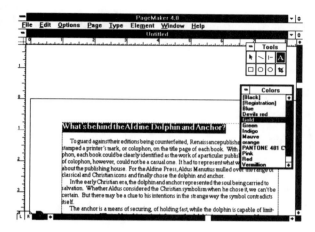

Figure 24. To apply a color to any element on the page, select the element and select a color from the Color palette. Although not visible on a monochrome monitor, the color has been applied to that graphic or text element.

EXERCISE:
COLOR

Color

In this exercise you will be working with color within PageMaker. A color screen or printer is not necessary to complete this exercise — but would only it a little easier.

This training material is structured so that people of all levels of expertise with Page-Maker can use it to gain maximum benefit. In order to do this, we have structured the material so that the bare exercise is listed below this paragraph on just one page, with no hints. The following pages contain the steps needed to complete this exercise, for those who need additional prompting. The **Color** module should be referenced if you need further help or explanations.

Module 13 exercise steps

1   *Open up the publication LES2DONE.PM4 from the lesson3 directory.*

2.   *Define three new colors — **orange**, **purple**, and **aqua**. Use the RGB method to do this. Orange will be 100% red, 40% green; purple will be 100% blue, 75% red; and aqua will be 100% green and 100% blue.*

3.   *Show the* Color *palette.*

4.   *Make the heading purple and the graphic orange. The Portrait graphic at the top of the page must be aqua.*

5.   *The frame around the page must also be aqua (you will have to move to the master page to do this).*

6.   *Create registration marks on the master pages, at the top and bottom of the page, and make sure they are correctly colored for registration.*

The steps to completing this exercise are on the following pages.

The steps in detail

1. Open up the publication LES2DONE.PM4 from the lesson3 directory.

This file is located in the lesson3 directory — it is accessed by selecting the *Open* command in the **File** menu once you are already in PageMaker.

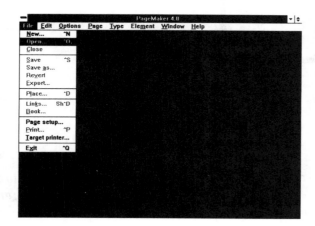

Figure 1. *Use the* Open *command (as shown here) to access the* Open publication *dialog box of Figure 2.*

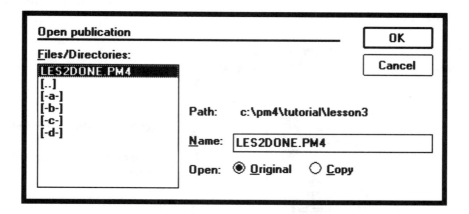

Figure 2. *Open the LES2DONE.PM4 file from the lesson3 sub-directory, within the tutorial directory.*

Figure 3. The publication *LES2DONE.PM4 will look like this on your screen in* Fit in window *view.*

2. *Define three new colors —* **orange, purple,** *and* **aqua.** *Use the RGB method to do this. Orange will be 100% red, 40% green; purple will be 100% blue, 75% red; and aqua will be 100% green and 100% blue.*

Defining colors is done through the *Define colors* command in the **Element** menu (Figure 4). Upon selecting this command, you will be greeted with the dialog box of Figure 5.

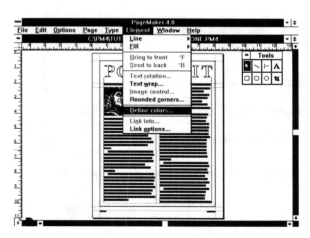

Figure 4. Choose the Define colors *command from the* **Element** *menu to create and use new colors.*

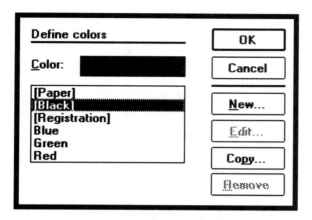

Figure 5. The Define colors *dialog box. Red, Blue, and Green may also be included in this box as default colors.*

The Figure 5 dialog box will have six colors defined by default — Paper, Black, Registration, Red, Blue, and Green. To create new colors, click on the *New* option. You will then be presented with the Figure 6 dialog box.

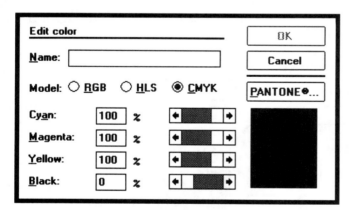

Figure 6. The Define colors New *dialog box is actually the same as the* Define colors Edit *dialog box. The only difference is that after clicking on* New *in Figure 5, you need to type in a new name in the* Name *rectangle.*

By default, the *Edit color* dialog box will be in CMYK mode when you first activate it. For this exercise, you are using the RGB method of applying colors, so select this method by clicking in the RGB button with the mouse. Before you actually create this new color you must name it. Type in the name of the new color in the rectangle at the top of the dialog box — in this case, orange (see Figure 7).

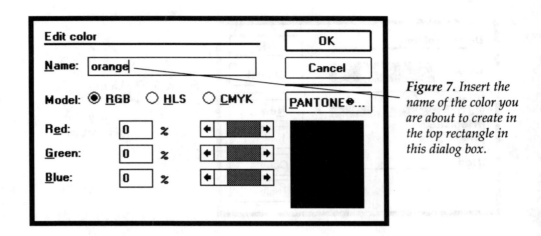

Figure 7. Insert the name of the color you are about to create in the top rectangle in this dialog box.

You have been asked to create three colors using the RGB method — the method selected in Figure 7. Using this method, you will see sliding scale bars — one representing Red, one Green, and one Blue. To create orange, move the red sliding scale to 100%, the green to 40%, and make sure that blue is at 0% (Figure 8). Although it is not noticeable on monochrome screens, the color orange has been created and is represented in the bar to the right of these sliding scales. Now click on OK.

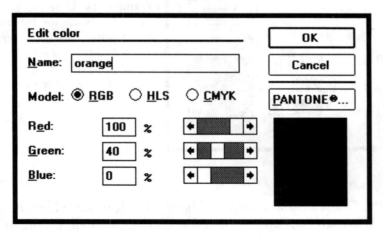

Figure 8. To create the color orange, use the scroll bars on the sliding scales to set the Red bar at 100%, the green at 40%, and the blue at 0%. You could also key these numbers directly into the boxes as shown.

You will then be returned to the previous *Define colors* dialog box (shown again in Figure 9), to which the color orange will have been added. From here, click on *New* again to create the next two colors. Creating purple is shown in Figures 10 through 12, while aqua is shown in Figure 13.

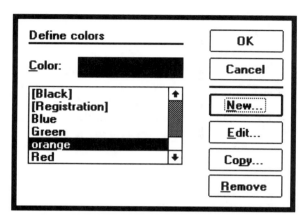

Define colors

Color: ▮

[Black]
[Registration]
Blue
Green
orange
Red

OK

Cancel

New...

Edit...

Copy...

Remove

Figure 9. After clicking OK in the box in Figure 8, you will be returned to this dialog box. The orange color you just created will be included in the list of colors.

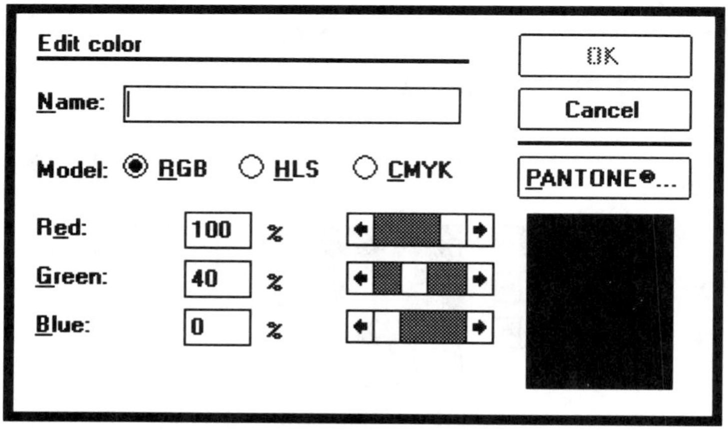

Edit color

Name: |

Model: ● RGB   ○ HLS   ○ CMYK

Red: 100 %   ← ▮▮▮   →
Green: 40   %   ← ▯ →
Blue: 0   %   ← ▯ →

OK

Cancel

PANTONE⊕...

Figure 10. You must click on New again in the dialog box in Figure 9. Once again, you will be presented with this dialog box.

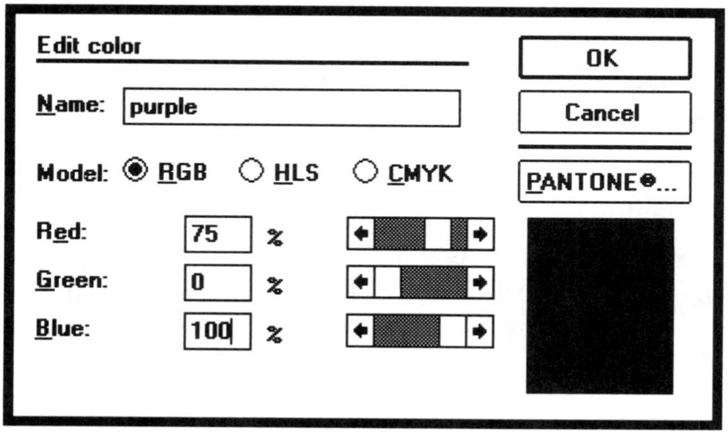

Edit color

Name: purple

Model: ● RGB   ○ HLS   ○ CMYK

Red: 75   %   ← ▮▯ →
Green: 0   %   ← ▮ →
Blue: 100 %   ← ▮▯ →

OK

Cancel

PANTONE⊕...

Figure 11. For the color purple, insert its name at the top and set the blue scale at 100%, the red at 75%, and the green at 0%.

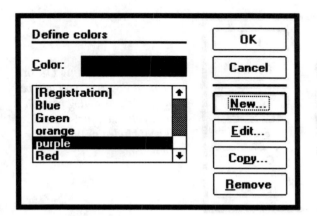

Figure 12. After clicking OK from Figure 11, you will once again be returned to this dialog box with the color purple added to it.

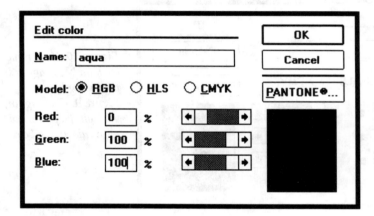

Figure 13. Match your dialog box with this one (after choosing New again from Figure 12) to create the color aqua.

After Figure 13, click on OK twice to get past the two dialog boxes and back onto the PageMaker page.

3. *Show the* Color palette.

The *Color palette* can be accessed via the *Color palette* option in the **Window** menu (Figure 14). In this *Color palette* will be listed all the colors you have just created. You may want to resize the *Color palette* so that you can see all the colors (Figure 15).

Figure 14. Choose the Color palette *command from the* **Window** *menu to display the* Color palette *on screen.*

Figure 15. Here the Color palette *has not only been displayed, but we have increased it in size a little to view all the colors listed.*

4. Make the heading purple and the graphic orange. The Portrait graphic at the top of the page must be aqua.

To make any text a certain color is quite a simple procedure. Select that text using the text editing tool and click on the required color in the *Color palette*. The selected text will then be registered as that color. Although these colors can be applied with style sheets, none has been defined for this publication, so we will apply colors manually. See Figures 16 through 21 for these operations.

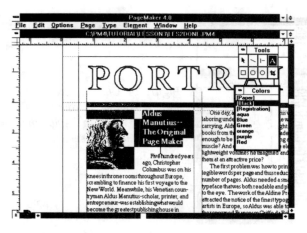

Figure 16. *75% view has been used here to allow us to read the text while viewing a good deal of the page. To make the heading purple, select it, as shown here, using the text editing tool.*

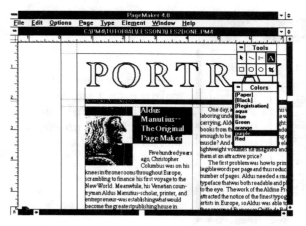

Figure 17. *Click on the color purple in the* Color *palette.*

Figure 18. *Select the graphic next to it with the pointer tool. . .*

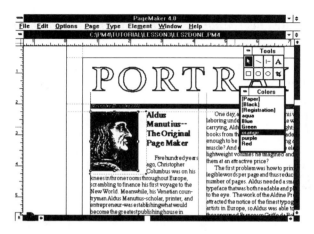

Figure 19. . . . *and click on the color orange from the* Color palette. *Repeat this step for every Bulletpoint encountered.*

Graphics must be selected using the pointer tool, but are applied colors in exactly the same way as text. Once the graphic is selected, click on the correct color in the *Color palette* and the graphic will then assume that color (Figure 19).

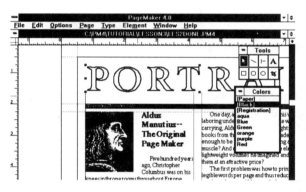

Figure 20. *Move to the top of the page and select the graphic at the top of the page with the pointer tool.*

Figure 21. *Click on the color aqua in the* Color palette *to turn the graphic this color. Note that EPS and color TIFF graphics are not displayed on screen in their assigned colors.*

5. The frame around the page must also be aqua (you will have to move to the master page to do this).

Because the frame is on the master page, you will not be able to select it from page 1. Click on the *R* icon in the bottom left-hand corner of the page to move to the master page (Figure 22).

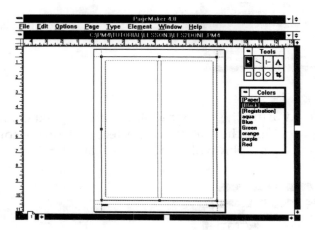

Figure 22. Note how the R icon in the bottom left-hand corner of the page has been selected — we are looking here at the master page. Note that the frame around the page has been selected.

Select the frame using the pointer tool and click on the color aqua from the *Color palette* (Figure 23). This frame is now treated as aqua, although once again not all of you will be able to see this.

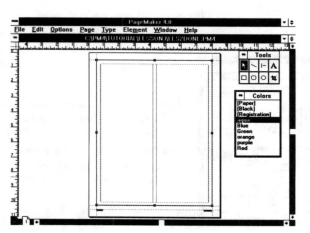

Figure 23. Select aqua from the Color *palette to turn the frame this color.*

6. *Create registration marks on the top and bottom of the master pages and make sure they are correctly colored for registration.*

These registration marks are only created as guides to the printer — they help align color separations. They are created on the master page and are very simple to do.

Create a fairly small symbol at the top of the master page (Figure 24) and repeat it at the bottom of the page (Figure 25). It does not matter exactly what you create: a typical symbol is shown in Figure 24.

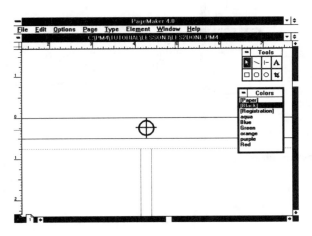

Figure 24. This symbol has been created using the graphic drawing tools within Page-Maker — it is two lines drawn through a circle. Copy this graphic and paste it at the bottom of the page as well.

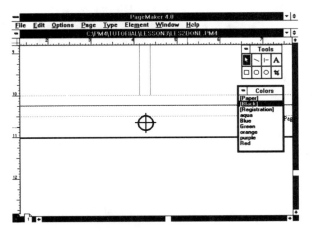

Figure 25. The graphic has been copied and pasted at the bottom of the page.

After creating a symbol and placing it at the top and bottom of the page, make sure that all parts of both symbols are colored Registration by selecting the Registration color from the *Color palette* (Figure 26). This ensures that these registration marks will print on every page if color separations are created at print time.

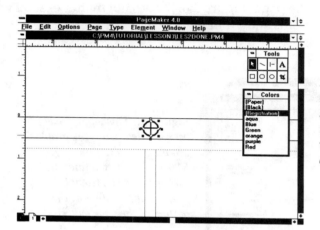

Figure 26. *Assign the color Registration to the special symbol marks. This ensures that these registration marks will print on every page of color separations.*

ADVANCED PICTURE FORMATTING

Advanced Picture Formatting

We have already described in Module 7 how you can import pictures, and also how you can resize and move these pictures in various ways. In this module we are looking at more complex wraparounds and also how you can alter the composition of the picture itself.

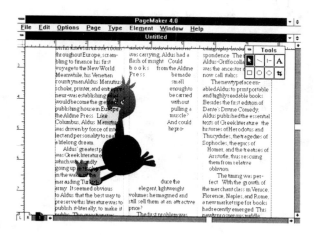

Figure 1. *An example of an irregular wraparound achieved using PageMaker 4's advanced features.*

Irregular wraparounds

In Module 7, we looked at creating simple wraparounds with graphics using the *Text wrap* command in the **Element** menu. Depending on the options you select with this command, text can be made to skip over a graphic, stop at a graphic, run through a graphic, or wrap regularly around the border of the graphic. What we are looking at now is how to make text wrap *irregularly* around the edge of the graphic.

To follow this example, load the text file LEADSTRY.RTF (lesson2 sub-directory) into a three-column page, then load the picture file ANCHOR.TIF (in lesson4 sub-directory, within the tutorial directory) somewhere on top of this text. Make the graphic about 4" (10 cm) square (see Figures 2, 3, and 4 for details). Before loading the picture file, ensure that your *Text wrap* command in the **Element** menu is set as shown in Figure 3.

Figure 2. The file
LEADSTRY.RTF will
not quite fill three
columns, but should look
something like this. This
is the page in 75% view.

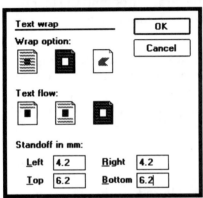

Figure 3. To make sure that the text
wraps regularly around the image
about to be loaded in, alter the Text
wrap command so that it reads the
same as shown here. Do this before any
pictures are loaded, and it will become
the default for this publication.

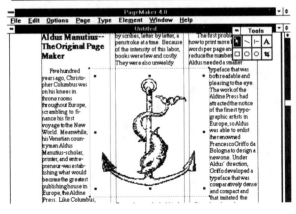

Figure 4. Size the
graphic so that it fits
nicely across two
columns. Text will flow
down both sides of the
graphic as long as you
followed the instructions
in Figure 3.

Click now on the graphic you have loaded in, as shown in Figure
4. Every picture, when selected, will have two sets of handles
around it. The inside handles are the ones used to resize the

picture. We have already looked at the use of these handles in previous modules. The outside graphic boundary handles, connected by dotted lines, are used to create a wraparound for the graphic . Before these handles can be used, however, the *Text wrap* command must be set up in a fashion similar to Figure 3.

If you failed to do this before loading the graphic, select it now and set up the wrap options as shown in Figure 3. Make sure your graphic fits across two columns as shown in the 75% view of Figure 4.

Most graphics placed in PageMaker will not be transparent and will sit on top of the text. Before we began altering the text wrap frame around this graphic, we sent the graphic behind the text by executing the *To back* command from the **Element** menu with the graphic selected.

Initially, the outside set of handles around a selected graphic consists of a diamond-shaped dot in every corner. You can hold the mouse button down on any of these corners, as if you were going to resize the graphic, and change the shape of the wraparound. Move the top right-hand dot a little to the right (Figure 5) and watch how, after a few seconds, the text will change its flow to compensate for this movement (Figures 6 and 7). Any of the four corner dots can be moved in this way, and the text will change its flow each time. The text flow can be altered so that it bears no relevance to the graphic originally within it.

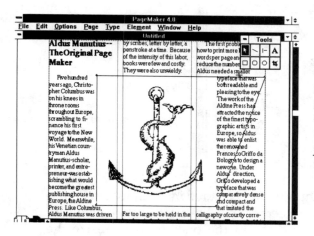

Figure 5. Here we are in the process of altering the position of the right-hand outside text flow margin of the graphic. See the next figure for the results of this movement.

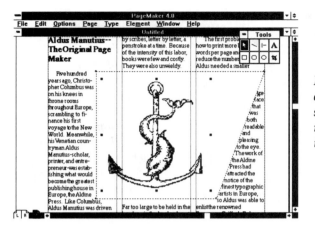

Figure 6. After moving one of the outside dots slightly, the text reformats to compensate for this movement.

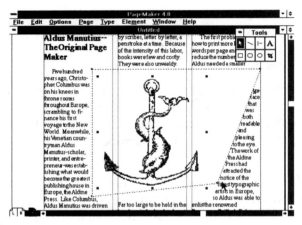

Figure 7. Here we have also moved the bottom right-hand corner dot up slightly. The text will now reformat to compensate for this.

Moving the four dots in this fashion will alter the way the text flows, but will hardly create an irregular wraparound. You need to have more than four dots to correctly achieve an irregular wraparound. You can actually create more dots to suit your purpose.

Move the mouse cursor to a point on the dotted outline where another movable handle would come in handy. Think of it as moving to a point where a bend in the outline would be necessary. Click once and a new graphic boundary handle will be created (Figure 8). After clicking once, hold the mouse button down on this handle and move it around. You will notice that you can now alter the shape of the wraparound at this new boundary point.

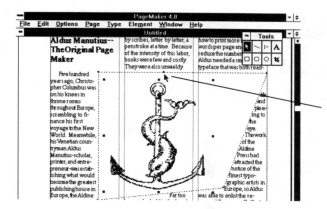

Figure 8. We have decided that the dotted outline, in order to best "hug" the graphic, needs a bend in it exactly where the mouse is. All you need to do is click on that spot, and a new handle, with all the properties of the corner dots, appears.

This new handle can be moved in any direction, including along the line itself. As many dots as necessary can be created to make an irregular wraparound. Simply click on the dotted outline of the graphic wherever you need to bend the line.

Figures 9 through 12 show additional manipulations to make the text wrap exactly as you would like. With this irregular wraparound, the graphic can still be resized and moved using the inside handles without losing the actual shape of the wraparound (Figure 13).

Every time a boundary handle is moved or created, the text reflows to compensate. If this is slowing you down, annoying you, or you simply don't want it to happen, hold down the space bar as you move or create boundary handles. The text will only reformat when the space bar is released. You can move several handles before the space bar is released.

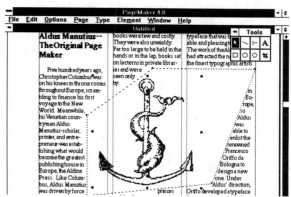

Figure 9. After we created a new handle in Figure 8, notice how, after we move the top left-hand handle, the line now bends at the new position.

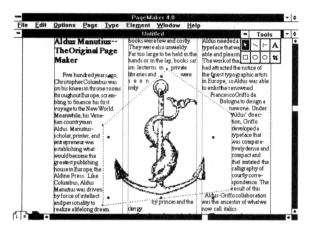

Figure 10. We can also move down the right-hand corner handle thanks to the new one we created in Figure 8.

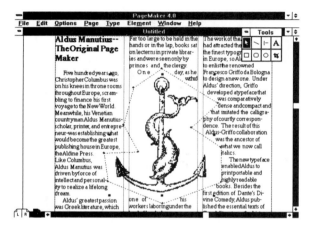

Figure 11. Almost finished. . . we have created several new handles, simply by clicking on the dotted line where we felt it necessary and moving these new dots around.

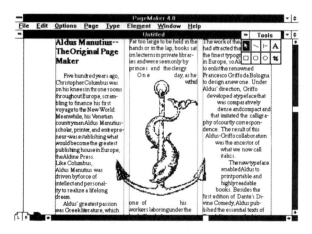

Figure 12. After we finished the wraparound, we deselected the graphic. This gives us a good indication of how the printed graphic will appear.

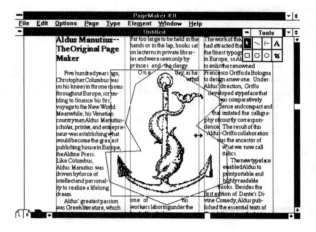

Figure 13. We can still enlarge the graphic without any worries about losing the wraparound. The handles used to resize the graphic may be a little hard to see.

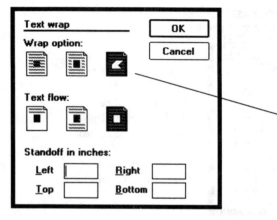

Figure 14. Once the text wraparound has been manually altered, the dialog box for the Text wrap command from the **Element** menu will reflect that change. This option will then be automatically selected.

Altering the appearance of graphics

Several controls exist to alter the appearance of certain imported graphics, such as scanned images or Paint-type graphics created in any of the packages compatible with PageMaker. Graphics imported in EPS format, Draw-type package images, or internally created graphics cannot be altered in this way.

The controls for altering these graphics are contained within the *Image control* command in the **Element** menu. Before this command can be activated, a graphic must be on the screen and selected.

Several aspects can be altered relating to an imported graphic. These include the lightness, contrast, and screen pattern of the graphic.

Adjusting the lightness of a graphic will affect the entire image. Blacks, for example, can be lightened until they appear a pale shade of gray. Light images can be darkened so that they appear totally black.

Adjusting the contrast of an image involves lightening dark areas and darkening light areas. A high-contrast picture is one in which there are very dark areas and very light areas — without much in between. A low-contrast picture is one in which there is little difference between the dark areas and the light areas of a picture — for instance, a photo that is taken in very poor light. Contrast can be increased or decreased using PageMaker's *Image control*.

For our examples in this module we have loaded the graphic PRACTICE.TIF from the basics directory and a scanned image, PHOTO.TIF, from PageMaker 3's getstart directory. This image is not available with PageMaker 4.

Figure 15. Here we are going to alter two different types of imported graphics — a black and white image and a scanned image with sixteen levels of gray.

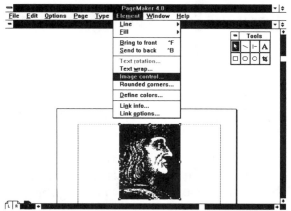

Figure 16. Select the image you would like to alter and choose the Image control *command from the* **Element** *menu. We have chosen to look at the black and white image first.*

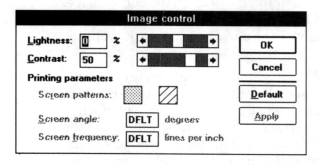

Figure 17. This is the
Image control *dialog box.*

In the top left-hand corner of the *Image control* dialog box, the default settings for *Lightness* and *Contrast* will be 0 and 50, respectively. These can be changed at any time. Next to these options are two horizontal scroll bars that represent the settings for *Lightness* and *Contrast*. If, for example, we change the *Contrast* figure to -50, the image will be inverted (Figure 18). Clicking on the apply button in the Figure 18 dialog box allows you to view the result of any changes on the screen without exiting the dialog box.

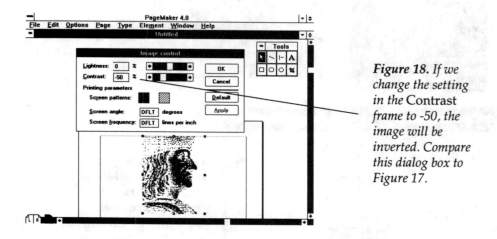

Figure 18. If we change the setting in the Contrast *frame to -50, the image will be inverted. Compare this dialog box to Figure 17.*

Changing the settings in the *Lightness* or *Contrast* frames will not effect the image until you click on the *Apply* button. Figures 19 through 21 provide further examples of changes to the *Lightness* and *Contrast* settings.

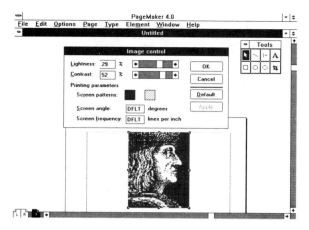

Figure 19. When you click on the right or left arrows of the horizontal scroll bars to adjust Lightness *and* Contrast *of the image, two things will happen. The scroll buttons will move and the* Lightness *and* Contrast *settings will change. After you click on* Apply, *the image will also change to reflect the adjustments you have made.*

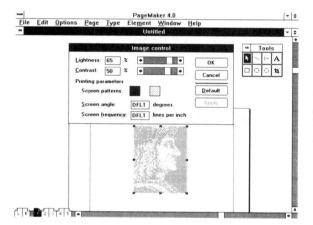

Figure 20. The higher the figure you have in the Lightness *frame, the lighter the image will appear.*

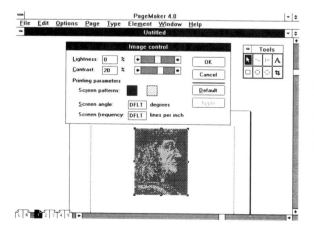

Figure 21. If you change the Contrast *setting to a lower value, such as 20, the contrast of the image will become poor.*

The *Lightness* and *Contrast* settings can also be changed (in 10% increments) by clicking the mouse button in the gray section of the horizontal scroll bars.

Remember that when dealing with screened images, results are often far better on a printer than they appear on screen. It would be a good idea to experiment with a few settings, when altering a picture, to see exactly which ones give the best results. In the following examples (Figures 23 through 26), we have included some printed results on exactly how two-tone, paint-type graphics can be manipulated using the *Image control* command.

Figure 22. This image has been printed exactly as it was created — no changes have been made. Its black and white dialog box is the same as in Figure 17.

Figure 23. This image was reversed before it was printed.

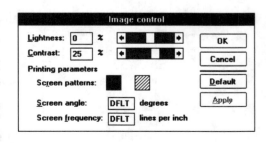

Figure 24. This image has had the contrast lowered.

 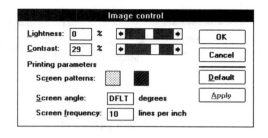

Figure 25. *Here we have changed the screen pattern to lines and the lines per inch to 10. The screen pattern options are described later in this module.*

Scanned graphics are a slightly different story. They may contain more shades of gray, and more precise manipulation of these graphics is possible.

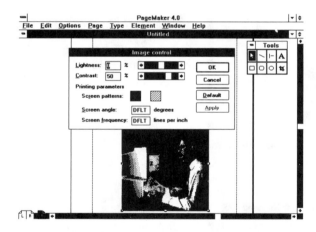

Figure 26. *This time we have selected a scanned photo to manipulate through the* Image control *dialog box.*

By default, the *Lightness* and *Contrast* settings are 0 and 50, respectively. The *Screen angle* and *Screen Frequency* are on the default settings as well.

Figures 27 and 30 show examples of the scanned photo after changing the settings in the *Image control* dialog box.

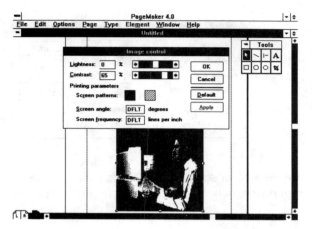

Figure 27. *Here we have changed the* Contrast *figure to 65 and clicked on the* Apply *button. The image has become more contrasty.*

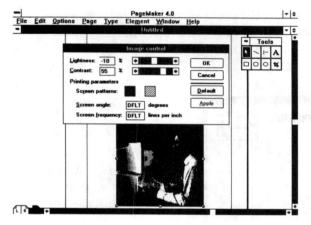

Figure 28. *If we change the* Lightness *to -10 and the* Contrast *to 55, the image becomes darker than the original image.*

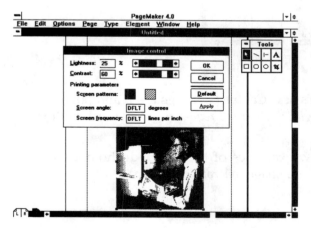

Figure 29. *As with two-tone graphics, the* Light-ness *and* Contrast *can be adjusted by clicking on the two horizontal scroll bars. Remember to click on* Apply *to see the result. Here we have increased the* Contrast *as well as the* Lightness *settings.*

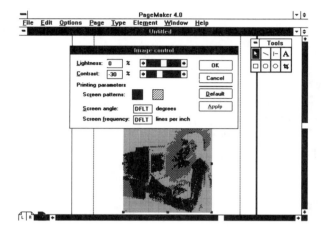

Figure 30. Here the image has been inverted by changing the Contrast *setting to -30.*

A scanned photo can also be adjusted by altering the screen pattern itself. Initially, the screen pattern consists of dots, but it can be changed to lines to create special effects. This is achieved using the controls under *Printing parameters*.

Apart from changing the screen pattern to lines or dots, you may also adjust the frequency of these lines or dots and the angle at which they lie. The controls for these commands are at the bottom of the dialog box (Figure 31). See Figures 33 and 34 for more variations.

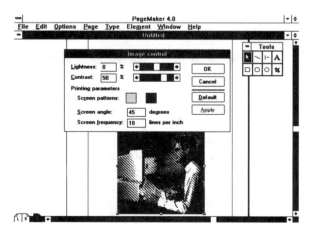

Figure 31. Here we have changed the screen pattern to lines rather then dots, the angle to 45, and the frequency of the lines to 10 per inch.

481

Figure 32. This is the scanned image as it would normally appear using the gray level box shown in Figure 26.

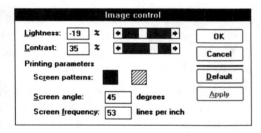

Figure 33. Here we have altered the image in the above manner.

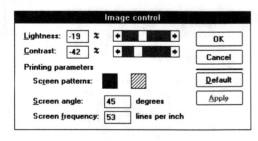

Figure 34. Here we have inverted the image and decreased the Contrast.

Inline graphics

Inline graphics are graphics that are added to your text to actually become part of the text. This enables your graphic to move with the text if you happen to change your page layout. This feature is best suited to small graphics used with body text. Text that a graphic is linked to will not wrap around the graphic. If your graphic is large and you insert it in the middle of your text block, it will act as a large text character and widely separate your lines of text. This graphic can be reduced in size, if necessary, to more easily fit within the text.

Inserting an inline graphic

To insert a graphic into the text so it becomes part of that text block, follow these steps. First, load the text file STORY2.RTF (lesson4 directory) onto a one-column page. Move the page to 75% view and, with the text tool, place the flashing cursor somewhere in the middle of your text. (Figure 35).

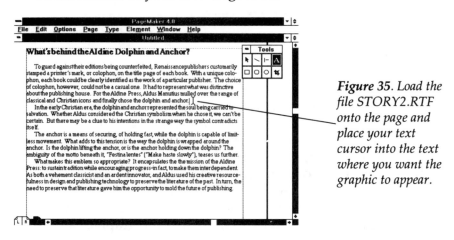

Figure 35. Load the file STORY2.RTF onto the page and place your text cursor into the text where you want the graphic to appear.

You are going to load the graphic ANCHOR.TIF onto the page as an inline graphic. Keeping the text tool selected, choose the *Place* command and find the file ANCHOR.TIF from the lesson4 directory. You will notice that, once this file is selected in the dialog box (Figure 36), you will be given two choices as to how to load this graphic.

As independent graphic is your first choice (Figure 36). If you select this option, the graphic you place will not be part of the text but will be a separate object on the page. Because you placed the text cursor in the middle of your text (Figure 35), *As inline graphic* is selected. If you hadn't placed the text cursor in the text, *As inline graphic* would not be available.

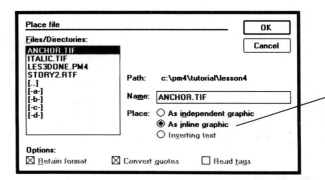

Figure 36. The Place *dialog box is giving you two choices on how to load the graphic. Because you inserted the flashing cursor into the text,* As inline graphic *is selected automatically.*

After clicking on OK in Figure 36, the graphic appears where you placed the cursor. You will probably notice that it is a little large (Figure 37). Before you shrink the graphic, notice that the flashing cursor next to the image is just as large, as though the graphic were a block of text. Double-click over the graphic with the text tool and you'll see that it can in fact be selected as text. Now move to the *Alignment* command in the **Type** menu, change the alignment to center, and you'll see that the graphic can be aligned just like text.

Inline graphics can be resized just like normal graphics. We suggest you try this. Select the graphic with the pointer tool and shrink it using the bottom right handle. Decrease it so it is just slightly larger than your text. The graphics may now be unrecognizable, but not to worry — you can still see what has happened. See Figures 37 through 39 for more details.

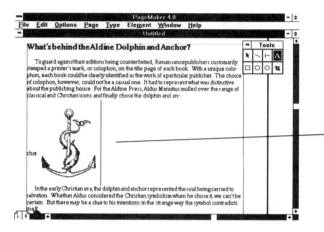

Figure 37. The graphic is placed as an inline graphic but also has certain characteristics of text. Notice the flashing cursor next to the graphic.

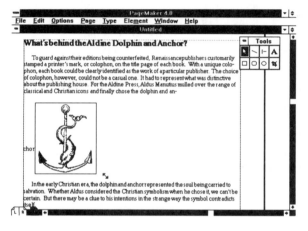

Figure 38. Generally, the graphic should be shrunk so it will not affect the layout of text. This, of course, depends on what effect you are trying to achieve. Select it with the pointer tool and change its size as though it were a normal graphic.

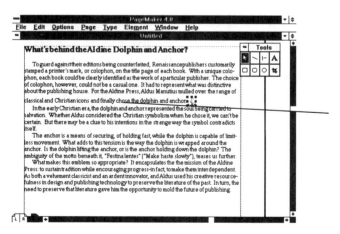

Figure 39. The graphic is reduced in size so that it fits into the text much better.

To prove that the inline graphic moves with the text, take your pointer tool, place it anywhere in the text, and keep your finger on the mouse. Now, move the mouse around and see how the graphic follows with the text (Figure 40). If you try to move the graphic on its own now, you'll see that it can't be done. It can be moved slightly up and down on the baseline, but because it's part of the text, it can't be moved to the left or right.

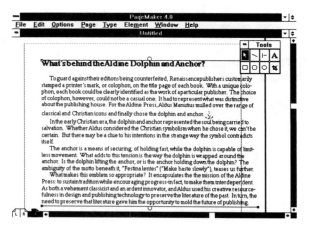

Figure 40. *You will see that if you move the text anywhere on the page now, the graphic will follow.*

Separating inline graphics and text

If you later decide you want an inline graphic to be an independent graphic, this is easily done. First, select the graphic with your pointer tool. Then, move to the **Edit** menu and activate the *Cut* command. Right after this, use the *Paste* command. Your graphic will reappear in the same position. Using the pointer tool, move in and pull the graphic away from the text, keeping your finger on the mouse button the whole time. You'll see that it is now an independent graphic and can be moved as such. Figures 41 through 44 illustrate this process.

Figure 41. After selecting the graphic with the pointer tool, activate the Cut *command.*

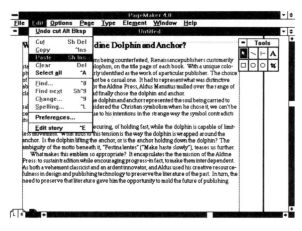

Figure 42. Next, choose the Paste *command so that the graphic will reappear on your page.*

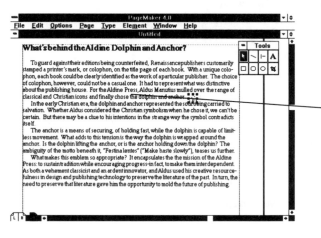

Figure 43. The graphic will reappear in exactly the same position, but as an independent graphic.

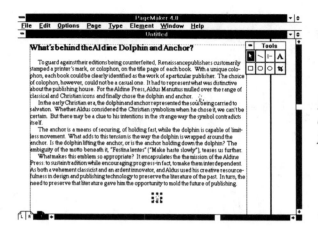

Figure 44. *The graphic can now be moved away from the text.*

Joining graphics and text already on the page

If your graphic and text are already on the page and you want to join them, you follow similar steps. First, select your graphic with the pointer tool and choose *Cut.* Next, select the text tool and insert it where you would like your graphic to be placed. Then simply choose *Paste,* and it becomes an inline graphic. Figures 45 through 48 illustrate this approach.

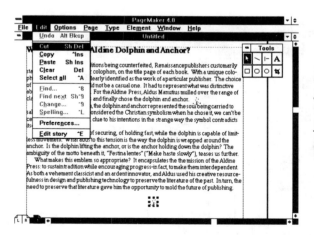

Figure 45. *When making a graphic that is already on the page an inline graphic, first select it with the pointer tool. Then activate the* Cut *command.*

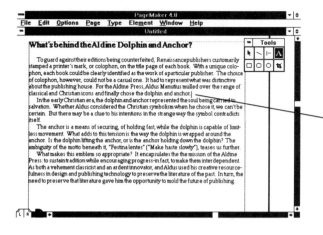

Figure 46. After cutting the graphic from your screen, select the text tool and place the flashing cursor where you want the graphic to be placed.

Figure 47. To bring the graphic back onto the page as an inline graphic, simply choose Paste.

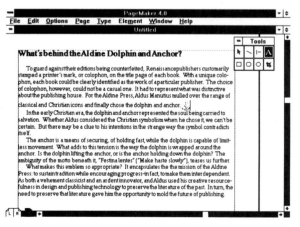

Figure 48. It is now an inline graphic at the location of the text cursor and will move with the text.

Inline graphics can be loaded in story view as well. Story view is part of the story editor discussed in Module 5. The procedure is almost the same. Place the flashing cursor in the text where you would like the graphic to appear. Then, instead of choosing the *Place* command, choose the *Import* command from the **Story** menu. The graphic, which shows up as a little marker, can only be manipulated outside story mode. See Figures 49 through 52 for details.

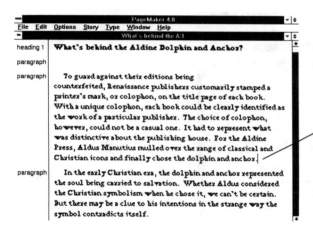

Figure 49. To place an inline graphic in story view, first place the flashing cursor somewhere in the text.

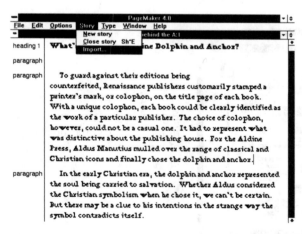

Figure 50. The Import command is selected from the **Story** menu.

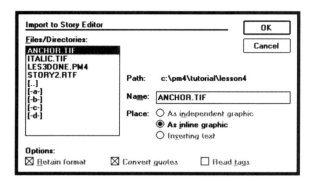

Figure 51. *The* Import to Story Editor *dialog box will appear. This is the same as the* Place *dialog box, so the same steps are followed. Again, because you placed the flashing cursor in the text, the* As inline graphic *choice is selected.*

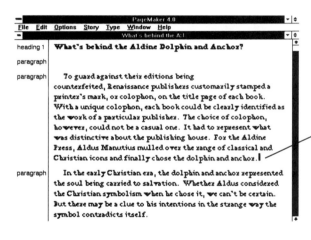

Figure 52. *The placed graphic in story view will show up as a marker and can only be manipulated once out of story view.*

Inline graphics are also affected by the *Leading* command. Your best option here is to have *Auto* leading selected. In some cases, the graphic may be too large, as we mentioned earlier, and your lines of text will be altered. Sometimes, moving the graphic slightly up or down, or shrinking it more, can alleviate the problem of breaking up text.

EXERCISE: ADVANCED PICTURE FORMATTING

Advanced Picture Formatting

In this exercise, you will import different types of pictures into PageMaker and look at the advanced options that are available to alter the look and properties of these pictures. You will also be working with irregular wraparounds of graphics.

This training material is structured so that people of all levels of expertise with Page-Maker can use it to gain maximum benefit. In order to do this, we have structured the material so that the bare exercise is listed below this paragraph on just one page, with no hints. The following pages contain the steps needed to complete this exercise, for those who need additional prompting. The **Advanced Picture Formatting** module should be referenced if you need further help or explanations.

Module 14 exercise steps

1.   *In this exercise, you are going to load three files — ANCHOR.TIF, PRACTICE.TIF, and LEADSTRY.RTF. Load these files now so that LEADSTRY.RTF is in two columns and the two graphics are positioned on the page. Text must also wrap regularly around these graphics. If you are unsure about what we mean, look at Figure 1 on the next page.*

2.   *Select the file PRACTICE.TIF and make it slightly darker. Now, invert the image — turn white black and black white.*

3.   *For the second graphic file, ANCHOR.TIF, create a wraparound with the image that will cause the text to run irregularly around the image — to hug the image. (See Figure 2 on the next page if you are unsure about what we mean here.)*

4.   *The second part of this exercise is to create an inline graphic. Open a new PM4 publication and load the file STORY2.RTF onto a one-column page. Place the file LOGOTYPE.TIF as an inline graphic anywhere in your text. (Preferably, beginning at the left-hand margin, as the graphic will most likely spread right across the page.) Shrink it slightly so it fits nicely on the page.*

5.   *Now make LOGOTYPE.TIF an independent graphic and move it so it sits under the text on the page.*

The steps for completing this exercise are on the following pages.

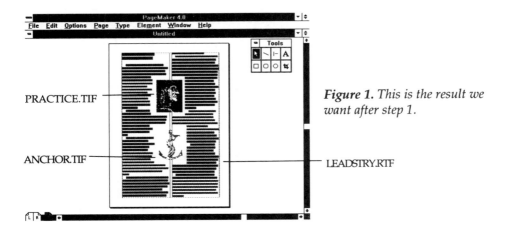

PRACTICE.TIF

ANCHOR.TIF

LEADSTRY.RTF

Figure 1. *This is the result we want after step 1.*

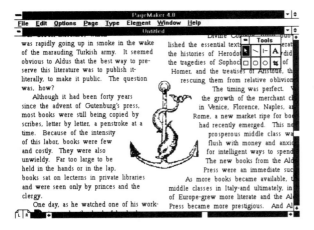

Figure 2. *This is the result we want after step 3.*

The steps in detail

1. *In this exercise you are going to load three files — ANCHOR.TIF, PRACTICE.TIF, and LEADSTRY.RTF. Load these files now so that LEADSTRY.RTF is in two columns and the two graphics are positioned on the page. Text must also wrap regularly around these graphics. If you are unsure about what we mean, look at Figure 1 above.*

To achieve the results shown in Figure 1, follow these steps.

Select *New* to create the publication, and choose an A4 or Letter size page.

Use the *Column guides* command in the **Options** menu to create two columns (Figure 3).

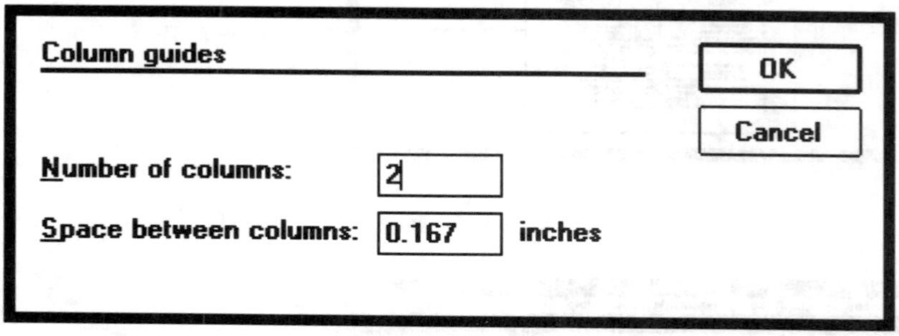

Column guides
         OK

         Cancel

Number of columns: 2

Space between columns: 0.167   inches

Figure 3. In the Column guides *dialog box, insert the number 2.*

Load the file LEADSTRY.RTF from the lesson2 directory into these two columns (Figures 4 and 5).

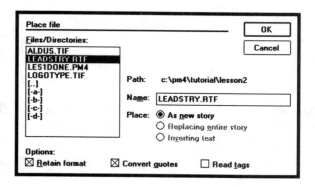

Figure 4. Load the file LEADSTRY.RTF from the lesson2 directory. This is the dialog box obtained from the Place *command in the* **File** *menu.*

Figure 5. The LEADSTRY.RTF file is loaded into two columns on an A4 or Letter size page.

Before loading any pictures, move to the *Text wrap* command in the **Element** menu and set up the dialog box for a regular wrap, as illustrated in Figure 6. Make sure the pointer tool is selected and that no text block is selected since the text wrap setting will then only apply to that text block.

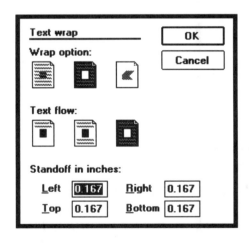

Figure 6. It is a good idea to set the Text wrap *dialog box up as such before actually loading any pictures. This ensures that all pictures, when loaded, will take on this setting automatically.*

Load both ANCHOR.TIF (lesson4 directory) and PRACTICE.TIF (basics directory) onto the page using the *Place* command from the **File** menu. Position them approximately as shown in Figure 1. Resize these pictures, if necessary, so that they are roughly the size of those in this figure.

If the text did not run around the pictures as in Figure 1, the step you took in Figure 6 did not work. Simply select both pictures with the Shift key depressed, choose the *Text wrap* command, and set it up as shown in Figure 6.

2. Select the file PRACTICE.TIF and make it slightly darker. Now invert the image.

Select the file PRACTICE.TIF on the page simply by clicking on it, then choose the *Image control* command from the **Element** menu (Figure 8). If this command cannot be chosen, make sure that the graphic is selected on the page. The *Image control* dialog box of Figure 9 then appears. Also, change to *Actual size* view as shown in Figures 7 and 8.

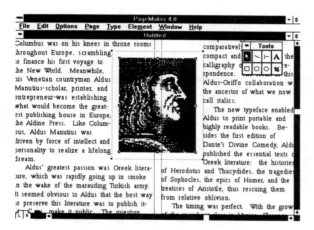

Figure 7. *Select the file PRACTICE.TIF. Also, make sure that you are in* Actual size *view to better see the changes you make to this picture.*

Figure 8. *After selecting the graphic, choose the* Image control *command from the* **Element** *menu.*

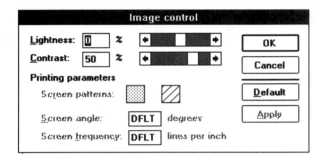

Figure 9. *The* Image control *dialog box.*

You now have to do several things — darken the image slightly and then reverse it. Also, if the Figure 9 dialog box covers the image, grab the dialog box title bar with the mouse and move it to a new position.

To alter the picture settings, change the figure in the *Lightness* frame to -20, hit the Tab key, and click on the *Apply* button (Figure 10). Alternatively, the horizontal scroll bar reflecting *Lightness* could have been used in conjunction with the mouse to get the same result.

To alter the image to a reverse video image, change the figure in the *Contrast* frame to -50, hit the Tab key, and click on *Apply* (Figure 11). The horizontal scroll bar could also have been used in this case. Click on OK to remove the dialog box from the screen.

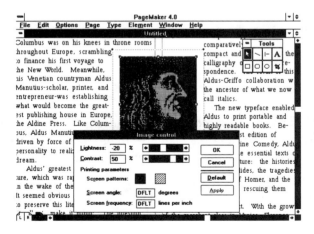

Figure 10. *Darken the image by adjusting the* Lightness *figure. Don't forget to click the* Apply *button to see the results.*

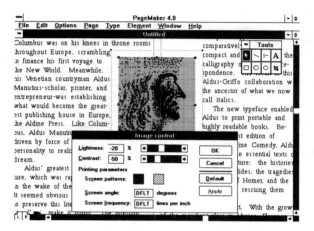

Figure 11. *Reverse the video of the image by changing the* Contrast *figure to -50. Note the change in the actual graphic.*

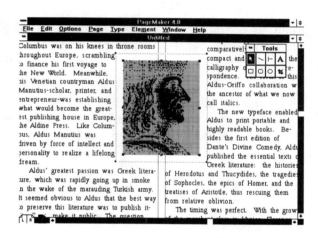

Figure 12. *The final result of your changes to the graphic.*

3. *For the second graphic file, ANCHOR.TIF, create a wraparound with the image that will cause the text to run irregularly around the image — to hug the image. (See Figure 2 at the start of this exercise, if you are unsure about what we mean here.)*

Stay in *Actual size* view and move down the page to view the graphic ANCHOR.TIF. Also, select the image so that you can see the handles around the image (Figure 13). In fact, there should be two sets of handles showing.

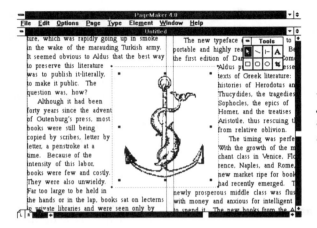

Figure 13. Move down to the second graphics file, ANCHOR.TIF, and select it. Note the two sets of handles showing.

The outside diamond handles are the ones joined by the dotted lines: these are the ones that control the irregular wraparound. You will use these to create your wraparound.

Every time you click the mouse button on the dotted line, a new boundary handle is created. Several of these handles will have to be created at strategic points on the dotted line in order to create the wraparound. From this point, however, we will guide you with pictures — which can explain the procedure far more easily than words alone can.

See Figures 14 through 25 for details.

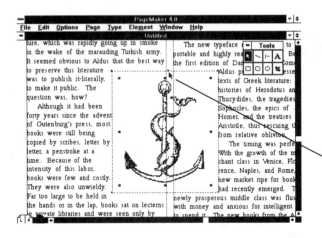

Figure 14. To add a corner, or handle, to the dotted line, simply click on it. In this figure we have added another corner (it looks at the moment like another handle on the dotted line) in the middle of the top horizontal line.

501

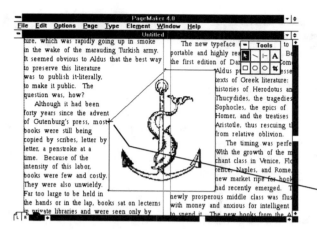

Figure 15. *In order to change the shape of the dotted square (and hence the wraparound), hold the mouse button down on one of its handles and move it towards the graphic. Here we are in the process of holding the mouse button down on the top left-hand corner handle and moving it towards the graphic. Be careful to hold the mouse button down only on handles on the dotted line — not the other selection handles inside the lines.*

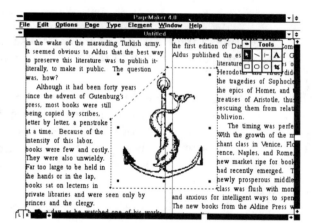

Figure 16. *When you release the mouse button after performing the step in figure 15, the text reflows around the new border of the dotted polygon. Some of the text will still be hidden, so select* Send to back *from the* **Element** *menu.*

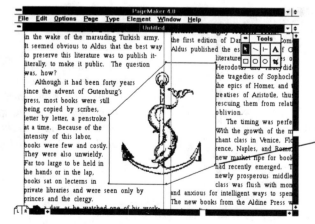

Figure 17. *Once again, we are in the process of changing the wraparound — this time by holding down the mouse button on the bottom right-hand handle and moving it towards the graphic.*

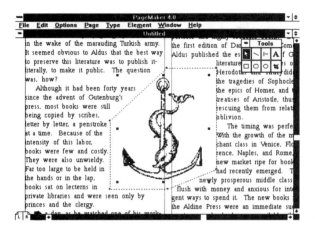

Figure 18. And once again, after releasing the mouse button, the text reflows around the graphic.

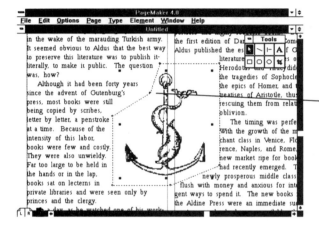

Figure 19. You must again add another handle to the dotted line — this time in the middle of the left-hand line. After creating the handle, move the line closer to the graphic so the text hugs the image.

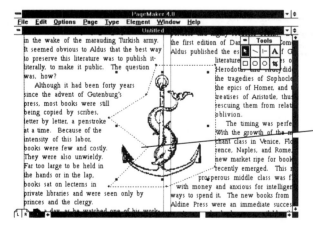

Figure 20. Keep adding as many handles as you need to complete the irregular text wraparound of the image. Because the shape of this image is so irregular, you may have to create quite a few additional handles. In this figure we are in the process of moving another one we created. Figure 21 shows you the final result of this move.

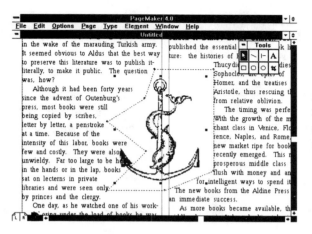

Figure 21. *Notice the text has reflowed to fit in with the direction we just moved our line.*

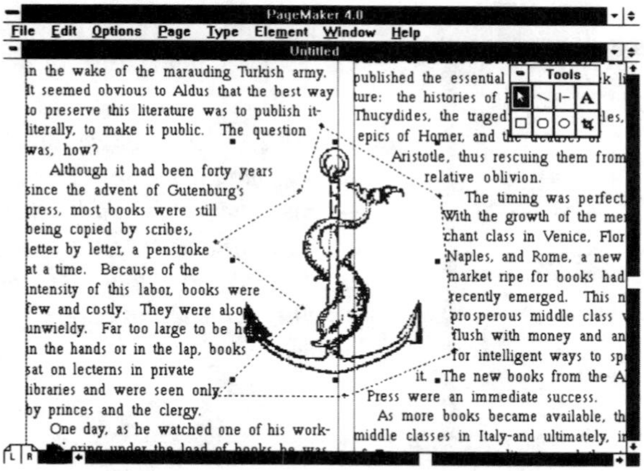

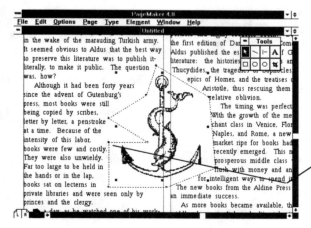

Figure 22. *This figure is the result of moving yet another handle towards the graphic — this time the top right handle.*

Figure 23. *Once again, another handle has been added near the bottom left of the graphic.*

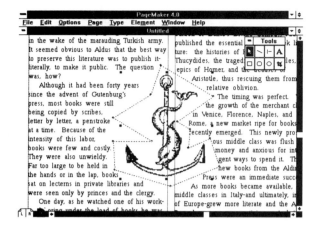

Figure 24. More handles have been added and moved to complete the wraparound...

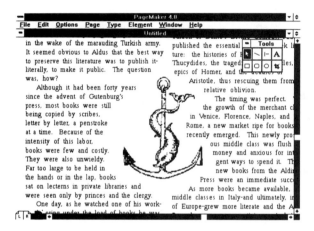

Figure 25. ... and here is how the wraparound finally looks on the screen, once guides are hidden and the graphic is deselected. (This simply gives a better view of the graphic — it is certainly not necessary.)

4. *The second part of this exercise is to create an inline graphic. Open a new PM4 publication and load the file STORY2.RTF onto a one column page. Place the file LOGOTYPE.TIF as an inline graphic anywhere in your text. (Preferably, beginning at the left-hand margin, as the graphic will most likely spread right across the page.) Shrink it slightly so it fits nicely on the page.*

On the new page, load in the file STORY2.RTF from the lesson4 directory (Figure 26) and move to 75% view for a better perspective. Place the flashing text cursor somewhere in your text, as in Figure 27. Because the graphic will be placed where you inserted the cursor, it is a good idea to position the text cursor against the left-hand margin. This will allow enough room for the placed graphic to load.

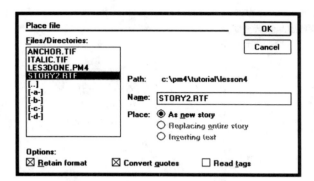

Figure 26. The STORY2.RTF file is located in the lesson4 sub-directory. Double-click on it for placement onto page 2.

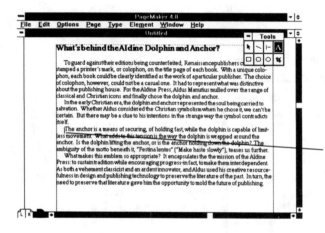

Figure 27. STORY2.RTF is loaded onto page 2. Move to 75% view and place the flashing cursor into your text. We placed ours at the beginning of the third paragraph.

The next step is to load in your inline graphic. Move again to the *Place* command and locate the file LOGOTYPE.TIF (Figure 28). Because you placed your cursor in the text, the *As inline graphic* choice will be available and automatically selected.

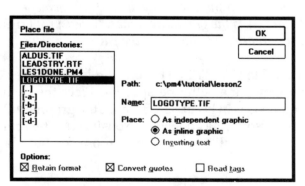

Figure 28. The LOGOTYPE.TIF file can be found in the lesson2 directory. Note that the As inline graphic choice is automatically selected.

Figure 29. The graphic is loaded into the text and is now an inline graphic. Whenever the text block is moved around the page, the graphic will follow.

After the graphic has been loaded onto the page, you will probably notice that it is a little wide and hangs over the right margin slightly. If it doesn't, all the better, you won't have to resize it. If it does, simply select it with the pointer tool and reduce it in size just as you would any graphic. Use the bottom right handle and push it back over the margin so it fits on your page (Figure 30).

Figure 30. The reduced graphic now fits into the margins of the page. If you reduce it too much, the text below will start to come up on the right-hand side. If this happens, just enlarge the graphic slightly to push the text down to the next line.

5. Now make LOGOTYPE.TIF an independent graphic and move it so it sits under the text on the page.

Now to make *LOGOTYPE.TIF* an independent graphic. First, with the pointer tool, select the graphic. Next, activate the *Cut* command from the **Edit** menu. The graphic will disappear from the screen. From the **Edit** menu once more, choose the *Paste* command. The graphic will appear in exactly the same position as it was before. Now that it is no longer part of the text, move the graphic down and place it underneath the text. Follow Figures 31 through 34 to see how this is done.

Figure 31. Cut *the graphic from the screen, but only after you have selected it with the pointer tool.*

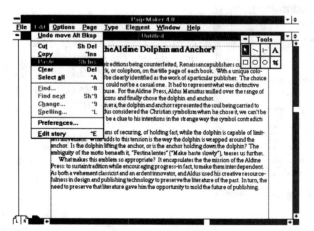

Figure 32. *The next step is to* Paste *the graphic back onto the page.*

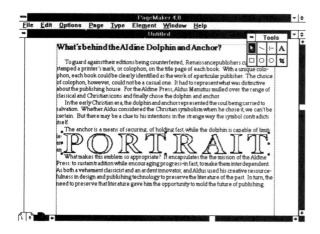

Figure 33. *The graphic is pasted back onto the page, but it is now completely separate from the text.*

Figure 34. *The graphic is moved away from the text and placed below it. This step simply reinforces the fact that the graphic is now independent of the text.*

LINKING FILES

Linking Files

PageMaker automatically links text and graphics that you place in a publication with the original, external files. This feature allows you to update the linked text or graphic files automatically, replacing them with changes from the most current version of the external file. It also gives you access to information regarding when the file was created, when it was last modified, and whether or not the linked element is up-to-date. This version control is especially valuable in a work situation in which several people may be working on a publication that is being revised continually.

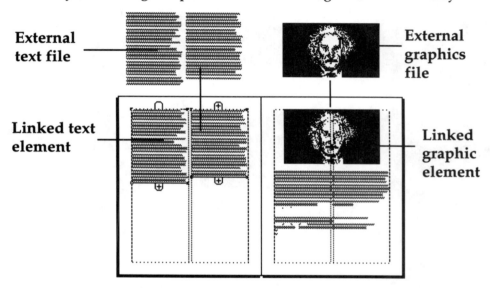

External text file

External graphics file

Linked text element

Linked graphic element

Figure 1. Publications can be updated when changes are made to external text or graphics files.

It is possible to change a graphic in the originating graphics program and have PageMaker notify you that the linked graphic is different from the revised external file. You can then update the linked graphic without having to place the file again manually.

Generally, all text or graphic files that you import into Page-Maker using the *Place* or *Import* command are automatically linked to their original, external files.

In order to find out status information on any linked file, select the *Links* command in the **File** menu (Figure 2).

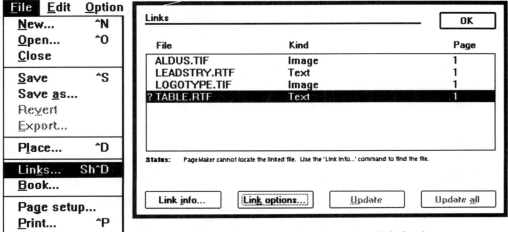

Figure 2. The Links *command and associated dialog box.*

When you select a file on the list, its status is displayed underneath (Figure 2). Below is a list of symbols that can appear to the left of a file name and an explanation of what these symbols indicate.

Link status indicator

No indicator	Link is up-to-date or not linked
†	Linked file has been modified and will be automatically updated
-	Linked file has been modified and will not be automatically updated
!	Both the linked file and the internal PageMaker file have been modified.
x	Publication does not contain complete copy
?	Cannot find the external file

The column which lists "Page" in Figure 2 may display the following symbols (as well as the actual page number):

UN	The linked inline graphic element is in a story that has not yet been composed; the page number is therefore unknown.
LM	The left master page
RM	The right master page
PB	The pasteboard
OV	The linked text element — an inline graphic, for example, is not displayed because it is part of a text block that is overset, or not fully flowed.

In the Figure 2 *Links* dialog box, there are four buttons available at the bottom. The first two, *Link info* and *Link options,* display dialog boxes and are described in the following sections.

The *Update* option is for updating single linked elements. This option will be dim if there is no existing linked file or if the highlighted file name is currently up-to-date.

The *Update all* option allows you to update all internal publication files that are linked to external ones, but only those that have *Update automatically* selected in the *Link options* dialog box (Figure 4 in the following sections). This option will be dim if the selected linked element is up-to-date, or if you have not selected *Update automatically* for that element.

Link info dialog box

When you select *Link info* from Figure 2, the dialog box in Figure 3 appears. This box can also be selected from the *Link info* command in the **Element** menu. It cannot be selected through the **Element** menu, however, unless you have a graphic or text block selected.

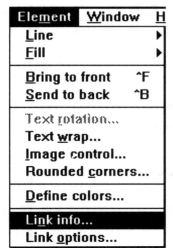
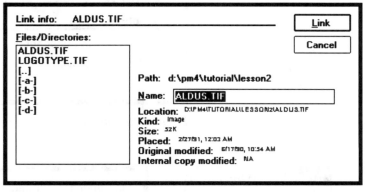

Figure 3. Link info *dialog box and the* Link info *command in the **Element** menu. This dialog box can also be selected by clicking on* Link info *in the Figure 2* Links *dialog box.*

In the Figure 3 dialog box, you can update or re-establish a link between a text or graphic element and its external file and you can display file information. Relinking may be necessary if the external file is moved to a different directory or if its name has been changed. To update a link, select the required external file and then click on *Link.*

To the right of the *Link info* dialog box of Figure 3, important information about the linked element is displayed.

Link options dialog box

There are two ways you can activate the *Link options* dialog box (Figure 4). First, you can select a file from the list in the *Links* dialog box of Figure 2 and then click on *Link options,* or you can select a linked element in the publication and choose *Link options* from the **Element** menu. Either way will get you to Figure 4(b). To select the *Link options: Defaults* dialog box of Figure 4(c), choose *Link options* from the **Element** menu when no publication is open or no element is selected.

In this dialog box, you can determine how PageMaker will store and update linked elements with external files. You can set up or change the default options for all publications you open during a session, or you can modify the options for a single linked element. Any settings you change for a single element will override the default settings.

Figure 4. The two
Link options *dialog
boxes and the* Link
options *command
from the* **Element**
menu.

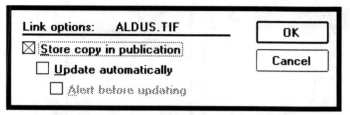

Figure 4(b). This box is displayed when a linked element
is selected.

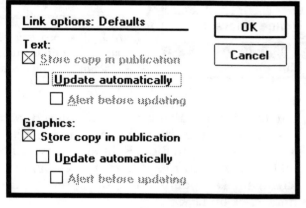

Figure 4(a). The Link
options *command in the*
Element *menu.*

Figure 4(c). This box is displayed when nothing is
selected and you choose Link options *in the*
Element *menu. It can be used to set default
values.*

The options in these dialog boxes are interdependent: each lower
option becomes available only when the one above it is selected.
Each option provides a different layer of control over how linked
files are updated.

Store copy in publication: This option is always selected for text
and EPS files. For graphics files, if this is deselected, it is necessary
for PageMaker to use the external files when printing. It is also
useful when the graphic file is large since this increases the size of
the publication considerably, slowing down processing time.

Update automatically: If you select this option, any changes you make to the external file will automatically update the linked version within the publication. Updating occurs whenever you open the publication or select *Update all* in the *Links* dialog box (Figure 2). With graphics files, you must have *Store copy in publication* checked before *Update automatically* is available.

Alert before updating: With this option selected, you can, if necessary, prevent a linked element from being updated (see Figure 5).

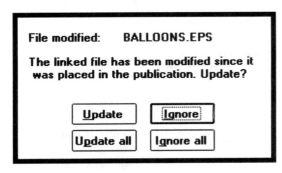

Figure 5. This alert appears if you have selected Alert before updating *in Figures 4(b) or 4(c).*

If you are placing a graphic in your publication that is larger than 256K, or if the updated version of the graphic file has increased beyond 256K, PageMaker will display an alert asking you if you want to continue storing a copy of that file in the publication. If you choose not to, you have the advantage of the publication's becoming smaller and easier to work with, but only a low resolution screen version of the graphic will then be updated.

Which files can be linked?

PageMaker can only establish a link to a file stored on a disk, where it has a definable location. For this reason, a text block or a graphic copied from one program (for example Microsoft Word) to the Clipboard and pasted into a PageMaker publication from the Clipboard has no link to an external file. However, if you cut a linked graphic or text file and paste into another publication, the link is transferred.

It is also possible to create a text file from within PageMaker and export it into a word processing program. This feature allows you to edit the text in your word processor, as well as giving you the option of being able to use the same linked document in more than one publication if necessary.

When you open a publication that has links to external files, PageMaker must find all these files before it can open the publication. If the file has been deleted or moved into a different directory, PageMaker will search the directory containing your publication. If it cannot find the file, it will display the dialog box of Figure 6.

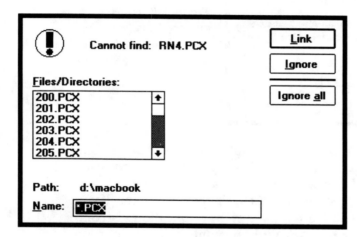

Figure 6. This dialog box will be displayed if PageMaker cannot locate a file while you are opening a publication.

From this dialog box, you can search through different directories to find the missing file. Once you have located it, highlight it with your mouse and click on *Link* to re-establish the link and automatically update the file.

If you select *Ignore* in the *Cannot find* dialog box, you are accepting a broken link. This file will not be updated with the current external file version until you re-establish the link. If a graphics link is broken, only a low resolution screen version of the graphic will be displayed until the link is re-established.

Printing a publication that contains links

When printing a publication that contains any linked elements, PageMaker searches for the linked external files, as it does when opening a publication. If there are any files not found, the dialog box of Figure 7 will be displayed.

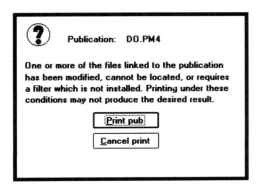

Figure 7. This alert will be displayed when PageMaker cannot find a link during printing.

If you are copying a publication to disk to take to a commercial printing house, make sure you select the *All linked files* option for the *Copy* command in the *Save publication as* dialog box (Figure 8).

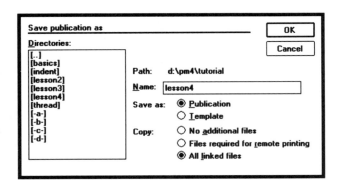

Figure 8. You must select the All linked files *option if you are taking your publication to a commercial printing house.*

Note: To keep link management tasks to a minimum, be careful when moving files into different directories or when changing the names of files, directories, or disk drives. All these changes break links between external files and their linked elements in a publication, which means you must re-establish the links with each individual file.

EXERCISE:
LINKING FILES

Module 15 Exercise

Linking Files

In this exercise you will be utilizing some of the features for linking publications with external files.

This training material is structured so that people of all levels of expertise with PageMaker can use it to gain maximum benefit. In order to do this, we have structured the material so that the bare exercise is listed below this paragraph on just one page, with no hints. The following pages contain the steps needed to complete this exercise, for those who need additional prompting. The **Linking Files** module should be referenced if you need further help or explanation.

Module 15 exercise steps

1. *In a new PageMaker publication, place the following files on the first page:*

    STORY2.RTF (located in the tutorial directory in lesson4 sub-directory) and ANCHOR.TIF (in the same sub-directory).

2. *In the* Links *dialog box, make the following changes:*

    For STORY2.RTF, in the Link options *dialog box, select the* Update automatically *option.*

    For ANCHOR.TIF, in the Link options *dialog box, deselect the* Store copy in publication *option.*

3. *Save the publication with the name "Linked," and select the option* All linked files *under the* Copy *command.*

The steps for completing this exercise are on the following pages.

The steps in detail

1. *In a new PageMaker publication, place the following files on the first page:*

STORY2.RTF (located in the tutorial directory in lesson4 sub-directory) and ANCHOR.TIF (in the same sub-directory).

Start a new single-page publication (your choice of specifications) through the *New* command in the **File** menu.

Go to the **File** menu, select the *Place* command, and locate the file STORY2.RTF in the lesson4 sub-directory (Figure 1). Place STORY2.RTF on the page in two-column format.

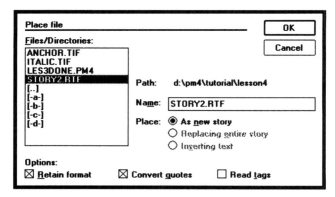

Figure 1. Locate STORY2.RTF in the lesson4 sub-directory.

Go to the **File** menu again, select the *Place* command, and locate ANCHOR.TIF in the same sub-directory. Place it at the top of the second column. Figure 3 indicates how your page will look in 75% view.

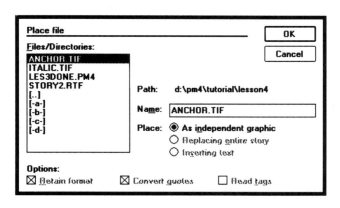

Figure 2. ANCHOR.TIF is also located in the lesson4 sub-directory.

Figure 3. Your page with the two files placed.

2. *In the* Links *dialog box, make the following changes:*

For STORY2, *in the* Link options *dialog box, select the* Update automatically *option.*

For ANCHOR.TIF, *in the* Link options *dialog box, deselect the* Store copy in publication *option.*

Now go to the **File** menu and select the *Links* command. The Figure 5 dialog box will now appear.

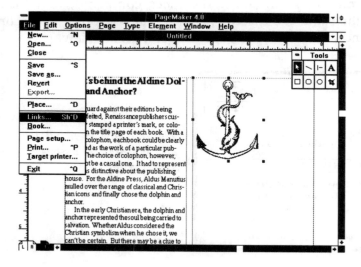

Figure 4. Select the Links command from the **File** menu.

Highlight STORY2.RTF with your mouse and then select the *Link options* button (Figure 5).

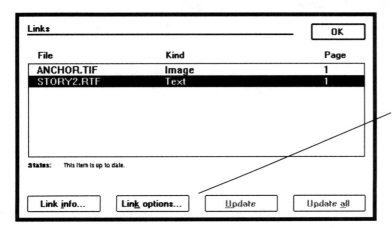

Figure 5. After highlighting STORY2.RTF, select the Link options *button with your mouse.*

When the *Link options* dialog box is activated (Figure 6), click your mouse on the *Update automatically* option and then select OK. This will ensure that any changes made to the text outside of PageMaker will automatically be included the next time this PageMaker document is opened.

Figure 6. Click on the Update automatically *option with your mouse.*

To modify the *Link options* for the ANCHOR.TIF file, highlight the file name, and then click the *Link options* button again (Figure 7).

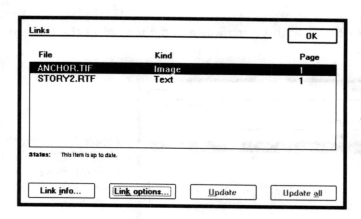

Figure 7. Make sure you highlight the ANCHOR.TIF file before you click the Link options *button for this next step.*

When the *Link options* dialog box of Figure 8 appears, deselect the *Store copy in publication* option. This option is useful to cut down the memory size of the publication so it is easier to work with. Select OK, and then OK again from the Figure 7 *Links* dialog box.

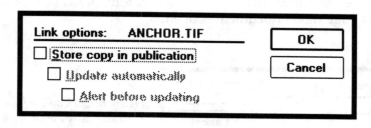

Figure 8. Deselect the Store copy in publication *option.*

3. *Save the publication with the name "Linked," and select the option* All linked files *under the* Copy *command.*

Use the *Save as* command in the **File** menu to save the publication with the name Linked (Figure 9). Click on the *All linked files* option in this dialog box. This option is essential if you are making a copy of your publication on a floppy disk. It copies all externally located files to the directory where you are saving your publication.

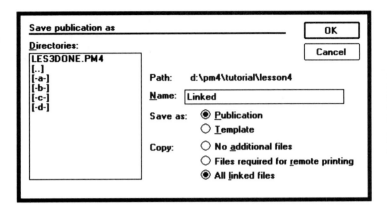

Figure 9. *Make sure you choose the* All linked files *option when you save this publication. Select OK.*

LONG DOCUMENT CAPABILITIES

Long Document Capabilities

PageMaker allows you to create large documents by linking many publications together. You may choose to do this for several reasons. Linking publications to form a long document allows you to generate a table of contents and an index that cross-references between publications.

Linking publications can also be used as a multiple printing device — you may set up many publications to print without operator intervention. The multiple publication features can be accessed via the *Book* command in the **File** menu (Figure 1).

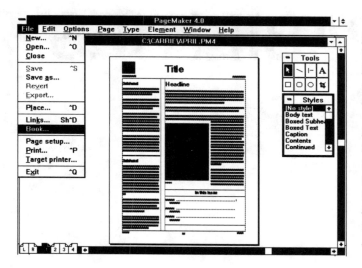

Figure 1. *Select the* Book *command in the* File *menu to access the multiple publication capabilities.*

If you wish to work through with us in this module, open a copy of the NEWSLTR2.PT4 template from the pscript sub-directory. We have named the copy APRIL.PM4.

Book command

After selecting the *Book* command from the **File** menu, the *Book publication list* dialog box of Figure 2 appears. Publications are linked together through this dialog box. The list of publications is normally included in the first publication in your book. As an example of this process, we have opened in Figure 1 a copy of the template NEWSLTR2.PT4 from the pscript sub-directory within the template directory and called it APRIL.PM4.

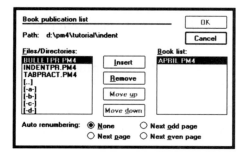

Figure 2. The Book *dialog box should look something like this. It does not matter if your list is empty.*

Note that in the *Book list* rectangle at the right of the dialog box, the publication APRIL.PM4 is already included. To add further PageMaker publications to your *Book list*, you must locate the specific documents on your hard disk (in the rectangle to the left in Figure 2), highlight the document name, and click on the *Insert* button (Figure 3).

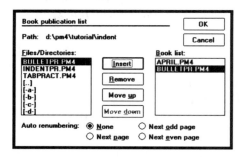

Figure 3. Once you have clicked on the Insert *button, the document name at the left will appear in the* Book list *on the right, as illustrated here.*

Using this procedure, you can keep adding documents to your *Book list* until it is complete. Double-clicking on a document name on the left causes it to be added to the *Book list* automatically. Deleting a document is just as simple. Highlight it in the *Book list* to the right and click on the *Remove* button (Figure 4).

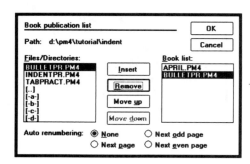

Figure 4. Highlight the document name that you wish to delete on the right, and then select Remove. *It will disappear from the* Book list.

The *Move up/Move down* options move the selected document up or down one position at a time in the *Book list*.

Auto Renumbering options: These options are for controlling the page numbering options of your book.

None: With this option, the start page of each publication in the *Book list* is controlled by the *Start page #:* option in the *Page setup* dialog box.

Next (odd, even) Page: The *Next page* option will number the pages consecutively beginning with the starting page number of the first publication in the book list. If you want all chapters to begin on an odd-numbered or even numbered page, choose *Next odd page* or *Next even page*. PageMaker may generate an extra page to ensure this.

Note: *A document's position in the list represents its position in the book, which is significant when creating a table of contents, an index, or printing out the whole* Book list.

Book list uses

Once you have created your *Book list*, you will be able to use this list in conjunction with the *Create TOC* and *Create index* commands from the **Options** menu and the *Print* command from the **File** menu.

If you wish to print your entire *Book list*, simply select the *Print entire book* option in the *Print* command, as illustrated in Figure 5.

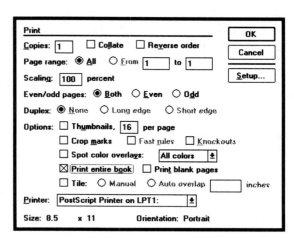

Figure 5. This is the selection that will allow you to print the entire Book list *(in the print command under the* **File** *menu). Multiple publications will then be selected and printed automatically.*

Both the index publication and the table of contents publication must include a copy of the *Book list*, as should the publication you wish to print from. To keep a copy of the *Book list* in every publication, open the publication in which the original *Book list* was produced. Then hold down the Control key and choose the *Book* command again. Every publication contained in the *Book list* will now have this *Book list* included in its own publication.

EXERCISE: LONG DOCUMENT CAPABILITIES

Long Document Capabilities

This short, but important, exercise will help you more fully understand the process of creating a *Book list*.

This training material is structured so that people of all levels of expertise with Page-Maker can use it to gain maximum benefit. In order to do this, we have structured the material so that the bare exercise is listed below this paragraph on just one page, with no hints. The following pages contain the steps needed to complete this exercise for those who need additional prompting. The **Long Document Capabilities** module should be referenced if you need any further help or explanations.

Module 16 Exercise steps

1. *Open up a copy of the NEWSLTR1.PT4 template from the pscript sub-directory in the template directory and call it APRIL.PM4.*

2. *Create a* Book list *containing the following example templates, in addition to APRIL.PM4 at the top of the list:*

   BROCHUR1.PT4
   BROCHURE2.PT4
   DIRECT.PT4
   FINANCE.PT4
   MANUAL2.PT4
   PRICE.PT4

3. *Remove the documents DIRECT.PT4 and MANUAL2.PT4.*

4. *Rearrange the order of the chapters so that they appear like this:*

   PRICE.PT4
   BROCHUR1.PT4
   FINANCE.PT4
   BROCHURE2.PT4
   APRIL.PM4

Read the following pages for the steps to complete this exercise.

The steps in detail

1. Open up a copy of the NEWSLTR1.PT4 template from the pscript sub-directory in the template directory and call it APRIL.PM4.

Figures 1 and 2 indicate how to open a copy of the NEWSLTR1.PT4 template. Once this is done, save the document as APRIL.PM4 using the *Save as* command in the **File** menu. You may choose where this publication is to be saved.

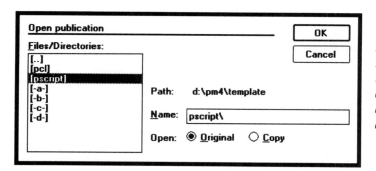

Figure 1. The template NEWSLTR1.PT4 is located in the pscript sub-directory in the template directory, within the pm4 directory.

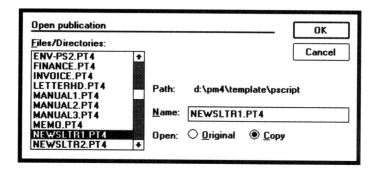

Figure 2. Before double-clicking on NEWSLTR1.PT4, make sure that you don't open the original template. Selecting Copy ensures you don't open the original.

2. *Create a* Book list *containing the following example templates, in addition to* APRIL.PM4 *at the top of the list:*

BROCHUR1.PT4
BROCHURE2.PT4
DIRECT.PT4
FINANCE.PT4
MANUAL2.PT4
PRICE.PT4

Figures 3 through 6 explain these steps.

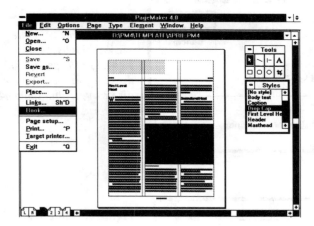

Figure 3. *Select the* Book *command in the* **File** *menu. By selecting this command with APRIL.PM4 open, you are telling PageMaker that APRIL.PM4 is effectively your first publication in the list. This command leads to the dialog box of Figure 4.*

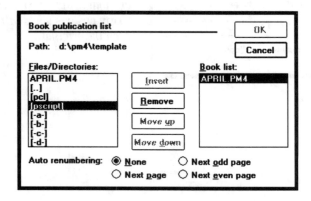

Figure 4. *By double-clicking on the pscript directory within the template directory, locate the list of files needed to compile this* Book list.

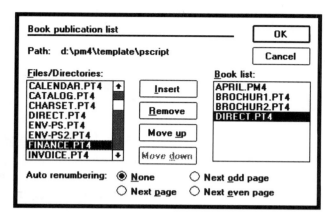

Figure 5. Select each document individually and then select the Insert *button so that the document appears in the* Book list *on the right. Alternatively, documents can be appended to the* Book list *by simply double-clicking on them. Remember, the order in which you select the documents is the order in which they will appear in the* Book list. *This sequence can be changed with the* Move up/down *commands.*

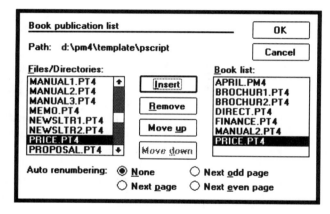

Figure 6. Once you have selected all six documents (plus the APRIL.PM4 document), your list will be the same as in this figure.

3. Remove the documents DIRECT.PT4 and MANUAL2.PT4.

Highlight DIRECT.PT4 in the *Book list* rectangle to the right and click on the *Remove* button (Figure 7). Repeat for MANUAL2.PT4.

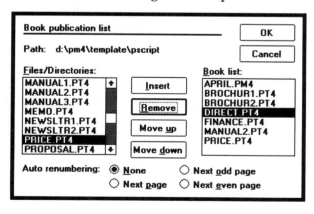

Figure 7. To remove a publication from the Book list, *highlight it and select* Remove.

4. Rearrange the order of the chapters so that they appear like this:

> *PRICE.PT4*
> *BROCHUR1.PT4*
> *FINANCE.PT4*
> *BROCHURE2.PT4*
> *APRIL.PM4*

Changing the order in which the publications appear involves highlighting the name and selecting either the *Move up* or *Move down* button. This will have to be done a few times to get the documents into the correct order (Figure 8).

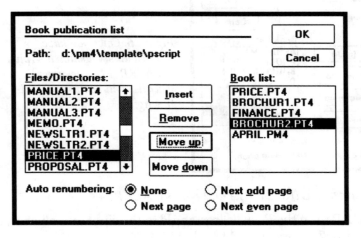

Figure 8. Arrange the documents in the required positions by selecting each one individually and choosing either the Move up *or* Move down *button.*

CREATING TABLES OF CONTENTS

Creating Tables of Contents

PageMaker can automatically generate a table of contents at the completion of your publication or publications. You can create a table of contents for a single publication or for multiple publications that make up the one long document.

A table of contents is the list at the start of a chapter, publication, report, book, or whatever, that lists both the major contents and the page number on which they start. The object of creating a table of contents automatically is to locate the important contents of your publication and note the page numbers on which they begin. This is what PageMaker does.

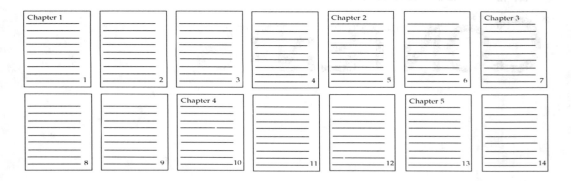

Figure 1. *This diagram shows every page of a book that would generate the table of contents shown on the next page.*

Let's assume you have a 14-page book. This 14-page book has five chapters in it. Chapter 1 starts on page 1, Chapter 2 on page 5, Chapter 3 on page 7, Chapter 4 on page 10, and Chapter 5 on page 13. If you were to create a table of contents for this book manually, it might look something like the example on the following page.

Contents of your Book

What we are going to look at here is how to get this same result using the automatic *Create TOC* command found in the **Options** menu.

The most effective way PageMaker is able to do this is through the paragraph styles found in the *Style palette*. When you create a table of contents, you are asking PageMaker to search through the document for the occurrences of a particular paragraph style, and then to compile them in order of sequence along with the numbers of the pages where they occur.

If you look at Figure 1 again, you can see that we have used two paragraph styles in the creation of this book. One style is **Body text**, and the other we might have called **Chapter Head**. The paragraph style **Chapter Head** would be applied to the paragraphs that read Chapter 1, Chapter 2, Chapter 3, Chapter 4, and Chapter 5 (Figure 2). This paragraph would have *Include in table of contents* selected as one of its attributes (found in the *Paragraph* command). The **Body text** style does not have this attribute. Apart from this selection, it does not matter how this paragraph style was set up, and it does not matter what the style was called. **Chapter Head** is only an example.

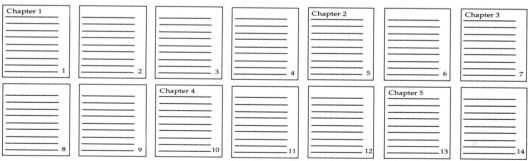

Figure 2. *In this simplified example, we have used only two paragraph styles —* **Body text** *and* **Chapter Head**. *To create a table of contents, select* Create TOC *and PageMaker will search for the paragraph style that has* Include in table of contents *selected.*

Creating your table of contents

In order for PageMaker to generate a table of contents, you must first apply a chosen paragraph style from the *Style palette* to every heading, subheading, and paragraph in your document that is to become part of the table of contents. PageMaker creates the table of contents by searching through the document for every paragraph style that has the option *Include in table of contents* as one of its attributes. (Refer to the module on style sheets if you are unsure how paragraph styles work.)

It is also possible to mark separate individual paragraphs (even without style names) to be included in the contents. This is not a recommended approach, as it may lead to inconsistent results.

For an example to work on in this module, we have opened a copy of the template MANUAL2.PT4 contained within the pscript sub-directory, within the template sub-directory. An *Actual size* view of the page is shown in Figure 3. In this document, go to pages 6, 7, and 8, and replace each "Level Head" using the text tool, as follows:

Replace "First Level Head" (page 6) with "Editorial"; replace "Second Level Head" (page 7) with "What's New?" (Figure 3); and the next "Second Level Head" (page 8) with "Tips and Tricks."

Figure 3. *This is a copy of MANUAL2.PT4 opened at page 7. We have selected "Second Level Head" on page 7 with the text tool to change it to "What's New?"*

After changing the wording on the three pages, make sure the *Style palette* is showing on your screen. If it is not, go into the **Window** menu and select *Style palette*.

Starting at page 6 of the document, select "Editorial" with the text tool and apply the **Head 1** paragraph style to it from the *Style palette*. It may already have this style by default. Select "What's New?" (page 7) and "Tips and Tricks" (page 8), and apply the **Head 1** style to each of these paragraphs separately (Figure 4).

Figure 4. *Here we are applying the style* **Head 1** *to the "Tips and Tricks" heading on page 8.*

Select *Define styles* in the **Type** menu. Highlight **Head 1** (use the scroll bars to locate it) and choose to *Edit* this style. This is after you have decided that these particular headings are to be part of the table of contents. Select the *Para* command from the *Edit style* dialog box, and click on *Include in table of contents* in the *Paragraph specifications* dialog box (Figure 5). Click on OK three times to return to the page.

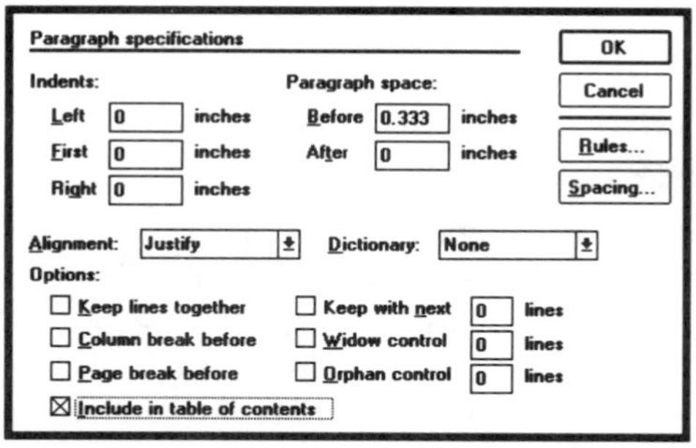

Figure 5. *We are editing the* **Head 1** *style through the* Define styles *command by selecting the* Include in table of contents *option.*

The method described above is the way of including, in the table of contents, paragraphs that have a particular paragraph style applied to them. But you may also wish to include a single paragraph that you do not wish to set up a new paragraph style for.

For example, in addition to all the headings you have applied the **Head 1** style to, you may also want to include the sub-heading "Third Level Head" which only occurs once in the whole document. In this case, you may select that particular item with the text tool (page 8), then select the *Include in table of contents* option (also found under the **Type** menu in the *Paragraph* command).

Select "Third Level Head" with your text tool and go to the *Paragraph* command in the **Type** menu (Figure 6). Select the *Include in table of contents* option and click on OK.

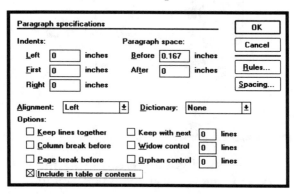

Figure 6. We have now selected the option Include in table of contents *for "Third Level Head" on page 8.*

It is also possible to have more than one paragraph style with the *Include in table of contents* option selected, as PageMaker will list each item in order of its appearance in the document when generating the table of contents (Figure 7).

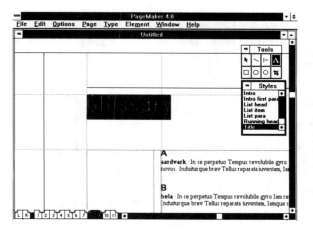

Figure 7. Both the Glossary (page 9) and the Appendix Contents (page 10) have the style **Title** *already applied (as do earlier headings in the document). We selected the* Define styles *command and then selected* Include in table of contents *option for the* **Title** *style.*

Note in Figure 7 that we will also include all paragraphs with the style name **Title** in our table of contents option.

The next step, after selecting all chosen paragraph styles for the table of contents, is to insert one or two blank pages at the beginning of your document (Figure 8). This is where the table of contents can be placed after it has been generated. Alternatively, the table of contents can be placed in a new or already existing PageMaker document. We will be placing the newly generated table of contents on page 5 (see Figure 8).

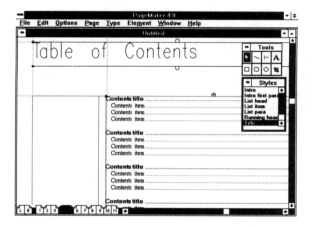

Figure 8. For our example, we deleted the two text blocks on page 5, which were the example table of contents. Our new table of contents will be placed here.

You are now ready to generate the table of contents. To do this, select *Create TOC* in the **Options** menu. The dialog box of Figure 9 will appear.

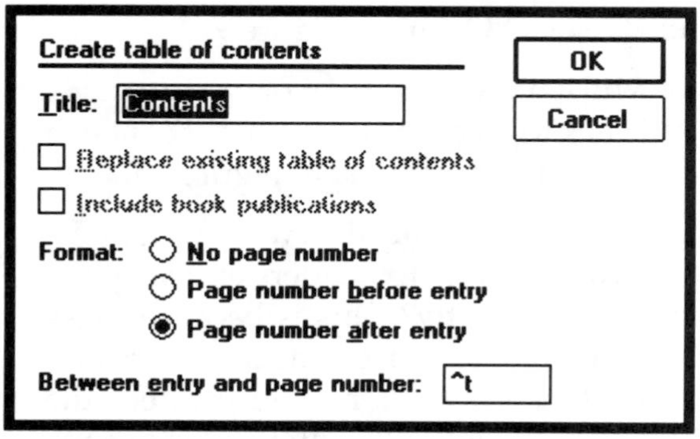

Figure 9. This dialog box will appear when you select Create TOC.

The *Title* option allows you to give your table of contents a title of up to thirty letters. Alternatively, you may delete "Contents" and leave it blank. The *Replacing existing table of contents* option will only be available if you have previously generated a table of contents, in which case you can replace it with a revised version.

If *Include book publications* is selected, PageMaker will generate a single table of contents for all the documents in the *Book list* (provided one has been created). Refer to Module 16, **Long Document Capabilities,** for more details on *Book lists*.

If you are creating a table of contents for multiple publications, you will need to follow the procedure described here for each individual document and then create a *Book list* including each publication name. Make sure, when you are generating your table of contents, that you have the publication opened where you wish to place the contents, or, alternatively, that you have a new untitled publication opened. If the latter case applies, the untitled publication must include the full *Book list* of publications.

The next three options refer to the formatting of the table of contents. You can select to have *No page number*, *Page number before entry*, or *Page number after entry* (default). It is not referring to the actual page that your table of contents is placed on, but to the entries themselves.

The default setting for *Between entry and page number* option is "^t^" — the symbol for a leader tab (.....). This will appear between each entry and the page number (see Figure 10). This symbol can be changed. The PageMaker Reference Manual Appendix lists other characters that can be used.

We chose to have the numbers displayed after the entry. Once you have made your choices, select OK from Figure 9.

After a few moments, you will have a loaded cursor on your page. Position the text cursor and click to place the new table of contents on page 5, which we chose as our contents page (Figure 10).

You will probably wonder (as we originally did) why some of the entries shown in Figure 10 do not have dot leaders and why the numbers are not right aligned correctly? This is because these entries had the style **Title** applied to them in our document before the contents were created. Once the contents are created, the heading at the top (in Figure 10, the word "Contents") is given a style called **TOC Title**. Unfortunately, any style in your document that is called "Title" and included in the table of contents, will also receive the style **TOC Title** once the contents is generated. This confuses PageMaker and causes incorrect formatting (as shown in Figure 10).

The solution — don't use "Title" as a style name in your publication if you intend to use this style as part of your table of contents. See the result of Figure 11 — this is the same document with the table of contents generated. The only difference is that we created a new style (**Heading**) identical to **Title** and reset all paragraphs originally styled **Title** to **Heading**.

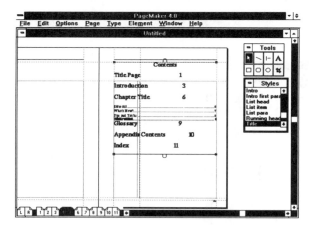

Figure 10. We have placed our newly generated table of contents on page 5. See text for an explanation of why the formatting is not correct.

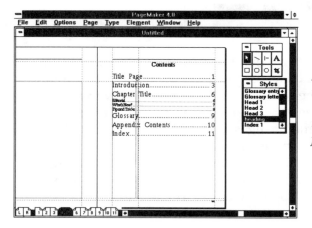

Figure 11. If you change the name of the style from "Title" to "Heading," the table of contents will be formatted correctly.

You will notice that PageMaker creates its own default paragraph styles for each entry that has had a paragraph style applied to it. For example, if the style **Head 1** is included in the table of contents, all **Head 1** table of contents entries will now have the style **TOC Head 1**. (As indicated above, this is why an original **Title** style ended up with **TOC Title**, once the contents were generated.)

To see the paragraph styles that have been generated, select the table of contents entries individually with the text tool, and each particular style will be displayed in the *Style palette*. By default, the generated styles are all in the Times font, but the point size and style (e.g. bold, italic) will be identical to the original paragraph style (Figure 12).

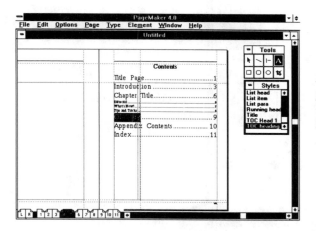

Figure 12. By selecting a paragraph, you can see the TOC paragraph style that has been generated by PageMaker.

These paragraph styles can now be edited and changed in the same way as you would change them for any text file. Be careful not to change the names of the paragraph styles, only the attributes, because subsequent regenerations of the table of contents will overlook the name changes while accepting the attribute changes (e.g. spacing, font, leading, etc.). If you do apply other paragraph styles to the table of contents, or if you make any other style changes that are not made through the *Define styles* command, these changes will be lost when you generate a new table of contents.

EXERCISE: CREATING TABLES OF CONTENTS

Creating Tables of Contents

This exercise is concerned with producing a simple table of contents.

This training material is structured so that people of all levels of expertise with Page-Maker can use it to gain maximum benefit. In order to do this, we have structured it so that the bare exercise is listed below this paragraph on just one page, with no hints. The following pages contain the steps needed to complete this exercise, for those who need additional prompting. The **Table of Contents** module should be kept on hand, in case you need further help or explanations.

Module 17 exercise steps

1. *Open a copy of the template MANUAL1.PT4.*

2. *Include the word "Subhead" on pages 6, 7, and 8 as part of the table of contents. (It occurs twice on each page.) Change each occurrence of "Subhead" in turn to a chapter number (Chapter 1 through Chapter 6).*

3. *Create a blank page at the beginning of the document on which to place the table of contents.*

4. *Edit the paragraph styles of **Subhead 2** and **Subhead 3** so that both have* Include in table of contents *selected.*

5. *Generate a table of contents.*

6. *Place the table of contents.*

7. *Change the style that has been generated for the first line of the contents page so that there is 0.2" paragraph spacing above and below it.*

8. *Go to page 4, select the word "Head," and change its attributes so that it will become part of the table of contents.*

9. *Regenerate the table of contents to replace the existing contents file on page 2.*

The steps to completing this exercise are on the following pages.

The steps in detail

1. Open a copy of the template MANUAL1.PT4.

Open a copy of the file MANUAL1.PT4 from the pscript sub-directory within the template sub-directory.

2. Include the word "Subhead" on pages 6, 7, and 8 as part of the table of contents. (It occurs twice on each page.) Change each occurrence of "Subhead" in turn to a chapter number (Chapter 1 through Chapter 6).

See the Figure 1 caption for details. Once this is complete, select one of the Chapter X insertions on your page with the text tool to see what style has been applied. You will see that pages 6 and 7 have **Subhead 2** and page 8 has **Subhead 3** (Figure 2).

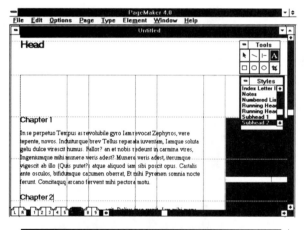

Figure 1. With your text tool, go to pages 6, 7, and 8, select every word "Subhead" (an actual bolded subhead), and replace each one with a chapter number (1 through 6). You should have six when you reach the end. (Do not change anything on page 5.)

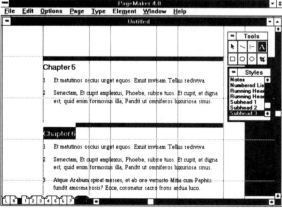

Figure 2. On selecting Chapter 6 on page 8, you can see that the **Subhead 3** style becomes highlighted in the Style palette.

3. Create a blank page at the beginning of the document on which to place the table of contents.

Go to page one of the document and insert one page after the current page by selecting *Insert pages* from the **Page** menu.

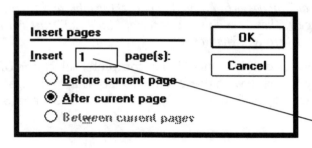

Figure 3. *On page 1, select the* Insert pages *command in the* **Page** *menu to get this dialog box. The final result will give you a blank page on page 2 for placing the table of contents on.*

Make sure you set this number to 1.

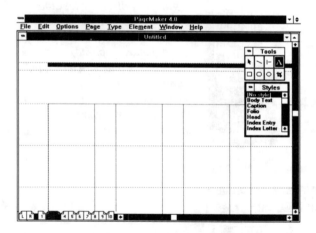

Figure 4. *Page 2 is a new blank page ready to receive the table of contents.*

4. Edit the paragraph styles of **Subhead 2** *and* **Subhead 3** *so that both have* Include in table of contents *selected.*

Go into the *Define styles* command in the **Type** menu and highlight the **Subhead 2** style (Figure 5). Then select the *Edit* option.

See Figures 6 and 7 for how to ensure this style is included in the table of contents. Now, on your own, repeat this process for **Subhead 3**.

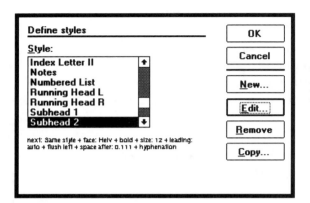

Figure 5. Highlight **Subhead** *2 and select the* Edit *option.*

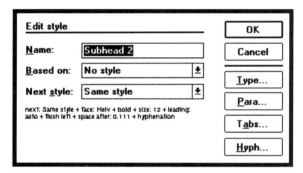

Figure 6. When the Edit style *dialog box appears, select the* Para *option.*

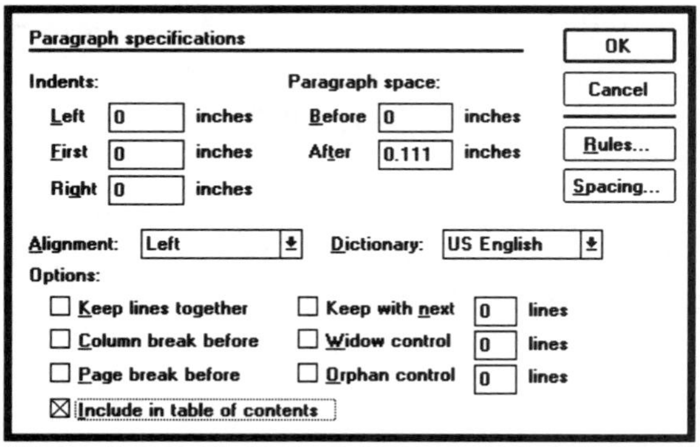

Figure 7. In the Paragraph specifications *dialog box, make sure the* Include table of contents *option is selected.*

Clicking on OK twice will bring you back to the Define styles *dialog box of Figure 5. Now select* **Subhead** *3 and repeat the Figures 6 and 7 procedures. Then click on OK the necessary number of times to return to your page.*

5. Generate a table of contents.

You are now ready to generate the table of contents. Go to page 2 of your document where the generated TOC will be placed. Select *Create TOC* from the **Options** menu (Figure 8) to get the *Create table of contents* dialog box (Figure 9). Leave the default settings of Figure 9 as shown in this example and click on OK.

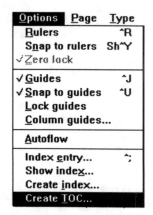

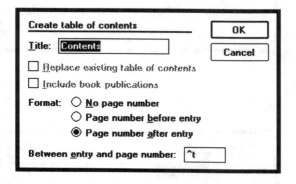

Figure 8. *Go into the* **Options** *menu and select* Create TOC.

Figure 9. *In this TOC dialog box, leave the default settings as your choice for creating the table of contents, then click on OK.*

6. Place the table of contents.

When the loaded cursor appears on your page, place the text. On placing the cursor in the top left-hand corner of the page and clicking the mouse, the generated table of contents file will flow down the first narrow column to the left. To ensure the text flows right across the page, draw an imaginary box from the top-left hand corner to the bottom right before releasing the loaded cursor. It will then look similar to Figure 10.

Note that the page numbers in this Contents file for chapters 1 through 6 will now list pages 7, 8, and 9 rather than 6, 7, and 8. This is because you added the extra page after page 1 (Step 3) to load in the Contents file.

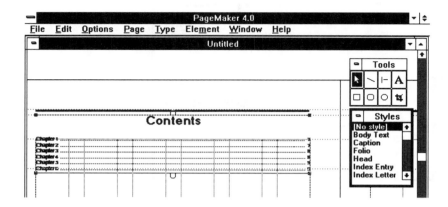

Figure 10. This is how your Contents page will look at this stage.

7. *Change the style that has been generated for the first line of the contents page so that there is 0.2" paragraph spacing above and below it.*

Select the first line with the text tool. The style **TOC Subhead 2** will be highlighted (Figure 11).

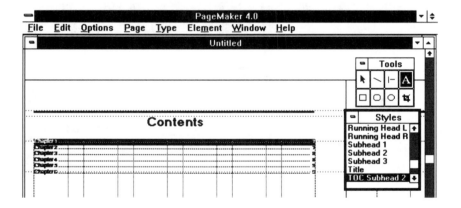

Figure 11. When you select the first line, the **TOC Subhead 2** style becomes highlighted in the Style palette.

Go into *Define styles* in the **Type** menu and highlight **TOC Subhead 2**.

You need to select the *Edit* option in the *Define styles* dialog box to change **TOC Subhead 2** paragraph spacing to 0.2" *Before* and 0.2" *After*. From the *Edit style* dialog box, select the *Para* command to get the Figure 12 dialog box for *Paragraph specifications*. See the Figure 12 caption for more details.

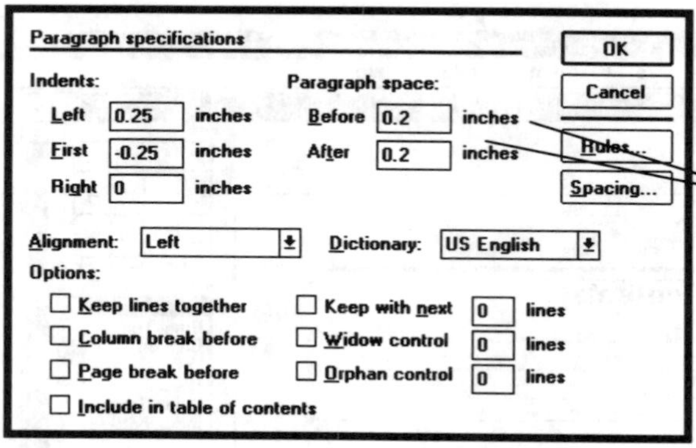

Paragraph specifications				OK

Indents: Paragraph space:

Left [0.25] inches   Before [0.2] inches

First [-0.25] inches   After [0.2] inches

Right [0] inches

Figure 12 After selecting the Para option, insert 0.2" of spacing Before and After. Select OK three times to get back to page 2.

Notice what has now happened to the contents. The lines starting Chapter 1, Chapter 2, Chapter 3, and Chapter 4 all have 0.2" spacing before and after. This is because they all use the same style — **TOC Subhead 2** — which you have just altered. The lines beginning Chapter 5 and Chapter 6 do not have the extra spacings because they use the style **TOC Subhead 3** (Figure 13).

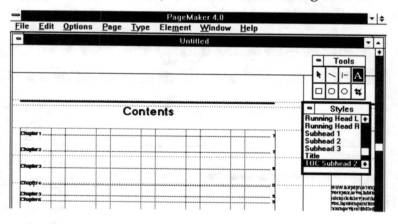

Figure 13. Your table of contents will now look similar to this.

8. Go to page 4, select the word "Head," and change its attributes so that it will become part of the table of contents

Select the word "Head" at the top of page 4 with the text tool (Figure 14). Choose the **Type** menu and select the *Paragraph* command. In this dialog box, select the *Include in table of contents* option (Figure 15). Note that we are changing this paragraph's specifications without altering its style definition. This is generally not good practice.

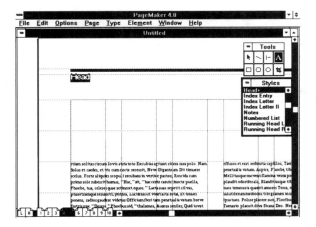

Figure 14. Highlight the text with the text tool on page 4.

Type	Element	Wir
Font	▶	
Size	▶	
Leading	▶	
Set width	▶	
Track	▶	
Type style	▶	
Type specs...	^T	
Paragraph...	^M	
Indents/tabs...	^I	
Hyphenation...	^H	
Alignment	▶	
Style	▶	
Define styles...	^3	

Paragraph specifications — OK

Indents: Paragraph space: Cancel

Left 0 inches   Before 0 inches   Rules...

First 0 inches   After 0 inches   Spacing...

Right 0 inches

Alignment: Left   Dictionary: US English

Options:

☐ Keep lines together   ☐ Keep with next 0 lines

☐ Column break before   ☐ Widow control 0 lines

☐ Page break before   ☐ Orphan control 0 lines

☒ Include in table of contents

Figure 15. Select the Paragraph *option in the* **Type** *menu. Click on the* Include in table of contents *option with your mouse. Select OK.*

9. *Regenerate the table of contents to replace the existing contents file on page 2.*

Go back to page 2 and select the *Create TOC* command in the **Options** menu. Make sure that *Replace existing table of contents* is checked (Figure 16). Select OK.

Create table of contents

Title: [Contents]

OK

Cancel

☒ **Replace existing table of contents**

☐ Include book publications

Format: ○ **No** page number
         ○ **Page number _before_ entry**
         ◉ **Page number _after_ entry**

Between _entry_ and page number: [^t]

Figure 16. Select Replace existing table of contents *in the dialog box. It may already be checked by default. Click on OK.*

The new contents page will still have the paragraph spacing and also the new addition ("Head") that was just selected for inclusion. Your table of contents will look like Figure 17.

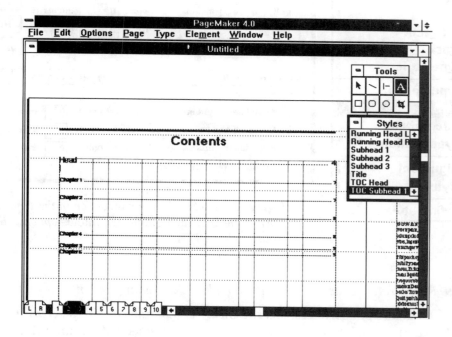

Figure 17. This is how your table of contents will now look.

GENERATING AN INDEX

Generating an Index

PageMaker can automatically generate an index from reference words that you select and identify in the text. From this selection, PageMaker searches through the text to generate a list of words which have been specifically chosen by you to become part of the index.

Creating an index involves:

- Identifying the important topics.

- Developing a hierarchy of related words for each topic.

- Identifying alternative wordings and related information for cross-referencing of each topic.

You'll need to spend time planning your index. Try to think of as many ways of describing each topic as you can. For example, "delete" may be described as "cut" or "clear." It is only once you have completed this stage that you will be ready to move on to the next step involving the "index entry."

PageMaker allows you enter up to three levels for each index entry. The primary entry will be the topic that you have selected, for example "Printer," the secondary level could be "PostScript" and the tertiary entry might be "Paper." PageMaker also allows you to cross-reference other index entries from the current document, and even from other documents that are part of a *Book list* (see Module 16, **Long Document Capabilities**).

Once you have a list of the words and related cross-reference words that are to become part of the index, the next step is to go through the document systematically and select each of these words for inclusion.

Each word must be selected individually (PageMaker does not, for example, search through the whole document for every occurrence of the word "Printer" — only the one you have selected). Each occurrence of a particular word may be in a different context.

For example, the first occurrence of the word "Printer" may be in relation to "laser printers" and the second occurrence may be in relation to "outside bureau printers." That is why every index entry must be inserted individually, although once you have built up a fair number of index entries, you are able to cross-reference entries of the same word very quickly. If you are creating index entries in story view, you can, however, use the *Find* command to assist in locating desired index words and phrases.

Once you have completed all the index entries and cross-references, you select *Create index* in the **Options** menu, choose the format you want, and PageMaker generates an index that you place onto a new page or into a new document.

If you add any text or graphics to your publication that cause the page numbering to change, PageMaker will allow you to generate a new, updated version to replace the old index.

Let's have a look, step-by-step, at how this is done.

Creating index entries

To illustrate index entry with a page reference, we have placed the text file LEADSTRY.RTF from the lesson2 directory in Figure 1. On the first page, if you want, say, *Aldus Manutius* as one of your index entry topics, you must "mark" these words for inclusion. There are two ways to do this. The first way is illustrated in Figure 1, the second in Figure 2.

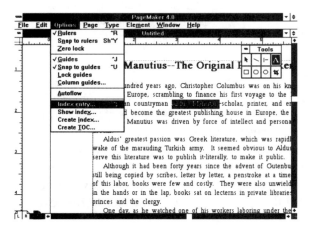

Figure 1. With the text tool, highlight the words Aldus Manutius. Select Index entry from the Options menu. The highlighted word will appear as shown in the Figure 3 Add index entry dialog box. It can then be edited, if necessary, with the text tool.

The Figure 1 method is used when the text you want in the index is the same as the text you have selected. The Figure 2 method opens up the Figure 3 dialog box but without, in this example, any words in the *Topic* rectangles. You are free to enter your own entry, which may differ slightly from the actual word or phrase in the text. It is also possible to enter an index entry using the *Topic* button of Figure 3. See the description of this approach below, with reference to Figure 5.

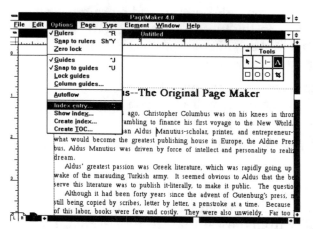

Figure 2. *With the text tool, insert the flashing cursor close to the words **Aldus Manutius**. Select* Index entry *from the* **Options** *menu and you can then type the required index word into the first* Topic *edit box of the Figure 3* Add index entry *dialog box.*

Note: *Each index entry topic can be up to fifty characters long.*

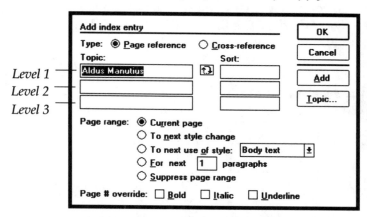

Figure 3. *There are three levels of index entry in the* Add index entry *dialog box for primary, secondary, and tertiary levels. Note that* Page reference *(next to* Type*) is the default mode of index entry.*

The *Add index entry* dialog box of Figure 3 contains three levels of index entry — primary, secondary, and tertiary. Secondary and tertiary are optional. When you insert an entry, as we have done in Figures 1 and 2, PageMaker places an index marker in the text which is visible in story view.

If you enter in the *Add index entry* dialog box "Desktop" as the first entry, "publishing" as the second entry, and "PageMaker"' as the third entry (as shown in Figure 4), PageMaker will display the generated index like this:

D

Desktop

  publishing

    PageMaker   **1**

Or like this:

D

Desktop: publishing: PageMaker **1**

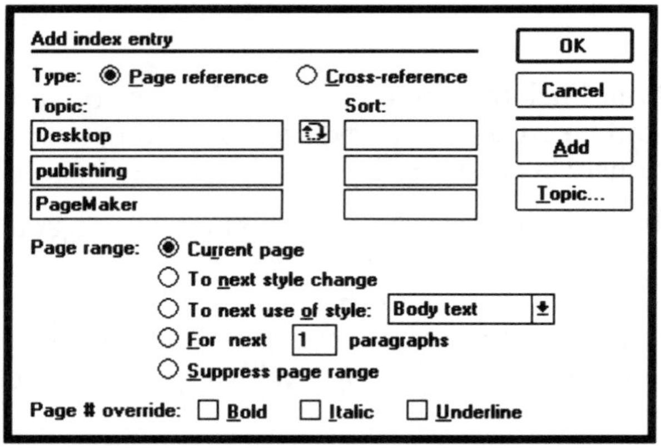

Figure 4. An example of the Add index entry *dialog box with all the levels utilized.*

You may want to create several primary entries for each topic to ensure readers will find what they are looking for. So, if it is necessary to create such a comprehensive index, you will need to enter, for example, "publishing" and "PageMaker" as first entries as well.

If you use the cross-reference option, no page number will be displayed at all. It could look like this:

D

Desktop

  See **publishing: PageMaker**

Let's look at the other sections of the *Add Index entry* dialog box of Figure 4. Using the *Sort* edit boxes allows you to specify how each corresponding entry will be sorted in the index. (Figure 5 displays an example of its use.)

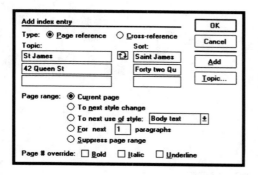

Figure 5. If the Sort *edit box is left empty, PageMaker will list the entry as it appears in the* Topic *edit box. However, if you have an entry such as a number, it is wise to spell out its sort details; otherwise it may not appear at the correct place in the index.*

Cross-reference option: Click this option to select the *X-ref* button so that your entry can be cross-referenced with any other index entry that has previously been entered.

X-ref button: This button only becomes available after clicking on the *Cross-reference* option to the right of the *Page reference* option. Clicking on this button will display the *Select cross-reference topic* dialog box. This box allows you to cross-reference what is in your *Add index entry* dialog box as an index topic with any other topic already entered.

We will look at these last two options in more detail in the next section. It is always advisable to leave cross-referencing until **after** all the major index entries have been made, as PageMaker provides a list of all existing index topics in your publication to make selection easier.

Add button: Use this option to complete the index entry if you wish to add more entries at this insertion point.

Looped arrow icon: Clicking on this icon automatically moves any entered text from one topic level to another in a circular fashion.

The options that follow the *Page Range* command in Figure 4 refer to the number of pages PageMaker will include for the current index entry listing. For example, if the topic "Desktop" is referred to continually on pages 1 and 2, then in the index you would want the "Desktop" listing to display, for example,

D

Desktop **1-2**

Current page option: If "Desktop" information is complete on this page, select this option.

To next style change option: If "Desktop" information continues until the next change in paragraph style, select this option.

To next use of style option: If "Desktop" information continues beyond the next style change, you can select the paragraph style that marks the end of this section with this option.

For next ☐ *paragraphs* option: Here you can enter in the specified number of paragraphs that include "Desktop" information.

Suppress page range option: When you want to create an index without a reference, click on this option. This is useful when you are in the process of revising an index and you want to create entries as a reminder to index later.

P# override option: These three options allow you to modify the style for the page numbers and cross-reference sections of the index. These selections remain until changed again.

Topic button: Clicking on this button will display the *Select topic* dialog box. This dialog box simplifies the multiple entry of identical topics. Simply select, in alphabetical order, from the list of index topics and click on OK.

One final note: If you choose *Index entry* without first selecting text or inserting the text tool, only the *Cross-reference* option becomes available at this point.

It is also possible to index across multiple publications using the *Book list* command. Upon clicking on *Topic* in the *Add index entry* dialog box of Figure 4, the *Select topic* dialog box appears. An *Import* button allows topics to be imported from other publications to ensure consistency of indexing.

Cross-referencing

Cross-referencing of new entries is done by highlighting the word with the text tool and selecting the *Index entry* command from the **Options** menu. Our example in Figure 6 is showing Page Maker selected from the heading of Figure 2. Next choose *Cross-reference* as the type in the *Add index entry* dialog box. Then choose the *X-ref* button (Figure 6), which brings up the *Select cross-reference topic* dialog box of Figure 7.

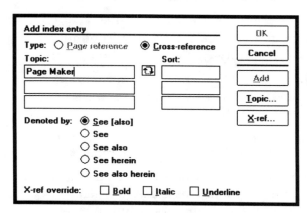

Figure 6. The Add index entry *dialog box with Page Maker in the Level 1 topic box and* Cross-reference *selected.*

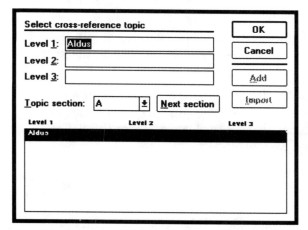

Figure 7. The Select cross-reference *topic dialog box with the Aldus entry showing.*

From this dialog box, you choose the entry you wish to cross-reference with. We currently have two index entries, both on page 1 — Aldus and Greek. Aldus is showing in Figure 7, as it belongs to the A section. We wish to cross-reference Page Maker with the word "Greek." The Greek entry can be found in either of two ways.

Click on the down arrow to the right of the letter A, next to *Topic section*. This will provide an alphabetical drop-down menu for you to locate the required word. A faster way is to click on the *Next section* button, which will bring up in turn each separate alphabetical entry. Figure 8 now shows the Greek entry.

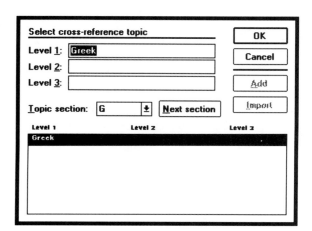

Figure 8. The Select cross-reference topic *dialog box with the Greek entry showing.*

Click on "Greek" and click on OK twice to return to the page. Your index, when generated, will then read:

A

Aldus 1

G

Greek 1

P

Page Maker. *See* Greek

It is also possible to cross-reference between entered index entries using the *Show index* command from the **Options** menu (Figure 9). Say, for example, in the sample index listed above, you wanted to cross-reference the Aldus entry also to the Greek entry: e.g., Aldus *See also* Greek. You would do it this way.

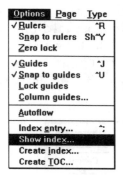

Figure 9. The Show index *command in the* **Options** *menu gives you the associated dialog box of Figure 10.*

From the *Show index* dialog box of Figure 10, first select the Aldus entry. Then click on *Add x-ref* in the bottom left corner. From the *Add index entry* dialog box that appears, click on *X-ref* again (see Figure 11).

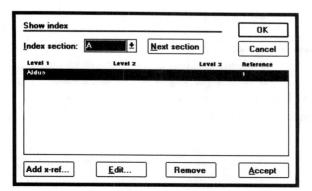

Figure 10. Once you have selected the Aldus entry in the Show index *dialog box, click on the* Add x-ref *button in the bottom left corner.*

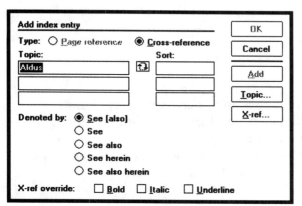

Figure 11. Once the Add index entry *dialog box appears, click on the* X-ref *button to activate the* Select cross-reference topic *dialog box.*

From the *Select cross-reference topic* dialog box of Figure 12, click on *Next section* until "Greek" appears, and then highlight this entry. Click on OK twice to return to the *Show index* dialog box of Figure 13.

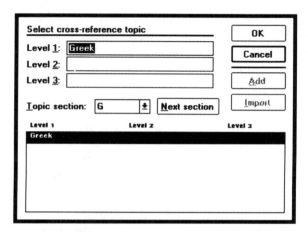

Figure 12. In this dialog box, highlight the Greek entry after clicking on Next section *until "Greek" appears.*

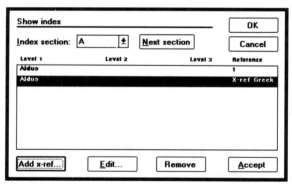

Figure 13. In the Show index *dialog box, the Aldus entry will now have an* X-ref *to the Greek entry.*

In the Figure 13 dialog box, the Aldus entry will now show an *X-ref* to" Greek." Your index would now look like this:

A

Aldus 1. *See also* Greek

G

Greek 1

P

Page Maker. *See* Greek

PageMaker also allows you to cross-reference topics from other publications. All selected publications must be placed in a *Book list* (described in Module 16) so that PageMaker will know which documents to display the index entries of for cross-referencing.

In the *Select cross-reference topic* dialog box (Figure 7), you have the option to choose the *Import* button. This option imports all the topics from the other publications to ensure cross-referencing is correctly performed. You are able to select the entry you wish to cross-reference with the original topic you chose.

Editing

When you have completed your index entries, as well as any cross references, you may still need to edit, add, or delete an entry at a later stage before creating your index.

This is simply done by selecting the *Show index* command in the **Options** menu (as we have already done above for creating cross-references). The dialog box that appears is shown again in Figure 14. Highlight the entry you wish to edit, add a cross-reference to, or remove, as shown in Figure 14 below.

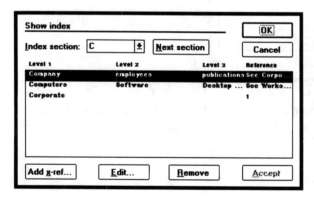

Figure 14. The Add x-ref *button allows you to add a cross-reference to the selected index entry as described above. The* Edit *button displays the* Edit index entry *dialog box, allowing you to edit any section of this. The* Remove *button removes the highlighted index entry.*

Adding a cross-reference has been described above. The *Edit index entry* dialog box is the same as the *Add index entry* dialog box already explained. *Remove* simply removes a highlighted index entry. The *Accept* button allows changes you have made to be accepted, but leaves the dialog box open for further changes, if necessary.

Creating the index

You are now ready to create the index. Before this is done, you need to decide if it is to go onto a blank page at the end of the document, onto the pasteboard area, or into a new document altogether.

Once you have the appropriate page of your document opened, select *Create index* in the **Options** menu. A dialog box similar to that of Figure 15 will appear on your screen. The title of the index, which can be edited with the text tool, can have up to thirty letters.

By selecting the *Format* button, a second dialog box (Figure 16) will appear.

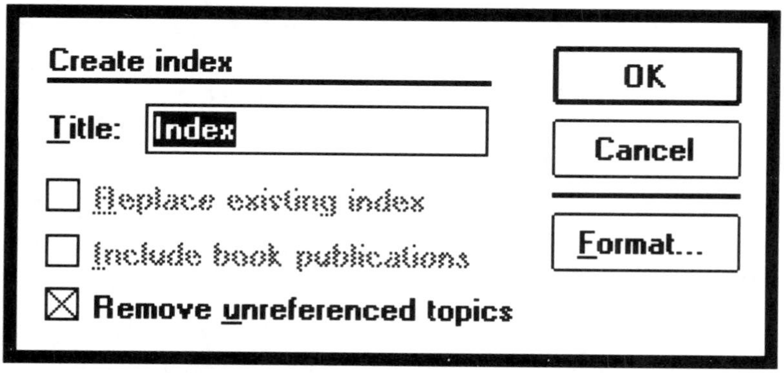

Figure 15. In the Create index *dialog box, the* Replace existing index *option will not be available if this is the first time you have asked PageMaker to generate this index. The* Include book publications *will also be unavailable if you have not set up a* Book list *previously. If you select* Remove unreferenced topics, *index topics imported from other publications that are not used as entries or cross-references in the current publication will be removed. Any index topics that have no references are also removed.*

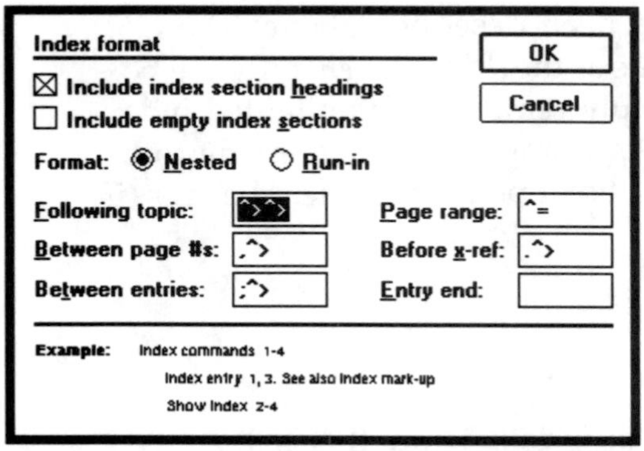

Figure 16. PageMaker offers you two default settings for the index format, Nested *and* Run-in. *By clicking on either alternative, an example of the format is displayed at the bottom of the dialog box.*

Because PageMaker automatically generates each section heading of the index (e.g. A, B, and C), you must deselect *Include index section headings* in Figure 16 if you wish not to have these included. PageMaker, however, will still insert spacing between each alphabetical section.

If you select *Include empty index sections*, PageMaker will list every section included in your index, but the empty sections will read "no entries."

Choose *Nested* or *Run-in* to determine the format of your index. Examples are shown at the bottom of the Figure 16 dialog box. With *Nested*, each entry level of the index is a separate paragraph. With *Run in*, all entry levels belong to one paragraph. The rest of this dialog box highlights the different characters used between index entries, page numbers, etc. The Appendix of the PageMaker Reference manual provides details of these characters.

Once you have made your selections in the *Index format* dialog box, click on OK. Then select OK again, and PageMaker will generate an index.

After a short time, you will have a loaded cursor on your page which you can place in the same way as any other text file. If you checked *Replace existing index*, your new index will automatically replace the old.

As with the generated table of contents, PageMaker creates its own paragraph styles for the index as well. You are also able to make additions and deletions to any index entries after the index has been created. To update the index, simply select *Replace existing index* in the *Create index* dialog box, and PageMaker will regenerate and replace the old version.

EXERCISE: GENERATING AN INDEX

Generating an Index

   This exercise is designed to illustrate the concepts of index generation within PageMaker. Although it only refers to a single-page publication, the major requirements to generate an index are covered.

   This training material is structured so that people of all levels of expertise with Page Maker can use it to gain maximum benefit. In order to do this, we have structured the material so that the bare exercise is listed below this paragraph on just one page, with hints. The following pages contain the steps needed to complete this exercise, for those who need additional prompting. The **Generating an Index** module should be referenced if you need further help or explanations.

Module 18 exercise steps

1.   *Open a new two-page publication and place LEADSTRY.RTF from the lesson2 sub-directory across three columns. This will be used to create an index.*

2.   *The items that are to be indexed are* **Francesco Griffo da Bologna**, *italics,* **Greek literature, Homer,** *and* **Aristotle.** *Some of these will be primary entries, others secondary.*

3.   *Index the items so that the resulting index file looks like this:*

   A
   Artist
           Francesco Griffo da Bologna *1*
   F
   Fonts
           italics   *1*
   G
   Greek literature
           Aristotle   *1*
           Homer   *1*
   I
   italics. *See Fonts: italics*

4.   *Place the created index text on page 2 and make sure that it looks similar to the example of Figure 16.*

The steps to completing this exercise are on the following pages.

The steps in detail

1. Open a new two-page publication and place LEADSTRY.RTF from the lesson2 sub-directory across three columns. This will be used to create an index.

Perform this simple step yourself to get the layout shown in Figure 1.

Aldus Manutius— The Original Page Maker

Five hundred years ago, Christopher Columbus was on his knees in throne rooms throughout Europe, scrambling to finance his first voyage to the New World. Meanwhile, his Venetian countryman Aldus Manutius-scholar, printer, and entrepreneur-was establishing what would become the greatest publishing house in Europe, the Aldine Press. Like Columbus, Aldus Manutius was driven by force of intellect and personality to realize a lifelong dream.

Aldus' greatest passion was Greek literature, which was rapidly going up in smoke in the wake of the marauding Turkish army. It seemed obvious to Aldus that the best way to preserve this literature was to publish it-literally, to make it public. The question was, how?

Although it had been forty years since the advent of Gutenburg's press, most books were still being copied by scribes, letter by letter, a penstroke at a time. Because of the intensity of this labor, books were few and costly. They were also unwieldy. Far too large to be held in the hands or in the lap, books sat on lecterns in private libraries and were seen only by princes and the clergy.

One day, as he watched one of his workers laboring under the load of books he was carrying, Aldus had a flash of insight: Could books from the Aldine Press be made small enough to be carried without pulling a muscle? And could he produce the elegant, lightweight volumes he imagined and still sell them at an attractive price?

The first problem was how to print more legible words per page and thus reduce the number of pages. Aldus needed a smaller typeface that was both readable and pleasing to the eye. The work of the Aldine Press had attracted the notice of the finest typographic artists in Europe, so Aldus was able to enlist the renowned Francesco Griffo da Bologna to design a new one. Under Aldus' direction, Griffo developed a typeface that was comparatively dense and compact and that imitated the calligraphy of courtly correspondence. The result of this Aldus-Griffo collaboration was the ancestor of what we now call italics.

The new typeface enabled Aldus to print portable and highly readable books. Besides the first edition of Dante's Divine Comedy, Aldus published the essential texts of Greek literature, the histories of Herodotus and Thucydides, the tragedies of Sophocles, the epics of Homer and the treatises of Aristotle, thus rescuing them from relative oblivion.

The timing was perfect. With the growth of the merchant class in Venice, Florence, Naples, and Rome, a new market ripe for books had recently emerged. This newly prosperous middle class was flush with money and anxious for intelligent ways to spend it. The new books from the Aldine Press were an immediate success.

As more books became available, the middle classes in Italy-and ultimately, in all of Europe-grew more literate and the Aldine Press became more prestigious. And Aldus, the publisher who put books in the hands of the people, eventually lent his name to the company that put publishing in the hands of the people.

Figure 1. LEADSTRY.RTF placed on a three-column page. This figure may make it easier for you to identify the parts of the text to be indexed in step 2 of this exercise.

2. *The items that are to be indexed are **Francesco Griffo da Bologna, italics, Greek literature, Homer,** and **Aristotle**. Some of these will be primary entries, others secondary. (See Figure 1 for their locations.)*

The first step when creating an index is to change to the text tool. This allows you to move through the text and select the index entries that you want.

The first item to index is around the middle of the center column. If you look at how this entry occurs in the example index on the front page of this exercise, you will see that it is actually a secondary entry — under the primary entry of **Artists**. See Figures 2 through 4 for the steps to achieve this.

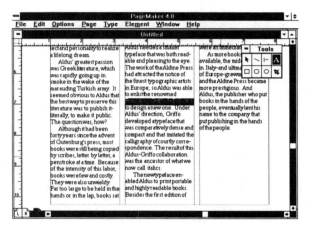

Figure 2. *Highlight the words "Francesco Griffo da Bologna."*

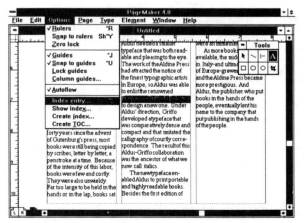

Figure 3. *After highlighting the words you would like to index, select the* Index entry *command in the* **Options** *menu.*

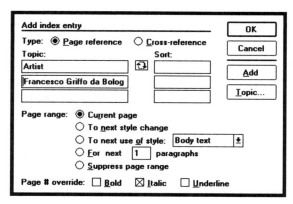

*Figure 4. Because **Francesco Griffo da Bologna** is a secondary entry under the primary entry **Artists**. The* Add index *entry dialog box should be filled out as illustrated in this figure. (Initially, the name Francesco will appear in the level 1 line from the operation of Figures 2 and 3. Click on the looped arrow once and it will move to level 2.) Also choose* Italic *for P# override to get italic page numbers. Select OK to record your entry.*

Move now to the next phrase to be indexed — "italics," just below "Francesco." As you look at the index example at the front of this exercise, you will see that this also is a secondary entry under the heading **Fonts**. See Figures 5 through 7 for the steps to do this.

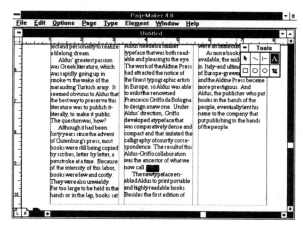

Figure 5. Highlight the word "italics," as shown here.

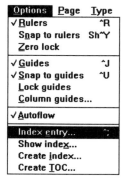

Figure 6. After highlighting the word, remember to choose the Index entry *command.*

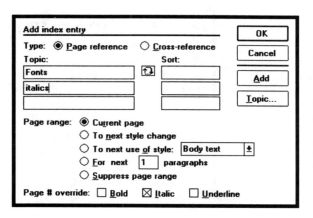

*Figure 7. Because **italics** is a secondary entry, it must be inserted in the correct box. (Click on the looped arrow to move it down to level 2.) The word "Fonts" should be inserted on the first line. Ensure that Italic is selected at the bottom and click on OK.*

The next two entries — **Homer** and **Aristotle** — occur as secondary entries under the same primary entry. To do this, you must be very careful to spell the primary entry correctly as it has to be entered twice (once for each secondary heading). Apart from being careful to spell everything correctly, these two phrases are notated as index entries in exactly the same way as the previous one (Figures 8 through 11).

Alternatively, for keying in the second secondary entry of **Aristotle** (Figure 11), you could have first chosen the *Topic* button and selected **Greek literature** from the *Select topic* dialog box that appears. That way you would have ensured that the spelling was correct.

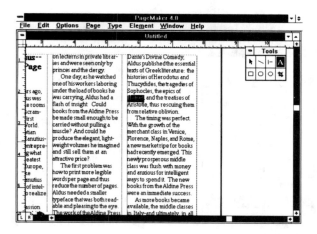

Figure 8. Highlight "Homer" with your text cursor.

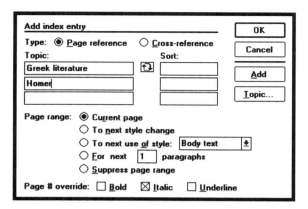

Figure 9. Fill out the dialog box as illustrated. Again, use the looped arrow option to move **Homer** down to the second level. Make sure **Greek literature** is spelt correctly, as it will be referenced again. Select OK.

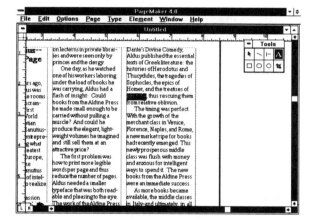

Figure 10. Highlight the word "Aristotle."

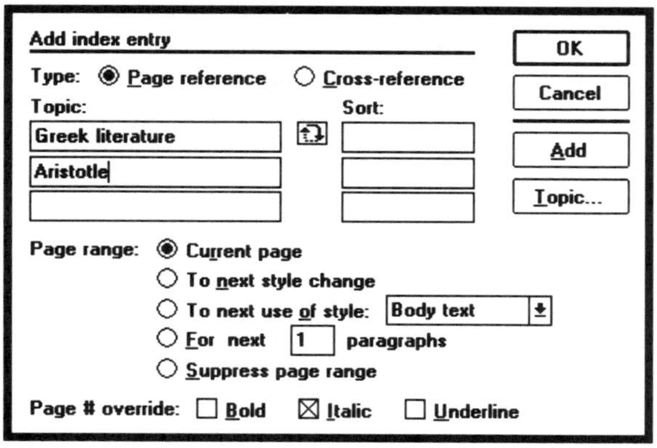

Figure 11. Under the **Options** menu select Index entry and, when the dialog box appears, fill it out as in this figure. Select OK.

The final index entry involves the *X-ref* option in the *Add index entry* dialog box. On the example index at the front, note the entry under *I*. It reads:

I

italics. *See Fonts: italics*

When you create this sort of index entry, you do not have to worry about inserting the text cursor anywhere near the words "italics" or "Fonts," although the cursor may be embedded in the text. You can also choose the *Index entry* command with the pointer tool selected, which by default only allows you to select the *X-ref* command in this dialog box. This is because there are no page numbers displayed with the **See** entries.

To complete this last entry, insert your text cursor anywhere in the document, or select the pointer tool, and then choose the *Index entry* command in the **Options** menu. This gives you the Figure 12 dialog box. Add the word "italics" in the level 1 topic box as shown.

Make sure *Cross-Reference* is selected, and also select the *See* option. Click on the *X-ref* button. In the *Select cross-reference topic* dialog box of Figure 13, you must then find **Fonts** under the letter F and highlight it. Select OK twice to get back to your page.

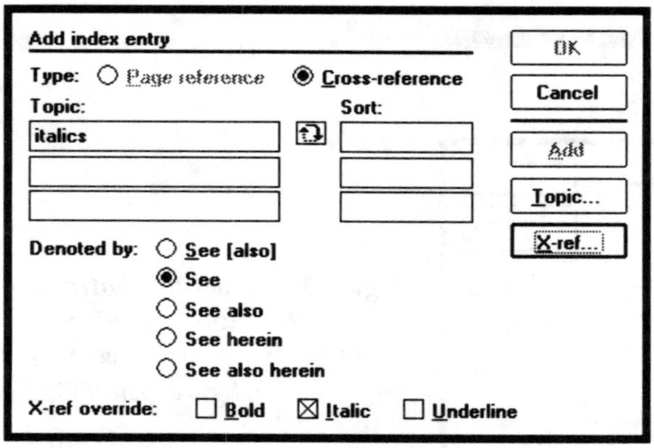

Figure 12. The entries should look like this for the ***italics*** cross-referencing. Select the Cross-reference *option and the* See *option, then click on* X-ref.

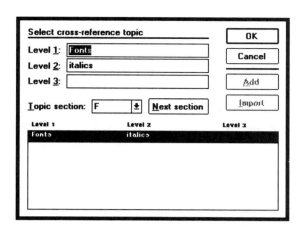

Figure 13. Once "Fonts" has been located and highlighted by selecting OK, PageMaker will list *Fonts* as a cross-reference to *italics*.

3. Index the items so the resulting index file will look like that shown below.

A

Artist

　　　Francesco Griffo da Bologna   *1*

F

Font

　　　italics　　*1*

G

Greek literature

　　　Aristotle　*1*

　　　Homer　　*1*

I

italics. *See Fonts: italics*

4. Place the created index text on page 2 and make sure that it looks similar to the example of Figure 16.

Go to page 2 and select *Create index* from the **Options** menu. See Figures 14 and 15 to complete this process.

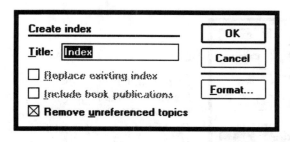

Figure 14. The options in the Create index *dialog box will look like this. Now select the* Format *button.*

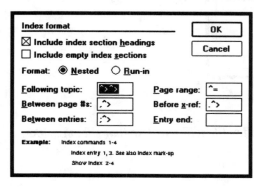

Figure 15. For this exercise, ensure that your Index format *box looks like this and click on OK.*

You are now ready to select OK in the *Create index* dialog box. When the loaded cursor appears on your blank page, place the text. Your final index page will look like the example in Figure 16.

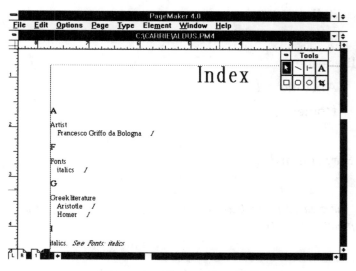

Figure 16. The completed index.

THE TABLE EDITOR

The Table Editor

The Aldus Table Editor is similar in operation to PageMaker, making it very easy to use. This program is designed to help you create professional looking tables, schedules, lists, worksheets, forms, comparison charts, etc. that you can import into your PageMaker documents.

Table Editor is like a spreadsheet program, allowing you to arrange information easily into rows and/or columns. Its features then give you the option to resize, insert, and delete any of these rows or columns.

The flexibility of this program lets you apply, format, and edit text attributes, as well as allowing you to change the line styles and fills to give your table more visual impact.

Citizens Applications 1985-1987			
	1985	1986	1987
January	7370	8250	4739
February	9931	8947	6397
March	9685	7542	5766
April	12302	8194	4539
May	11126	8313	5067
June	8394	7622	5668
July	10042	8897	n/a
August	11727	7997	n/a
September	7099	6827	n/a
October	7655	5189	n/a
November	8277	3775	n/a
December	5504	4763	n/a
Total	109112	86298	32176

Figure 1. This is an example of the sorts of tables that can be created in the Table Editor program.

Once you have created your table, you may save it in its native format (.TBL) for importation into PageMaker, or export it either as a text or a graphics file into another application. If you bring it into PageMaker as a text file, you can edit it with the text tool directly on the page; if you import it as a graphics file, you may resize and crop the image as you would any other graphic.

Creating a table

Before you use Table Editor, make sure that it has been installed using the correct installation procedures from the installation guide notes. To start the program, double-click on the Table Editor icon in the Windows environment. Select *New* from the **File** menu (Figure 2).

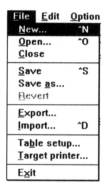

Figure 2: Select New *from the* **File** *menu to create a new table.*

The *Table setup* dialog box (Figure 3) will appear, allowing you to specify the number of columns and rows you would like in your table. Remember that you can add, delete, or modify the number and size of columns/rows at any stage, so don't be afraid to experiment. We will now briefly explain each section within this dialog box (refer to Figure 3).

Number of columns: Specify here the number of columns you would like in your table. Remember, columns are vertical.

Number of rows: Choose the number of rows you require. Rows are horizontal.

Table size: This option allows you to determine the height and width of the overall table, regardless of the number of rows and columns.

Gutter in inches: Column/Row: This option determines the space between text from one column/row to the next. You may need to experiment with values in this option until the text is correctly positioned.

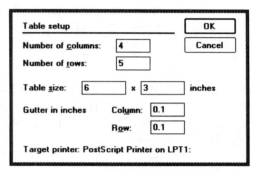

Figure 3: The Table setup *dialog box allows you to pre-determine the basic setting for your table. We have changed the default settings for the number of columns and rows to 4 and 5.*

Typing in text

To enter text into a table "cell," first select the text tool, click the cursor inside a specific cell so that the flashing text cursor is visible, and simply start typing (Figure 4). The text will wrap to fit inside the cell, expanding vertically to accommodate the text. If required, hold down the Shift + Enter keys to create a new line.

To move from cell to cell within your table, there are a couple of options. If you press the Enter key, you will move down to the next row. Pressing the Tab key will move you to the right, while the Shift + Tab keys will move you to the left. Alternatively, you can click the cursor into another cell.

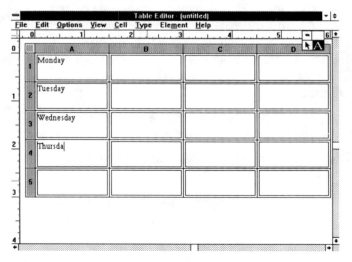

Figure 4. Select the text tool, click the cursor inside a cell, and start typing. Here we have typed text into a number of cells to illustrate the principle.

Resizing rows and columns

This feature allows you to experiment with rows and columns of varying widths and lengths. As you will see, whenever you modify the height or width of a column or row using these methods, the text reflows automatically. There are two ways to modify rows and columns.

The first method is to select a particular cell by clicking inside it with the pointer tool selected. Alternatively, clicking inside any of the defined gray areas to the far left or far top of the table (known as grid labels) will select a whole column or row. Once you have made your selection, go to the **Cell** menu and select either the *Row height* or *Column width* command, depending on which option you have decided to vary. Inside this dialog box, you can change the value (Figure 5, 6, and 7). For our example, we selected one cell and chose to modify its row height.

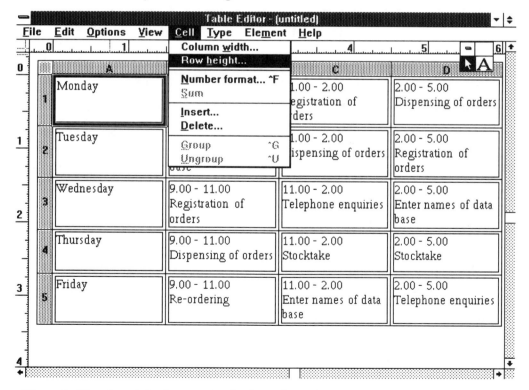

Figure 5. *We selected the first row in the first column in order to modify its row height. We then selected the* Row height *command from the* **Cell** *menu.*

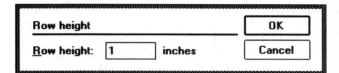

Figure 6. This is the dialog box that is invoked after selecting the Row height *command. We substituted the value of 1 inch here and selected OK.*

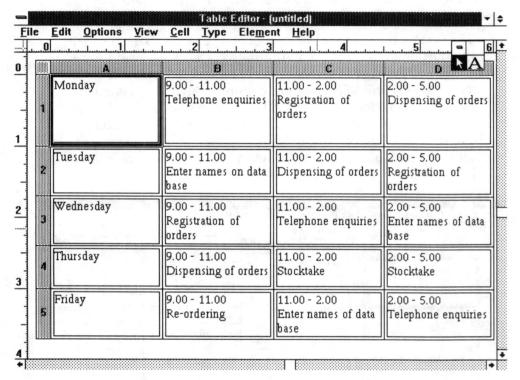

Figure 7. This is the result of the changes we just made. Note how the depth of the table has been adjusted.

Note: It also possible to select more than one cell, row, or column by holding down the Shift key as you are making the selection. (Alternatively, you can keep the mouse depressed as you make your selection). This allows you to modify more than one cell, row, or column at the same time.

The second method is the manual way to modify the sizes of rows or columns. It involves moving the boundaries of the rows and/ or columns with the mouse placed in the grid label area. Follow Figures 8 and 9 to see how this is done.

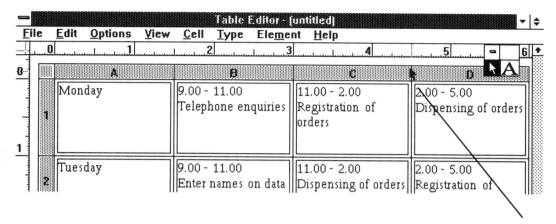

Figure 8. *We are going to change the width of column C manually to make it wider. Position the mouse on the line between columns C and D until a double-headed arrow appears, hold the mouse down, and drag it to the right. Release the mouse.*

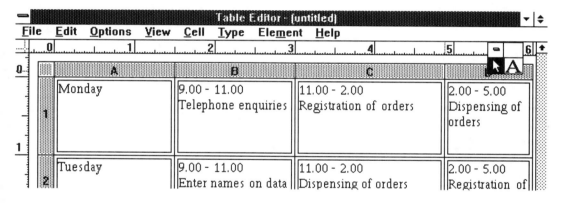

Figure 9. *After releasing the mouse, this will be the new width of the third column. Note how the fourth column width has also changed, becoming smaller.*

Formatting text

You will find this particular section of table editing very simple if you are familiar with the **Type** menu and the text tool within PageMaker. They both work in a similar way; the idea is that you select the text you wish to format, and then use the commands from the **Type** menu to effect this change.

There are two methods for selecting text — with the text tool and with the pointer tool. We will look at both.

The text tool is used if you only wish to format text in an individual cell, as it will not allow you to select any more than this. The easiest way is to simply insert the text tool inside the specific cell, move to the **Type** menu, and make your command selection. Any changes you make in this way will apply to all the text in the cell. It is not possible to apply any more than one font or type size in a cell. Follow Figures 10 and 11 for our example.

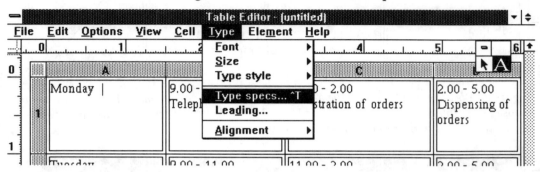

*Figure 10. We have inserted our text cursor in the first row of the first column of our table. We have then gone to the **Type** menu to select the* Type Specs *command to make our changes.*

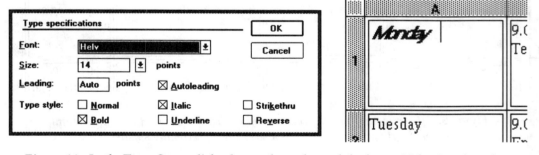

Figure 11. In the Type Specs *dialog box we have changed the font to Helvetica, the point size to 14, and the style to* Bold *and* Italic. *The result can be seen in the diagram to the right.*

The second method involves using the pointer tool to select text. This method allows you to select more than one cell at a time, and even the whole table if necessary. To select the whole table, click in the top left corner of the grid labels. To select an entire row or column, click on its corresponding grid label area. To select one or more cells, either hold down the Shift key or keep the mouse button depressed and drag to include the other cells.

Follow Figures 12 and 13 to see our example.

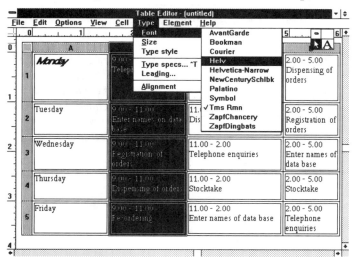

*Figure 12. After selecting the second column by clicking on B in the grid label, we have gone to the **Type** menu and invoked the Font sub-menu to choose Helvetica.*

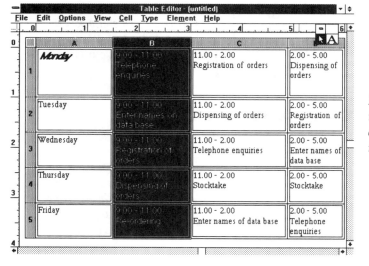

Figure 13. This is the result of the font change we just invoked.

Inserting rows and columns

With Table Editor, you can insert and delete rows and columns at any time, making it very easy to edit your table.

As you may have guessed, there are a number of ways to insert and delete rows or columns. To insert a row or a column using the pointer tool, follow Figures 14 through 16.

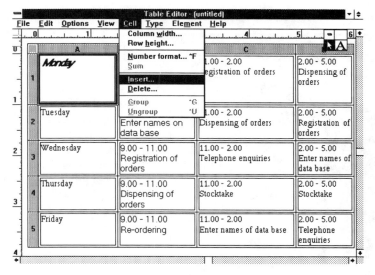

Figure 14. We selected
the first cell in the top
left of the table and
then chose the
Insert *command from*
the **Cell** *menu.*

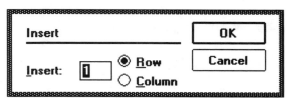

Figure 15. This invoked the
Insert *dialog box. We are going to*
insert one row in our table.

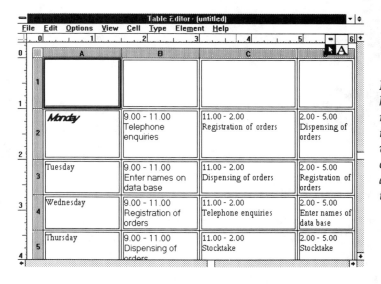

Figure 16. Note
how the new row
now appears above
the selected cell. If
we had inserted a
column, it would
appear to the left of
the selected cell.

You may also use the text tool to insert rows and columns using the *Insert* command. Simply insert the text cursor inside a cell, and then select the *Insert* command from the **Cell** menu. The same procedure shown in Figures 15 and 16 applies.

The last method is to use the *Table setup* command from the **File** menu. The new rows are added to the bottom of the table and the new columns are added to the right side.

Deleting rows and columns

To delete a row or column, use the text or the pointer tool to select a cell in the same manner that has just been described, and then select the *Delete* command from the **Cell** menu. You may delete multiple rows or columns at one time.

Grouping cells

The grouping of cells is useful for creating headings that stretch across a table, and also for combining certain cells together to create one large cell within the table itself.

With the pointer tool, select the cells you wish to combine. Then go to the **Cell** menu and select the *Group* command (Figures 17 and 18). To ungroup combined cells, select the cells and then choose the *Ungroup* command from the **Cell** menu.

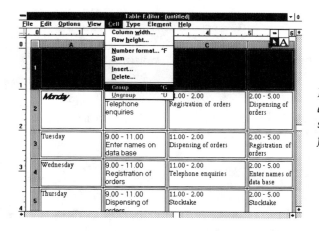

Figure 17. After selecting all the cells in the top row, select the Group *command from the* **Cell** *menu.*

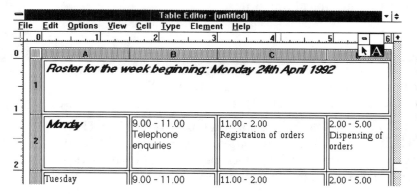

Figure 18. Grouping these cells together allows us to type in a table heading.

Changing line styles and shading tables

Varying the line styles within a table can often clarify and enhance the look of your table. By default, all the cell borders are 1 point in thickness, but the *Borders* command from the **Element** menu will allow you to vary this thickness in selected parts of the table.

Before selecting the **Borders** command, you must first select the whole table or section of the table that you wish to affect. Let's say for example, that you want to create a 2-point line thickness for the border around the table, and you also want to delete all internal vertical rules. After selecting the whole table and the *Borders* command from the **Element** menu, follow the steps as illustrated in Figure 19.

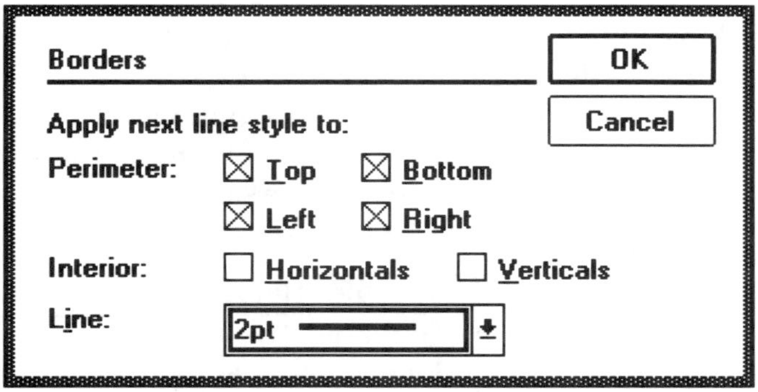

Figure 19. We have deselected the Interior Horizontal *and* Vertical *rules so that only the outside border will be changed to a 2-point thickness. Select* OK.

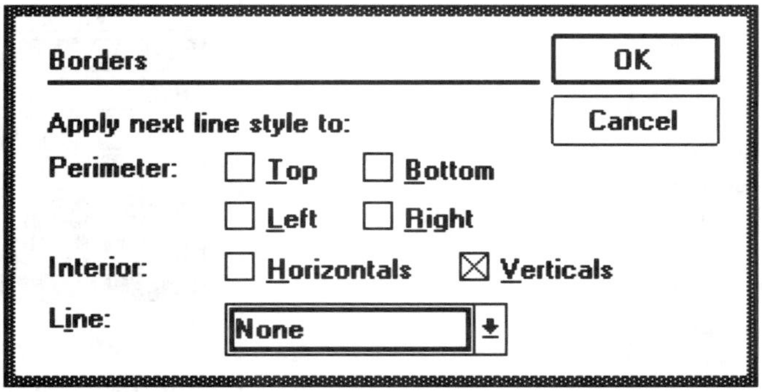

Figure 20. In order to delete all the Interior Vertical *rules, we need to reselect the* Border *command, deselect all options except for the* Verticals *option, and change the line thickness to* None.

Roster for the week beginning: Monday 24th April 1992			
Monday	9.00 – 11.00 Telephone enquiries	11.00 – 2.00 Registration of orders	2.00 – 5.00 Dispensing of orders
Tuesday	9.00 – 11.00 Enter names on data base	11.00 – 2.00 Dispensing of orders	2.00 – 5.00 Registration of orders
Wednesday	9.00 – 11.00 Registration of orders	11.00 – 2.00 Telephone enquiries	2.00 – 5.00 Enter names of database
Thursday	9.00 – 11.00 Dispensing of orders	11.00 – 2.00 Stocktake	2.00 – 5.00 Stocktake
Friday	9.00 – 11.00 Re-ordering	11.00 – 2.00 Enter names of data base	2.00 – 5.00 Telephone enquiries

Figure 21. This is the final result of the changes we just made. We also deselected the Grid lines *and* Grid labels *from the* **Options** *menu.*

The *Line* command from the **Element** menu can be used to vary the line thickness of the border of a selected cell or cells (Figure 22(a)). The chosen line style only applies to the options last checked in the *Borders* dialog box. The *Fill* command (Figure 22(b)) allows you to shade any selected cell or cells in the same way as you would change the line thickness in the *Line* command.

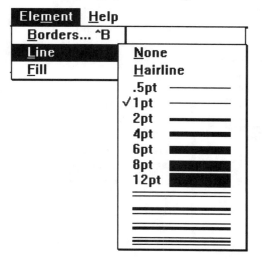

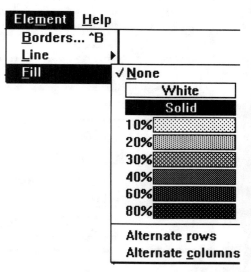

Figure 22(a). The Line *command allows you to change the line thickness of any selected cell or cells.*

Figure 22(b). The Fill *command allows you to shade any selected cell or cells.*

Roster for the week beginning: Monday 24th April 1992			
	Karen	David	Andrew
Monday	9.00 - 11.00 Telephone enquiries	11.00 - 2.00 Registration of orders	2.00 - 5.00 Dispensing of orders
Tuesday	9.00 - 11.00 Enter names on data base	11.00 - 2.00 Dispensing of orders	2.00 - 5.00 Registration of orders
Wednesday	9.00 - 11.00 Registration of orders	11.00 - 2.00 Telephone enquiries	2.00 - 5.00 Enter names on data base
Thursday	9.00 - 11.00 Dispensing of orders	11.00 - 2.00 Stocktake	2.00 - 5.00 Stocktake
Friday	9.00 - 11.00 Re-ordering	11.00 - 2.00 Enter names on data base	2.00 - 5.00 Telephone enquiries

Figure 23. This is an example of the kind of effect you can achieve just by varying line thickness and shading certain parts of your table.

Importing, exporting, and pasting tables

Once you have completed your table in Table Editor, the next step is to bring the file into PageMaker.

This is a simple procedure which involves saving the file in the usual way. Just select the *Save* command from the **File** menu and give the file a name (Figure 24). All files created within Table Editor will have a .TBL extension.

Once you are in PageMaker again, use the *Place* command as you would for any file and locate the .TBL file in the *Place* dialog box. The table file will be in a graphic format, which means you can resize and crop the image as you would for any graphic, but you cannot edit the text.

Alternatively, you can export the Table Editor file in a .TXT format and load this into PageMaker. This approach is generally not recommended unless you absolutely need to edit the text within PageMaker.

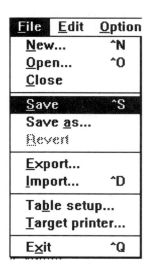

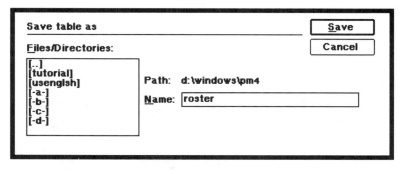

Figure 24. In the Save *dialog box, you must name the .TBL file.*

We will look at using the *Place* command for our example. Follow
Figures 25 through 27.

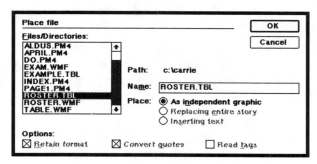

Figure 25. After choosing the
Place *command within*
PageMaker, select the
ROSTER.TBL file to bring it
into PageMaker.

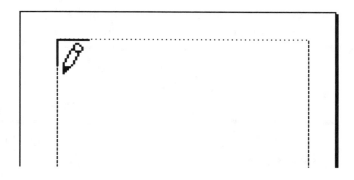

Figure 26. After a
couple of minutes, the
loaded cursor will
appear with this icon,
ready for you to place
the graphic onto the
page.

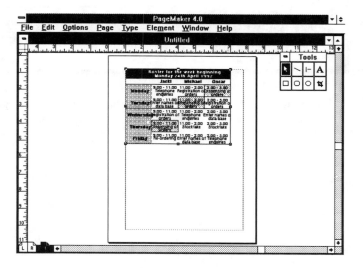

Figure 27. Once the
graphic has been
placed, you can
move, crop, and
resize as you would
any other graphic,
but you cannot edit
the text.

The Windows environment allows you to cut, copy, and paste between programs by moving the cut or copied text or graphics into a pasteboard area. You can use this feature to cut and paste tables from Table Editor into PageMaker.

By following Figure 28 through 30, you will see how easy it can be to paste tables from Table Editor into PageMaker.

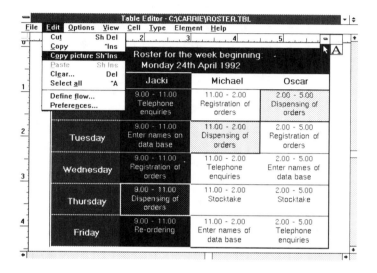

Figure 28. We have both a PageMaker document and a Table Editor document open, and are using the Alt + Tab keys to alternate between the programs. In the Table Editor program, we have selected a portion of the table with the pointer tool, and have then selected the **Edit** menu. We are going to select the Copy picture *command which will copy the table as a graphic. The* Copy *command will only copy the text.*

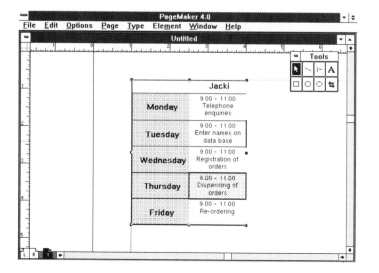

Figure 29. By using the Alt + Tab keys to move to the opened PageMaker document, move to the page you wish to paste the table onto, and then select Paste *from the* **Edit** *menu The copied area has now been pasted onto the page and can be resized, cropped, and moved just like any other graphic.*

Updating Table Editor files

To update tables that have been imported as .TBL graphics files into PageMaker, hold down the Control key and double-click with the mouse on the table. This activates the original .TBL file in Table Editor, allowing you to make any edits that you require. Once you have saved the changes and exited from Table Editor, these changes will be reflected in the PageMaker document.

Note that you must have the *Update automatically* option selected in the *Link options* dialog box for this updating to take place automatically.

EXERCISE: THE TABLE EDITOR

The Table Editor

This exercise is designed to illustrate the concepts of table generation within the Table Editor program.

This training material is structured so that people of all levels of expertise with Page-Maker can use it to gain maximum benefit. In order to do this, we have structured the material so that the bare exercise is listed below this paragraph on just one page, with no hints. The following pages contain the steps needed to complete this exercise for those who need additional prompting. The **Table Editor** module should be referenced if you need further help or explanations.

Module 18 exercise steps

1. *Recreate the table shown below in Figure 1 using Table Editor.*

2. *Import it into a new PageMaker file and place it on a page.*

Hours Worked Per Day By Week						
	Mon	**Tues**	**Wed**	**Thu**	**Fri**	**Sat**	**Sun**
8 May 1999	6	7	12	4	9	2	2
15 May 1999	4	8	8	7.5	9	0	1
22 May 1999	8	9	10	11	2	0	0

Figure 1. This is the table you are going to create using the Table Editor.

The steps to completing this exercise are on the following pages.

The steps in detail

1. Recreate the Figure 1 table using Table Editor.

The first step you must perform is to go into the Table Editor program. You can either double-click on the Table Editor icon from within Windows or activate the Files program (also from within Windows), locate the file TE.EXE (which will probably be in the pm4 directory), and double-click on this file. Either method will bring you into Table Editor.

The next step is to go to the **File** menu and select *New*. Once you select *New*, you will be confronted with the dialog box of Figure 2. You will need to change the number of columns to *8* and the number of rows to *5*, as we have already done in Figure 2.

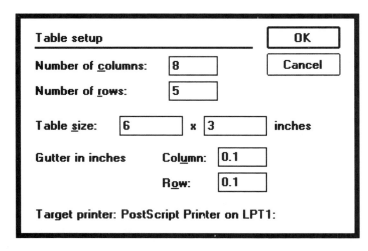

Figure 2. Change the number of columns and rows as we have done in this dialog box.

After selecting OK and returning to your page, a table with eight columns and five rows will appear, as shown in Figure 3.

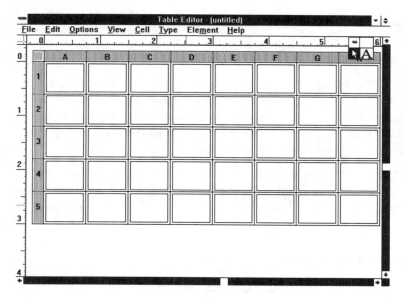

Figure 3. How the table should look so far on your screen.

The next step is to create a header row. To do this, select all the cells of the top row and then select *Join* from the **Cell** menu (Figure 4). The easiest way to do this is to click on the number 1 grid label.

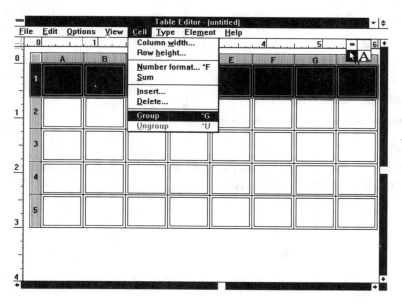

Figure 4. Select Group *from the* **Cell** *menu after selecting the top row of cells.*

To shade the header row, make sure that it is still selected and then select 10% black from the *Fill* sub-menu in the **Element** menu (Figure 5).

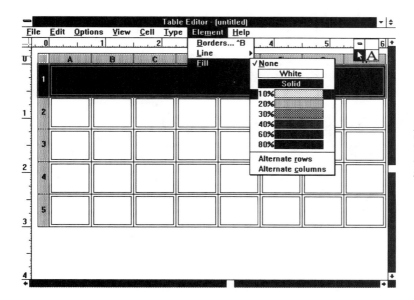

Figure 5. *Activate the* Fill *sub-menu from the* **Element** *menu and select 10% black.*

Now it is just a matter of inserting the text in the correct cells. Select the text tool and click the text cursor in the first cell. Type in "Hours Worked Per Day By Week." At this stage, don't worry about bolding, italicizing, or centering the text.

Now, enter all the text in the appropriate cells (Figure 6). Use the tab and return keys to move around the cells. You will find it quicker than using the mouse.

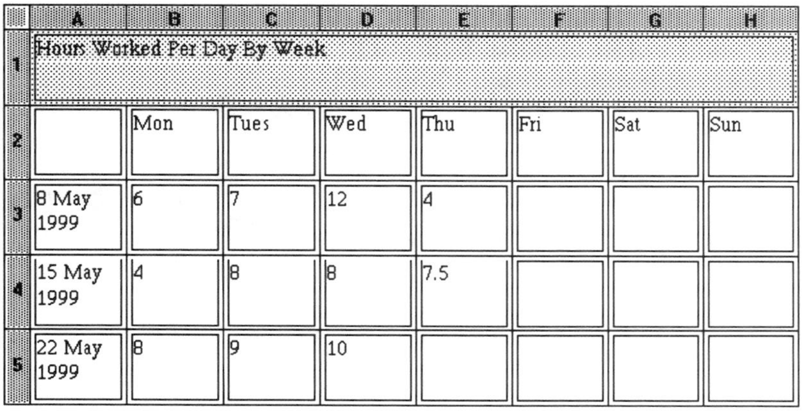

	A	B	C	D	E	F	G	H
1	Hours Worked Per Day By Week							
2		Mon	Tues	Wed	Thu	Fri	Sat	Sun
3	8 May 1999	6	7	12	4			
4	15 May 1999	4	8	8	7.5			
5	22 May 1999	8	9	10				

Figure 6. *Enter the text in the correct cells as we are doing here.*

The next step is to format the text. Click in the top left corner of the grid label to select the whole table. Go to the **Type** menu and change the *Font* to Helvetica, and in the *Alignment* sub-menu change the text alignment to *center* (Figure 7).

607

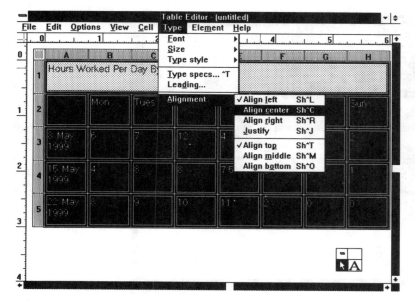

Figure 7. Change the Font *to* Helvetica, *and the* Alignment *to* center.

What is needed now is to apply styles to selected text. This can be done by selecting the text with the text tool, or selecting the cell containing the text with the pointer tool. The header row is bold italic so, after selecting this, invoke the *Type style* sub-menu from the **Type** menu (Figure 8) and select *Bold* and *Italic*. (This will have to be done separately.)

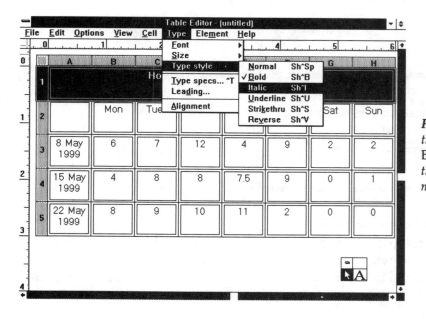

Figure 8. Change the heading to Bold and Italic through the **Type** menu.

The weeks are italic, the days are bold, and the rest is normal. Use the pointer or the text tool to modify the rest of the text in the table, as we have done with the header. Your table will now be similar to Figure 1.

2. *Import it into a new PageMaker file and place it on a page.*

To perform this step, first you must save the table. Go to the **File** menu and select *Save*. The dialog box of Figure 9 will appear.

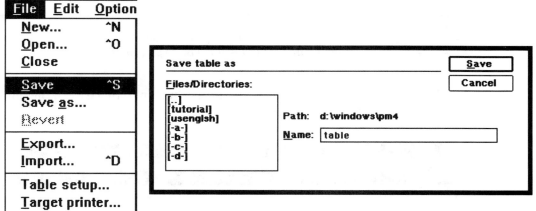

Figure 9. Type in the name you wish to give to the file.

Call the file "TABLE." Make a note of which directory you have saved the file in.

To leave this program, select *Exit* from the **File** menu. Open up a new Page-Maker document and then select *Place* from the **File** menu.

When the dialog box of Figure 10 appears, locate the file TABLE.TBL and double-click on it.

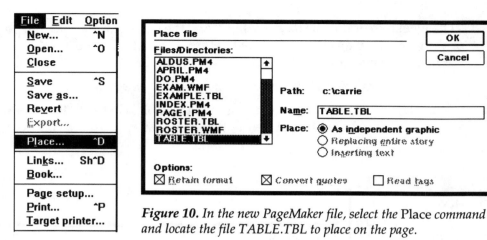

Figure 10. In the new PageMaker file, select the Place command and locate the file TABLE.TBL to place on the page.

On returning to the page, click the mouse button to place the table onto your page. It will now look like Figure 11.

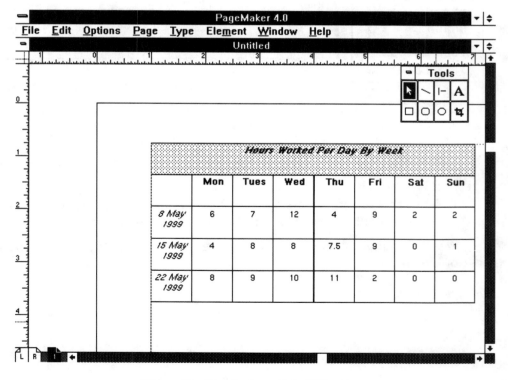

Figure 11. The final result in 75% view.

About the Authors

Tony Webster was awarded the 1986 McGraw-Hill award for Distinguished Achievement in New Product Development for his work in publishing. He is the author of several books, including *PageMaker 3 By Example* (M&T Books, 1989) and *Dynamics of Desktop Publishing Design* (M&T Books, 1989).

Paul Webster has worked extensively with PageMaker for several years and has come to be an expert with the package. After leaving school in 1986, he obtained a Diploma in Commercial Art and went on to work in both the photographic and desktop publishing industries. Paul is the author of *CorelDRAW! by Example* for Version 1.2 of the package as well as *Teach Yourself CorelDRAW!* He is currently head PageMaker trainer at Webster & Associates.

Index

A

Actual size command 41
Adobe Illustrator 53, 263
Alignment 153, 154
Alignment command 154, 176
Autoflow command 54, 93

B

Backspace key 129
Bit-map graphics 262
Book command 530
Book list 531
Book list printing 532
Book publication list 530
Bring to front command 228

C

Cancel button 22
Change command 206
Clear command 95, 226
Close command 43, 415
Color
    Applying 450
    Creating 439
    CMYK 443
    Editing 447
    HLS 442
    Palette — See Color palette
    Pantone 444
    Printing — See Printing
    RGB 441

Color palette 29, 437
Column guides command 80, 295
Command shortcuts 19
Copy command 136, 226
Copy master guides command 301
Create index command 563, 573
Create TOC command 543, 547
Cut command 95, 136, 226

D

Defaults
    Application 415
    Graphics 238
    Publication 416
Define colors command 437, 439, 450
Define styles command 174, 373, 385,
    387, 545
Dialog box 20
Dictionary 154
Display master items command 301

E

Edit menu 17, 42, 95, 226, 237
Element menu 17, 221
EPS Format 47, 53, 263, 474
Exit command 44
Export command 178

S

T

U

W

Z

A Library of Technical References
from M&T Books

Fit to Print with PageMaker 4
PC Edition
William Lomax, Maire Masco, and Mark Justice

PC users: enhance your PageMaker knowledge as you sharpen up your design skills! Get inside this hands-on guide to designing printed materials with PageMaker 4 and you'll take a quantum leap to better layout ideas, smart design tips, and practical exercises that pay off. Companion disk contains ready-to-use templates. Includes eight pages of full-color illustrations. 351 pp.

Book/Disk $32.95   #1989

Level: Beginning-Advanced

PageMaker 3 By Example
PC Version
by Tony Webster and David Webster

A complete guide for users who want to tap into the power of PageMaker. Teaches how to use the many features of this premier desktop publishing program. Includes easy-to-follow instructions and hundreds of screen shots. 464 pp.

Book $22.95   #0508

Level: Beginning - Advanced

ORDER FORM

To Order: Return this form with your payment to M&T books, 501 Galveston Drive, Redwood City, CA 94063 or **call toll-free 1-800-533-4372 (in California, call 1-800-356-2002).**

ITEM #	DESCRIPTION	DISK	PRICE

Subtotal

CA residents add sales tax _____ %

Add $3.50 per item for shipping and handling

TOTAL

Charge my:

☐ **Visa**

☐ **MasterCard**

☐ **AmExpress**

☐ **Check enclosed, payable to M&T Books.**

CARD NO. _____

SIGNATURE _____ EXP. DATE _____

NAME _____

ADDRESS _____

CITY _____

STATE _____ ZIP _____

M&T GUARANTEE: If your are not satisfied with your order for any reason, return it to us within 25 days of receipt for a full refund. Note: Refunds on disks apply only when returned with book within guarantee period. Disks damaged in transit or defective will be promptly replaced, but cannot be exchanged for a disk from a different title.

8023

Tell us what you think and we'll send you a free M&T Books catalog

It is our goal at M&T Books to produce the best technical books available. But you can help us make our books even better by letting us know what you think about this particular title. Please take a moment to fill out this card and mail it to us. Your opinion is appreciated.

Tell us about yourself

Name _____

Company _____

Address _____

City _____

State/Zip _____

Title of this book?

_____

Where did you purchase this book?

☐ Bookstore
☐ Catalog
☐ Direct Mail
☐ Magazine Ad
☐ Postcard Pack
☐ Other

Why did you choose this book?

☐ Recommended
☐ Read book review
☐ Read ad/catalog copy
☐ Responded to a special offer
☐ M&T Books' reputation
☐ Price
☐ Nice Cover

How would you rate the overall content of this book?

☐ Excellent
☐ Good
☐ Fair
☐ Poor

Why?

_____

_____

What chapters did you find valuable?

_____

_____

_____

What did you find least useful?

_____

_____

_____

What topic(s) would you add to future editions of this book?

_____

_____

_____

What other titles would you like to see M&T Books publish?

_____

_____

_____

Which format do you prefer for the optional disk?

☐ 5.25"   ☐ 3.5"

Any other comments?

_____

_____

_____

☐ Check here for M&T Books Catalog

M&T BOOKS

2950